Culture on Ice

Culture on Ice

Figure Skating
& Cultural Meaning

ELLYN KESTNBAUM

Wesleyan University Press   Middletown, Connecticut

Published by Wesleyan University Press, Middletown, CT 06459
© 2003 by Ellyn Kestnbaum

Printed in the United States of America
ISBN 0-8195-6641-1 (cloth)
ISBN 0-8195-6642-x (paper)
Design and composition by Julie Allred, B. Williams & Associates
All photos © by J. Barry Mittan
Additional information is available at www.jbmittan.com

Cataloging-in-Publication Data appear on the last printed page of the book

Contents

Introduction

The popularity of figure skating as a spectator sport increased enormously during the past decade, leading to expanded television coverage of the sport's existing events and a proliferation of new competitive opportunities and shows for both Olympic-eligible and professional skaters. Figure skaters and skating also feature more prominently than ever in books, newspapers, magazines, and television. There have even been scholarly articles published about the cultural significance of the spectacle figure skating provides. And the Internet teems with chat rooms, mailing lists, and newsgroups devoted to discussing skating or individual skaters.

Much of this discourse surrounding figure skating is celebrity oriented, treating high-profile skaters much like well-known figures in other sports or entertainment fields, encouraging casual skating fans and other members of the general public to understand skating in terms of media-shaped parables about broader cultural issues—for instance, anxieties about femininity or masculinity, about nationalist contests on the field of sport, or about individuality versus conformity.

Networks often shape their skating broadcasts to highlight these broader issues—most blatantly in made-for-television professional team events such as "Ice Wars: USA vs. the World" or "Battle of the Sexes"—and even the expert commentators often focus their commentary during competitions such as the Olympics and World Championships more on questions of the images that skaters represent than on their technique. Although skating broadcasts are usually produced by the sports divisions of their respective networks, even the most serious competitions are often packaged with more emphasis on the aesthetic qualities of the skating—or of the female skaters —and on the pleasures of rooting for a home-country hero than on the technical details that determine the winners. Because of the need to condense a week's worth of competition into only a few hours of broadcast time and to avoid overloading viewers with too much information at once, even those educational segments about skating technique or competition rules that do make it to the airwaves are, of necessity, brief. Viewers who look to television coverage for their understanding of skating are thus limited in their access to information about what makes skating competitions interesting as sport.

Journalists and scholars who have written about figure skating have there-fore tended to focus on these broader cultural issues as well.[1] The best sports-writers who cover skating for America's major newspapers have taken the time to learn the rules of the sport and to understand some of the technique. More often, especially in local papers, if the sports editor agrees to cover a skating competition at all (for instance, during the Olympics or when a major skat-ing event happens to be occurring in town), the newspaper accounts tend to misidentify jumps and to devote more column inches to the skaters' costumes than to what actually transpired on the ice. Readers who turn to their local sports pages for news of figure skating have thus been more likely to en-counter sportswriters who would rather be covering football editorializing without real knowledge about why skating is not a legitimate sport or ex-pressing amazement at the athleticism that skating actually involves once they got to see it up close than to find real information about why one skater placed higher than another at any given competition.

With the mass media thus offering so little information about what skat-ers and judges actually do, scholars who have relied on these sources of in-formation in their attempts to analyze what skating means have generally ended up analyzing not so much the skating itself as the media frame sur-rounding it. At the start of my project of analyzing skating myself, I too fell into the trap of relying on media generalizations for my subject matter. But the more I delved into the real world of skating, the more time I spent at rinks skating myself, watching practices and competitions, and talking to coaches, judges, young skaters and their parents, and devoted fans, the more my focus has turned to understanding the sport on its own terms. To resort to semiotic jargon (see chapter 1), there has already been much interesting work analyz-ing figure skating as a signifier within the signifying system that is Ameri-can popular culture, and there is much yet to be done; along with this analy-sis, in this book I also wish to look at the subject matter more closely to theorize how figure skating can also work as signifying system itself.

The best way to learn about skating, of course, is to skate. Analysts or fans who want to understand better what they see when they watch elite skaters would do well to sign up for a course of lessons at the nearest rink and to observe and befriend other skaters working on their own skills. Of course, not everyone has access to ice or the time, money, and physical ability to be able to skate at all. It takes a wealth of all these factors, along with good coaching and hard work, to make a champion skater. Most of us, even with all the resources we could ask for, could never approach the skill level of the elite skaters we see on television. But, given a pair of skates and a surface to skate on, almost anyone can learn the basics. And once you've struggled to control an edge and look reasonably coordinated while doing so, or to center a two-foot spin or control the landing of a single salchow jump, it's that much easier to understand what makes a skating move difficult, what makes a move well done, and why skaters who are able to do very difficult moves very well deserve to be rewarded. The viewer who has had even a few skating lessons brings to her watching a much more intimate knowledge of what skating technique is all about.

The next best way to learn is to attend live events in person. Especially up close, the sights and sounds of live skating make it a completely different experience than the televised version and make differences in quality of the kind that affect competitive placements much more apparent.

If traveling wherever elite competitions happen to be held each year proves impossible, look for opportunities closer to home. A touring skating show may appear at a local city arena. Depending on the tour, production values such as theatrical lighting and intensively designed costumes will probably be higher than in competitive skating, and the skaters involved will have been chosen for their ability to entertain an audience. Tours that feature well-known star skaters offer opportunities to see favorites in action and to observe high-level skating skills up close and personal.

If there is a local skating club nearby, look for opportunities to observe practices or to attend (or volunteer at) any club competitions or shows that they may sponsor. Observing skaters at intermediate or lower levels struggle with double and single jumps is a very different experience from watching the skill levels and production values of elite competitions and shows, but for understanding skating as a set of athletic skills and competition from athletes' or judges' perspectives, club-level events can provide an enlightening look into the skating world at its grassroots level.

There are numerous supplementary resources describing the technique and rules of figure skating and the culture surrounding it. See the bibliography for a list of books, magazines, Web sites, and commercially available videos that offer information and discussion of skating from knowledgeable insider points of view, including those of star skaters, coaches, and others involved with the sport at the highest levels; lower-level judges, accountants, and other officials; parents of competitive skaters; recreational figure skaters, including many who took up the sport as adults; and knowledgeable long-time fans. The neophyte who wants to learn the recent history of elite skating and skaters would also do well to cultivate friendships with more experienced fans who have kept past skating broadcasts on videotape. Much of this material was nonexistent or not readily available a decade ago, but the growth of popular interest in skating and advances in communications technology have encouraged these sources to proliferate in recent years.

Because different audiences bring different types of knowledge and different understandings of what they're seeing when they watch elite skating on television or at the local city arena, there can never be any single fixed meaning to a given skating performance or occurrence—as observers we can interpret what we see only in terms of what we already know. From the outside, this fact often leads to misunderstandings about the values that the skating establishment represents or promotes; from the inside, it can lead to a lack of perspective about how skating imagery connects to larger forces within Western culture.

This book's aim is to bridge the gap between technical knowledge and cultural theory, to synthesize these various perspectives and knowledges about figure skating, and to offer analyses of general trends and specific events that have contributed to skating's public meanings as the twentieth century gives way to the twenty-first. My purpose is not to propose definitive answers, but rather to provide strategies by which readers with an interest in figure skating can derive a richer understanding of this fascinatingly complex sport and art form.

In the first section of the book, "Meaning and Figure Skating," I develop a theory of how skating carries meaning before examining in more detail in later sections some of the specific meanings it has carried. Because figure skating is above all a form of human movement, the first question to address is how movement means. Because audiences and even participants usually encounter figure skating within a structuring framework of competition or show, the structure both introduces and limits meaning. Chapter 1 therefore discusses theories of meaning in relation to systems of bodily practices and paradigms by which they are organized, with particular reference to figure skating. I then survey some meanings that have accrued to skating within the wider cultural system. Chapter 2 sets forth a more detailed theory about how individual skating performances convey meaning within the signifying system of figure skating practice as a whole.

From the perspective of late-twentieth/early-twenty-first-century American culture, many of the rules and traditions observed within the sport of figure skating appear quaint, incongruous, or out of touch with mainstream values (as evidenced by the casual portrayals of skaters and skating in the mainstream media mentioned in chapter 1). To understand contemporary skating practice, it is useful to examine the social and technical realities attending the development of the sport as the context underlying these practices.

The second section of the book, "How Figure Skating and Its Meanings Developed," addresses a number of strands in the history of skating that account for how a sport originally developed primarily by adult men has come to count adolescent and pre-adolescent girls as the vast majority of its practitioners, and how a sport formed under adherence to strict upper-class ideals of amateurism has become one in which the most successful competitors can emerge from any class to become millionaire celebrities. These changes in the meanings associated with figure skating reflect tensions or contradictions inherent in the nature of skating itself as well as opposing cultural forces in the external context in which it has thrived. Throughout this section, I trace the gender and class associations of the various intersecting strands of skating as athletic endeavor, physical discipline, organized competitive sport, and performing art that have woven together to create figure skating as we know it today.

If there is one aspect of figure skating that has received analytical attention from academics and journalists interested in cultural criticism, it is the issue of femininity. Specifically, the central concern of much of this work has been the ways that figure skating practice itself and media representations thereof reinforce disempowering stereotypes of female skaters and female viewers of skating.

Many of the articles written by feminist scholars since the Tonya Harding/ Nancy Kerrigan scandal in the mid-1990s have relied, as I have, on Laura Mulvey's formulation of the split between the gaze as male and the object of the gaze as female, with femaleness thus connoting "to-be-looked-at-ness."[2] These notions have permeated feminist film criticism in the decades since Mulvey's article on visual pleasure in classic Hollywood films and have entered the discourse of theatre and dance scholarship as well. At the most general level, I find Mulvey's terminology useful for describing gendered patterns of looking that recur in many cultural practices, including skating. Mulvey's discussion, however, rests on psychoanalytic arguments that, however much they may decry this situation, accept masculinity and femininity as inescapable products of males' and females' histories of psychic identifications within patriarchal family and social structures. Debates within film studies that adopt Mulvey's concept of the male gaze have often spent as much time arguing fine points of psychoanalytic theory as they have applying the concept to the workings of specific film experience.

The danger in adopting any such theory wholeheartedly is that any analysis of cultural phenomena will fit all the real-world details of the object of analysis into a preexisting schema and will ignore conflicting details or adapt them to fit. In the case of analyses of skating by scholars trained in feminist theories, and especially film theories, the questions they bring to analyzing skating often relate only to questions of skaters as objectified, commodified objects of a spectatorial gaze. These analyses generally make reference only to the highly mediated and narrativized television coverage of skating events and occasionally to attendance at slickly produced exhibition tours. Both television producers and tour producers indeed package the skating with non-skating spectators in mind, using conventional codes of representation, including representations of gender.

Thus within these analyses we get repeated versions of the story that skating defines and rewards women on the basis of their physical beauty, femininity, or sexual appeal to male viewers, as if the belief that skating disempowers women by valuing these qualities alone is the only correct feminist reading of figure skating as a cultural practice. Reliance on the results of recent Olympic competitions as indicative of what the skating world in general values allows critics to point to the relative success and failure of opposing sets of skaters. Such exemplary sets include Katarina Witt and Rosalynn Sumners compared to Elaine Zayak in 1984; Witt over Debi Thomas in 1988; Kristi Yamaguchi versus Midori Ito, and Nancy Kerrigan versus Tonya Harding and Surya Bonaly, in 1992. All function as evidence that skating values women's appearance more highly than it does their athletic accomplishments. In 1994, the most frequent understanding of the Olympic results was that Harding had suffered in the standings in previous competitions as well as at Lillehammer because she did not meet skating's accepted standards of femininity, that Kerrigan came closer to the ideal than Harding and was rewarded accordingly, but that she lost at the Olympics to a young woman—Oksana Baiul—who proved more feminine, more of a victim, more adept at wielding her personal charm and beauty, and also less athletic than Kerrigan herself.[3]

But other meanings are available. Looking at skating itself rather than at mediated representations *of* skating and focusing on questions that have concerned the skating community and informed fans rather than (or in addition to) the questions that have preoccupied outside analysts produces different sorts of readings of skating's meanings about gender and the implications for female skaters and viewers. This is the project of this book's third section, "Cultural Meanings of Ladies' Figure Skating."

Chapter 6 traces the feminist critiques of skating as an activity that seems to measure women less on their athletic accomplishments than on how well they live up to prevailing standards of femininity. Insofar as the questions asked concern issues of how skating represents meanings about femininity in the context of other representations of womanhood in American popular culture and sport, the critiques offered have merit and are worth detailing here. However, within the context of skating practice in all its manifestations, not just the few top skaters who have represented the sport on television, such critiques often prove to be simplistic and beside the point. This chapter also addresses the skating world's reactions to feminist critiques and suggests some of the meanings of skating to skaters that outside observers may be missing.

Chapter 7 focuses on the question of maturity in skating presentation and how the body practices and images expected of "mature" skaters in some ways work to enmesh female skaters further in the traps of feminine stereotypes and in other ways offer escape routes out of those traps. As a case study, the chapter focuses on the ascent of Michelle Kwan and Tara Lipinski as the premier skaters of the mid- to late 1990s and the questions raised within the skating world by the dominance of young teenage girls within this sport for "ladies." As the outcome of Kwan and Lipinski's final confrontation at the 1998 Olympics and the shifting successes of both older and younger skaters in the ensuing Olympiad show, which qualities of skating and of self-presentation skating judges value enough to reward with gold medals are not as easily predictable as one might believe: they depend very much on the specific mix of qualities in the particular skaters and their particular performances at a given competition. The chapter concludes by detailing a handful of programs by female skaters that have bridged or sidestepped the perennial dichotomy between stereotypes of "artist" and "athlete."

As detailed in parts II and III, public perceptions of figure skating increasingly came to focus on those aspects of the sport associated with values that are stereotypically gendered as feminine, particularly the emphasis on grace, beauty, and to-be-looked-at-ness. For female skaters, these images are consonant with their gender identity and therefore welcome to binary understandings of gender, whereby successful females must exhibit primarily so-called feminine attributes and successful males must exhibit so-called masculine attributes, although the "overdetermined" nature of these feminine images has been problematic for feminist observers who profess a more complicated understanding of (particularly female) gender identity.

With regard to male skaters, however, the dissonance between popular conceptions of masculinity and the feminine connotations that have accrued to figure skating has led to assumptions that male skaters must somehow participate in a feminine, effeminate, or less-than-truly-masculine gender identity simply by virtue of participating in figure skating. Such assumptions have led to public discomfort with skating as an activity for males and to negative stereotypes, often homophobic, about male skaters. Skaters themselves, skating officials, and television networks or skating promoters attempting to market male skating work to counteract these assumptions, at times by insisting on external signifiers of masculinity even more compulsively than those feminine signifiers discussed in chapter 6.

If the project of gender studies is to unmask the mechanisms by which male and female bodies are socialized into displaying masculine and feminine gender traits, respectively, it is as important to interrogate social constructions of masculinity as those of femininity. To investigate femininity as a problem against a context of masculinity as the norm would be to reinforce the very masculine normativeness upon which patriarchy depends. Figure skating offers a useful field in which to examine questions of masculinity precisely because masculine identity has become so precarious and provisional within this context.

In the book's fourth part, "Masculinity on Edge," chapter 8 addresses the problematic status of masculinity in figure skating and discusses a variety of strategies that the skating world has adopted to combat negative public perceptions. Chapter 9 takes up the question of gay men in figure skating.

Both pair skating and ice dancing have roots in the "combined skating" practiced by nineteenth-century organizations of skating enthusiasts mentioned in chapter 3 and in simple hand-in-hand skating that any minimally accomplished friends, or courting or married couples, might engage in while skating together for fun. Although both disciplines developed over the course of the twentieth century into sports performed by one male and one female partner, the divergent paths each has taken account for the differences in meanings about gender that each is equipped to convey according to its history and its underlying techniques as currently practiced.

In the case of pairs, athletic techniques tend to serve as the limiting factor, so that pair skating has not produced the same kinds of crises of meaning that inspired my chapters on the singles disciplines and the fifth section, "Compulsory Mating Dances," on ice dance. In the case of ice dance, on the other hand, the history of the discipline itself and the definitions of "dance" that it seeks to translate to the ice prove the most powerful determinants of the meanings about male-female relationships that it depicts. Ice dancing actively discourages the bravura athletic feats of pairs or singles freestyle skating. There are no multi-revolution jumps or extended spins, and no overhead lifts as in pair skating. Only "dance lifts" in which the man does not fully extend his arms are allowed.[4] In terms of technique, then, the sine qua non of ice dance is the curve of the blade edges on the ice and the difficulty and precision of the steps and turns. In essence, an ice dance program is all footwork.

There is thus much less necessity for ice dancers, compared to pair skaters, to possess a given body type or for the sizes of the partners to differ drastically. For instance, there is no physical reason why the steps designated "lady's steps" or "man's steps" in the compulsory dances can be performed only by skaters of the specified sex. Indeed, within teaching contexts it is not uncommon for a coach or another skater to demonstrate steps to a skater of the opposite sex, or even to partner a skater of the same sex.

Ice dance maintains, however, a strong tradition of sex differentiation and of heterosexual narrative, even stronger than that in pairs, deriving from the discipline's origins as ballroom dancing on ice. This tradition has persisted even through an experimental phase that ice dance experienced from the mid-1980s to early 1990s, when ice dancers began to experiment with thematic material far removed from the original ballroom sources of inspiration. During this period, the sister-brother team of Isabelle and Paul Duchesnay went further than most in redefining the types of narratives and imagery possible within the ice dance medium, in the process challenging the gender norms of the discipline and throwing its assumptions about masculinity and femininity into question. By the mid-1990s, the traditional definitions were once again officially in place. At the turn of the twenty-first century, eclecticism reigns.

Chapter 10 examines briefly the development of pair skating technique and the types of gendered meanings it has created, in order to provide a contrast to the way gender is performed in ice dance. The remainder of the chapter examines practices that contribute to the performance of gender difference in ice dance. Chapter 11 analyzes how recent developments in international competition reveal the uneasiness surrounding challenges to a binary understanding of gender within this cultural practice.

The final section, "Spectatorship," offers an analysis of the pleasures of skating fandom.

Note to the reader: To avoid interrupting the discussion throughout the book with definitions of skating terms each time they appear, the appendix provides an overview of skating technique and technical terms. Key terms are highlighted in boldface within this appendix on the occurrence closest to their definition. For readers not already familiar with skating technique, I recommend reading this appendix *before* beginning the first chapter.

I need to thank all the people whose time and expertise have contributed to my knowledge of skating, particularly Jo-Jo Starbuck for offering advice; competitive skaters, especially Mark Naylor, who responded to my inquiries;

judges Robert Horen, Jeroen Prins, Joyce Komperda, Sharon Wright, Debby Fortin, Angi Carhart, Janet Swan Hill, Nancy Iida, Jean Scholes, Ed Russell, and all the judges with whom I have trial judged for articulating what evaluating skating is all about; and coaches Tina Chen, Sandy Galbraith, Susi Wehrli, and Cesca Supple for sharing their experiences and knowledge (and expanding my own repertoire of moves on the ice). Long-time skate watchers Sandra Loosemore and Trudi Marrapodi shared useful memories and observations. Fellow obsessives Nichole Gantshar, Julia Ridgely, Morag Carnie, Eda Tseinyev, Amy Mossman, Sita Ismangil, Jonathan Singer, Severine Chanduloy, Lorrie Kim, Ellen Kittell, Karen Frank, Sylvia Yu, and others have aided my research and conceptualization by sharing tapes of hard-to-find performances and hours of analysis. Thanks are also due to the skaters and parents of the Figure Skating Club of Madison and others I have skated with in Madison and Washington, D.C. In addition, I thank the manuscript reviewers and my dissertation advisor, Sally Banes, for all her feedback and recommendations.

PART ONE

Meaning
and Figure
Skating

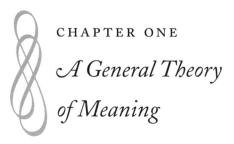

CHAPTER ONE

A General Theory of Meaning

*A*ccording to structuralist linguistic/semiotic theory based on the work of Swiss linguist Ferdinand de Saussure, meaning derives from difference or distinction within a system of signification.[1] Within the realm of all possible human activities, those structured under the category of "sport" derive their meaning as sport from their distinction from all other forms of activity. Figure skating suggests meanings different from other sports according to the ways that it differs from other sports. And an individual skating performance derives meaning from the choices the skater makes about which moves to include from the repertoire of known and original skating moves and how to link them together, as well as from how and how well the skater performs these moves compared to other skaters.

In Saussurean terms, we can think of a skating performance as an "utterance," an example of *parole* within the *langue,* or signifying system, of figure skating practice as a whole, or of the entire realm of sport, or of popular spectacle. Just as language is a cultural system that communicates meaning through symbols (words) that represent particular concepts and that can be combined according to grammatical conventions, so too other cultural systems communicate according to their own conventions of representation and combination. We understand each utterance according to our competency in applying the conventions within the system. Defining the system, or the universe of discourse, differently results in bringing different conventions to bear, so that in skating the same series of movements might mean something very different when considered as an aesthetic statement or as an expression of athletic achievement.

My goal throughout this book is to identify the conventions (what semioticians call the "codes") by which we can understand skating "utterances." Operating on the theory that meaning is always a product of the interactions among the sender of a message (the skater) and the person (viewer) who receives it, and thus can never be fixed, at no point do I claim to offer definitive readings of what a skater or skating performance represents. What I do hope to do is to provide tools that will help viewers to read skating performances on multiple levels and skaters to consider the various ways their performances can be interpreted.

An important question in literary and media studies in recent decades has been whether meaning resides within a message or work, such as a novel, television broadcast, or any other intentionally produced system of signs through which the work's creator encodes the intended meaning according to the conventions of prose fiction and its various genres, television programs and their genres, and so forth, and readers or viewers simply decode that meaning according to these same conventions. The problem with this explanation is that different readers (to use a term that emphasizes the active process of decoding on the part of the receivers of the message, whether the signs used to represent meaning are written words or otherwise) often arrive at meanings that differ slightly or significantly from each other even while displaying equal competence in using the conventions of the genre.

An alternative is therefore to locate meaning within the reader's interpretive process. Carried to an extreme, this theory would lead to meaning being completely independent of the message and solely created in the mind of each interpreter. This is what literary theorist Stanley Fish calls "solipsism," in which there is no possibility of communication between individuals and no authority to what the creator of the message intended. Instead, Fish posits the notion of "interpretive communities" or "communities of readers" who share common understandings of the literary conventions involved and common strategies for interpretation.[2] We can also speak of interpretative communities among figure skating audiences, who bring to their understanding of what the skaters perform for them various knowledges of skating conventions or, in their absence, of conventions and strategies for understanding sports performances or performing arts in general.[3]

Strategies for interpreting televised skating broadcasts often draw on similar strategies for understanding other types of mediatized narratives. The fields of media studies and, more broadly, cultural studies offer theoretical approaches toward understanding how audiences make sense of mass media messages. An early focus on the ways that institutional power structures maintain their hegemony through their control of these media has largely given way to an emphasis on the ways that audiences representing nonpowerful groups can interpret the materials of mass media to serve their own interests rather than those of the power structure.[4]

A study of skating meanings, therefore, should look both at the systems of power within the sport and its interface with popular culture and also at resistances to that power. Skating's governing bodies impose rules that limit the possibilities for meanings that skating can express, and individual skaters can negotiate those rules to convey new or oppositional meanings instead. Television networks package skating into meanings that support the dominant culture, and communities of skating fans produce alternative meanings by framing their experience of skating according to questions and interpretive strategies other than those privileged by the broadcast producers.

Figure skating is a complex form of movement that encompasses a variety of contradictions. By simultaneously encompassing opposites such as control versus freedom, effortlessness versus power, art versus sport (i.e., representation versus fact), and masculine versus feminine, skating occupies an "anomalous category" particularly fraught with cultural meanings related to the intersections or clashes of these categories. The inability to categorize skating as belonging to either one side or the other of these oppositions reveals pervasive cultural anxieties about the need to structure reality by imposing distinct categories.[5]

By exploiting the physics of steel blades traveling across ice, skating opens potentials for human movement impossible in other media. Most specifically, the minimal friction between a narrow steel blade and the ice melting beneath it allows for the effect of sustained gliding. This gliding motion is achieved by stroking continuously and evenly across the ice or especially by holding the body still but continuing to move across the ice after taking one or many strokes to gain speed, so that the body is simultaneously motionless with respect to itself and in motion with respect to its surroundings and to a fixed visual point of view. The lack of friction also allows for sustained rotational as well as linear motion, allowing a skater to spin continuously in place faster and for longer than is possible without blades and on other surfaces. The skater can either hold a single position or move body parts around the spinning center, in either case presenting a constantly changing three-dimensional picture to a fixed observer. Translating the horizontal momentum achieved by stroking across the ice surface into a vertical direction at the takeoff of a jump allows skaters to jump higher and further, and to stay in the air longer, than they could without ice and blades. It is thus possible to produce a clear body position frozen at the apex of the jump or to combine rotational momentum along with the horizontal and vertical directions to achieve multiple revolutions (double, triple, and even quadruple jumps) in the air. The use of special dance floors and shoes or equipment and media such as bodies of water, skis, trapezes, and trampolines can also enable people to achieve many of these effects, but none allows for combining them with quite the fluidity of ice skating. (See the appendix for further details on skating technique.)

The sense of transcending natural forces appeals to skating practitioners who get a rush from the nearly effortless speed and temporary weightless-ness, which can feel like the next best thing to flight.[6] But none of these ef-fects is possible without sufficient mastery of directing the blade on the ice. The exacting muscle control necessary for perfecting difficult moves is the chief appeal in and of itself for those who value precision and painstaking attention to detail, qualities particularly emphasized in the discipline of school figures, but required for edge control in all disciplines and for freestyle feats such as centering a spin or controlling a jump landing. Thus the nature of skating movement itself contains contradictory meanings: the body is simul-taneously bound by technique and empowered by freedom from restrictions of mundane existence. These opposing preferences may also be true of spec-tators who prefer the appearance of either freedom or control.

The contradictions multiply when the issue of structure comes into play. Skating historian Nigel Brown distinguishes between two late-nineteenth-century trends in the development of the sport: "To the Viennese, skating meant primarily something to see, to the English it was something to do."[7] This distinction can apply simply to the difference between participatory and spectator sports, but it also points to skating's perennial status as both sport and performing art.

Because figure skating consists of difficult physical feats, it falls under the category of sport, "something to do," and also something to measure, by means of proficiency tests and competitions comparing one skater against another. The discourse of sport is one of quantitative fact and record keep-ing, comparison and judgment, and defeat and victory. It is also a realm tra-ditionally associated with masculinity, as are the instrumental use of equip-ment (blades) to transform the environment by cutting tracings into the ice and the speed and athleticism required to perform spectacular moves such as jumps and spins.[8]

But skating also has a qualitative dimension, based on the aesthetic prop-erties of skating movement. This side of skating led to the development of skating performances outside of any competitive context, from the pioneer-ing performances of Jackson Haines and Charlotte Oelschlagel to the hey-day of large traveling ice shows such as Ice Capades and Holiday on Ice in the mid-twentieth century to more intimate shows such as John Curry's ice theatre and the current Stars on Ice. Such shows, aimed at entertainment and artistic value, are primarily a professional phenomenon but exist in the world of amateur skating in the form of skating club carnivals and the ex-hibition performances associated with major competitions. Appreciation of skating for its beauty and expressiveness tends to ally skating with femininity according to Western conventions of looking that structure the gaze or the action of looking as masculine and "to-be-looked-at-ness" (to borrow a phrase from film scholar Laura Mulvey) as feminine.[9]

Traditionally within Western culture, according to art theorist John Berger, a man's social status or presence "is dependent upon the promise of power which he embodies. If the promise is large and credible his presence is striking. If it is small or incredible, he is found to have little presence. The promised power may be moral, physical, temperamental, economic, social, sexual —but its object is always exterior to the man." A woman's presence or value as a woman, on the other hand, is seen to inhere within her body, and to manifest itself in the visual appearance of that body, by which she is judged. "Men act and women appear. Men look at women. Women watch themselves being looked at."[10] Looking is thus a gendered activity. As Mulvey sums up, "In a world ordered by sexual imbalance, pleasure in looking has been split between active/male and passive/female."

Certainly women do watch men, women watch other women, and men watch other men, on the ice as well as in day-to-day life. Not all or even the majority of acts of looking follow this gendered paradigm, as Mulvey acknowledges. But the cultural history of the spectatorial gaze has been structured so that the looking role is coded as male, even if the actual looker is not, and the looked-at role is coded as female. Stereotypically, there has been a pervasive cultural tendency, which Mulvey and Berger point to, to consider the condition of being evaluated on visual appearance as a feminine condition. This stereotype, I would argue, has led to the characterization of figure skating as a "feminine" sport. (I also argue in chapter 6 that this characterization derives primarily from those who know skating more as spectators rather than as participants.)

The aesthetic qualities of skating as "something to see" are not entirely divorced from the athletic components of skating as sport, however, but rather are incorporated into the very structure of skating competition. Unlike other judged sports such as gymnastics or diving, figure skating has long had a dual scoring system, with separate marks given for "technical merit" and "artistic impression" or "presentation." At one time, skating governing bodies precisely specified what was considered good or correct form for competitive freeskating as an indication of correct technique, and judges could score skaters according to how well they approximated this ideal.[11] As competitive skaters developed more variations to the standard skating positions in order to add aesthetic interest to their programs, however, and adapted the rhythms and postures of their skating to interpret a wider range of musical styles rather than simply choosing music suited to the accepted style of skating movement, more flexible standards became necessary for evaluating the aesthetic form of the body as an indication of good skating technique. The artistic impression/presentation mark is thus necessarily ideological and representational, as judges award scores and governing bodies enact rules based on implicit judgments about what are appropriate or "artistic" ways for different types of skating bodies to present themselves. Skaters' performances on (and, often, off) the ice are always being read, by officials as well as by the viewing public, as performances of identity that may be defined in terms of nationality, race, class affiliation, and, most saliently, gender.

By "performing" gender, I do not mean adopting qualities of movement and other signifiers that are extrinsic to the skater's everyday modes of movement and self-presentation. Nor, on the other hand, do I mean simply allowing one's putatively essential, natural gender qualities to appear. Rather, I am drawing on Judith Butler's characterization of gender identity as a "stylized repetition of acts" instituted through "bodily gestures, movements, and enactments of various kinds [that] constitute the illusion of an abiding gendered self."[12] This understanding of gender implies that there is no preexisting essential masculinity or femininity inherent in the body that an individual either possesses or not, once and for all; rather, it is constituted or constructed through the moment-to-moment and day-to-day ways in which the individual lives his or her body, subject to some degree to the individual's conscious choice but perhaps far more to the prevailing cultural norms of inhabiting the male or female body. In the case of figure skaters, these ways of "living the body" are to a large degree a product of the conscious repetition of posture and alignment necessary for the development of technical skills, much in the way that a ballet dancer's or martial artist's gait and carriage away from the studio are permanently affected by years of repeating technical exercises. Skaters, like anyone else, have a degree of choice regarding how much effort they wish to put into cultivating posture, free leg extensions, and so forth to the point that they become second nature. They may also make choices regarding which particular bodily practices to so cultivate, strongly influenced by the cultural norms within the skating community, which may or may not be in accord with those in the outside culture. (In the case of individuals whose métiers are not dependent on consciously chosen control of the body to the same extent as athletes, dancers, or actors, the stylized repetitions Butler speaks of would likely be less subject to conscious cultivation and more to mere habit.) And, like dancers or actors who can adjust their bodily deportments according to the role or genre they are performing in, skaters too vary their positions and movement qualities in accordance with the character of the music and other thematic or stylistic characteristics of a given program. Thus, an individual's body style is an accretion of a lifetime of practice—that is, of repeating socially created body practices through the means of the genetically given body, subject both to the individual's chosen will and to physical and social forces outside her control and capable of variation from one occasion to another.

THE BODY, MOVEMENT, AND MEANING

Anthropologists and philosophers of the body have noted an intimate connection between how human beings perceive and use their bodies and the social formations surrounding these perceptions and uses. A "constructivist" approach to explaining this relationship focuses on human behavior not as determined by biology but as produced or *constructed* through the workings of social relationships. Human beings must learn "techniques of the body"; what and how we learn differs within different cultures.[13] Bodily practices thus serve as representations of social realities. We learn what our bodies mean and how to use them through existing social categories, and these meanings and practices in turn sustain a particular view of society.[14]

For example, according to Michel Foucault's notion of discipline, producing efficient use of the body through drill both allows individuals to achieve greater control and productivity and also creates more predictability as to how bodies will behave, making them more susceptible to social control and regulated social order. Figure skating has long represented a highly ordered world, most obviously through the discipline of school figures, with each individual tracing his or her own individual circles over and over again until the body became a perfect drawing instrument. Even after the elimination of figures in 1990–1991, the values of the sport have remained those of the highly controlled body, one that fits Foucault's definition of the "docile" body as one "that may be subjected, used, transformed, and improved."[15] The skating body has been used not only for drawing circles or other patterns on ice, but also for the aesthetic appreciation of virtuosity, for presenting an image of what the human body can accomplish when subjected to years of rigorous training.

The International Skating Union (ISU) and the various national governing bodies, such as the United States Figure Skating Association (USFSA), have established a hierarchy of tests and competitions to measure individuals against established norms and against each other. In competition, ranking of skaters often depends in effect on judging how nearly they approximate an implicit ideal or norm.[16] In Foucault's terms, "the power of normalization imposes homogeneity; but it individualizes by making it possible to measure gaps, to determine levels, to fix specialties and to render the differences useful by fitting them one to another."[17] The very concepts of testing and of competition are based on measuring gaps and fixing levels. When a new skater enters the world of skating instruction, she also enters a world of constant measurement and comparison. Skating training is for the most part geared toward testing and competing. It is rare for any young skater to study skating for several years and get beyond the stage of learning the single jumps without ever taking tests or entering competitions.[18] Coaches teach "presentation" skills to meet judges' expectations, but those who wish to make an artistic statement with their skating must develop artistic sensibilities on their own, or by studying other arts outside of their skating training or seeking out skating choreographers or coaches who specialize in style and artistry.

Through this process of normalization, skating practice has traditionally rewarded and therefore produced bodily practices associated with an upper-class European and Euro-American repertoire of movement, often drawing on classical ballet as a source of movement imagery, in conjunction with an associated repertoire of "high-art" ("classical") musical accompaniment, the style and values of the dominant class being considered "good skating" and reinscribed on the bodies of every skating student.

Skaters who do not or cannot approach the existing norm suffer through lack of competitive advancement. Or, if they are particularly gifted at necessary competitive skills, such as landing advanced jumps or skating expressively in movement genres other than those already established in skating tradition, they may even succeed in spite of their failure to conform. In so doing, they provoke controversy by calling into question assumptions that the existing accepted practice is implicitly more correct than any possible alternatives. Examples include the use by Debi Thomas and Tonya Harding, and more successfully by Kurt Browning and Elvis Stojko, of movement imagery from hip-hop or other contemporary urban dance styles rather than traditional classical or folk dance. When combined with enough competitive success to attract the attention of other skaters and/or of skating audiences, such deviations from the norm constitute a form of resistant practice that often inspires imitations and thus expands the definition of what constitutes good skating—the trends or traditions that we take for granted today, insofar as they differ from accepted practices of earlier skating generations, can usually trace their origins to skaters who dared to differ from existing norms.

THE STRUCTURE OF COMPETITIVE SKATING

Competitive figure skating at the international level currently consists of four disciplines: ladies' and men's singles (freestyle), pairs, and ice dance; the latter two events are competed in teams of one female and one male. Up through the 1989–1990 competitive season, singles competitions consisted of both compulsory school figures and freestyle components. Indeed, these school figures were originally considered the technical core of the sport, especially in the English-speaking nations, and gave figure skating its English name. (Other European languages emphasize the "something to see" aspect by referring to the sport as "artistic skating," e.g., *patinage artistique* in French, *Eiskunstlauf* in German.)

Since 1990–1991, school figures have no longer been competed internationally. Some national governing bodies also dropped figures requirements for their skaters immediately; others phased them out more gradually, so that in the United States, for instance, figures existed as a separate competitive discipline up until the 1999 season. Competitive precision skating, now known as "synchronized skating," by teams of up to twenty-four skaters in physical contact with each other is growing in popularity and is competed at the national and international level, but at separate competitions from the more established disciplines. Local club competitions may also offer categories for interpretive skating, similar (same-sex) pairs (because most skaters in the United States are girls concentrating on freestyle technique, the similar pairs event offers these skaters an introduction to the process of skating with a partner), solo compulsory dance, Moves in the Field (the USFSA's replacement for school figures in the required test sequence for competitive skaters), and the like. Professional competitions exist in a variety of formats, some of them resembling amateur interpretive events by emphasizing expressivity and theatricality rather than technical difficulty, and the ISU now sponsors and allows skating federations or, occasionally, outside promoters to sponsor "pro-am" or "open" events allowing top-ranked eligible skaters to compete against professionals under similar formats.

But at the level of the Olympic Winter Games, the World Figure Skating Championships sponsored by the ISU, and the various national and regional championships leading toward these goals, it is singles freestyle, pairs, and dance that matter.

The decisions of sports ruling bodies as to which skating disciplines to favor (e.g., with Olympic status), the once-rigid distinction between amateur and professional status, and the relative esteem accorded to competitive versus show skating also all carry ideological meaning. Which elements within a competitive discipline (e.g., jumps versus footwork, pair moves versus side-by-side moves) the rules tend to encourage, which an individual judge chooses to reward most highly, and which each individual skater chooses to cultivate also reflect value judgments with wider implications, including the kinds of meanings the average nonskater thinks of when encountering the words *figure skating.*

Singles and pairs competitions consist of two phases: a "short program" (which at various points in its history has also been known as the "original" or "technical" program), worth one-third of the total competition, and a "long" or "free program," worth two-thirds.[19] Ice dance competitions at the senior and junior level consist of three phases: compulsory set-pattern dances, an original dance to specified rhythms and tempos, and a free dance. Ice dance is discussed in more detail in chapters 10 and 11.

In the short program, skaters must perform a specified number of required moves (jumps, spins, and step sequences; also lifts and death spiral for pairs), with no additional moves allowed other than connecting steps. Judges award short program scores for "required elements" and "presentation" by assigning a base mark determined by the difficulty and quality of the elements and then applying specified deductions for errors or omissions in completing the elements.[20]

In the free program, skaters are free to include whichever elements they choose, within guidelines for what constitutes a well-balanced program (with less credit given for repeated moves), and with prohibitions against repeating more than two triple or quadruple jumps and against excessive two-footed skating, knee slides, and other moves that detract from the amount of time spent demonstrating true skating ability. Prohibited moves also include backflips and certain pair moves that rely more on acrobatic than skating techniques but that serve as effective crowd pleasers in exhibition and show skating. Free programs receive marks for "technical merit" and "presentation" (formerly referred to as "artistic impression" or, in the United States, "composition and style").[21]

Because the presentation score formerly included such considerations as "speed" and in the short program "difficulty of the connecting steps," it is not, strictly speaking, a measure of how much artistry goes into constructing and presenting a program, although factors such as originality and musical expressiveness are also included. Rather, it might be more accurate to think of the first mark as representing how difficult the program was and the second how well it was performed (although the program's structure would also be a consideration under the second mark and the technical mastery demonstrated in executing the elements under the first). An international judge explains:

> The criteria to which I am marking are described in the ISU Regulations so I am following them strictly. It is important that you use the same criteria for all skaters, so your procedure how to find the marks for a skater should be exactly the same for all skaters. It is a bit machine-like behavior, in a way.
>
> Basically, it is the difficulty and quality of the elements that make out the first mark, but also the easiness, sureness, quality of the basic skating, distribution of the elements in a program (not all difficult triples in the first minute). Sometimes I see judges marking only the difficulty of the jumps and not the quality of these jumps and of the whole rest of the performance (spins, basic skating, step sequences, connecting steps). You should not give much credit to badly landed triple jumps, and there should be no credit at all for elements with a fall, or jumps landed on two feet.[22]

Figure skating involves a highly complex set of skills, and one skater may excel at some aspects while another skater may be weak in those areas and strong in others. In close contests, judges must make value judgments about which aspects to reward most highly. In this sense, figure skating judging is necessarily subjective and ideological; it is not, however, arbitrary, as naive observers sometimes conclude. The scoring system is designed to elicit an agreement on each skater's ranking based on the often disparate opinions of the individual judges and to prevent unconscious bias or active attempts at manipulation on the part of any single judge from skewing the results. As one international judge puts it, "In figure skating it's not what one judge does that's important. In fact, it is the group truth or the group consensus that counts."[23]

So how is this group truth arrived at? How does a panel of judges (always an odd number, nine at major championships but sometimes seven at smaller international meets or five or even three at a local club competition), who may be of differing opinions as to the relative merits the various skaters, arrive at a decision as to which one is the best? The operative concepts underlying the various permutations of the scoring systems to date have always been that majority rules, judges compare skaters to the other skaters in that competition rather than to a fixed standard, and consistency or well-roundedness counts for more than a single outstanding skill.

After the scandal at the 2002 Olympics, when the admission by the French judge in the pairs competition that she had been pressured by the French federation president to favor the top Russian team over the Canadian cofavorites provided confirmation of judging improprieties in front of a worldwide audience, the ISU took drastic action. For the 2002–2003 season, an interim scoring system was put in place for senior international events under which five, seven, or nine judges are randomly selected by computer from a larger panel of up to fourteen judges, and each set of marks is displayed in ascending order so that no one—skaters, fans, media, the judges themselves, and most to the point anyone who might have attempted to exert pressure on judges to vote against their honest evaluation of the skating—would know which judge gave which marks or which ones actually count toward the official result. For further anonymity to be the solution to dishonest judging presupposes that any judges who had acted dishonestly in the past had done so under pressure, bribes, or threats from their national federations, referees and other ISU officials, or outside sources, rather than from personal initiative. The lack of accountability is worrisome to observers who fear that anonymity will just give any judges so inclined further scope for dishonesty.[24]

Also in development is a radically new scoring system that will do away completely with the traditional 6.0 scale and the ordinal system by which each judge's evaluation of each skater is ultimately converted to a ranking, in favor of a cumulative system in which skaters receive technical scores for each element based on difficulty and quality of execution combined with scores for the various presentation criteria.[25] This approach, promoted by ISU president Ottavio Cinquanta, a former speed skater, may hold greater appeal to those who believe that sport should be more about quantitative than qualitative achievement. It remains to be seen whether the new system will be officially adopted at the 2004 ISU Congress, and, if so, whether it will prove flexible enough to reward quality and intricacy of skating between jumps and spins, whether it will in fact minimize or exacerbate the effect of overly biased or otherwise out-of-line judges on the final result, and whether scores will be reported in such a way as to provide viewers with more or less information about how the judges, as a group if not individually, rate the various aspects of each skater's performance.

"SKATING" AS A SIGNIFIER

Within the broad context of mainstream American mass culture, figure skating appears from time to time as a cultural reference point intended to evoke particular associations or values. As audience awareness of the sport has grown, so too have the uses of skating to symbolize a larger idea.

The process of using skating to represent a given meaning is most obvious in television commercials, where a limited number of images must convey strong positive ideas and feelings about the product being advertised. The Campbell's Soup company, for instance, has been a corporate sponsor of the United States Figure Skating Association since the early 1980s. In addition to event sponsorship (primarily of the American offshoot, produced by impresario Tom Collins, of what was originally the ISU's spring tour of champions) and print ads in skating publications and event programs, Campbell's has also used an image of skating to sell soup to the American public by featuring prominent skaters in a series of television ads. Shots of Rosalynn Sumners or Nancy Kerrigan at work on the ice and then enjoying a steaming bowl of soup play on a notion of ice skating as wholesome cold-weather activity to promote hot soup as equally wholesome and warming.

Other TV ads have emphasized glamour (e.g., Katarina Witt's pitch for Diet Coke, Dorothy Hamill and, more recently, in Canada Josée Chouinard, both in ads for shampoo), power and energy (a Texaco ad featuring Tonya Harding), or international fellowship and pursuit of excellence as qualities associated with skating as part of the Olympic movement (a 1988 Coca-Cola ad depicting then-unknown Nancy Kerrigan as a Russian figure skater sharing a Coke with an American hockey player; a U.S. Postal Service ad from 1992 featuring a young male Olympic hopeful, portrayed by then–junior skater Michael Weiss, receiving overnight video instruction on double axel technique from his grandfather; ads from event sponsors State Farm Insurance and Office Depot saluting the hard work and dedication of competitive skaters and champions). Kerrigan's Reebok ads associated the athlete's hard work and rewards more with qualities enhanced through use of the product. In each of these cases the advertiser uses skating as a signifier for positive values associated with the sport in order to associate those values in viewers' minds with the product or the company as well.

In television shows (e.g., references to skaters and skating in episodes of sitcoms such as *Cheers, Friends, Just Shoot Me,* and in monologues by *The Tonight Show*'s Jay Leno and other comedians) and other forms of mass entertainment (for example, Moss Hart's 1948 stage play *Light Up the Sky,* films such as *While You Were Sleeping* and *To Die For*), references to figure skating often rely on stereotypes of male skaters as gay, female skaters as scantily clad sex objects, or skating shows as corny entertainment.

Articles and columns in print media that discuss skating, especially surrounding the Olympic Winter Games when skating is on the minds of many who in other years don't give it a thought, also tend to sum up figure skating or a particular skating discipline (e.g., pairs or ice dance) into a single meaning, whether positive, negative, or neutral. For instance, ice dancing may be summed up as romantic passion on ice: "Ice dancing is the most sensuous of sports. Partners glide across the rink—limbs entwined, faces enraptured—balanced on a blade roughly one eighth of an inch wide, a precarious state that adds danger to their practiced ardor."[26] Attention to skating in general often focuses on the human interest stories surrounding the athletes: For example, "Yes, even before the attack on Nancy Kerrigan, it was safe to say that if we ever run out of soap operas, we'll still have figure skating,"[27] and male columnists often dismiss it as not a real sport: "Figure skating—Should be dropped altogether. What used to be a genuine competition is now what *Cats* is to musical comedy, a costumed, overwrought, pretentious joke. And what kind of game is it where the winner gets to wear cosmetics and skate on tour?"[28]

The conceit of a performance or feat of any sort being reduced to a series of numbers bestowed by forbidding-looking individuals is instantly recognizable as a reference to figure skating judging in numerous cartoons or sight gags showing a panel of judges holding up cards with scores in contexts as varied as political campaigns and couples' lovemaking. In the movie *Flashdance,* the audition by the heroine's skating friend for an ice show in front of a panel of producers is framed as a now-or-never opportunity for failure and rejection, borrowing significance from the association with career-making (or -breaking) competition. Skating judging as a signifier of a politicized, inherently corrupt system of power can be seen in references to "the East German judge" even postdating the existence of East Germany;[29] in the wake of the pairs judging scandal at the 2002 Olympics, the signifier of choice has become "the French judge."

In each of these cases "figure skating," or a particular inflection thereof, signifies a simple, readily accessible meaning. These meanings change from use to use but draw on recognizable imagery associated with skating from the contexts in which the public most often encounters skating directly and in more depth—touring (and televised) ice shows and televised competitions.

Narratives that deal with skating as primary subject matter of course are apt to show a more nuanced view of it, but they inevitably distill the messy reality of a complex sport into a few enduring images that contribute as much as actual skating events to the public's perception of the sport. A number of themes recur: a vision of personal excellence; the sacrifices competitive skaters make to achieve this excellence and the abnormality of their resultant lifestyle; the transformation of a working-class protagonist from an ordinary member of the masses to a champion; romance, especially between pair partners or between a male protagonist and a female skater whose commitment to skating is an obstacle to the romance.

In Noel Streatfeild's 1951 children's novel *Skating Shoes* (originally published in England as *White Boots*), for instance, Harriet is a lower-middle-class girl who takes up skating as part of her convalescence from a long illness.[30] At the rink, she befriends Lalla, a wealthy orphan from a higher social class whose aunt is grooming her to become a skating champion as her father had been before her. Because Lalla's friendship with Harriet helps her to concentrate on her training, Lalla's aunt offers to pay for skating lessons and ice time for Harriet, who soon begins to catch up with Lalla's achievements in passing figure tests. Harriet is the more serious and hardworking of the two girls, temperamentally more suited to the painstaking repetition necessary for perfecting the school figures that represented the majority of the score in skating competitions at the time, while Lalla is a talented freestyler and entertainer. By the end of the novel, it appears that it is Harriet who is destined for a successful competitive career and that Lalla can look forward to success as a professional performer, a career with less prestige according to the upper-class standards of amateur skating at the time.

In the 1979 film *Ice Castles,* an unknown but talented Iowa skater suddenly becomes a national skating sensation, leaving behind her small-town coach and hometown boyfriend to work with a high-powered coach who wants to groom her for the upcoming 1980 Olympics and to become romantically involved with a television sportscaster covering the story of her rise.[31] From its opening sequence, the film sets up sharp contrasts between, on the one hand, the serenity and freedom of skating for pleasure alone on the natural ice of a frozen pond and the gritty humbleness of the local ice rink–cum–bowling alley where Lexie, the heroine, initially trains in isolation, and on the other hand the glamorous, cutthroat world of the Olympic training center at the Broadmoor in Colorado Springs, where Lexie is overwhelmed by the demands of stardom, including being constantly "on display," as she puts it, even—or especially—when off the ice. During a fashionable party, she gazes wistfully at an ice surface outside, decorated with strings of lights and wrought-iron furniture. She leaves the party, laces on skates, tries a few moves with frustration, then with sudden determination begins to pick up speed to attempt "a triple,"[32] trips over a horizontal pipe supporting the outdoor furniture, and crashes headfirst into the furniture, sustaining an injury that leaves her blind and no longer able to compete. The remainder of the film recounts the efforts of her father and hometown boyfriend and coach to ease her depression by helping her learn to skate again without seeing. The story concludes when she is able to enter a competition again, not necessarily to win but to show that she can skate as well as she did at the start of the film, well enough that the spectators at the competition are unaware that she can't see until she trips over the flowers thrown on the ice after her performance. Ultimately, the story is a melodramatic cautionary tale celebrating the virtues of the simple life over the lure of fame and fortune, and then a story of triumph over obstacles.

In 1992's *The Cutting Edge*, a working-class Olympic hockey player from Minnesota, known for his skating ability, is unable to find work with a professional hockey team after losing a significant portion of his peripheral vision in a hockey accident. He is, however, recruited in a last-ditch attempt to find a suitable partner for an upper-class pair skater from Connecticut who has driven or sent away a string of previous partners whenever things didn't go her way. The story follows a traditional sports movie trajectory of melding these two athletes with little in common—the down-to-earth, regular guy and the pampered, spoiled rich girl—into a successful team. At the same time, the film also follows conventions of romantic comedy in which bickering colleagues become romantic lovers. The use of pair skating, with its male-female team format, allows both these narratives to proceed as one, with the sports team and the romantic coupling serving as metaphors for each other.

How skating is framed for the public—the images and metaphors used to advertise skating events, in print previews and reports of competitions, and in network lead-ins to event coverage—creates a horizon of expectations that focuses viewers' attention on particular aspects of the event as meaningful at the expense of other possible interpretations of the same event. In print coverage, especially headlines, puns on words associated with the sport such as "blade" or "spin" are frequent.

The fantastic nature of skating movement, its upper-class European origins, and the association with the glitter of ice and precious-metal medals seem to inspire a great deal of fairy tale and royalty imagery. So we read often of "ice queens" and "ice princesses"; articles previewing the competition at the 1992 Olympics are headlined "Spinning Gold" and "The Jewel of the Winter Games"; Brian Boitano and Nancy Kerrigan become spokespeople for Disneyland; NBC's lead-in montages to coverage of the World Championships in Munich, Germany (1991), Prague, Czech Republic (1993), and even Birmingham, England (1995), feature castles and other picturesque old-world architecture in and around the host cities, and voice-over introductions to championship coverage resonate with phrases such as "a new champion will be crowned" and question whether a challenger can dethrone "the king." During his reign as world champion—a phrase so common that its metaphoric value is practically imperceptible—Elvis Stojko was often referred to as "the king" out of association via his first name with "king" of rock-and-roll Elvis Presley.

Military metaphors including references to the number of triple and quadruple jumps a skater has in his "arsenal"—1988's "Battle of the Brians" being the best known—are frequent in coverage of men's events, and the skaters are often associated with nationalistic emblems such as flags or their nations' respective positions in Cold War rivalries. Coverage of the ladies is more likely to highlight delicacy, beautiful appearance, and young girls' dreams with soft-focus photography and images of music-box ballerinas, using musical accompaniment such as the Disney song "A Dream Is a Wish Your Heart Makes" or Frank Sinatra singing "The Way You Look Tonight." Profiles on foreign or nonwhite skaters often render them exotic, from American "China Doll" Tiffany Chin of the mid-1980s to made-in-Japan Midori Ito, black French skater Surya Bonaly's supposed origins on the remote African island of Reunion (later revealed to be a tale invented by her coach), and 1995 world champion Chen Lu, "the skater from the other side of the world." Images of winter emphasizing the mysteries of nature or the wholesomeness of days gone by—snowcapped mountains, horse-drawn sleighs, or old-time skaters on frozen ponds—are of course also common.

Television and print media don't invent these images and associations out of thin air. They pick up on imagery inherent in the nature of athletic-aesthetic competition on ice. Much of this imagery is also already present in the way the skating community represents itself to itself and to the outside world through publications such as the USFSA's *Skating* magazine and the event programs sold at competitions, through the kind of costumes and other aspects of personal appearance encouraged in skaters and even tuxedo-clad Zamboni drivers, and through the long-standing practice of referring to female competitors as "ladies." Large-scale ice shows and television specials for "family audiences" reinforce images of fantasy and romance by enacting the plot of *Cinderella, The Wizard of Oz,* and various Disney films, or translating ballets such as *Sleeping Beauty* and *The Nutcracker* to the ice.

Media narratives about skating tend to encourage viewers to identify with skaters as individuals submitting themselves to judgment by mysterious beings (the judges) with the power to decide their fate. This structure echoes a common theme in American popular culture of the individual pitted against a faceless power structure, with narrative identification always on the side of the individual being judged. Although skating judges focus primarily on what each skater does on the ice, particularly in the case of ladies' skating this judgment is often cast rhetorically in terms of being found worthy or wanting in appearance and "artistry"—on the basis of who one is rather than what one does. How this kind of media narrative structures gendered meaning in ladies' and men's skating, respectively, will be addressed in chapters 6 and 8.

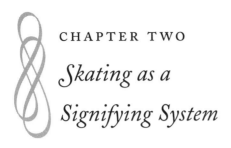

CHAPTER TWO

Skating as a
Signifying System

Skating need not "mean" anything in the sense of representing something other than itself. A skater might move in a particular way simply because it feels good, or because it's an efficient way to get from point A to point B. In the context of competition, however, specific moves are very clearly performed in order to denote a level of competence to the judges and thereby garner the appropriate score for technical merit.

Freeskating programs are judged simultaneously for their artistic impression, and to the average spectator, unfamiliar with the individual moves and their respective difficulty, it is on this level that skating means something, connoting what Roland Barthes calls "myths" or "second-order meanings" about nationality, class, and gender.[1] In professional or show skating and occasionally in competitive programs, skaters may attempt to convey an artistic statement of some sort. In most competitive programs, however, especially among skaters who have not yet reached the top ranks, choices about the kinds of images to convey are conscious or unconscious efforts to evoke associations between image and meaning that already exist within the cultural system, so that the individual skater becomes an example and symbol of an existing cultural type, for example, the "lady."

There may also be a level, corresponding to Barthes's "third meaning,"[2] of direct kinesthetic perception of the movement quality, the stretch of a leg or the suspension of a jump in the air, that communicates to the viewer on an emotional plane separate from any denotation of the skater's flexibility or strength or any connotations of, for instance, Russianness or masculinity that it may carry. This "third" level of meaning may in fact be the first that attracts skating fans, but once the issue of choosing between skaters in competition is brought in, of judging and of rooting for favorites, the second level of connotation and myth takes precedence.

Judges, skaters, and coaches often speak of the need for competitors to present "the entire package"—meaning both well-balanced technical content and the style and confidence with which these elements are presented. As judge Jean Senft puts it, "There are many factors that determine a winning performance. It's not just the program with the most triple jumps. It will also contain a balance of well-performed spins, connecting steps, choreography, and artistry that all complement each other to create that special package of overall ability."[3] Skaters and coaches need to put together competitive programs that do more than simply showcase athletic skills. The techniques of professional show business, once relegated to the ice-show side of figure skating, now proliferate within the competitive milieu. Increasingly skaters hire professional sound technicians, choreographers, and costume designers to help choose and edit music to skate to; choreograph the technical moves into a program and link them with transitions to highlight each one or to blend them into a relatively seamless flow of movement; develop a pattern of interaction between the skater and the spectators; and design costumes, hairstyles, and makeup. By these means each skater constructs a performance persona in order to create an image on the ice of what a skating champion should be. Through this process, individual skaters negotiate the rules and traditions to make a case for their version of the ideal skater as exemplar of the ideal young man or woman (or couple). In deciding between such "packages," judges in effect choose between competing ideals. Each package of course must contain the necessary technical goods, but decisions to favor, say, quality of jumps over quantity, or intricate edge work over powerful straight stroking, are just as ideologically laden as preferences based on appearance and are equally meaningful to knowledgeable observers.

In the eligible competitive context, the types of movement, music, and costuming are strictly regulated. What can or cannot be "said" proves very revealing of the cultural values underpinning the practice. For instance, there are specific rules stating that costuming should be appropriate for an athletic competition and not theatrical in nature. Traditionally, though, the skating world has considered good grooming, clean-cut appearance, and simple well-tailored clothes reminiscent of figure skating's origins as an upper-class club sport to be most appropriate for competition and respectful of the judges and the occasion. In recent decades, skaters have often opted for show-biz glitter or costumes depicting dramatic or historical characters. Athletic wear such as leotards, tights, or sweat pants may be acceptable for practice at some clubs, but for tests and competitions the tradition is to dress up. The image of the ideal athlete promoted is very specifically not one of sweaty struggle.

In eligible competition, skaters make choices with an eye toward meeting the judges' written and unwritten expectations, developed through the specific history of the sport, more than toward audience appeal. Ostensibly a competitive program is designed to demonstrate skating competence, with the assumption that superior skill allows for a wider range of expressive choices. Thus, unlike performances (including skating performances) that aim at entertainment value or artistic integrity, competitive performances fall under the ideology of sport, concerned with the establishment of a denotative fact—who is the better skater. The connotative "artistic" elements of competitive performance are meant to signify seriousness of purpose. Which particular signifiers (such as skirts for female competitors and a well-groomed appearance) have come to represent seriousness in this particular sport indicate the historically constructed nature of the ways different sports represent themselves as bastions of truth.

What we see on the ice, the whole packaged program of skating moves, gesture, gaze, music, and so on, presents on the body of the skater a performance persona that stands as a symbol of a particular way of being in the world, including very much a particular way of being male or female. Our preferences for one skater over another, as fans or as judges (in reality or imagination) reveal a lot about our ideologies. Ideologies about gender in particular, about what is acceptable self-representation for females but not for males and vice versa, have frequently been points of contention throughout skating's history.

A given competitive skating performance carries meaning along several channels or subcodes. Dance theorist Susan Foster offers a "blueprint" for reading dance performances according to categories of conventions: frame, mode of representation, style, vocabulary, and syntax.[4] For looking at skating performances, particularly in the competitive context, I find it more useful to distinguish these subcodes as Technical Content, Program Design, and Execution—all of which contribute to the technical score—and Movement Genre or Style, Music, External Appearance, and Relation to Spectators—which contribute to the presentation score. The latter also contribute to spectators' appreciation of skaters as performers and as embodiments of particular ideals or ways of being in the world, meanings that affect which skaters we root for or prefer but that have little if any effect on the scores or outcome of a given competition. Extrinsic sources of information about the performance or the performer, which as another source of material with which viewers build an understanding of the performance could be considered an additional subcode, would correspond to Foster's frame category. Mode of representation (the way the dance refers to the world) and style (the way the dance achieves an individual identity in the world and in its genre) would both fit under my Movement Genre/Style subcode; vocabulary (the basic units or "moves" from which the dance is made) would refer to technical content, with at least as much emphasis on the basic vocabulary of edges and turns that the blade makes on the ice as on the more distinctive elements or tricks such as jumps, spins, or pair lifts; and syntax (the rules governing the selection and combination of moves) would correspond to Program Design.

Each subcode contains information or messages intentionally encoded by the skater and additional information that the skater may not have intended or even be aware of. For convenience's sake, I will often speak of choices that "the skater" makes, with the awareness that, especially with younger competitors, it is often coaches, parents, and hired choreographers or costume designers or sound technicians who make many of the choices. Any choice may carry multiple meanings according to more than one subcode, and these meanings may be interrelated or they may be independent of each other.

In discussing collaborative works such as films and stage performances, it is customary to refer to the director, playwright, choreographer, or composer, and not the performers, as the individual responsible for its conception. For competitive skating performances, the comparable figure would be the coach, especially with regard to the athletic content of a program, and the choreographer (if not the same person) with regard to the artistic content. Skaters compete as individuals or as permanent pairs or dance couples and all competitive performances are constructed toward showcasing the abilities of that skater or team more than toward expressing an auteur's artistic vision.[5] The exact contribution of the skater and each of her advisors is rarely public knowledge, and even the names of the coaches and choreographers, much less those of costumers or music experts, are not always available to viewers. It therefore makes more sense to consider the individual skater (or team) as the focus, if not necessarily the source, of each program concept and of continuity from one program to the next. We can perceive similarities among approaches shared by different students of the same coach or between a choreographer's programs for different skaters, but ultimately it is the skaters themselves who bear the public meanings that accrue to them through the history of their program choices and competitive results.

As viewers, each of us will interpret a given performance slightly differently, according to our knowledge of skating technique and current practice; our broader cultural literacy, particularly regarding the source of the music used in the program and the stylistic basis of the movement; and our own priorities about which details to pay attention to and how to value them. The skater directs the messages within the program toward at least two different sets of receivers, which we could broadly categorize as those concerned with the athletic aspects of the performance and those concerned with its entertainment or artistic aspects. In competitive programs, the first group takes precedence; in exhibitions or shows, the second.

The first set of receivers is the judging panel for the event in question, along with other officials who may be in a position to affect the course of the skater's competitive career. These include the referee for the event, judges in the audience who may judge the skater at some future event, federation officials who determine which skaters to send to which international or developmental competitions, and, potentially, high-level coaches or choreographers who might be sufficiently impressed to propose working with an up-and-coming skater, offering their prestige and expertise. Rival competitors and their coaches and parents would also fit into this category as being interested in the standard of technical difficulty and presentation necessary to win competitions at a given level. The messages directed at this audience would primarily be concerned with the written and unwritten criteria for competitive success. Knowledgeable fans, especially those who skate at some level themselves, also read these messages, although they are not the primary receivers.

The other set of receivers is the general public, from friends or interested observers who might stop in at the rink to watch a local competition or club show to fans who buy tickets to elite-level competitions and exhibitions or watch them on TV. Television executives and tour promoters would also be interested in the messages sent to this audience and in the feedback, such as applause, indicating how much the audience appreciates each skater. The messages directed at this audience fall into the category of entertainment or artistic statements. Members of this audience may have little or no knowledge of skating techniques and competitive procedures, and so they will read each program according to interpretive strategies derived from other forms of art or entertainment performance. Members of the first audience will also receive this set of messages, depending how much attention they direct toward the performative aspects of the program. Judges actively evaluating a program may have little attention to spare for details irrelevant to the judging criteria. For example, skating fashion provides a major source of interest to many spectators, who enjoy discussing what each competitor is wearing (just as the clothing worn by celebrities proves a perennial topic of discussion for viewers of the Academy Awards), whereas a judge would likely notice the costume only to make sure it doesn't violate any rules and might note the color or another distinguishing feature in order to recall later which skater was which.

In few areas is skating denotational in the sense of strict one-to-one correspondence between what the skater does or displays on the ice and a specific external meaning. We could say that a technical move performed in a

Irina Slutskaya demonstrates a classic layback position.
Available meanings could include "flexibility and bal-
ance," "femininity" or "submissiveness," or "circular
patterns of life." Photo © by J. Barry Mittan.

program signifies the skater's ability to do this move (with qualifications as noted under "Technical Content" below), and specific gestures or poses and costume elements might refer to off-ice activities and relationships. Beyond this narrow range, skating programs convey meaning primarily through the associations and connotations of the images they produce, Barthes's second-order meanings. For example, the denotative or first-order meaning of a lay-back spin would be the skater's flexibility and ability to center a spin with the back and head arched backward; possible connotative or second-order meanings might be "gracefulness," "femininity," "submissiveness," or "circular patterns of life."[6]

TECHNICAL CONTENT

From the competitive point of view, the most important of these channels is the attempted technical content of the program—what the skater does. With guidance from the coach, the skater designs the program to convey the factual information to the judges and anyone else with the requisite technical knowledge that she can perform the included moves with a fair degree of reliability; including a move in a program implies that the skater expects to complete it.[7] Because repeating the same elements within a program does not add additional information about what a skater can do, the rules encourage variety and balance by setting forth guidelines for a "well-balanced" senior, junior, or novice free program and explicitly limit the number of triple and quadruple jumps that a skater may repeat.[8]

In addition to the bare elements, skaters also often include variations or unusual entries or exits to standard elements to signify added difficulty. Performing a jump with one arm (or both) overhead or at the hips indicates ability to generate rotation from the takeoff edge and from the whole body rather than relying on the arms, and the back strength and technical control to check the rotation without assistance of the usual arm position.

Unexpected entries into jumps and spins indicate sufficient control both of the jump or spin and of the preceding move to make the transition with little preparation. Holding the landing edge after a jump longer than necessary, especially with an unusual position of the free leg or torso, indicates superior control of the jump landing, as does performing well-controlled, intentional turns or changes of edge on the landing foot. Variations in spin and spiral positions can indicate additional flexibility and balance.

The very fact of including such variations, especially variations seldom or never before seen, signifies "creativity" on the part of the skater (or her choreographer). Television commentators sometimes point out variations they find particularly appealing or intriguing, thereby contributing to a skater's reputation among the viewing public for creativity or even "artistry." The specific variations included may of course also carry meanings within the style subcode.

Even within the purview of the first mark, there is room for difference of opinion as to what constitutes greater technical difficulty or which areas of difficulty should receive greater emphasis, and these differences often have ideological or second-order components.

For example, the ability to generate and to maintain high speed across the ice is one sign of efficient stroking technique. Speed across the ice generates forces that the skater can harness to assist in some moves, but greater speed also produces greater forces that the skater must work against in order to position the body correctly for a given move. Higher speed is therefore generally a mark of higher difficulty. On the other hand, the essence of figure skating is the use of the blade edges to create bold curves across the ice. The very best skating demonstrates high-speed ice coverage along deeply curving paths with little sign of visible effort. Skaters vary, however, in the degree to which they demonstrate each of these qualities.

In ranking the footwork and connecting moves of a skater who uses deep edges and difficult turns at moderate speed against another who covers the ice more quickly but uses less difficult steps and turns, which should take precedence: Power or intricacy? Athleticism or refined technique? In broader terms, these distinctions could be seen as representing choices between freedom and control.

And where would a skater fit in who attempts difficult moves at high speed but often skates on shallower curves or flats and often jumps through or scrapes her turns rather than using the edges carving into the ice to advantage? One judge or other knowledgeable observer might focus on the difficulty attempted as "risky" or "valiant." Another might pay more heed to the sloppiness of the result, interpreting careful attention to the quality of interaction between blade and ice and commitment to performing simple moves well as respect for the medium and imperfect attempts at moves the skater has not yet mastered as impatience and disrespect.

Similarly with jumps. A superior jump has more speed and flow along a bold curve on both the entrance and exit edges, attains more height off the ice, and covers more distance across the ice. Purists who value strong edging as the sine qua non of figure skating above the acrobatics of rotation in the air would prefer a well-performed double jump to a tentative triple (or, at the lower levels, a good single to a marginal double). Proponents of athleticism, on the other hand, might favor less-than-perfect attempts at triples as a necessary step toward perfecting them and as representing physical courage as opposed to caution.

"In the case of [all] jumps," according to the rulebook, "(including toe jumps) special attention must be paid to a clean spring starting from a true edge and to a clean landing."[9] A jump that rotates on the ice as well as in the air may look clean to the untrained eye, but technically it is "cheated" and should not receive full credit. Judges and other viewers who are particularly affronted by these forms of cheating may be more attuned to noticing them, whereas others may be more inclined to give skaters the benefit of the doubt.

In spins, what should be the relative importance of rotational speed, centering (rotating in place instead of traveling across the ice surface), the difficulty of the body position, the attractiveness of the position(s), in combination spins the number of positions or the ease of transitions between them, and in flying spins the height of the fly or the clarity of the air position? Should spiral sequences, especially as required elements in the ladies' short program, emphasize edge quality and flow, difficulty of transitions between edges, flexibility, or attractive positions?

Each of these factors is a consideration in performing elements well. For tests, judges develop a sense of the degree of competence in each aspect expected of a preliminary- or an intermediate-level skater and will not pass tests that do not meet or exceed the minimum expected level for most of these aspects. In competition, judges compare skaters with each other. Different skaters excel at different aspects, so value judgments come into play. These decisions, whether articulated in official rules and guidelines or merely in each judge's (and skater's, and fan's) conscience, represent judgments about whether to reward risk-taking or caution, quantity or quality, brute strength or technical finesse.

Members of the skating community care deeply about the answers to these questions. Mutually reinforcing trends in what skaters include in their programs and what judges reward represent different viewpoints about responsibility toward the medium and by analogy different views on similar questions of responsibility in all forms of human activity. They also contribute to public perception of skating's place within the realm of sport (or art).

American television commentators, for instance, tend to exclaim approvingly over the beauty of extended arabesque positions in spirals or of a perfectly turned-out attitude in the layback spin and to tsk over weaker, less aesthetically pleasing positions from skaters who do not approach the ideal. With this constant media emphasis on position, it has become a common joke among American coaches to correct skaters' layback positions by noting that Dick Button would not approve, and many of the top American ladies have striven to outdo each other with exquisite positions. Listening to such commentary concerning short program spiral sequences, viewers will be directed to note the beauty and originality of Sasha Cohen's positions and the relatively weak positions of Russian Irina Slutskaya, whereas one must look beyond the commentary to be wowed by the fact that Slutskaya can cover three-quarters of the ice surface on one foot with no additional push and a difficult backward-to-forward turn between positions and to note that Cohen requires multiple crossovers between spirals to maintain speed. Slutskaya's short program spirals are at least as much a technical and athletic tour de force as Cohen's are an aesthetic one, a fact that is doubtless not lost on the judges even as it is lost on fans who rely on the likes of Button and Peggy Fleming to tell them what to look for. Privileging of position over speed in this instance takes on overtones of nationalism in addition to establishing beautiful appearance as the norm by which to value these traditionally feminine moves.

PROGRAM DESIGN

Where and when an element appears in a program also carries meaning. A program as a whole, especially a free program, must be well balanced. To quote Jean Senft from one of the "Judge's Seat" segments she contributed to CBC skating broadcasts in the mid-1990s:

> Judges look for *what* the program includes. It's essential there be an equal balance of jumps to footwork sequences and connecting steps—those all-important movements between the elements. A program with many jumps and just a few spins in terms of sheer numbers is not balanced.
>
> *How* the elements are performed also adds to the balance. If the jumps are solid but the spins are weak with poor positioning, this is not balanced skating.
>
> *When* the elements are performed is equally important. Sometimes skaters will place their elements all at the beginning, when they are fresh, but that tends to leave a hole in the latter part of their performance, where lack of technical content is evident. Elements need to be evenly interspersed throughout the program to achieve balance.
>
> Balance also deals with *where* the elements are placed on the ice surface, the layout of the program. Judges watch that the whole ice surface is used and that the jumps, spins, and footwork sequences are attractively placed. Programs where the jumps are always by the boards or at one end of the rink, or where the spins are always in the center, are not balanced in layout.[10]

To demonstrate versatility, skaters have traditionally skated to several different pieces of music in a variety of different tempos within the same program, usually alternating fast and slow sections. Senft notes that "the pacing of the program also needs to be considered. A high-spirited section which allows quickness of feet needs also to be balanced with a slower section that gives time to display basic skating skills like edges and flow and field movements. There's a lot to achieving balance in a program, and if the structure allows it, it can be very effective."[11] The most common arrangement is fast (or powerful and majestic)—slow and lyrical—fast and upbeat. This sequence allows the skater to make a strong statement at the beginning with the big jumps when he is least tired. He can then catch his breath literally and give viewers a chance to do so figuratively while he displays sensitivity with a more lyrical section filled with sustained movement qualities, such as camel spins, spirals and spread eagles, edge jumps, and connecting steps using deep edges. The finish might include flashy high-energy moves that are less taxing in terms of technical precision, such as quick footwork, split jumps, or arabian cartwheels. Skaters will also often save a fast combination spin or scratch spin for the end of a program, both to create an impressive finish and to obviate the effect of any dizziness or exhaustion that such spinning feats might occasion. Because it is effective, this pattern is seen so frequently that it is something of a cliché. A choice to vary the approach—for instance, by starting or ending with a slow section—therefore stands out as an individual statement of aesthetic impact, as does using a single piece of music or a single movement from a larger work for a long program. In a short program there might be a single tempo throughout, although two- and three-part short programs are not uncommon, and free programs with four or five sections are also performed.

The spatial patterns that the skating lays out across the ice have an aesthetic effect that is one component of the second mark. Skating choreographer Ricky Harris encourages skaters to think in terms of spatial design "through body designs and through tracing designs" as well as design in time, giving circles, squares, figure eights, curves, and lines as examples. She urges skaters to "consider the overall shape of your movement sequences as to structure, content, and form."[12]

In the short program, footwork sequences must be either straight line (barrier to barrier along the long axis or diagonal of the rink), circular, or serpentine (two- or three-lobed S shape), covering the whole surface of the ice, and a "well-balanced" long program should contain at least one such sequence as well. For spiral sequences, to emphasize curving edges and not flats, the patterns should be circular, elliptical, or serpentine. But interesting patterning throughout a program, with frequent changes of direction and highlights such as jumps and spins dispersed to various points on the ice surface, also adds to the visual impact. A program that stays entirely within the center section of the ice, or that consists largely of gathering speed from one end to the other with the jumps at each end, or that proceeds counterclockwise around the rink with no prolonged travel on clockwise arcs, would lose points for the simplicity and predictability of its composition. Unusual entrances to jumps and spins that allow for these moves to occur unexpectedly and at unusual points on the ice surface (e.g., a lutz in the middle of the rink rather than in the corner) increase the visual interest.

In terms of technical information, placing a jump at a point on the ice where the judges have an obscured view of the takeoff might suggest to some judges that the skater is trying to hide a flaw in her technique, so they would be on the lookout for the likely error. Placing a move directly in front of the judges' seats could indicate particular confidence in the technique. It might also provide an opportunity to interact visually with the judges and as such might refer to the fact that the skater's future (to one degree or another, depending on the competition) is dependent on the judges' approval in ways that similar interaction with other spectators would not. Performing a difficult jump or combination late in the program indicates sufficient mastery of the technique that fatigue does not interfere with the ability to complete it successfully and enough stamina that three or four minutes of continuous skating is not debilitating.

For spectators who know which highlights to expect in a program, their temporal arrangement can also create a degree of anticipation and suspense. In the short program, of course, spectators may consciously keep track of the required elements or may unconsciously find themselves waiting for the remaining spin or step sequence. Skaters may consciously choose an unusual sequence of elements to play on audience expectations of the more usual patterns. Of his decision not to end his 1996–1997 short program with the combination spin, Todd Eldredge said, "That gets the audience going. Usually, they expect the spin at the end. To throw it in the middle throws them off, mixes it up so everything doesn't seem the same all the time."[13] The focus of attention is usually the jump combination, because it tends to be the riskiest, most difficult element the skater includes in the short program and the one that can have the greatest effect on her placement in this phase of the competition.[14] Until the jump combination is out of the way, it is likely to hang like a question mark over the concentration of skater, judges, and spectators alike. A skater who chooses to delay the combination until the third or fourth element of the required eight and to perform the preceding elements with such commitment that they take focus for themselves and don't appear as mere warm-ups to the combination is making a statement about her confidence and ability to sustain concentration evenly throughout the program. Leaving the combination or even the isolated triple (or, for senior men, quadruple) jump until even later in the program may have the effect of drawing more attention to it by prolonging the suspense.

The same is true in the long program of jumps that will separate the medal contenders from the also-rans, be it a triple axel or quadruple jump for senior men or a double axel or triple for intermediates, and of any additional element of particularly high risk that a given skater is known to perform, such as a quad or a triple axel from a female skater. The choreography preceding such a highlight may suddenly reduce to simple crossovers to gain speed; the high speed combined with the tension and focus of the skater's body in approaching the element, facial expression if visible, and gestures of the arm or gaze all point the viewer's attention to the jump and add to its significance in the rhetorical structure of the performance. Because an elite long program may contain as many as seven or eight triple jumps, for each one to be highlighted as a source of risk would put the skater's overall command of her technique in question, but such tension accompanying only the hardest elements can add a degree of excitement and a sense of the skater's triumph when she succeeds.

EXECUTION

Skaters, of course, always intend to perform every move attempted as well as they possibly can. How well they succeed depends on a variety of factors that function as "noise" disturbing the signal the skater intends the program to project.

Some of these factors are completely extrinsic to the skater's actions while performing (e.g., a rut or foreign object on the ice; failure of the sound system and/or lighting in the arena; a skate blade or lace coming loose; a costume coming unfastened; distractions from photo flashes from spectators or other unexpected stimuli, such as a fire alarm going off). If the problem is one that would continue to pose a safety risk throughout the remainder of the performance or would otherwise prevent the performance from continuing, either the skater or the event referee would halt the performance, the problem would be fixed if possible, and depending how far into the program it occurred and the current rules governing such interruptions, the skater would start again either from the beginning or from where the problem arose. According to the rules, judges should not penalize the skater for any disruption in the program due to halting the program or for any fall that is unquestionably the result of such an extrinsic factor.[15]

Other reasons for less than optimum transmission of the message the skater intends a program to convey have everything to do with the skater's own actions and condition, whether under her control or not. Strictly speaking, judges should base their marks only on the performance a skater actually gives during competition. Knowledge of the skater's past performances and practices that week, knowledge of other factors in the skater's life, and the skater's facial expressions and body attitudes during performance, however, may allow observers to attribute an error-filled or cautious performance to improper technique, lack of training and conditioning, nervousness, fatigue, injury or illness, apathy, or the like. If the explanation a judge comes up with is one that does not reflect unfavorably on the skater's ability and approach to the sport, she may be inclined to give the skater the benefit of any doubt when assigning marks.

Television commentators and viewers, too (who often have a better view of the skater's facial expression thanks to close-up camera work) and coaches, parents, and others who know a skater personally and so have greater knowledge of her life and her personality, may also attribute a particularly poor or a particularly inspired performance to emotional reasons. Skaters may add spontaneous signals, such as smiles or fist-pumping after landing an important jump, that comment on the performance and further encourage reading each performance as an episode in a narrative of personal triumph or defeat. These narratives that observers tell themselves about why a skater performs as she does may or may not be related to the "real" reasons. Often the skater herself cannot say why she performed better or worse than expected on a given occasion, or why she missed a particular jump, and observers with only the externals of the performance and a few surrounding facts have much less to go by. But especially when the rest of a skater's season or even the rest of his career may depend on the results of a given competition, there is a natural tendency to try to make sense out of the available facts.

This tendency is not unique to figure skating. Television sports coverage often attempts to narrativize athletes' performances in terms of motivation, mental attitude, and so forth. Figure skating particularly lends itself to this kind of analysis for several reasons. The performing art aspects of the sport encourage viewers to watch skating programs according to narrative codes in the first place, and television with its close-ups and running commentary further encourages this tendency in all sports.[16] In reading body posture and facial expression for aesthetic intentions, it is also possible to read these cues as signs of whether the skater is approaching the program in a nervous, confident, or aggressive manner and to track changes in manner over the course of the program. The fact that skaters perform one at a time makes the athletic struggle one of the individual against the challenges he has set for himself more than against anything his opponents do.

Also, the extreme youth of many of the competitors means that they are often in the process of learning how to handle different conditions and results from one competition to the next, allowing spectators to follow the public aspects of an individual's learning and maturation process and parents and coaches to follow the private aspects as well. The narrative of growing up, making the transition from dependent child to independent adult, is one of perennial interest and one particularly suited to the structure of competitive figure skating. Each jump or other risky element within a program, and on a larger scale each competition, is an obstacle or test that the individual must face and from which she emerges, victorious or defeated, having learned lessons that will help her to meet the next such test.

MOVEMENT GENRE/STYLE

The variations in types of movement—the individual choreographic decisions that skaters and choreographers make intentionally and intuitively—are what gives figure skating its expressive capabilities. These variations include structural decisions about which connecting moves to use to link jumps and spins together; how predictably or suddenly to change direction and whether to do so in the simplest, most unobtrusive way or whether to highlight more difficult turns such as brackets or choctaws (a point judges would take note of under the technical subcode); and how fast to skate to a particular passage. There are also local decisions about how much effort to put into each stroke; how long to hold each edge; how deep to make each edge; and whether, how, and how much to vary the knee bend and lean while holding a given edge. Taken together, these factors contribute to the rhythm of a series of strokes or steps, which can be meaningful in relation to the music accompanying the skating and in relation to rhythms of movement and feeling in everyday life.

Skaters also make decisions about what position to hold the torso, arms, free leg, or other body parts in; how much tension to hold in each part; which body part positions to change when; and with what rhythm to change them. This complex of elements together creates the associations that lend meaning to a skating performance. The skater may create shapes that relate to each other formalistically (e.g., creating a series of intersecting curves both in the lines of the body and the path across the ice), shapes that suggest recognizable off-ice objects or patterns (folding and then unfolding the body in simulation of a flower blossoming), positions and gestures that recall recognizable human activities (bowing a violin or wielding a sword),[14] or rhythms and patterns of tension and release that mimic or represent natural rhythms.[18]

The relationship of organism to environment and to self, over the course of diegetic time, seems a useful framework within which to understand movement-based performances such as skating programs, particularly solo performances, with patterns of tension and release in the performing body representing (connoting) patterns of arousal and awareness, growth or decline. Similarly, stability or precariousness of balance over skate blades, which skaters must constantly adjust to generate movement, might represent stable or precarious conditions in life.[19] Apparently effortless flow as a desideratum of skating movement thus might stand for an idealized strife-free existence, unattainable in real life but imaginable through easy skating movement, whereas a preference for acknowledging the muscular effort involved in generating the movement might reflect a recognition of the necessity of effort to achieve results in real life.

Skating movement and positions can also evoke specific emotional qualities. Dutch psychologist and skating coach Peter Paul Moormann discovered that although some emotions such as anger are "difficult to recognize without facial expression and without the *dynamism* of movement (often *stereotyped,* for example, making a fist) . . . for some emotions, like tenderness, joy, grief, and pride, body posture alone can be sufficient for a high recognition rate. These emotions are extremely suitable for being portrayed in large theatrical gestures. Therefore they are highly effective in figure skating programs, given that subtle facial expressions will be blurred by distance and speed."[20]

He also found that arm positions were particularly crucial for recognizing emotions in body postures and that emotions producing symmetrical body postures were easiest to recognize. "However, in dance and figure skating," he notes, "to achieve a balanced performance a combination of symmetrical and asymmetrical postures has to be used" because otherwise "the program will be boring to watch."[21] Moormann classified emotions as demonstrated by his experimental subjects along continua from extraversion to introversion or expansion and contraction, correlated with positive to negative emotion; sharing with others to tolerating no intervention by others; and stereotyped to natural gestures. He found "a remarkable similarity" between the body postures for each emotion in his experiments and "the emotion-illustrations from old handbooks on gestures."[22]

Understanding aesthetic movement as stylizations or abstractions of everyday gestures or of emotional states recalls Rudolf Laban's understanding of all movement in terms of effort shapes, combinations of weight (firm or gentle), time (sudden or sustained), and movement through space (direct or flexible) characteristic of all behavior. Movement toward or away from the center of the body represents the "fundamental urges" of possession and repulsion. All dance, Laban believes, develops from "thinking through movement," organizing the movement efforts significant in everyday life into symbolic actions that become the characteristic dance forms of a community. Any form of stylized, aesthetic movement becomes representative of the real-life forms of movement the community values and may come metonymically to represent that community to the outside world.[23]

A skater may adopt patterns of movement associated with particular styles of dance drawn from social and folk dance styles (the basis of ice dance), ballet, or vaudeville and Broadway idioms, for example. Specific moves, gestures, or poses may be borrowed wholesale, as when a program skated to music from *Swan Lake* or *West Side Story* adopts elements directly from the choreography of the original stage work. In these cases, the meanings associated with the source carry over into the skating performance, according to the specificity of the borrowing or adaptation and to each viewer's familiarity with the original work. So too with programs that employ movements characteristic of generic (e.g., cowboy or sailor) or specific (Charlie Chaplin's Little Tramp) characters.

An individual movement or sequence may be meaningful at the level of direct perception (kinesthetic for the skater, visual for the observer) and appreciated as pure sensual experience without referring to anything outside of itself. The effort-shape qualities of the movement will evoke emotion or mood, so that one arm gesture might suggest anger and another serenity, one stroking or jumping style might suggest sensuality and another aggressiveness. Any attempt to describe the movement in words will usually rely on likening it to other forms of movement, shapes, or rhythms, attaching additional meanings to the movement so described, many of them value laden (e.g., "flowy and feminine" or "elegant"). Such likenesses may in fact be the reason for the skater or choreographer including the movement in the program in the first place, at either a conscious or an unconscious, intuitive level. This process may sometimes occur indirectly through one skater emulating another without awareness of where the earlier skater's movement ideas originated. The sum of these images over the course of a passage, the program as a whole, or the course of a skater's career contributes to what that skater represents as distinguished from her competitors.

Gestures, especially flourishes with the arms, can punctuate a program by rounding off the rhythm of a movement sequence. They can also point toward the place on the ice where a highlight such as a jump is about to occur or has just been completed.

MUSIC

In ice dance, skaters are required to display movement that reflects the characteristic rhythms (as well as body shapes and partner holds) of existing social dance forms, so that authentically portraying the feel of a waltz or tango or polka and the existing meanings already associated with these forms (e.g., the aggressive opposition, often with sexual overtones, between the partners in a tango) is built in as a primary source of meaning in ice dance. In singles and pair skating, musical expression is also a criterion, but a less emphasized one and not so specifically compared to an existing ideal of how a given piece of music should be interpreted.

Music can highlight the technical elements of a program, for instance by timing the apex or landing of a jump to coincide with a musical accent and so emphasizing its height or solidity (or, more rarely, by placing jumps in the pauses between musical phrases to set them apart, as in Kurt Browning's 1993 short program to Led Zeppelin's "Bonzo's Montreux"). With edge jumps, a legato musical passage might emphasize the flow of the takeoff and landing edges, whereas a more sharply accented accompaniment might emphasize the pop of the jump itself. A pause between musical phrases can also serve an indexical function at a point where the skater halts travel in one direction and sets off in a new one—for instance, at the start of a required step sequence in the short program, to make sure the intended sequence stands out from the connecting steps allowed between required elements. Such a pause, particularly at an edit between separate musical selections, also alerts both skater and spectators to a shift in mood and movement quality. Musical cadences and conventional ending gestures usually signal the end of a program or program section.

Music often suggests emotional qualities and moods that the skater tries to match through the rhythmic and effort-shape qualities of the movement. With only subtle adjustments, a skater's crossover or stroking technique might read as "powerful" or "soft" according to the kind of music accompanying the movement. If the choreography and execution of the program key the movement more specifically to the beat-by-beat musical inflections, the music will dictate the emotional and other connotations of the program to a large degree, and the performance as a whole will signify the skater's "musicality." The wise skater of course would have chosen music that particularly well complements movement styles that come easily to her or that expresses the kinds of affective meanings she wishes to convey.

Movie soundtracks have become popular for skating music because they are specifically designed to evoke emotional states on first hearing without intensive listening or analysis. Young skaters without much musical training can thus understand the musical ideas underlying their programs, and they can expect judges and audiences to understand their interpretations with ease. Depending on their degree of musical knowledge, listeners can often identify musical genres (e.g., nineteenth-century Russian Romanticism, or Big Band swing, or action-movie soundtrack) even without familiarity with the specific piece being played; specific genres and styles thus evoke specific cultural milieux.

Skaters may choose a musical style and a movement style appropriate to it in order to signify national, generational, or class affiliations. For instance, a Finnish skater might skate to Finnish folk tunes or to compositions by Jean Sibelius to demonstrate national pride, whereas an American might choose works by John Philip Sousa or (as Brian Boitano did for his 1994 long program) Aaron Copland. A teenage competitor might use rock instrumentals to reflect her own off-ice music interests and those of her peers as opposed to the musical tastes of older judges, while another skater might opt for symphonic music to demonstrate upper-class artistic aspirations.

With music derived from a narrative performance such as an opera, ballet, musical comedy, film, or television score, the skating program may reproduce meanings from the source, especially if the skater makes an attempt to tell the story, portray a specific character or character type, or reproduce signature moves from the original choreography of a stage work. How far such meanings transfer to the skating performance will vary from spectator to spectator according to their familiarity with the original work. Viewers aware of the provenance of a musical selection may seek to make meaningful connections even when the skater has made no such effort and may not be familiar with the music except as music.[24] Or the program may piece together music from a variety of sources to serve thematic purposes that start from movement ideas rather than starting from the music. For instance, Kurt Browning describes his choreographer choosing several pieces of music from widely divergent sources for his portrayal of a Hindu war god in the short program he used for the 1990–1991 and 1991–1992 seasons.[25]

Moormann notes that "Deciding on a theme means that the trainer is more dramatically oriented: the program has to say something—the audience gets a chance of becoming involved in the story and to identify with the skater(s). Deciding for a potpourri-approach has a complete other intention: the pieces of music have well known melodies and strong rhythms."[26]

EXTERNAL APPEARANCE

Visual cues such as costume, hairstyle, and makeup, and less alterable physical characteristics such as height, weight, or skin color, contribute to the persona a skater projects on the ice and the values that persona represents. Off-ice image, including aspects of personal grooming as well as behavior, may affect judges' and the public's perception of which skaters they prefer to see representing a skating club or a nation to the outside world. So when Nicole Bobek, then seventeen, appeared at the 1995 U.S. championships in Providence somewhat slimmer than she had been at competitions earlier in the season and sporting a deep all-over tan in the middle of February, visible through the open back of her elegantly cut long program costume, she projected an image of a fit athlete and mature young woman worthy of the national ladies' title, in contrast both to her own reputation as a flighty, erratic, hell-raising teenager and to the less sophisticated image of her fourteen-year-old rival Michelle Kwan.

Unkempt appearance, on the other hand, even the tousled hair that can result from high-speed skating, can carry a suggestion of overall sloppiness. Long hair is thus rarely worn loose for reasons of image as well as those of safety. Short hair, french braids, and buns, controlled as necessary with hairspray, tend to suggest formality and sophistication; neat ponytails and pigtails, which fly about during movement, come across as more youthful or informal. Because clean-cut appearance is highly prized within skating tradition, short hair and lack of facial hair have been the norm for male skaters, and deviations from this norm suggest a degree of iconoclasm or rebelliousness on the part of the skater. In recent years, however, many of the top ice dance men have chosen to adopt shoulder length hair, sometimes accompanied by trim goatees, in an apparent effort to cultivate a romantic appearance.

Noticeable makeup for males reads as either effeminate or theatrical, although strategic application of base and eyeliner, for example, can help facial expression to carry.[27] Tasteful makeup that looks like street makeup from a distance is considered appropriate for female skaters, including prepubescent girls. Very heavy lipstick, eyeshadow, and so forth might be considered overly theatrical, whereas an older girl who forgoes makeup entirely might appear slovenly or unsophisticated. Some prominent skaters (for example, 1996 ice dance and ladies' world champions Oksana Grishuk and Michelle Kwan) have sometimes applied rhinestones or other ornaments to their faces as a theatricalizing gesture, and the use of spray-on glitter or hair color, popular particularly among adolescent and pre-adolescent girls as a fantasy dress-up accessory, has found its way to the ice as well, and not only among the adolescent girls.

Costume can add considerable information to a skater's image. Traditionally the standard competitive wear for female skaters is a one-piece "skating dress" consisting of bodice, trunks, and short skirt, worn over flesh-colored tights. A 1989 ISU ruling states that "Clothing for Ladies cannot be theatrical in nature. They must have skirts and pants covering the hips and posterior. A 'unitard' is not acceptable. A bare midriff is not acceptable. Clothing must be without excessive decoration, such as beads, sequins, feathers, and the like."[28] Because garments of this nature are rarely encountered in everyday life, the most salient meaning of any skating dress to an observer unaccustomed to seeing them is "female figure skater."

The typical short skirt and simulated bare legs might also suggest, depending on the design of the dress and the physique of the skater, a young child's playsuit or a costume of the sort worn by nightclub and Broadway showgirls and chorus girls, circus performers, cheerleaders, and other female performers whose function consists in part or in whole of displaying their pulchritude. As worded, the costume regulations do not specifically forbid female skaters from displaying their legs and the upper part of their chests under sheer or flesh-colored "illusion" fabric, or even from leaving these parts bare, and indeed tradition has encouraged them to do so. Within a fairly lenient interpretation of modesty (extremely high-cut pants or low-cut necklines might strike judges as "theatrical," immodest, or in bad taste and so risk a 0.1–0.2 penalty deduction in the second mark), the skating community expects women to display their bodies.

The only legal alternative for skaters who do not wish to call attention to their bodies and particularly to the sexualized regions of groin and buttocks highlighted by the pants of the typical skating dress ending there is to wear opaque leggings or tights, usually of the same fabric and often attached to the lower part of the dress. This design has been fairly common for practice clothing (where skirts are not required in any case) and figures competition, much less so for freestyle competition (although it is slightly more common in pairs, to allow the lady's and man's legs to be the same color). Even in these cases, though, the contour of the lady's legs is fully revealed. Long sleeves and high necklines are, of course, perfectly acceptable.

The required skirt, however, does not serve the purposes of modesty (since it will fly up during movement to reveal the area it is required to cover) so much as a symbolic function, signifying both femininity and formality. The need for athletic maneuverability precludes female skaters (except sometimes ice dancers) from wearing skirts that reach to the lower thigh or below, which would include most skirt lengths seen in off-ice social contexts. The requirement to include a skirt also restricts the possibilities for female skating costumes to approximate clothing worn by girls and women in many other athletic and social contexts, from the streamlined, skirtless garments worn by racers on speed skates, skis, or bicycles, and skirtless leotards or unitards worn for many dance, gymnastic, and circus performances, to shorts, trousers, or jumpsuits worn for leisure pursuits, in school, and even as business or formal wear. Any attempt to replicate such images for a themed competitive program would be complicated by the need to include a skirt. In exhibition and professional performances, there are no rules to preclude other costume possibilities, but skating dresses still predominate.

Aside from tradition, another reason for the popularity of including short skirts in skating costumes is that the rippling of the skirt produced by the skater's movement draws attention to that movement; male skaters' use of loose shirts that also ripple may derive from similar considerations.

To those who watch skating often and have become used to the traditional skating dress, its difference from typical women's street clothes becomes less salient and the differences between one skating dress and another take on stronger significance. The cut, color, texture, and ornamentation may resemble forms of off-ice apparel appropriate to the musical theme of the program. For instance, rich fabrics such as velvet and satin, elegantly cut and trimmed with rhinestones or beads to simulate jewels, could suggest a ball gown or other evening dress; a halter-type top covered with bright sequins or trimmed with feathers might suggest a chorus girl's costume; puffed sleeves and a dirndl waist might accompany a program of central European folk tunes.

Bright, shiny colors catch the eye and turn the covered portion of the skater's body into a shining, whirling object, evoking associations between the skater and a bauble or toy, pretty but frivolous. A less bright, mostly solid-colored dress, especially if composed of stretch fabric with attached leggings or if trimmed with broad strips of contrasting color or other simple geometric ornamentation, would carry connotations of greater seriousness, sedateness, and precision, even severity, perhaps of school uniforms or athletic garb worn in other sports, or of formalist movement-based performing arts such as mime or some forms of ballet and modern dance. In school figures competition and figure and compulsory dance tests, these more somber variations have prevailed, often accompanied by sweater and gloves or mittens, since skaters can get cold on the ice when moving at the deliberate pace required for tracing figures. The traditional cardigan of Alpine or Scandinavian design recalls the pre-television era of figure skating as an outdoor, school-figures-based, winter-resort activity.

Whereas the costuming rules and traditions for females intentionally or unintentionally encourage sexualized display and objectification of the body and limit the potential for imitating everyday wear on the ice, the trend for male costuming has been in the opposite direction. According to the rulebook, "Clothing for Men cannot be theatrical in nature, men must wear full-length trousers; no tights are permitted, and the clothing must not be sleeveless, must have a neckline which does not expose the chest and be without excessive decoration, such as beads, sequins, and the like."[29] In other words, under the current guidelines males are forbidden to reveal the flesh (and, often, hair) of their chests, armpits, and upper arms and shoulders or to reveal too accurately even the contour of their legs, buttocks, and external sex organs. The insistence on trousers, not tights, reduces the degree to which costumes can emphasize the formal shapes of the body in space or evoke many dance or acrobatic performance contexts, meanings that were more prevalent in the 1970s and 1980s, before these options were explicitly forbidden. It also encourages costumes that resemble off-ice attire in ways practically impossible for female skating wear. The simplest form of acceptable clothing would be slacks and a button-down or t-shirt-style top, perhaps supplemented by a sweater (especially for figures, although this look was also fairly common for freestyle in the days when competitions were still held on outdoor rinks), tie, vest, suspenders, and/or close-fitting jacket. The shirt might have a strap or extension to fasten between the legs and the bottoms of the trouser legs might have straps to fasten below the sole of the boot, to keep the garments from shifting too much during athletic maneuvers, but these practical expediencies would likely not be noticeable enough to affect the visual impression of the costume. Strictly speaking, blue jeans or other styles of work pants are not forbidden (although freedom of movement might be a problem unless special stretch fabrics were employed), but in practice skaters most often eschew these rough images in favor of costumes that suggest business or evening wear, or (often through the use of sequined vests and bowties) a circus ringmaster or vaudevillian, or with looser shirts a romantic poet or lounge singer. For a theme program, a skater might affect the garb of a cowboy, soldier, or sailor.

The other option for men is the one-piece costume, along the lines of a jumpsuit. A similar effect may also be achieved with pants and shirt of the same fabric. Sometimes the upper part of the costume is designed to simulate a jacket (as in a tuxedo or a bolero jacket for a Spanish-themed number) or vest over shirt as if separate from the pants, but with a sleeker, more aerodynamic line than separate garments would allow. Solid colors overall with bold geometric designs suggest athleticism or give a formalist, sometimes futuristic effect. Solid bright or pastel colors adorned with patterns of sequins or beads, which came to prominence during the disco era of the 1970s and lost favor in the 1990s, present the skater's body as an ornamented surface of superficial visual interest, a meaning that most male skaters have lately rejected but that many females continue to embrace. Russian men have tended to favor more elaborate, ornamented, theatrical attire than their North American counterparts, for whom simplicity seems to signify masculinity and/or good taste.

In pair skating and ice dance, the visual relationship between the two skaters' costumes takes on meaning. Often a team will wear costumes of matching fabrics and trim. The primary images might be of romance and fantasy (here is where it has been most common to find men wearing pastels, because the feminine associations of these colors are balanced by the need to match and the sexual division of labor in pair skating), of bold athleticism, or of the ethnic character of the music. In ice dance it is more common for the man to wear normal everyday or formal wear, such as one might wear to a dance, and the lady to wear the skating dress equivalent of a ball gown or popular dress styles from the era the music represents. Some of the extreme-themed free dances of the late 1980s and early 1990s employed more fantastic costumes now forbidden—using unitards, for instance—although there has been a trend in ice dance at the turn of the twenty-first century toward large masses of flowing fabric (and loose long hair) on the one hand and on the other hand, primarily but not exclusively for the women, illusion-fabric-based costumes with strategically placed opaque elements that treat the body surface as a site for ludic fantasy and formalism. If the man wears relatively simple, dark colors and the lady wears brighter colors, especially with "bare" legs and a skirt full enough to flow with the movement, viewers' eyes will be drawn to the lady as the object of the gaze, with the man there merely to support and present her.

RELATION TO SPACE AND SPECTATORS

A skater may or may not make eye contact or otherwise interact with the spectators while competing. The form such interaction takes establishes a relationship between the performance persona of the skater on the one hand and the spectators and judges on the other, particularly with regard to their relative status.[30] As with any performance, the skater is subject to audience approval and, in competition, is even more explicitly subject to the opinion of the judges. A star skater (for instance, a defending national champion) may also know that her presence on the ice is one of the chief attractions accounting for the presence of the spectators in the arena and might explicitly acknowledge her power to command such attention.

A skater might actively solicit approval, through sex appeal, cheeriness, or other means, or he might seem to take it for granted. He may timidly smile up at the judges or haughtily stare them down. As the focal point of attention for all eyes in the arena during the performance, the skater may seem to submit herself to the position of being the object of the spectators' gaze, to be judged on the attractiveness of what she looks like, constantly drawing attention to the shapes she makes with her body through the direction of her own gaze and the tilt of her head, shoulders, and arms. She might direct her own gaze and gestures back to the spectators or judges (or home viewers, by looking directly into a TV camera) as a challenge or invitation or offering. If so, is what she seems to be offering her program or herself? Does she seem to worry or care whether they will accept?

Spectators may interpret the performer's relationship to themselves according to codes of body language familiar from everyday interactions and other forms of performance, and spectators who bring different associations to their viewing might derive different interpretations for the same behavior. Imagine, for example, that a skater glides past the boards, her body turned above the waist toward the stands, chest and chin lifted, smiling broadly as she opens her arms from in front of her chest to spread wide apart, palms up. One spectator might focus on the upraised breasts revealed as the hands move away from the chest and read the gesture as one of sexual display. Another might focus on the path of the hands and the proud angle of the shoulders to read the gesture as a flourish punctuating the difficult jump just completed; a third might note the open palms as indicative of hospitable welcome. The rhythm of the movement and the exact angle of the skater's head and eye line relative to the viewer's vantage point might reinforce or contradict any of these meanings.

A skater may decline to engage directly with the audience because his attention is entirely consumed with the technical requirements of the skating, or because he is too shy or self-conscious to acknowledge the presence of the onlookers, or because his choreography has been intentionally designed to feature an introverted gaze. If his own focus is intense or concentrated enough it may draw in the spectators' attention to share an apparently intense inner experience; if not, he may appear devoid of affect or personality. A viewer who has a prior inclination to identify with this particular skater is more likely to be drawn in; one uninterested to begin with is likely to remain uninterested.

A skater might also focus her gaze and gestures outward not toward the spectators, but projecting energy out past her own body, across the ice surface and into the arena space, calling attention to her activity, her movement through space, and metaphorically her movement through the world. She may seem to impose herself aggressively into the space around her, or to give herself over to the space and to the ice (and to the music) as media supporting her movement and her very existence.

In a pair or dance program, creating a pattern of interaction between the partners establishes for the duration of the program what I call a relationship-persona, which may or may not reflect the skaters' actual relationship outside of performance. This on-ice relationship between the skaters complicates the relationship between skaters and spectators. Both members of a couple might smile at and make gestures of invitation or offering to the audience, or this task might be left to the female member of the team while the man remains focused on the technical relationships between the skaters' bodies. The man might actively display to the audience the extreme shapes the woman's body creates; occasionally these roles are briefly reversed within a program. The skaters might interact with each other as lovers in various forms of heterosexual relationship, or as partners providing mutual support, or as rivals, and so forth.

Vague, tentative, or flat focus on the part of the skater tends to suggest lack of confidence, nervousness, and shyness and may negatively affect the presentation score. Any of these other possibilities and more, if consciously chosen and executed with commitment, can contribute to the effect of a strongly presented program, one that captivates audiences and judges alike. There is no "right" or "wrong" style of program presentation, but certain approaches have histories of association with various social identities. For instance, American skaters have tended to favor an upbeat and outgoing style, whereas Russians are more likely to take an introspective or dramatic approach. Male skaters are less likely than female ones to engage in flirtatious behavior while competing; when they do, it generally has an aggressive or tongue-in-cheek quality.

Female skaters, especially North Americans, often learn to smile as much as possible, whereas males are more apt to maintain a serious expression. Smiling is believed to put both skaters themselves and judges at ease, projecting a cheery sense of confidence and competence. At local and qualifying competitions where fellow skaters make up a large proportion of the audience, and even occasionally at Nationals, it is common for friends and clubmates of the skater on the ice to cheer her on as she takes her opening position by yelling out, "Go [name of skater]!" followed by the reminder "Smile!" Friends of male skaters will also cheer them on in this way.

EXTRINSIC CODES

In addition to what actually happens on the ice once a skater is announced, ancillary information about the skater and the performance can also affect the meaning of a given performance. This information may include details about the skater's personal life and competitive history, available from television commentators during a performance or as background knowledge gleaned from following a skater's career through personal acquaintance and rink gossip, attendance at competitions and practices, or print and electronic media. Except for purely nationalistic allegiance in international competitions, *which* skaters we root for or identify with and the way the media characterize the skaters to distinguish them from each other depend largely on the persona each skater projects on the ice, the type of young woman or man or couple the skater or team represents or embodies. On a broader scale, the context and perceived intention of all the individual performances that make up a skating "event" inform us whether to read those performances and the event as a whole according to codes appropriate to sport and/or to performing arts.

How a performance is framed—for instance, whether as a test or competition to be judged, as practice for such an occasion of judgment, or as part of an exhibition or show for the delight of audiences; how the event and its participants are advertised or promoted; whether a live event makes available a printed program and, if so, what it includes—also affects the way we read its meanings. As Foster notes of dance performances, these framing conventions "all arouse in the viewer a set of expectations about the event" and also "help to define the viewer's role—as spectator, voyeur, or witness—in watching the event."[31]

Print articles or television profiles previewing an imminent competition, television commentary, and even the choice of whom to show off-ice preparing to skate or watching other competitors can position one or more skaters as objects for audience identification in their quest for validation through medals. Merely acknowledging the existence (or not) of other competitors, by name or often just by nationality, positions them as obstacles in that pursuit rather than as subjects engaged in quests of their own. Print and televised previews or advertisements for upcoming broadcasts or live shows tend to reinforce existing perceptions of which skaters are already stars who will attract audiences and which are not (or not yet) perceived to possess such drawing power. The skating order in post-competition exhibitions is usually defined more or less by protocol according to medals won at that event, whereas the television broadcasts of those exhibitions or a tour such as Champions on Ice may pick and choose which skaters to include at all and which order to present them in so as to create a rhythm of performance that offers variety of mood and also, perhaps most importantly, establishes its own hierarchy of stardom and keeps viewers in their seats until the end by building up to the skaters deemed to possess the most appeal.

In competition, skaters are announced by name and as representing a particular country (underscoring the nationalistic basis of international competition) or a particular skating club (providing prestige to those associated with clubs that have produced numerous past champions, and also perhaps evoking longstanding interclub rivalries). Sometimes music titles are also announced, providing an additional key to making meaning from the program to come. In exhibitions, including exhibition tours, and professional competitions, skaters are most often introduced by their most prestigious amateur/ eligible competitive titles, a process that further validates the importance of competition and of winning medals.

The comparative aspects of competition may carry over to noncompetitive formats, as witnessed by half-joking comments that a particular skater "won the practices" or "won the exhibition" or assignment of scores to a show performance or practice run-through. High-profile skaters sometimes give titles to their programs or make public statements in the press explaining their artistic intentions or dedicating their performances to particular individuals or causes, thereby shaping the way viewers interpret the programs. When applied to competitive programs, as when in the 2001–2002 season ice dancers were allowed the option of announcing a program theme to their free dances, this practice brings strategies of meaning making common to the performing arts into the sporting arena.

READING A PROGRAM

Noticing patterns of meaning within the various subcodes of a given performance and relating them to additional knowledge about the skater, her competitors, and the sources of the program choices allows viewers to interpret skating performances just as one might interpret any other cultural product. No reading can be definitive, because neither the creator(s) of the program nor any individual viewer brings all possible relevant knowledge to bear in forming an interpretation. My aim here is to provide a model of what a detailed interpretation might entail, to articulate the varied considerations that go into understanding what a program "means." The chapters that follow will often refer to such meanings without analyzing them in comparable detail.

At the 1995 World Championships, fourteen-year-old Michelle Kwan, skating last in the ladies' long program, gave the best performance of her life so far, completing all seven of her attempted triple jumps and exuding joy and enthusiasm. She finished third in the long program, behind winner Chen Lu and second-place finisher Surya Bonaly, and ahead of U.S. champion

Nicole Bobek, who had started out impressively but had succumbed to two falls later in her program. Because Bobek had won the short program, however, and Kwan had been only fifth in that phase, it was Bobek who stood on the podium at Worlds wearing the bronze medal. Kwan had completed more difficult jumps than any other lady in the competition except for Bonaly (whose skating draws criticism for its sloppiness and lack of finesse), and yet she had failed to win a medal. "I knew when I saw technical marks around 5.8 dropping to 5.5 in the second (presentation) mark there was something wrong with what we were doing," Kwan related later. "When I finished fourth, I said 'What can I do to move three places higher?'"[32]

At Skate America the following autumn, Kwan revealed her solution. In practices as well as during performance, she wore her hair in a sophisticated bun instead of her familiar ponytail and heavy theatrical makeup including rhinestones pasted beside the corners of her eyes. For her long program, skated to "Salome's Dance" from Miklos Rozsa's *King of Kings* film score and "The Dance of the Seven Veils" from Richard Strauss's opera *Salome,* she wore a short-sleeved rich purple dress with rhinestone-studded flesh-colored fabric across the midriff and deep front and back necklines, ornamented with elaborate sequined floral patterns in gold and bright pastels.

Kwan was portraying the role of Salome, the media told us, the "biblical temptress" as Dick Button put it.[33] Repeated broadcasts of Kwan's long program throughout the season and numerous articles about her in the mainstream and skating press quoted coach Frank Carroll's explanation of the change in Kwan's image since the previous season: "The judges [at the 1995 Worlds] were looking for the ladies' champion of the world, not the girls' champion of the world."[34] The conclusion suggested by these framing comments, especially when they draw particular attention to the heavy makeup and pseudo-flesh-baring costume and to the titles of her musical selections, is that Kwan was demonstrating her maturity, and thus her worthiness of winning championships, by revealing herself as a sexual being. The overt sexual cues of the performance, however, lay almost entirely in these externals. A feature on Kwan's artistic maturation,[35] however, showed her improvising to this music at the suggestion of choreographer Lori Nichol (and performing moves that do show up in the program) before she was aware of the music's source, which would suggest that as far as Kwan's early input into the choreography is concerned, her inspiration was music-based rather than narrative.

The program begins with Kwan posed with her knees slightly bent, left heel lifted to shift her hips to the right.[36] To a slow, haunting melody she circles left, elbows bent inward, then skates a circle to the right in forward

*Michelle Kwan as Salome. Elaborate makeup with a so-
phisticated hairstyle, a sensual costume, and complicated
choreography all add up to signify "maturity." Photo © by
J. Barry Mittan.*

spiral position, turns in place, then makes another circle to the left on two
feet with her left hip canted outward and torso and head twisted out and up.
Throughout this sequence her arms twist at the shoulders, forearms, and
wrists so that her arms, her body as a whole, and the elaborated figure eight
she draws on the ice create a series of curves within curves. The motifs of
movement path and body shapes thus suggest from the outset images associated both with femininity and with complexity or elaboration. Her visual
focus remains within the space described by her body, which, along with the
localized path of her slow, sensual circles, might suggest self-absorption or
sheltered existence.

She straightens, stepping forward with her arms floating slightly ahead, then turns backward and lets her arms float back as well, gazing outward now around her with an expression of innocent curiosity as she ventures out into the space, as if actively seeking wider experience. Stroking toward the far end of the rink, she gains speed for a triple lutz–double toe loop combination, losing speed on the landing, but clean and well controlled. She spreads her arms and allows a broad smile to appear on her face, the skater's pleasure at this athletic success momentarily displacing the role she is playing.

The music changes to a more densely textured, rhythmic passage. Kwan skates a circle of steps around the end of the ice, twisting her arms and free leg. Simpler strokes take her down the center of the ice at her highest speed into a triple toe–triple toe combination with good flow on the landing of the first jump and even more height in the second triple than in the first, again followed by a big smile. Her speed and power here connote confidence and competence in conquering the difficult triple-triple combination.

With arms bent upward from the elbow to open her hands above her face, Kwan twists into a flying camel, changes to a sitspin, and then rises with her one arm holding up her leg in a high side attitude position with the other arm snaking above her head. This final position creates a distinctive, Middle Eastern–flavored body shape. Kwan weaves her way back toward the other end of the ice, holding a brief backward attitude with knees and elbows bent at right angles and wrists flexed up, another Eastern-style shape. She circles one arm around her head to signal a third difficult jumping feat, a triple flip. A circular step sequence follows, with more emphasis on complex curves as her arms spiral around her waist first in one direction, then the other. Next comes a double axel, with a sustained edge on the landing folding into a back outside pivot with arms wrapped around her middle and her gaze focused down as the music changes to a lyrical, almost tragic-sounding selection.

In a series of wide steps and weight shifts on two feet, Kwan repeatedly reaches out with her arms, chest extended, then pulls her hands back to her chest, folding her body inward to give an appearance of mourning or pleading. She turns backward into a spiral with one arm behind her waist, then steps directly and unexpectedly into a layback spin, changing arms behind her in another example of arm positions both adding difficulty to the moves and signifying "complexity" as a thematic motif.

She exits stepping forward into upright walks on her toes, collapsing over forward as she comes down onto a full blade, twice, an image that again suggests grief or some such visceral emotion. She loops around the ice surface in an Ina Bauer, triple loop jump out of rolling threes, and forward spiral.

Broad turns down the length of the rink lead into a triple salchow followed by a combination spin as this legato passage builds then gives way to rhythm and dissonance.

A straight-line step sequence with several reversals of direction concludes with a final surprising reversal into another triple lutz—more emphasis on complexity. Star turns into a butterfly flying sitspin and strong forward crossovers build to an energetic peak with the music, which then thins out into a single sustained note as Kwan glides past the judges and TV camera, arms bent up to frame her face with flexed wrists and splayed fingers, eyes wide and intense. A thinner, smoother musical texture accompanies a serene denouement of spread eagle and back spiral, with a quick run of descending notes supporting a final double axel and a pose with one arm reaching up, the other crossed over her chest to the opposite shoulder, gaze focused proudly upward.

If one wanted to construct a linear narrative from the performance, it would be difficult to find explicit images within the choreography of a seductive Salome enticing Herod through a dance of veil removal. The moves and movement qualities might better represent a young woman venturing confidently into the world, encountering loss and confusion, but ultimately finding peace and triumph.

To observers familiar with Kwan's skating in the past, her increased speed and technical difficulty, particularly in the strong debut of her triple-triple combination, combined with better poise, posture, and precision in her positions, say more than her hairstyle or makeup about her new maturity as a skater. She was still no match in speed and flow across the ice or in the height of her jumps for the women who defeated her the previous year, her skating appearing cautious and controlled in comparison to theirs even as it carried new power and excitement compared to her younger self.

Seven successful triple jumps, especially the two triple lutzes (one in combination, one preceded by intricate steps) and the triple-triple combination, asserted Kwan's challenge to be ranked with the best in the world. The complexity of the steps linking the elements and the originality and variety in the spin positions further add to the program's difficulty and also to its artistic impression, signifying that Kwan was not just a young jumper but a well-rounded, artistic, and mature skater worthy of skating's highest honors. Her consistency in landing the jumps cleanly while others often falter, and her ability to perform complex steps and spins with ease, allowed her to defeat these skaters and others at Skate America and repeatedly throughout the 1995–1996 season.

This consistency marked Kwan's skating as solid, reliable, and technically sound in contrast to Bonaly's eccentric technique, Bobek's reputation for wildness, and Chen's apparent emotionality (and, as became apparent over the course of the season, Irina Slutskaya's relative lack of sophistication).

The intricacy of the choreography, with its frequent reversals of direction often leading unexpectedly into jumps or spins, and the emotional depth of the heavier passages convey the sense of an increasingly complex personality. The elaborate twists of skating path, torso, and especially arms, combined with the music and costume, evoke images of a sensual, luxurious, exotic Middle East. Through orientalist tendencies for Westerners to view this region of the world as feminized other,[37] the signifiers that mark the program as "Middle Eastern" indirectly also mark it as feminine and sexualized. These meanings may be unconsciously reinforced for some viewers by Kwan's ethnically Chinese facial structure—the orientalist theme both acknowledges Kwan's difference from the traditionally white image of the American skating darling and also elides that difference by shifting the frame of reference from Far East to Near and from Kwan the athlete/performer to Salome the character being portrayed.

This phenomenon may account for the repeated descriptions of her development from girl into "lady" in terms of her hypersexualized, hyperfeminine costume and makeup. Performed in practice clothes without the external accoutrements, Kwan's movements themselves would not seem to portray a Salome inciting a viewing Herod to lust, but the total context brings those meanings to the fore. Ironically, then, the Chinese American teenager became America's best hope for unseating Chinese world champion Chen by embodying a Westerner's fantasy about the sexual allure and danger of the East in order to prove that she was grown-up enough to merit the title of world champion.

PART TWO

How Figure
Skating and
Its Meanings
Developed

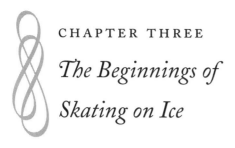

CHAPTER THREE

The Beginnings of Skating on Ice

*B*efore there was figure skating, there was skating, on whatever frozen body of water happened to be at hand, an age-old means of transportation and a leisure pastime.[1] Bone skates up to 4,000 years old have been found throughout various parts of northern Europe, shaved to a taper at one end and with holes at each end through which leather thongs could pass to attach the skate to the foot. These most likely were used for sliding with the aid of a "little picked staffe" for pushing against the ice, as mentioned in Fitzstephen's 1180 *Description of the most noble City of London.* Iron skates that would bite into the ice and allow the side-to-side skating motion known as the Dutch roll were in use in the Netherlands by 1498, according to the evidence of a woodcut by Johannes Brugman that depicts a man in the background advancing across the ice by such a method. The subject of the woodcut is Lydwina, a young woman of a century earlier who had been invited by her friends to go skating, fell to the ice and broke a rib, and suffered the aftereffects for the remaining thirty-eight years of her life. Canonized in 1890, St. Lydwina became the patron saint of ice skating; her story and Brugman's woodcut serve as evidence that in Holland of the late fourteenth and fifteenth centuries skating was an established wintertime activity for both males and females. Prints and written accounts from the sixteenth and seventeenth centuries indicate that activities of many sorts by participants of all ages and classes took place on the frozen canals and that organized speed skating races by both men and women were taking place by the sixteenth century.

Dutch aristocrats and the British royal family who lived in Holland while exiled during the Commonwealth introduced the elegant, dignified posture appropriate to the court to the process of gliding across the ice. The Princess of Orange evoked remark—but not scandal—when she removed her long skirt and tucked up her petticoats in order to allow herself greater freedom of movement while skating. Nevertheless, the relative encumbrance of women's apparel compared to men's, as well as cultural expectations that males would be more daring and more competitive in their athletic endeavors than females, ensured that the early development of figure skating would be primarily a male pursuit.

When the Stuarts returned to England upon the restoration of the monarchy, they introduced iron skates and the Dutch techniques of skating. In winter 1683, when the Thames froze solid for two full months, a fair was constructed on the ice, where Londoners enjoyed skating along with entertainments such as bull- and bearbaiting and foxhunting. Dutch sailors anchored at the Thames demonstrated "tricks and feats" on skates to the Londoners.

Skating at this point consisted primarily of the "Dutch roll" on forward outside and inside edges with occasional variations in the positions of the free leg and upper body. Because skating in Great Britain took place mostly on frozen ponds and fens rather than on the long canals connecting one town to another in Holland, racing and distance skating had less appeal, and refinement and expansion of skating techniques for use on relatively confined ice surfaces took precedence. During the eighteenth century, Englishmen of scientific bent developed curved blades that allowed easier turns and improved methods for fastening blades to boots. These improvements permitted further development of skating backward and skating circles on smaller radiuses, which would prove necessary for later systematic development of techniques of using the body to direct the blades in all the directions it was theoretically possible for them to move (i.e., all the possible edges and turns, as outlined in the appendix). Determining these possibilities and then working out the physical movements necessary to achieve them would be further manifestations of the English approach to skating as a matter of mathematics and physics.

Sometime before 1784, the Edinburgh Skating Club was formed, with a proficiency test for admission that required prospective members to demonstrate control and flow on edges by skating a complete circle on each foot (as in the figure eights that later became so important as school figures, except that the circles were not required to be joined together) and to demonstrate athletic daring by jumping over one, two, and three hats placed on the ice.

In 1772, Robert Jones wrote a *Treatise on Skating* that outlined "plain skating" on outside edges, including a "long roll," and on inside edges (easier for beginners to achieve but disdained in both England and Holland for prolonged use) and stopping. The latter part of the book described more advanced moves such as spirals, inside and outside circles and spread eagles, the "Serpentine Line" (repeated change of edge on one foot), backward skating, the "Salutation" for two skaters passing each other with a joining of hands while crossing, and a "figure of a heart on one leg," the principal component of which was what later came to be known as the three turn. Emphases on arm positions and finishing each move and illustrations of elegantly dressed and posed skaters indicated that the image skaters conveyed to onlookers was at least as important as accomplishing the moves. People who took up skating learned, from experts such as Jones and from the more accomplished skaters they encountered on the ice, not only to enjoy the kinesthetic experience of skating movement but also to convey messages about their standing as skaters through such codes as controlled posture and polished movement on the ice. The upright torso and gently curved free leg visible in portraits of skaters of the period such as Benjamin Rush and Johann Wolfgang von Goethe participate in a tradition of semiosis that aligns these bodily deportments with ideals of nobility.

Jones also lamented the fact that skating did not attract many female participants and encouraged women to take up the sport, noting that "A lady may indulge herself here in a tête-à-tête with an acquaintance, without provoking the jealousy of her husband; and should she unfortunately make a slip, it would at least not be attended with any prejudice to her reputation." The participation of women in skating was thus conceived in terms of potential social advantages for innocent interaction between the sexes.

The simple turn on one foot became known by its modern name of three, because of the 3-shaped mark it left on the ice. Joining two circles made on either foot produced a tracing that looked like an 8. Inspired by the ease of drawing these numerals, skaters in Holland and elsewhere on the continent began to develop methods for carving other numerals and letters of the alphabet into the ice. Writing one's name and drawing elaborate patterns became celebrated feats among accomplished skaters. In these practices was an impulse for self-assertion or self-expression by leaving one's mark on nature (traditionally stereotyped as a masculine urge) and by producing creative designs on the ice surface (the decorative function thereof being traditionally stereotyped as feminine). Throughout the nineteenth century and into the twentieth, one thread of skating development continued to consider the patterns left on the ice, more than the shapes the body made while doing so, as the locus of artistic expression in skating. Within this strand, "artistry" in skating would not be connected with the feminine associations of beautiful physical appearance, as discussed in chapter 5, on specularity, but with the masculine agency involved in transforming a medium outside oneself.

Skating techniques spread to Germany and France, which also saw textbooks published: *Ueber das Scrittshuhfahren* in 1790 and *Le Vrai Patineur* in 1813. J. Garcin, author of the latter book, along with fellow advanced French skaters known as "Gilets Rouges" on account of the red jackets they all affected, enthusiastically developed backward skating and moves that covered large expanses of ice. The Gilets Rouges considered skating an art comparable to dance, with attention to artistic positioning of arms and hands. Garcin gave fanciful names to the moves he described, such as Courtisane (forward outside three), Nymphe (back outside eight), Jump of Zephyr (waltz jump), and moves for two skaters known as Turtledove and Garland. A primitive spin or pirouette consisting of two or three revolutions was also included, but because it was difficult to exit gracefully it was generally used at the end of a series of moves rather than in the middle.

For Garcin and his compatriots, the form of the skater's body in performing each move was indeed central to artistry in skating. The imagery he drew on for the names of moves, and thus for the type of corporeal imagery aimed at, derived from aristocratic traditions of pastoral art and literature—a fantasy world populated by idealized lovers and supernatural beings and highly formal, conventionalized gestures.

This emphasis on grace and style was anathema to early-nineteenth-century English skating enthusiasts, who disdained concern for the decorative in favor of what they considered a more straightforward, practical scientific approach. A book published during an extended 1814 freeze on the Thames suggested such exercises as "When practicing the outside edge, the righthand pocket of the skater's jacket should be weighted with shot and a bag of shot or weighty article should be carried in the right hand." British skating authority G. Herbert Fowler objected to Garcin's approach, declaring that "toe steps, spins, and pirouettes, can hardly be described as skating, in the English sense of the word."[2]

The Skating Club was formed in London in 1830, with royal patronage and admission to membership by recommendation of members and later by proficiency test in order to ensure that only accomplished skaters would represent to the outside world the standard of skating espoused by the club. They pioneered "combined skating"—that is, patterns of moves for two skaters around a common center marked by a ball and later an orange placed on the ice. This served as the impetus for some of the symmetrical patterns later used in pair skating (and "fours" and synchronized skating), but more importantly it occasioned the development of the technical control necessary for returning to a fixed point and repeating the same movement immediately following in symmetrical fashion on the opposite foot, an organization of skills that would prove fundamental to the development of school figures.

Skating was now establishing itself as a club sport with official standards for inclusion (or exclusion). On the surface, these standards were based on skating ability. However, because both access to frozen bodies of water suitable for skating and ample leisure time to devote to skating whenever ice was available were necessary to achieving high levels of skill, not everyone had the means to achieve high proficiency, however talented they might have been. This necessity for flexible leisure time ensured that the greater proportion of expert skaters would come from the gentry and professional classes. And as the body of knowledge related to skating techniques grew, access to this knowledge through association with more advanced skaters skating together in such clubs led to ever-widening gaps between what casual recreational skaters and devoted, usually upper-class, enthusiasts could achieve.

Also in the 1830s, clubs were formed in Oxford, where skating proved popular among local "mechanics, tradesman and College servants"[3] after local resident Henry Boswell invented an improved blade that allowed greater control, particularly of backward maneuvers. Skating thus maintained a working-class affiliation in this town, one that furthered the mechanical advances of the sport. A newly formed club in Glasgow saw its club president George Anderson publish under the pseudonym of "Cyclos" an instructional book called *The Art of Skating*, which was soon published in translation in Germany and Sweden. Skaters in all these clubs proceeded with developing the technique necessary for performing combinations of threes, double threes, changes of edge, and loops both forward and backward.

Skating had been known since the eighteenth century in North America, where the artist Benjamin West had been one of the most well-known and accomplished exponents of the sport. In 1848, a Philadelphia skater named E. V. Bushnell improved on Boswell's blade by devising a method for permanently clamping blades to boots, thus providing greater stability. Philadelphians in 1849 formed a skating club that, because of the apparently frequent necessity of rescuing skating enthusiasts who fell through the Schuykill River ice, has been known since 1861 as the Philadelphia Skating Club and Humane Society, still in existence as the oldest club in North America. Like the Gilets Rouges, early members affected a uniform dress style, consisting of top hat, swallow-tailed coat, pantaloons, and white tie, an elegant costume that would distinguish the serious club members from casual skaters on the river. As members moved from Philadelphia they spread knowledge of skating techniques across the northeastern United States.

Throughout the nineteenth century, skating clubs continued to spring up across Europe and North America, with more accomplished skaters passing on established techniques and standards. Improved skate blade technology combined with mass production and the introduction of artificial ice and covered rinks led to increasing popularity of ice skating as a leisure activity, with some skating enthusiasts becoming serious practitioners of speed skating and/or figure skating techniques. Women as well as men participated, and various forms of hand-in-hand skating that would become the basis of pair skating were developed.

Not many names of individual nineteenth-century female skaters have been preserved, however, beyond the acknowledgment that several female members of European royalty gave impetus to the fashion for skating by taking to the ice, suggesting that during this period women were less likely than men to take leadership roles either in developing or preserving advances in skating technique, or at any rate to receive credit for such leadership. Fear of falling—initially of the physical consequences, and later of the social embarrassment occasioned by being seen to fall—appears to have played some role in the hesitance of women to take up skating.[4]

In their 1869 treatise *A System of Figure Skating*, H. E. Vandervell and T. Maxwell Witham include a chapter "for the ladies." They "rejoice to think that within the last few years the girls of England have been taking to skating in considerable numbers" and offer remarks based on their experiences teaching their female friends and relatives to skate. Along with questions of what to wear, and before proceeding to summaries of the basic edges and three turns, this chapter addresses the question of relying on some form of support while learning to skate. The authors first "divide our fair friends into two classes: those whose temperament is naturally timid, and whose physical powers are a little under the usual standard (and in which class we include those with weak ankles), and those who are courageous and strong. The former class will probably require artificial support to enable them to learn." They mention having once come across a suggestion of "a kind of basketwork crinoline or petticoat, and therefore of a bell-shape, tightly strapped round the waist, and reaching within a few inches of the ice. With this it would certainly appear impossible to fall, but we have never heard of its having come into practical use." Instead they recommend the use of a chair or a light wooden framework to lean on and express strong opposition to the use of "the ordinary stick." In addition to these "artificial" means of support, Vandervell and Witham also discuss a "natural" means: "By far the most agreeable . . . aid, is for the young lady to be supported by the arms, or by the elbows, or hands, either by two or a 'single' gentleman." This option, the authors note, offers the drawback that social interaction may interfere with actually learning to skate: "We have known several hours to pass by, almost as rapidly as the proverbial five minutes, without being able to detect that much progress has been made—that is, in 'the skating department.'" For "the second class of our fair skaters, namely those whose temperament is ardent, and whose courage and ankles are strong," the authors earnestly recommend relying on outside support as little as possible.[5] In the earlier part of the book, presumably addressed to male readers, the authors discourage the use of artificial support but "refer, however, those who require such aid to the ladies' chapter."[6]

These Victorian skating proponents thus reflect an expectation that even among those women who might adopt their preferred form of exercise, some will be too timid or too physically weak to progress from merely taking the ice in skates to actual figure skating. The majority of the chapter, however, is addressed to young women who do possess the temperament and either possess or are able to acquire the strength to pursue the sport fully. The authors also express expectation that the presence of female skaters will result in heterosexual interactions between the young men and women on the ice at the expense of actual skating. Their statement to their female readers that "should we find you wearing a dress rather short, we should smilingly approve,"[7] suggests, at least through its smiling, that putting on display more of the female body than was commonly revealed by the fashions of the day would be one benefit, to these male experts, of more females taking up the sport.

A generation later, an 1894 instructional book by a male expert contained a "Ladies' Chapter" written by an accomplished woman skater of the day, Miss L. [Lily] Cheetham. Cheetham reassured her readers that through practice they could overcome weak ankles and fear of falling. After offering instruction on some of her favorite moves, she concluded by recommending the sport on both practical and aesthetic grounds: "I can only hope that anything I have said may encourage all young skaters of my own sex to appreciate at its true value what has been one of my greatest pleasures and recreation during the past few years. Skating is not an expensive amusement, much less so than riding, for example; less tiring, and, I think, much prettier than lawn-tennis; and I am quite sure that it is decidedly beneficial from a health-giving point of view."[8]

An article in the January 28, 1860, issue of *Harper's Weekly* provides early examples of gendered meanings of skating, several of which would turn out to have lasting influence. The author noted that New York's Central Park offered two sites for skating. The "Gentlemen's Pond" was "a large space, which when the skating is good, may be seen covered with a couple thousand people. Here everyone may try his skill and tumble about on the ice as he pleases." The "Ladies' Pond" was "reserved for the fair sex, and no gentlemen are allowed to skate on it unless they are accompanied by ladies. It is kept in good order, and policemen on skates effectually repress all tendencies to rowdyism. . . . The scene when the ladies are on the pond is attractive in the extreme, and usually draws a large concourse of visitors."[9] The article goes on to catalog in imaginative detail eight varieties of falling on the ice, each described in terms of a male victim of his own overconfidence. Although most of the skaters probably evinced merely rudimentary skills at maneuvering around the ice for recreational purposes, the author does associate one variety of fall with "the phenomenon known to skaters as the 'outside edge,'" indicating that at least some of the pond skaters of the day were aware of the technical basis of what they were doing.

Men's skating, as depicted in this article, seems to have involved a degree of reckless athleticism, high speed, and a tendency toward showing off. It is not clear how many women, if any, ventured onto the Gentlemen's Pond in Central Park, and if so what they did there. The Ladies' Pond, by contrast, was a realm where orderliness reigned. It presented an attractive scene, the writer tells us, demonstrating a tendency to describe the women's activities in terms of visual appeal. Falls doubtless occurred among the ladies as well as the gentlemen, but, since they are not described as such, they were likely less frequent and less spectacular, suggesting perhaps that the female skaters were less likely to take the same kinds of risks by skating fast or attempting difficult maneuvers. Because gentlemen were permitted on the Ladies' Pond if accompanied by a lady, it likely served as a site for well-policed social interactions between the sexes. The fact that the orderliness of the ladies' domain was enforced by rules and policemen associates femininity and order with imposed restraint on a natural masculine wildness.

North American skating found an equally welcome home in Canada. Canadian skaters developed the technique of "grapevines," intricate two-footed maneuvers that remained of interest to skaters into the 1930s and have occasionally turned up since then as linking moves in freeskating programs (see, for example, Brian Boitano's 1988 short program to *Les Patineurs,* with its deliberate evocation of old-time skating images). Also in Canada, the practice arose of erecting covered sheds over sheets of ice in order to protect skaters (and the ice) from interference by wind and snow. British officers stationed in Canada brought back to London's Skating Club in the 1870s a "small tricky style of skating" they learned from Canadian enthusiasts, one not looked upon as good form by the devotees of the English style.[10]

North Americans had experimented with the possibilities for artificially producing ice surfaces, but the first successful rink so produced was built in London in 1876. "There was a gallery for spectators where on occasion an orchestra played for the benefit of the skaters. A noted artist from Paris was brought over to decorate the walls with Swiss Alpine scenery. The rink was not open to the public, but noblemen and gentlemen subscribed."[11]

Further attempts at rink building followed in a number of European and North American cities, with "ice palaces" providing a new venue for public entertainment that created a brief skating craze. The town of Leadville, Colorado, built a particularly grand Ice Palace in 1895, attracting visitors from throughout Colorado. "The skating master was Otis Richmond, a local miner who rather enjoyed himself observing all the talented young ladies in their colorful skating costumes. . . . Skating competitions were held and prizes were given to the neatest, the fanciest, the prettiest, the swiftest and most clever skaters."[12] The expert skater here was male (and working class; it is not clear how many of his pupils would have represented higher social classes), but the majority of the participants appear to have been female skaters, for whom fashion and appearance proved equally important as skating ability.

For the more technically minded skaters, who from the records appear to have been predominantly male, the crowds attracted to artificial rinks during the late-nineteenth-century skating craze interfered with serious practice. One solution, undertaken by the Princes Skating Club in London, was to build its own artificial rink for the exclusive use of its members. As the fad for recreational indoor skating waned, commercial rinks remained paying propositions by catering to growing interest in ice hockey and by leasing ice to figure skating clubs. How much time a skater could spend on the ice perfecting skills was now determined less by the climate where he or she lived than by whether there was an indoor rink nearby and how much ice time the skater could afford to purchase.

Informal or local competitions seem to have developed by midcentury. None have been documented before the 1870s, but a number of skaters who demonstrated their skill professionally for money advertised themselves before then as "skating champions."

The most important of these professional performing skaters was Jackson Haines, an American who had been trained as a ballet dancer and who as a young man during the Civil War performed in various capacities on the variety stage as well as in skating exhibitions. Haines's emphasis on body line and the positions of arms and legs—including the spin in sitting position, which he invented—and his use of theatrical costuming delighted audiences but drew scorn from American skating experts who found his skating technique wanting and considered his posing and theatricalism to be mere "fancy skating" rather than a serious demonstration of skill. Perhaps inspired by this criticism of his technique, Haines continued to work on learning and mastering the latest skating turns and other such maneuvers being developed in American and British skating clubs. In 1864 Haines left for England, where his skating met with similar criticism of his style, but he found greater approval on tours through continental Europe until his death in Finland circa 1875. Although Haines apparently spent his last years teaching skating in Scandinavia, he made his greatest impact in Vienna, where he entertained enthusiastic audiences with his interpretations of musical rhythms and theatrical characters on the ice and also attracted a number of disciples to his style of skating.

The difference in reception Haines encountered in the English-speaking countries and on the Continent is attributable to fundamental differences in how the various nationalities approached the sport. The "English style" (and the somewhat less advanced version of it practiced in America) focused on the scientific development of skating technique. It was during the third quarter of the century that a handful of Englishmen invented, or discovered, the advanced turns now known as brackets, rockers, and counters (see appendix). Vandervell and Witham's 1869 book *A System of Figure-Skating: Being the theory and practice of the art as developed in England, with a glance at its origin and history* was the first to address skating technique from a solid scientific point of view, including a chapter on "The Theory of Skating," with such subheadings as "Motion" and "Centre of Gravity."[13] Victorian skaters held combined skating to be the highest attainment of the medium. With symmetry considered the highest ideal in this practice, uniformity in carriage and dress (top hats, black frock coats, and trousers) and accuracy in tracing curves on the ice were paramount, leading to establishment of a standardized, somewhat rigidly mechanical use of the back, arms, and free leg. There was a correct way to perform the various moves, and any deviation was therefore incorrect and inferior.

For the Viennese or "International" style, as it came to be known, developed in the wake of Jackson Haines's sojourn in Vienna, by contrast, the gracefulness and expressiveness of the skater's movement to the eyes of spectators took precedence, with music a popular adjunct to the practice, inspiring skaters to think of what they were doing as dancing on ice. The presence of onlookers was taken for granted, and so the appearance of the skater's body, rather than the accuracy of the tracings left on the ice, defined the technique employed. Austrian skaters had discovered the bracket turn independently of the British and quickly adopted rockers and counters once introduced to them. Combinations of turns, loops, and changes of edge formed the basis of both English- and International-style skating, but moves such as spins and long held edges emphasizing body position (i.e., spirals) and stationary posing had a greater place in the International style, while accuracy and cleanness of turns held less importance.

As Nigel Brown put it, "To the Viennese, skating meant primarily something to see, to the English it meant something to do."[14] As I discussed in chapter 1, deriving meaning from appearance as opposed to action or deeds has long held connotations of femininity in Western culture, and with regard to skating this connotation may have been particularly salient for the nineteenth-century British. There is no reason to believe that Garcin and the Gilets Rouges or Haines and his Viennese disciples considered their pursuit of grace and attractiveness in skating in any way feminine; rather, it was simply a manifestation of refined taste. The British and, to some extent, American disdain for this approach to skating, however, may bear witness to an association between skating for show (as opposed to accuracy) and the lower social status accorded to feminine decorativeness compared to masculine action, as well as to the performing professions compared to upper-class leisure or to productive work.

As the body of skating technique and the expertise of its best practitioners advanced, some skaters became interested in comparing their skills formally to those of others. Competitions utilizing figure skating skills, as an alternative to speed skating races, appeared in the second half of the nineteenth century. Brown reports that a Danish race meet included an "artistic skating competition" that took the form of an obstacle race and that a series of competitions between North German and Viennese skaters included artistic events for ladies (1875) and men (1879).[15]

A landmark international competition held in Vienna in 1882 established a precedent for formal competitions to come. At this competition, Viennese skaters took first and second place, with winner Leopold Frey, a disciple of Jackson Haines, establishing the performance-oriented International Style as the standard to be emulated. Third place went to Axel Paulsen of Norway, a speed skater who was active in establishing the Christiana (later Oslo) Skating Club. A panel of judges evaluated the contestants on twenty-three prescribed moves or "compulsory figures," a four-minute freeskating performance, and a section of the event called "special figures" that allowed each contestant to present moves or combinations of moves that highlighted his own most advanced skills. Frey "linked an outside spread Eagle to a back outside eight and terminated on a Jackson Haines sitting pirouette."[16] Axel Paulsen performed a single spectacular feat, demonstrating the one-and-a-half revolution jump that bears his name, introducing the athletic component of transitioning from one edge to another by means of rotating in the air.

Another entrant, Theodor Langer, drew a filigree design of a symmetrical four-point star. The body movements required to produce this drawing were jerky and unpleasant to watch, and according to Brown were "anti-skating" in the sense that they did not use the flow of the blade across the ice.

The pattern traced on the ice, however, was aesthetically pleasing, and the feat of producing it demonstrated a high degree of skill and control. Other skaters were inspired to develop their own elaborate patterns, and tracing these designs, which came to be known as "special figures," became an important part of the sport for the remainder of the nineteenth century and into the first three or four decades of the twentieth. By producing something beautiful outside of himself, the skater demonstrated a degree of aesthetic refinement without the feminizing component of becoming the object of beauty himself. This practice was akin to the mechanical nineteenth-century "English style" of skating that was gradually being replaced even in England by the more eye-appealing and musical international style within the free-skating branch of the sport.

In the components of this landmark competition, we see three strands of meaning, which we might label as "technique," "athleticism," and "artistry," woven into the origins of figure skating as an organized sport. First, the compulsory and special figures represented technical skills of controlling the path of the blade on the ice, feats primarily of biomechanical engineering carrying with them the masculine associations of such activities. They also relied on a highly disciplined or "docile" and carefully measured use of the body to produce a predetermined, normative result, which suggests—at least to American ideologies of rugged individualism—domestication and an adherence to cultural authority that tended to associate the repressive aspects of civilized culture with the feminine sphere. Freeskating, on the other hand, involved both the masculine-coded athletic components of speed and jumping and the more feminine attributes of grace and beauty through the curving, flowing qualities of skating movement itself and through its alliance with the fine arts of music and dance.

In 1892, representatives of speed and figure skating organizations from various European nations convened to form the International Skating Union, one of the first such international governing bodies for any sport. In the 1892–1893 season, the ISU held its first racing championships, and in 1896 it sponsored the first annual World Figure Skating Championships, in St. Petersburg, Russia, to determine (in theory, at least) who was the best figure skater in the world. The competitions consisted of compulsory or "school" figures and freeskating. All the early competitors were male—until 1902, when Madge Syers, an Englishwoman, entered the championship and placed second in the field of four. No one in the ISU hierarchy had anticipated that women would wish to engage in competition at that level, but in the face of one who did, the 1903 ISU congress quickly rewrote the rules to prohibit women from competing in the existing championship, because "(1) the dress prevents the judges from seeing the feet; (2) a judge might judge a girl to whom he was attached; and (3) it is difficult to compare women with men."[17] At the following congress two years later, they instituted a separate ladies' championship, beginning in 1906, in which Syers defeated four other female competitors. In 1908 a pairs championship was added, and in October of that same year figure skating debuted as one of the first winter sports included in the (summer) Olympic Games. Figure skating was thus one of the first organized sports to include female participants on a nominally equal footing with males and one of the first to offer women the opportunity to participate in the Olympics.[18]

By the end of the first decade of the twentieth century, then, figure skating as an internationally organized competitive sport existed in the form that was to shape its meanings throughout the remainder of the century. How these meanings have changed, along with changes in the technical advances of the sport and shifts in the surrounding social context, constitutes the subject of the subsequent chapters of this book.

To appreciate skating as it is practiced in the twenty-first century, it is useful first to examine the meanings inherent in skating as practiced at the beginnings of its consolidated form a century earlier. As we have seen, the types of skills and images associated with figure skating involved a blend of masculine and feminine qualities, as evidenced by the gender associations of its technical (largely gender-neutral), athletic (masculine), and artistic (feminine) aspects. The varying proportions that each of these aspects has contributed to the gender mix that skating exhibited at any point in its history can be traced through the history of school figures and multi-revolution jumps as they have respectively waned and waxed in importance throughout the century, and through the history of what we might call the "specular" or visual aspect of skating as represented in the second mark awarded in free-skating competition for "artistic impression" or "presentation." Later chapters of this section will address each of these strands.

In addition, figure skating's meanings have been shaped by the social practices and values of its founders, that is, primarily northern Europeans and North Americans of European ancestry from the upper- and upper-middle social/financial strata. For obvious reasons, ice skating plays a larger part in the culture of civilizations located in cold climates and has less resonance for people living in warmer parts of the world, where natural ice is infrequent or unknown and artificial ice an expensive extravagance. It has not been until the latter part of the twentieth century, in the era of global mass communications, that skaters from Asia (most notably the relatively cold and wealthy nation of Japan since the 1960s) have achieved standards of skating comparable to those of the Europeans and North Americans, with skaters from China, Australia, and Korea entering international competitions beginning in the 1980s and 1990s and one Chinese lady, Lu Chen,[19] and one pair, Xue Shen and Hongbo Zhao,[20] also capturing world and Olympic medals. Chinese men, notably Zhengzhin Guo, Chiangjing Li, and Min Zhang, have been at the forefront of the quadruple jump trend. There have been few if any skaters of international caliber from Africa or south and southeast Asia or Central and South America, or even from southern Europe, primarily because very few ice rinks exist in these regions and skating even at a recreational level plays virtually no part in the local cultures.

A growing population of Americans and Canadians of Asian descent have also been attracted to figure skating in recent decades, more girls than boys, as is true of the skating population as a whole in these countries, with notable success particularly in U.S. champions Tiffany Chin, Kristi Yamaguchi, and Michelle Kwan, the latter two of whom have also won major international titles.

A number of people of African descent living in Europe or North America have also taken up skating where interest and proximity to ice have allowed, the most famous international competitors being American Debi Thomas[21] and Frenchwoman Surya Bonaly,[22] with 1998 junior world champion Derrick Delmore the most decorated African American man.[23]

On the whole, however, skating is widely perceived as a "white" sport because of its greater proportion and longer history of European and Euro-American exponents. The traditional movement vocabulary and body imagery employed in international-style freeskating has largely drawn on European genteel traditions, primarily the ballet since the days of Jackson Haines and the Viennese school, along with such social dance forms as the waltz and the march. Other forms of popular and stage dance have since made their way onto the ice, although African and Latin American rhythms and movement styles have generally first been filtered through white adaptations on the mainstream musical stage and in ballrooms.

In the parts of the world where skating on ice is a well-established form of recreation, only a minority of those who ever put on skates take up figure skating, and of those only a few reach the elite competitive levels. One effect of organizing an activity in terms of competition is to drive those who are good at the activity to aim at being the best. As we have seen, access to ice itself often entails considerable expense, and perfecting skating skills to a high competitive level demands many hours on the ice over a period of many years, all the more so as skaters at the highest levels of the sport continually push each other toward even higher levels of attainment. The insistence on amateur status through much of competitive skating's history has further re-stricted those who excel at the sport to be self-selected from the pool of those who can financially afford the costs of training. In addition, as the people shaping the sport draw on their own cultural backgrounds for its rules, val-ues, and traditions, it has tended to attract new participants of similar back-ground or those who aspire to this cultural stratum. One manifestation of upper-class culture within skating traditions has been the types of clothing skaters (and their families) wear on the ice and off to mark themselves as members of the skating community, in many cases occasioning further ex-pense. The following chapter traces the history of amateurism as it has shaped the sport's cultural meanings, and discussions of skating fashions appear at relevant points in subsequent chapters.

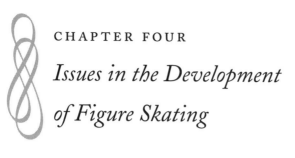

CHAPTER FOUR

Issues in the Development of Figure Skating

AMATEURISM

During the nineteenth century, as figure skating and other athletic pursuits began organizing at local, national, and international levels, the distinction between amateurism and professionalism in athletes was largely based on social class. "Gentlemen" who pursued athletic pastimes as part of developing a well-rounded personality, without thought of pecuniary gain, avoided competing against men who indulged in physical labor (and therefore might have an unfair strength advantage) or forsook well-roundedness in favor of specializing in a single sport.[1] Professional sports in the second half of the nineteenth century also attracted betting on outcomes and the use of unfair and corrupt means to win at any cost. From the point of view of the upper-class amateur athlete, *professional* was a dirty word, suggestive of money-grubbing and corruption. The ideal of amateurism in sport was to create a venue for competition and pursuit of excellence "untainted" by material reward, where upper-class athletes could indulge their love of sport and of what they considered "fair play." The rules for defining amateur status also resulted, not coincidentally, in sparing these upper-class sportsmen from having to associate with or compete against those they considered their social and moral inferiors. When the National Skating Association was formed in England around 1879–1880 and offered members the opportunity to pass proficiency tests in figure skating and receive badges in recognition for doing so, many English skaters saw this move as "violating the pure amateur status of the art," so much did they pride themselves on skating being "one of the few sports in the country 'untainted by professionalism and betting in any shape or form.'"[2]

The growth of interest in amateur sport intersected with Baron Pierre de Coubertin's goal in the 1890s of establishing the modern Olympic Games in emulation of the ancient Greek sports festivals. The International Skating Union, formed in 1892 to govern both speed and figure skating, was one of the first international governing bodies formed in any sport. In conjunction with the meetings by national sports leaders connected to formation of the Games, many other sports quickly organized at the international level. Because the issue of amateurism was of such pressing concern to amateur sport enthusiasts of the day, regulations of amateurism as a prerequisite for participation in the Games occupied a large part of Coubertin's organizational congresses and the early days of the International Olympic Committee. Enforcement of these regulations was largely the responsibility of each nation's Olympic committee and of the individual governing bodies for each sport.

At the time of the 1908 London Olympics, the fourth of the quadrennial events inaugurated in 1896 and the first in which figure skating events were held, the internationally accepted codes of amateurism stated that one ceased to be an amateur:

1. by accepting a cash prize;
2. by competing against a professional;
3. by receiving a salary as a teacher or instructor of physical exercise;
4. by taking part in competition open to all comers.[3]

Figure skating, then, almost from its beginnings as an organized sport, was associated with these strict ideals of amateurism. These codes made it impossible for an athlete to support himself (or herself) financially by teaching for money the skills at which he competed, thus making it practically impossible for those who had to earn a living by other means to attain the same level of skill as those who were independently wealthy or who practiced professions that allowed for flexible scheduling. This was particularly true for school figures, which required long hours of practice on pristine ice in order to become intimately familiar with how subtle shifts of the body's balance over the blade affected the tracings left on the ice. It is also true of the multi-revolution jumps that have become so crucial to competitive figure skating success in recent decades. Both types of feats require very precise body control and leave little room for error, which becomes objectively visible in erratic tracings on the school figures and poor landings or falls on the jumps. With artificially produced indoor ice available nearly year-round by the time figure skating competitions were established at the end of the nineteenth century, access to ice itself for long hours of practice, free from the distractions of crowds of unskilled skaters and the vagaries of the weather, further favored the skaters who could afford to join private skating clubs and to purchase multiple hours of ice time. Winter resort towns such as St. Moritz, Switzerland (favored by British skaters), or Sun Valley, Idaho, in the United States became popular destinations of well-to-do skating enthusiasts in the years between the world wars.

Under the codes of amateurism, skaters who achieved a certain level of expertise and competitive success but who could no longer afford the expenses of training, and who had not also prepared for careers in business, the professions, or the like, might "turn pro" in order to realize a financial return on their investment in developing skating skills. Their options, for the most part, were to teach skating or to perform with traveling ice shows. In either case, the fees they could command and their opportunities for advancement were largely dependent on the impressiveness of their amateur competitive titles.

Competitions for professional skaters were organized from time to time, but the level of competition where the most highly developed skills were to be seen has always been in the amateur arena. Until very recently, the number and frequency of professional competitions and the amount of money to be earned by entering them were negligible. Often they served more as an outlet for coaching and performing professionals to test their skating skills against their peers, and the demands of coaching and of touring generally meant that these professional skaters had less time to devote to their own training than they had had as amateurs.

Over the years, the governing bodies of the sport have enforced the prevailing understanding of principles of amateurism by defining certain activities as incompatible with amateur status and thus with eligibility to participate in the activities of the association, including the championships they sponsored. This effort led at first to a growing number of rules prohibiting certain actions, then, as ideology about amateurism in sport changed, to amendments and relaxations of most of those rules. Even in today's looser environment, however, the associations continue to define the territory and to require specific paperwork to document the now-approved activities.

Within a year after its founding in 1921, the USFSA adopted amateur status rules, based on those of the Amateur Athletic Union, defining an amateur as "a person who participates in Figure Skating for the sake of the pleasure afforded by the occupation itself and not for any pecuniary gain, being a person for whom the pursuit is solely a recreation and in no sense a business."[4]

In the 1930s, the USFSA Governing Council added a ruling that prohibited amateur skaters from "capitalizing on one's athletic fame" by appearing in movies and receiving direct or indirect compensation, or from allowing their names or skating titles to be used whether or not they received any compensation. In later years, that rule has been relaxed to allow such appearances provided that the association approved the contracts. Rules clarifying which sorts of club carnivals skaters could or could not participate in without jeopardizing their amateur status first appeared in 1936. The determination was based on the percentage of amateur versus professional skaters appearing in the show and on whether the show was controlled by the club, on the one hand, or by any professional skater or rink manager, on the other. Although such mere association with professionals appearing on the same ice is no longer itself a source of contamination to the purity of one's amateur status, activities such as club shows still require official sanction from the USFSA. Another rule disqualified skaters from amateur status if they received compensation for coaching, instructing, or exhibiting at a rink, or for designing and selling skates, clothing, or other sporting goods. Rulings in 1935 and 1945 allowed skaters who had lost their amateur status to be reinstated after a waiting period following their last professional act and clarified restrictions against reinstated former professionals competing in sanctioned competitions.[5]

These rules had different consequences for skaters in different situations. Once they abandoned amateur competition to turn pro, champions with impressive titles and public name recognition could earn considerable fees through professional appearances. The most successful skater to do so was Sonja Henie of Norway, the ten-time world champion (1927–1936) and three-time Olympic champion (1928, 1932, and 1936). In the 1930s and 1940s Henie widely popularized figure skating by starring in Hollywood films that showcased her skating ability and by touring North America with her own professional show. In so doing, she amassed considerable personal wealth and, in popularizing the ice show form, opened up professional performing opportunities for other less-decorated skaters in her own vehicles and in such shows as Holiday on Ice and Shipstad's Ice Follies, also begun in the 1930s. Henie, like many skaters, came from a well-to-do family, but her success (and the plot of several of her films, as discussed in the analysis of *One in a Million* that concludes this part) set the pattern of skating ability serving as a means to achieve wealth rather than as a result of being wealthy.

For not-yet-famous competitive skaters who wished to make a professional career of performing and/or teaching skating, the decision when to turn pro would involve weighing one's competitive success so far, the likelihood of achieving more impressive titles in the future by continuing to compete for another year or several years, and the availability of financial resources for training, travel, and so forth to allow further efforts at amateur competition. Under the code of amateurism, no such resources could derive from any skills or recognition achieved through skating or, in many cases, from participation in other sports-related activities. This presented the talented but not independently wealthy competitor with the dilemma that money was necessary to improve one's skating in order to compete successfully, but the only ways to earn money were either to engage in a profession that would occupy more of one's time than skating, or else to earn money through skating—and thus render oneself ineligible to compete.

For others, skating never had been anything but a form of recreation, whether because they did not have the time and money, or the talent, to reach the highest levels in the first place, or because they had always intended to make their life's work elsewhere and might or might not continue to skate throughout their lives at a less-than-competitive level. The vast majority of people who take up skating would of course fall into this category, if only because a small minority of those who aim at competitive success can actually win medals. Should these skaters teach skating or perform for pay at any point before the 1990s, however, they forfeited their eligibility to engage in amateur competition at any level. In addition, mere participation in a club show for which the organizers had not completed the appropriate paperwork or in which the appropriate ratio of professional to amateur performers was not observed could jeopardize a USFSA member's status, as could participation in an amateur competition that had not been sanctioned by the USFSA, for instance Ice Skating Institute events, even though such actions involved no act of professionalism or profit on the part of the skater concerned. (The ISI, a recreational skating association, provides an alternative source of skating instruction, testing, and competition for skaters not aiming at world-class recognition. At most times the USFSA has been willing to sanction ISI-run events to allow participation by USFSA members, but proper sanctioning procedures must be followed.)

The values underlying the ideology of amateurism derive from this recreational approach to sport and have been figured as a matter of honor. Amateur rules restricted not only the athletes' ability to profit financially from their sport, but also the amount of time they could devote to training. The noblest values of athletic competition—that is, the pursuit of excellence and the highest possible standard of achievement—are, however, fundamentally at odds with such principles. As good skaters strive to be the best in order to win competitions, and to be the best they personally are capable of in order to satisfy their own sense of honor and self-respect, the trend has been for the most successful competitors to devote more and more hours to training from an earlier and earlier age, supplemented by dance classes, weight training, and any other types of off-ice activities that will lead to demonstrable improvement on the ice, often at the expense of a normal education or social life during childhood and adolescence.

Avery Brundage, president of the International Olympic Committee from 1952 to 1972, sought to keep amateur values a pressing concern of the Olympic movement even as the growth of electronic mass communication offered successful athletes further fame and opportunities to capitalize on it commercially. In the realm of figure skating, ice shows might wish to secure the services of popular skaters at the height of their amateur careers, yet the skaters were not permitted to formalize any such arrangement while they still intended to compete in national, world, or Olympic competition. Any hint that a skater had done so was a cause for controversy, as when Ronnie Robertson (perennial silver medalist in U.S. and international competition behind Hayes Alan Jenkins during the mid-1950s) was rumored to have signed a contract with Ice Capades prior to the 1956 National Championships—the results of the men's competition at that Nationals were thus not made official until the USFSA had investigated the rumor and failed to discover sufficient evidence to disqualify Robertson.[6] A more complicated scenario arose in the pairs competition at the 1964 Olympics in Dortmund, West Germany, when silver medalists Marika Kilius and Hans Jurgen Baumler of Germany were alleged to have violated their amateur status and were required to return their medals, which were then redistributed to third-place finishers Debbi Wilkes and Guy Revell of Canada, with the bronze medals going to the fourth-place American team Vivian and Ron Joseph. In light of the failure of the West German or International Olympic Committee, or the ISU, to investigate the allegations thoroughly, years later Kilius and Baumler were awarded replacement medals.[7]

Beginning in the late 1950s, the Soviet Union, and shortly thereafter the German Democratic Republic, started sending skaters to international competitions. Within a decade, Soviet skaters were winning medals in the pairs and dance events, which they have dominated ever since, while East Germans ignored ice dance but produced ladies' world champions in the 1960s, 1970s, and 1980s, as well as champions in the men's and pairs events. These entrants were products of intensive government-supported sports programs, with successful competitors often awarded special privileges by their governments or comfortable salaries as members of the armed forces when their military service consisted solely of representing the nation in international competition. As with Eastern-bloc athletes in other sports, these skaters were often seen by their Western competitors as benefiting from an unfair training advantage that violated the spirit if not the letter of the amateur rules.

Meanwhile, Western skating federations and skaters were wrestling with questions of how to comply with the spirit of amateurism inherited from the nineteenth century in an increasingly commercial and competitive world in which the mass media were evincing and attracting growing interest in the sport. In 1963, the USFSA Governing Council revised its amateur rules, among other things making it "possible for news reporting of figure skating activities on the part of amateur figure skaters to be carried on with much less restriction than in the past" and to "worry about policing their own members without attempting to police those outside the membership."[8] In a *Skating* article clarifying revisions to the amateur status rules in 1970, Charles De-More noted that "Amateur Status, to a great extent, is a matter of honor and integrity," suggesting that although amateur status might indeed be defined largely by following rules and completing appropriate paperwork, mere adherence to those rules still carried a moral value.[9]

In 1976, Toller Cranston of Canada (that year's Olympic bronze medalist) referred to himself as "the last true amateur," referring not only to the state sponsorship his eastern European rivals enjoyed, but also to British Olympic champion John Curry's sponsorship by commercial entities.

The skating associations themselves began to turn to corporate sponsorship in the 1980s to help finance high-profile competitions and other association activities. Revenues from television contracts had been available since the 1960s, but in the 1980s and 1990s advertising by sponsoring companies began to appear on the rink barriers during televised competitions, and the events themselves began to bear titles such as "Campbell's Soups Tour of Champions" or the "State Farm U.S. Figure Skating Championships."[10] In the 1980s, individual top skaters could earn payments for appearances in exhibitions such as the Tour of Champions and from corporate sponsorship agreements, but such income had to be deposited in a trust fund administered by the skater's national governing body and the skaters could have access to the funds only for approved training expenses. During the 1980s, it also became a frequent practice for prominent skaters to sign with sports agents while they were still competing as amateurs. The USFSA also initiated the Eligible Skater Instructor Program, whereby skaters who had passed their junior tests could earn money for coaching lower-level skaters while still maintaining their own eligibility to compete, provided they filed the appropriate paperwork with the association. In 1994, the trust funds were finally eliminated, and skaters were allowed to earn and control their own money without restrictions.

The most drastic change in the distinction between "amateur" and "professional" skaters took place following the 1992 ISU congress, at which it was decided that each national governing body would have the authority to determine its own skaters' eligibility and that professional skaters would be allowed to reinstate their eligibility one time only, with approval from the association. This decision responded in part to a campaign by Brian Boitano, who had turned professional following his gold medals at the 1988 Olympics and World Championships, to be allowed to compete in another Olympic Games, should he qualify to do so. The reinstatement option came too late to affect the 1992 season and the Albertville Olympics, but with the next Winter Games in Lillehammer scheduled only two years later, Boitano and a handful of other well-known professional skaters did take advantage of the offer. In addition, a number of lesser-known skaters who had turned pro for financial reasons before they had achieved as much as they believed themselves capable in amateur competition also sought to regain their amateur status. The "window of opportunity" for reinstatement lasted from the 1993 to the 1996 season, with paperwork needing to be filed the previous spring and the skater needing to refrain from all unapproved activity during that time. Some applications for reinstatement were denied because the skater had not met all these requirements, and during the final year of reinstatement the USFSA failed to forward to the ISU in time to meet its deadline the paperwork that would have established the skaters' eligibility to represent the United States in international competition, effectively eliminating the incentive for several of the skaters involved actually to return to amateur or, as it was now referred to as, "eligible" competition.

The same 1992 ISU congress also authorized national governing bodies to sponsor "pro-am" competitions in which both "pro" (professional or "ineligible") and "am" (amateur or "eligible") skaters could compete against each other for prize money. The USFSA has held such competitions for American skaters each spring and fall since the 1992–1993 season, using ISU-certified judges. Often the format included an amateur-style short program followed by an "artistic" program similar to professional competitive programs or exhibitions in that vocal music is permitted, as are moves illegal in eligible competition, such as backflips, while the number of triple jumps allowed is further limited in number. The first program thus favors eligible-style skating and the second the professional, more entertainment-oriented approach. In other years, these pro-ams have sometimes included only the artistic phase and have sometimes been held as team events, on occasion using a "battle-of-the-sexes" format of men versus ladies, so that these events serve primarily as an opportunity for the skaters to perform their programs for judges in a relaxed atmosphere without having to worry about the effect of their performances on their national or international rankings and for both the skaters and the association to earn money.

In light of the surge of public interest in skating following the 1994 season and the proliferation of new professional competition opportunities developed at that time, the ISU sought to discourage the top eligible skaters from turning pro and abandoning ISU competition by offering prize money at its championships for the first time. ISU officials also organized their own pro-am competitions beginning in 1995–1996 and structured the major eligible fall competitions into a "Champions Series" or "Grand Prix" circuit. ("Grand Prix of Figure Skating" was the name originally chosen for this circuit, but the ISU was not able to obtain legal rights to use this name until 1998–1999.) During the fall competitions, skaters earn not only prize money but also points based on their finishes at these competitions, with the top point earners competing against each other in a series final (with larger prizes) that rewards consistency over the course of the season. This Grand Prix acts as a preview of Worlds, though not always with the same results.

In the 1998–1999 season, the ISU expanded its series of pro-am or open competitions ("open" in the sense of permitting both eligible and ineligible skaters to participate with no penalty to the eligible skaters' eligibility—but invitational, favoring skaters with world and Olympic medals or other prominent titles, not "open" to anyone who wishes to enroll). They also agreed to sanction, as long as they could provide judges for, a number of formerly unsanctioned professional competitions produced by Dick Button's Candid Productions in conjunction with the International Management Group (IMG), a large corporation that both produces sporting events and serves as agent to athletes, including many prominent skaters. This agreement increased the number of open competitions with high prize money available to eligible as well as ineligible skaters, effectively reducing the incentive for skaters who no longer wish to compete at the World Championships and similarly run competitions to give up their ISU eligibility while pursuing more art- and entertainment-oriented opportunities. Several professional skaters, including Boitano, however, decided that they no longer wished to be judged by ISU judges and declined to enter any of these newly sanctioned events. This ISU experiment in more or less taking over the existing professional events proved unsuccessful enough that a year later they relinquished control of most of these events, which either returned to an all-professional format or simply ceased to exist.

In 1997, the USFSA eliminated the Eligible Skater Instructor Program, reducing the amount of paperwork involved and allowing eligible skaters (or judges) at *all* levels to teach without losing eligibility, with the sole exception that judges could not serve on a panel judging any of their students for at least a year after last teaching them.

By the start of the twenty-first century, then, "amateurism" is no longer about money or about profiting from one's participation in sport. The only kind of activity that would necessarily compromise one's eligibility is participating in an unsanctioned event—in other words, the various professional competitions run by commercial promoters, many new since 1994 and a few with longer traditions dating back to the 1970s or 1980s. Sanctions are available for club shows and for amateur competitions such as State Games or Ice Skating Institute competitions, and for some open noncommercial competitions such as the figure skating event at Gay Games, so for all skaters except the elite handful who are offered opportunities to compete in pro competitions, the only reason to lose eligibility would be failure to obtain the necessary sanctions. Even for that handful of skaters, there are now more-than-adequate opportunities to compete for money in sanctioned invitational competitions. Because reinstatement to eligibility to compete internationally is no longer an option, some skaters may have lost the opportunity to do so through the timing of their own professional activities and the rule changes throughout the 1990s. For those who are currently still eligible, however, performing in touring shows or television specials, coaching, endorsing commercial products, and the like are now viable ways to finance advanced training. Skaters at lower or intermediate levels can also earn income by teaching learn-to-skate classes or low-level private students without compromising their eligibility to compete in USFSA competitions. The distinction between "eligible" and "ineligible" has become one of the governing bodies' retaining some control over how skating is run in their name and deriving some profit (through sanction fees, etc.) from their members' activities. Whether the distinction will ever be erased completely so that skaters who participate in unsanctioned, unstandardized competitions will also be permitted to qualify for and compete in national and international championships remains to be seen, but at present there is no significant movement to allow that option.

FIGURES

As noted in chapter 3, early competitions and proficiency tests generally required skaters to perform specified ("compulsory") moves ("figures") in order for those judging the competition or overseeing the test to compare each skater to the others or to an established standard. In 1868, for instance, the American Skating Congress adopted a series of various types of movements to be included in competitions between American and Canadian skaters. Other late-nineteenth- and early-twentieth-century competitions included special figures and/or freeskating in addition to the compulsories. Freeskating was also referred to as "free figures," since early free programs consisted largely of the same kinds of established moves used in the compulsories, freely arranged around the ice surface by the skater, and the word "figure" was often used by English-speaking skaters during that period to refer to any skating move. The bulk of what was judged, however, were standard moves that everyone was expected to perform, with comparisons being made as to who performed each move best, second best, and so forth.

In 1897, the ISU adopted a schedule of forty-one "school figures" of progressively greater difficulty, proposed by the British representatives. These remained the standard compulsory figures used in testing and competition throughout the skating world until 1990, and which the USFSA continued to offer as a separate discipline in the 1990s. These figures all consist of two or three tangent circles with one, one and a half, or two full circles skated on each foot, in some with turns or loops included on the circles.

From the first World Championships in 1896, organizing officials drew six of these figures by number to be competed at that competition. Since most of the figures used at the international level involved versions beginning on both the right and the left foot, that meant skaters were required to take the ice up to twelve times each, not including the freeskating. The figures portion of the competition was worth 60 percent of each skater's total score and freeskating 40 percent. "Special figures" were never included in the World Championships, although they were competed as a separate discipline at other competitions, including the 1908 Olympics.

For each start, the skater performed the figure three times on each foot, for a total of six, a practice that gave rise to the system of awarding marks based on a standard of 6.0 as perfection. Judges rated the skaters on the ease and flow of their movement around the circles and the correctness of their body form and also on the accuracy of the prints left on the ice, taking notes of any wobbles or other deviations from a perfect circle, scrapes, double tracks indicating that both edges of the blade had been in contact with the ice at the same time, and other such errors, as well as how closely the tracings from each repetition followed each other and how well the turns or loops lined up.

It might take one to two minutes for a skater to complete three repetitions of a single figure, compared to the four or five minutes for a freeskating program, but adding in the time the judges took to examine the tracings and the number of figures involved, this was clearly the most time-consuming phase of competition. With competitions mostly held outdoors in Europe until the 1960s, weather also was often an issue. After World War II, when the number of countries sending skaters to the World Championships increased, the ISU decided to cut the number of figures to a maximum of six, alternating right- and left-foot starts rather than requiring both. The relative importance of figures and freeskating to the final result remained 60 percent to 40 percent until the 1969–1972 seasons, when the balance was changed to 50/50.

Throughout this first seventy-some years of organized competition, while school figures carried the most weight and remained the deciding factor in most championships, skating authorities held differing opinions on the true value of these exacting exercises. As early as 1927, USFSA president A. Winsor Weld wrote, "By no means would I go so far as to advocate the complete elimination from competitions of 'school figures': although good arguments might be advanced even for this, I do suggest, however, a distinct reversal of their present rating as compared with free skating."[11] Evelyn Chandler Baier, a headliner with Ice Follies in the 1930s, expressed the belief that the best figures skaters rarely made successful show skaters and the best free skaters rarely excelled at figures, whereas multiple U.S. champion and later coach Maribel Vinson Owen remarked, "Take the school figures out of skating and you have an undisciplined sport. There can be no substitute technique— there are no short cuts."[12] By the 1950s, former champions whose strengths and preferences had been for the freestyle side of the sport, such as Dick Button and the artistic Frenchwoman Jacqueline DuBief (who won the ladies' world title in 1952, the same year that Button won his last men's title), were arguing in favor of freeskating-only competitions.[13]

How-to books aimed at beginners devoted the bulk of their instruction not simply to the skills of edges and turns that school figures were designed to teach, but to their execution specifically on the circles as required for testing and competition.[14] The USFSA did not include freestyle requirements in any of its tests until the 1960s, beginning with the eighth (senior) test and adding freestyle components to the sixth and seventh (junior) tests, and finally to the fourth (novice) test in 1970, before introducing a separate freestyle test stream at all levels in 1977–1978. Not only did the figures carry greater or equal weight in competition until the 1970s, but when there were many entrants in a given competition—for instance, in the lower level ladies' events at U.S. regional competitions and at some points in the history of the World Championships—figures were used as the elimination portion of the competition. Under such a system, strong freestylers who were not among the best in the compulsories never even got the opportunity to demonstrate what they did best.

The skater who wished to advance and receive recognition for her accomplishments through passing tests and placing in competitions thus had to devote the majority of her practice time to the dozen or so specific figures that made up the next test she was aiming to pass and the pool from which figures would be drawn in competition at her competitive level. To be able to check her tracings and to stay on the circle without having to watch out for other skaters, figures were generally practiced on "patch sessions," in which each skater would contract to rent a patch of ice fifteen or so feet wide and extending halfway across the rink. For an hour at a time, several times a day, the rink would be filled with skaters, each on her own patch of ice, skating around and around her own set of circles with exacting attention to how each tiny body movement affected the precision of the results on the ice. These sessions would alternate with freestyle sessions (as well as with periods when the ice was used for ice dancing, public skating, hockey, or other uses), and, once frequent resurfacing became feasible with the invention of the Zamboni resurfacing machine, patch sessions would always begin with clean ice to allow skaters to see their tracings.

Some skaters found the sedate pace and repetition calming and the visible results of one's efforts rewarding. Many others who preferred more athletic or expressive qualities of the sport found the amount of practice necessary to produce perfect circles and perfect turns tedious, to be suffered through in order to be allowed to indulge in freestyle. Most coaches and judges extol the virtues of figures practice for learning the skills and control necessary for high-quality freestyle skating, but most children learning the sport lack the patience and interest to enjoy the process, at least until they reach a fairly high degree of proficiency.

By the 1960s, as television increased freestyle skating's popularity as a spectator sport, and in view of the fact that the standards of freeskating had risen continuously over the years while skaters continued to perform the same school figures with little improvement in quality, proposals to do something to change the situation took on more urgency. T. D. Richardson, a British champion of the 1920s who later published ten books on the subject, noted that figures constituted the majority of what determined a competitive skater's career. His solution to the lack of advance in figures performance was to introduce yet more difficult figures with more complex turns on the circles.[15] Per Cock-Clausen, a World-level referee from Denmark, agreed that figures were not being performed to a sufficiently high standard, lamenting "that compulsory figures are performed with insufficient lean and speed and that too little attention is paid to style." He suggested requiring competitors to compose "a creative figure containing certain prescribed elements such as rockers, brackets or others" that could be performed "in a graceful style" (in distinction to "the old Starfigures" or special figures with their jerkiness and contortions), to eliminate the triple repetition but to restore the practice of skating the figures starting on both the right and left foot, and to allot more marks in all figures "for style, lean and speed."[16]

For the 1969 season, the ISU did reduce the value of figures in singles competition to 50 percent, equal to that of the freestyle component. Under the scoring system then in use, however, judges scored skaters for each figure and for the free program, and then the total score each judge gave a skater determined that skater's ordinal placement from that judge for the competition as a whole. This meant that a skater who excelled consistently at all the figures continued to have an advantage over those who placed only moderately well in the figures and higher in the freestyle. This effect was seen with Jeannette Altwegg of Great Britain, who won the 1951 World Championship with unanimous first-place scores in figures and only a sixth placement in freestyle. Under the revised weighting, Beatrix "Trixi" Schuba of Austria achieved similar results in 1971 and 1972.

Schuba's reign coincided with the career of American Janet Lynn. Lynn was consistently judged the best freeskater, and she enchanted fans who witnessed her performances live and via television but who had difficulty understanding why she placed no higher than third or fourth while the gold medal went to the skater whose freestyle performance was judged no better than sixth. Largely in response to the system's failure to reward the skater who shone in the most public portion of the competition, beginning with the 1973 season the ISU instituted a freestyle short program of required moves (along the lines of the pairs short program that had been introduced a decade earlier) and to reduce the number of figures skated to three. The weightings were at first 40 percent for figures, 20 percent for the short program, and 40 percent for freeskating, revised as of 1976 to 30/20/50, further lessening the value of figures skills compared to freestyle. This balance obtained until 1988, with championships going to "well-rounded" skaters who could place relatively well in all phases of the competition.

Triple jumps were taking on more and more importance in the ladies' competitions as well as the men's, and artistic or performance aspects of freeskating combined with increasing television coverage were raising the standards in the second mark of the freeskating portion of the events and attracting more fans to the sport (see the following section of this chapter, on jumps, and chapter 5 on specularity and artistry). It was becoming evident that the ability to skate precise figures and the ability to meet the athletic and presentation criteria of freestyle competition did not necessarily go together and that talented freestylers were being held back by the necessity to demonstrate high-quality figures before advancing to the next test level or phase of competition.

As mentioned earlier, in the 1978 season the USFSA introduced a separate series of freestyle tests beginning at the preliminary level. Also during this period, they introduced elimination rounds at the regional competitions, wherein all skaters entered in large events would be divided into smaller groups to perform their free programs, with the top few skaters from each group advancing to a final round that would include both figures and freestyle. The ISU later instituted a similar system at its World and Junior World Championships. These changes increased the importance of freeskating in determining what level a skater could compete at and also prevented strong freestylers from being eliminated from competition after the figures without having had an opportunity to perform their free programs.

Throughout this period, international medals were won primarily by representatives of a small number of countries (the United States, the Soviet Union, East Germany, Canada, and, to a lesser extent, Great Britain and West Germany), all of which boasted either a large affluent middle class or intensive government support for athletic training. Meanwhile, more countries with fewer ice rinks and fewer financial resources to support skaters' training were joining the ISU and sending skaters to its competitions. With limited ice time available for training figures, these skaters were at a competitive disadvantage. By the late 1970s, there was talk of eliminating compulsory figures from international competitions, and discussions on the matter continued through the following decade. Reasons for getting rid of figures in competition included the facts that practicing figures takes up too much training time and conflicts with school; figures are very costly to run at competitions (because of the long hours of ice time required); they are boring to watch (and therefore don't attract paying spectators or television sponsorship); and limited practice ice in Europe put European skaters at a disadvantage.[17]

At the June 1988 ISU Congress, a vote passed to reduce the figures in international senior and junior competition to only two for the 1989 and 1990 seasons. Figures would now count for only 20 percent of the total score and the weight of the short program proportionally was raised to 30 percent.

More shockingly, they also voted to eliminate figures entirely from international competition beginning with the 1991 season. As skating historian Benjamin Wright put it, "The die was cast and the sport, in Singles skating at least, was changed forever."[18] Only the United States, Canada, Great Britain, and New Zealand dissented; although the Soviet Union had also produced skaters strong in the figures portion of competitions and might have been expected to favor retaining figures, when it came to the vote they sided with the European majority.

Reactions to this decision were strong. American skaters anticipating the imminent removal of figures from competition voiced their allegiance to the discipline:

The whole reason figure skating is called figure skating is because of figures. (Debi Thomas)

Honestly, I think that figure skating would really be at a loss. It's heritage. You can't just cut off something. It's part of the sport. (Jill Trenary)

I think definitely if you drop figures you're going to find a different kind of sport. I think it's going to go professional. (Brian Boitano)

Who knows what the economic ramifications are going to be. I mean, coaches aren't going to be teaching as many lessons. Rinks aren't going to be selling as many hours of ice time. It could really hurt the sport. It could kill the sport. The ISU being what they are, they don't care. It costs them money to have figures at a championship. They don't care what it does to the rest of the sport as long as they can have another cocktail party. (Scott Hamilton)

Sonia Bianchetti, the Italian chair of the ISU technical committee, countered:

Well, may I say that only the English-speaking people called our sport figure skating. That is not the right word for our sport, that all the rest of the world call it artistic skating. . . . They are really basically like the scales for a pianist. But as for the pianist that plays these scales to learn to play the piano, when he gives a concert he just plays the symphony and not the scales.[19]

Coaches tried to put the change in competitive focus, and the place of figures in training, into perspective. Some pointed out the benefits of figures for training and for competition:

My major thing now with my students is that these kids realize that without compulsory figures there would be no jumps, there would be no footwork, there would be no program. (Robin Cousins)

I'm very unhappy, very unhappy, because I think it changes the picture of the sport. It'll be much more difficult to judge. The judging's already controversial, it'll be even more, and I think they take away something that discipline [*sic*] the kids when they were young and I think they take away also the basics. (Carlo Fassi)[20]

Others looked to the future and to potential advantages the elimination of figures might bring:

An old friend. You lived with them all your life as a skater, competitor, and coach. However, I feel that it's an economic issue and it reduces the cost of our sport and it opens our sport up to many many more people. (Evy Scotvold)[21]

In hindsight a decade later, a coach recalled their value:

It's a tedious thing but it teaches tremendous self-discipline. I think that helped a lot because figure skating really is a sport based on discipline. (Frank Carroll)[22]

With figures no longer a component of international competition, how to handle their inclusion in domestic programs became a topic of hot debate. The USFSA chose to separate figures and freestyle entirely in its test and competition streams beginning at the novice level, but to leave them combined at the lower levels in order to ensure that all skaters demonstrated a grounding in the fundamental skills represented by school figures. Thus, once a skater had passed the fourth figure test and novice freestyle test, she could continue to test either freestyle or figures independently of each other and to enter competitions in one discipline or the other without the requirement to have passed the test for the corresponding level in the other discipline. At intermediate level and below, both freestyle and figure tests for the respective level were required for competition, which continued to include both figures and freestyle components in a combined competition. For 1993, the fourth test requirement was dropped for freestylers moving up from intermediate to novice competition.[23]

Finally, as of the 1995 season, figures were entirely separated from freestyle at the lower levels as well. In place of school figures as a testing requirement, the USFSA introduced a new series of "Moves in the Field" tests that evaluate stroking and combinations of the various one-foot and two-foot turns to be performed at freestyle speed, with focuses on power, edge quality, extension, and quickness. These sequences of moves test similar basic skills to those included in figures, but within a freestyle context. Judges do not examine the tracings on the ice at close range for flats and scrapes or the exact placement of the turns as when judging figures, and there is no requirement to repeat one part of the pattern directly on top of the tracings of the previous repetition. Instead, movement across the ice with good carriage and flow, and in most cases with more speed, is if anything more important than in the figure tests. Many of the moves, or portions of them, could be incorporated directly into a freestyle program without appearing out of place.

The elimination of figures requirements at the lower freestyle levels effectively put an end to figures as a living discipline in the United States, much as they had already disappeared in most of the rest of the world. Among those who had gotten well into the figure test structure, some skaters had grown to enjoy and appreciate the discipline or to recognize a greater talent in figures than in freestyle and continued to test and compete, but the numbers steadily dwindled. New skaters, particularly children, who take up skating are unlikely to be attracted to studying figures now that they are not required to do so, and most skaters who had been partway through the figure test structure when the requirements were dropped chose not to continue.

With the sudden drop in demand for patch sessions, many skating clubs eliminated them entirely or severely reduced the number of hours per week devoted to patch, thus making it difficult for figures specialists in the late 1990s to achieve the same standards as the best figures skaters of even a decade earlier.[24] The USFSA stopped certifying new judges to judge figures and dropped figures from regional competitions, allowing competitors to proceed directly to sectionals in 1998 and 1999 and combining the men's and ladies' competitions because the number of boys still competing at figures anywhere in the United States was insufficient to hold a competition. Beginning with the 1999–2000 season, figures events are no longer offered at U.S. qualifying competitions.

The endless tracing of adjacent circles, the figure eight that has long stood as an emblem of skating itself and that turned on its side serves as the symbol for infinity, carries a number of meanings both phenomenologically inherent in the activity and symbolic of broader social meanings. I have heard fellow adult skaters describe the process, with its endless repetition and minute concentration, as meditative and zenlike. A column in *Skating* magazine marveled:

> Eight-making has emotional, as well as mental symmetry. The confusion of the world is pushed aside for awhile as the path stretches endlessly, seamlessly, and the body sings a soothing melody as the flow of the blade produces one vast muscular hum. . . .
>
> But there is that incredible roundness to circles. You laugh! But consider: earthly motion is straight lines. A thrown ball will not return to the thrower. Whirled objects released will not stay "in orbit." Even a boomerang does not make a real circle. But we can. A push, a slight "falling" of weight, a minute tip of blade and voila! le cercle.[25]

Nowhere more than in the practice of school figures, in which the very object of the exercise is the pursuit of the perfect circle, is the symbolism of the circle as representing perfection to be strived for more evident: "Figure skating . . . is about the creation of perfect circles which simulate the orbs of the universe. It is about the achievement of flow, which simulates the cycle of nature: movement (life); stillness (death)."[26]

Once school figures had been cemented into their standardized form by the start of the twentieth century, the sense of scientific or creative exploration of the different ways it was possible for the human body to direct the blade that had characterized their development during the preceding century diminished. Coaches and other experts might seek to refine understandings of why the biomechanics of certain body positions and muscle tensions produced the results they did; for the average skater, however, the practice of school figures had become not a source of discovery, but rather one of rote repetition of a limited set of already-established moves. Because there was a "correct" way to perform them, the social value implicit in this discipline is that of conformity to established standards, or norms, which normalizes a particular set of bodily images along with the social meanings attendant on these images.

Even within the seemingly most objective aspect of the sport, the tracing of compulsory figures, not only the tangible evidence carved into the ice but also the visual impression of the skater's movement while performing these feats took on significance—it mattered not merely *what* was performed, but *how*. The value system by which the founders of the sport determined what constituted "good" skating required that skaters perform the required moves in a manner that made them look easy and that presented a visual image of grace. Because this ease of movement can be achieved only through "correct" technique, usually requiring long hours of practice, the appearance of such ease serves as an indexical sign of the skater's technique and the work she has engaged in to achieve it. Paradoxically, this work is manifested through the *lack* of visible effort in her movement.

Ease of movement also, however, serves a symbolic function, with each correctly schooled skater embodying an image of ease and grace as the ideal of human movement or, at a higher level of abstraction, of human existence. As social symbolism, such images accord well with an upper-class or well-to-do lifestyle in which means exist to find solutions for most problems of daily living and the avoidance of social friction or tensions is a desideratum of the ideal life. The ordered discipline of a patch session, with skaters tracing predictable paths and not getting in each other's way, might appeal most to those who similarly desire orderly and predictable social relations. As an ideal, of course, these images would appeal not only to individuals who already enjoy such a lifestyle, but also those who aspire to it. And as an idealization, such fantasies leave out those struggles or tensions that not even wealth, or secure skating technique, can prevent.

Easy movement holds less symbolic value for individuals from social strata where struggle is an unavoidable and acknowledged part of daily existence —for such individuals, visible effort in human movement may seem a truer representation of the nature of human life. The effortless ideal of skating would hold less appeal for these individuals, who would either dismiss skating entirely as unworthy of their interest or else prefer aspects such as jumps in which risk, effort, and freedom are more salient aspects of the movement.

JUMPS

As we have seen, jumping on ice skates had long been a component of the athletic side of freeskating practice, from the early feats of jumping over objects such as hats or barrels placed on the ice (or, quite likely though undocumented, natural objects such as logs), to the waltz jump or "Jump of Zephyr" and other such small jumps as ornaments to the artistry of graceful freeskating, and later, in the 1880s, to Axel Paulsen's foray into multiple revolutions with his eponymous jump. It was not until well after the establishment of organized skating competition, in the early years of the twentieth century, however, that the various ways of jumping were formally categorized and the one-revolution jumps with their standard back outside edge landings—to which, like the axel jump, it later became possible to add more revolutions—were invented. Multiple world champion Ulrich Salchow of Sweden and Alois Lutz, an Austrian skater who never competed at the world level, introduced the jumps that bear their names during the years preceding World War I, along with German skater Werner Rittberger's loop jump, which is sometimes referred to in Europe as a Rittberger. The toe loop (or cherry flip) and flip (toe salchow) jumps, toe-assisted versions of the loop and salchow, respectively, seemingly did not appear until they were introduced after the war by American Bruce Mapes. These single versions of the current multi-revolution jumps soon became standard elements in the athletic freeskating repertory, but unlike the later technical importance of double and triple jumps they received no more emphasis than the half- and no-revolution jumps that emphasized spectacular air positions such as split or crossed legs, serving similar purposes in punctuating the gliding movements of the skating with explosive movements above the ice. The 1920s also saw the introduction of the flying sitspin by Swedish champion Gillis Grafstrom and the first double jumps performed in practice by Grafstrom and Austrian Karl Schafer, as well as refinement of rotational technique for the axel jump. It was not until the 1930s that skaters, led by the Austrian men, began including double jumps in their competition programs.[27]

These athletic components of skating at first were considered inappropriate for female practitioners of the sport; in 1920, American Theresa Weld received reprimands for performing a single salchow jump because her skirt would fly up to her knees, creating an image deemed too risqué. In 1924, however, eleven-year-old Sonja Henie made her first appearance in world and Olympic competition. As a child, she could properly wear a short skirt and bloomers, as opposed to the ankle-length skirts her adult competitors wore, and thus she was able to demonstrate the same kinds of jumps and flying spins performed by the more athletic of the male skaters. Because Henie at that point was not yet as accomplished at school figures as her older rivals, she finished eighth out of eight competitors in the 1924 Olympics and fifth at that year's World Championships. By 1927, however, at age fourteen, she won her first world title and went on to dominate the sport for the next decade, winning every competition she entered until turning professional at the end of the 1936 competitive season. During her reign, skating saw an increase in athleticism for both male and female skaters, including the prevalent use of short skirts to allow female skaters the necessary maneuverability. With this new athleticism came the beginning of a trend toward youth, with many of the most accomplished skaters, especially among the ladies, still in their teens.

In 1930, Maribel Vinson included an Axel Paulsen jump in her free program, and in the mid-thirties Cecilia Colledge, successor to Henie's world title in 1937, became the first woman to perform a double salchow jump. By the time international competition was interrupted once again by World War II, double jumps had become commonplace in men's skating and unsurprising from the ladies but not yet required or expected of top competitors of either sex. Because moves such as jumps that required high levels of athletic exertion were considered less central to skating technique than long gliding moves such as spirals and spread eagles, "for the skaters of that period a very good physical condition was not necessary," according to a Czech expert. "Figure skating was then considered primarily a sport for ladies as a weaker sex, and it was recommended as an easy and not too demanding sport for boys who were less physically capable."[28]

North American skating lost many of its male practitioners to military duty during World War II and then to adult careers when they returned, leading to a shift in favor of a female majority among both skaters and volunteer officials such as judges and referees, a trend that has continued ever since.[29] Under the prevailing system of amateurism and volunteerism, the majority of such officials consisted of women and older male retirees who did not hold full-time jobs and thus had sufficient time available for volunteer activity. Professionals such as doctors and lawyers who could control their own schedules have also been well represented among officials. These demographics can account to a large degree for the feminine and conservative values that have prevailed among those who set and enforce the rules and standards of the sport. As skaters learn to develop those skills that judges value most highly, these values also become ingrained among the skaters, some of whom then go on to pass along these values to the next generation as they become judges, coaches, or parents of skaters when their own competitive days are over.

During the war, international competition was suspended, and European and North American skating lost contact with each other. The development of rotational technique required for axels and double jumps continued on both sides of the Atlantic, particularly in the United States and Czechoslovakia. When skating competition resumed in 1947, the sport saw its first North American champions, with Barbara Ann Scott of Canada winning the World Championships in 1947 and 1948 and the 1948 Olympics. Dick Button of the United States won the freeskating portion of the 1947 World Championships to place second, and during the next five years he went on to remain unbeaten until winning his second Olympic and fifth world gold medals in 1952. (Both Scott and Button also captured the 1948 European titles, as a result of which representatives of non-European nations have since then been disqualified from entering the European Championships.)

Just as undefeated champion Sonja Henie had set the standards athletically, as well as sartorially and artistically, for ladies' skating in the 1920s and 1930s, Dick Button served a similar function for the men during the post–World War II era. Born in 1929, Button had been too young to be affected appreciably by the war and was just reaching his athletic peak when international competition resumed afterward. Double jumps were now a staple of postwar freeskating, but Button, who is on record as having intentionally tried to bring a greater athleticism to men's skating,[30] raised the stakes still higher by performing the first double axel jump (two and a half revolutions) in 1948 and the first triple jump, a triple loop, in 1952. He also introduced the flying camel spin, for some time known as the "Button camel," and made the forward camel spin a regular part of male as well as female skaters' repertoire.

During the 1950s and early 1960s, triple jumps, particularly triple salchows, became increasingly common among male competitors, and the top female competitive freeskaters included the full repertoire of two-revolution jumps, with North Americans continuing to lead the way. Carol Heiss, the 1960 Olympic champion, became the first woman to perform the double axel. David Jenkins, who also won gold in 1960, was known to have performed triple axels in practice, although it would be another two decades before such a feat was successfully accomplished in competition. Donald Jackson of Canada included the first official triple lutz to win the 1962 world title. Petra Burka of Canada and Janet Lynn of the United States were among the first women to complete triple jumps in competition, but in the absence of records of domestic and junior competitions, the honor of who was the very first remains undocumented. By the late 1960s and early 1970s, in any case, male medal contenders were expected to perform at least triple salchows and toe loops and females to include the double axel. Triple loops, lutzes, and flips began to show up more regularly among the male contenders and triple salchows and toe loops among the females. Dorothy Hamill became the last woman to win major international titles—world and Olympic championships in 1976—without including any triple jumps.

As we have seen, freestyle skating took on increasing importance compared to school figures during the 1970s, with the introduction of the short program for senior singles skaters in the 1973 season and the introduction of a separate freestyle test track by the USFSA five years later. The USFSA test requirements have always included jumps only of a difficulty that all skaters at a given level are expected to be capable of; even today the double lutz is the hardest jump required, and not until the senior test. The most athletic skaters have been performing double lutzes at the juvenile level since the 1970s, if not earlier. However, expectations at that time were less that skaters would continue to add more and more difficult jumps with each level of competition, but rather that the size and quality of the jumps would continue to improve and that skaters would develop the command to include the double jumps in more complex combinations with other jumps or other skating maneuvers.

In the competition track, on the other hand, the ISU sets standards for senior- and junior-level competitions at an international level, and the rules for competitive requirements in domestic competitions at these levels must conform to international standards. The jump requirements in the short program have attempted to keep pace with what the majority of credible senior- and junior-level competitors had demonstrated themselves capable of in long programs, so even from the beginning in 1973, ladies were required to perform double axels, and triple jumps were permitted for the men in the jump combination from the beginning, then were soon after permitted for the ladies and required for the men. Thus, a skater competing at the senior level twenty-five years ago was obliged to include jumps that are not actually required in the USFSA senior test a quarter century later. (Other countries do now require double axels and triple jumps in upper-level tests, and USFSA test rules now acknowledge that skaters *may* perform triple jumps in their senior test programs. Canada solves the problem of the discrepancy between test level and competitive level by maintaining two separate test tracks, one for competitors and the other for recreational skaters.)

The year 1978 saw two more milestones in jumping standards when Vern Taylor of Canada performed the first successful triple axel in competition at the World Championships and Denise Biellmann of Switzerland became the first woman to perform a successful triple lutz. With the arrival of the 1980s, it became generally expected for male medal contenders to perform four or five different triple jumps and females to perform the two easier triples, with a third triple—most commonly the loop but sometimes the lutz or flip—the mark of an exceptional female jumper.

As understanding of the biodynamics of jumping increased, fueled in part by scientific studies sponsored by skating associations in countries such as the Soviet Union, East Germany, and the United States, coaches have been able to teach ever greater percentages of advanced students to do jumps that once only the truly exceptional jumpers could dream of attempting. The tucked or straight-leg air position once deemed acceptable was gradually superseded by a recognition of the crossed-leg position, or "backspin in the air," as most advantageous for efficient rotation and control and therefore as "correct" form.[31]

In free programs, skaters who could perform triple jumps with ease tried to include as many as they could safely expect to complete in order to gain credit for their jumping skills. To remain competitive with rivals of comparable overall skating ability who included more jumps, less talented jumpers also needed to attempt the same jumps, leading to a situation in which the highest level of jump difficulty current at a given point of time soon became prevalent throughout the competitive field and the most talented jumpers of the time push the boundaries still further by attempting more difficult feats, which in their turn eventually become the norm. This pattern has held true throughout the history of the sport and at each competitive level, but most notably with triple jumps.

In the 1950s and 1960s, triples served as a marker of masculine athleticism in a sport that had already established a reputation as "feminine," differentiating the men's approach to the sport from that of its lady participants. Male body types had proved more efficient at generating the necessary forces for jumping high enough and rotating fast enough to achieve three revolutions in the air, but female skaters' jumping achievements continued to lag considerably behind their male counterparts', in large part because judging and training of female skaters placed more emphasis on graceful movement, while triple jumps carried more weight on the male side of the sport.

In the 1970s, the era of the women's liberation movement, Title IX, and the Billie Jean King–Bobby Riggs tennis match, when women sought parity with males in all areas of endeavor including sport, girls training as figure skaters welcomed the challenge of matching the boys' athleticism. Those who had mastered the double jumps went on to begin learning triples rather than simply turning to polishing the jumps they could already do.

The best male jumpers continued to push their own abilities forward, perhaps partially in response to female skaters beginning to close the gap in jump content. With the mere fact of doing triple jumps at all no longer an exclusively male preserve, male skaters who wished to underscore their difference from females needed to include ever more and more difficult jumps.

Also during the 1970s and 1980s, many skaters of both sexes began to cultivate images related more to powerful athleticism and less to refined gentility, and to skate with more speed and less attention to precise body positions, along with including more triple jumps. Even the most conservative of judges who deplored the triple jump trend and the declining attention to other aspects of skating could not fail to reward speed and successful jumps. Since the 1990s, with school figures gone from the equation, jumps serve as the most objective measure of technical merit, and successful triples constitute the greatest contribution to each skater's technical scores.

In 1982, Elaine Zayak won the world championship with a free program that included five triple toe loops or toe walleys, a nearly identical jump. In order to encourage variety and balance rather than allowing a skater to rack up credit for demonstrating the same skill over and over throughout the program, the ISU instituted what is popularly known as the "Zayak rule." This provision states that no triple jump may be repeated in a program unless it is performed as part of a jump combination or jump sequence one of those times and that a maximum of two different triple jumps may be repeated. Because there are six different jumps that can be performed as triples (explicitly counting the toe loop and toe walley as the same jump for purposes of this rule), if a skater performs all six and repeats two of them, the maximum number of permitted triple jumps would be eight. For those who have mastered only the triple toe loop and salchow, the maximum number of triples would be four. In other words, a skater can legally attempt two more triple jumps than the number of different triples in his or her repertoire. The intention of the rule was not to prevent female skaters from performing as many triple jumps as the men. But because, on average, female skaters tended to have command of fewer different varieties of triple jumps, the effect is that female skaters on average can legally include fewer triple jumps than the men.

A handful of advanced jumpers among the men, led by Brian Orser of Canada, began including triple axels as a regular part of their jump repertoire during the early 1980s, although it was not until after the retirement of the unbeatable Scott Hamilton in 1984 that this jump became virtually mandatory for an international medal in men's figure skating. Thus, since the mid-1980s, the top male skaters have indeed been attempting all six triples in their programs, with two repeated for the maximum of eight, not always successfully. For those who could not master the triple axel, as well as for those who could, jump combinations of two triple jumps served as yet another option for demonstrating extreme jumping ability; beginning in 1990, the triple axel–triple toe combination became the benchmark of the championship-winning men's short program. By the beginning of the new century, the number of male skaters including all six triples including the axel in their repertoire has increased to the point that almost every skater who progresses as far as the final round at the World Championships will at least attempt a triple axel, as opposed to the small minority who did do so a decade and a half ago.

The mid-1980s also saw sporadic attempts in competition of the quadruple toe loop, with Canadian Kurt Browning completing the first attempt recognized as successful by the ISU at the 1988 World Championships. Elvis Stojko, also of Canada, continued that country's tradition of jumping firsts by landing the first official quadruple jump combination, a quad toe–double toe, in 1991, and a quad-triple combination in 1997. Attempts at quadruple salchows remained much rarer in competition and always unsuccessful until a junior international event in 1998, where American Timothy Goebel completed the first official quad salchow and the first successful quad by an American skater. During the same season, American Michael Weiss, in quest of similar "firsts," had been including quadruple lutz attempts in his long program, but none with complete success. As of the 1998–1999 season, senior male competitors have the option of including a quadruple jump in the short program. The "Zayak rule" has also been reworded to include quadruple as well as triple jumps.

As more young skaters have been attempting quads in competition and some of them succeeding, predictions surfaced throughout the 1990s that quads would become the new standard of men's jumping. Since 1999, spurred by Stojko's example, by the rivalry of the two young Russians Aleksei Yagudin and Evgeny Plyushenko, and by the emergence of several Chinese men as masters of the quad, more and more men have been attempting quadruple jumps in their programs, with variable success; world medals have still been won without successful quads, but only with creditable attempts being made or near-perfection in the triple jumps and other elements. At the 2002 Olympics and World Championships, all of the men's medalists included at least one successful quadruple jump in the short and/or long programs.

Meanwhile, even in the early to mid-1980s, female skaters such as Zayak, Elizabeth Manley of Canada, and Midori Ito of Japan reportedly were landing triple axels in practice. In 1989, Ito became the first woman to complete this jump in competition, winning the World Championship that year with all six different triples in her free program. In 1991, Tonya Harding won the United States title and a world silver medal with a triple axel in her long program, and during the 1991–1992 season both Ito and Harding were attempting the triple axel–double toe as their short program combinations. Harding continued to plan this jump in her long program through 1994; Ito performed several in pro competitions and attempted it during her return to eligible competition in 1996 (successfully only at the Japanese national championships). But since Ito at the 1992 Olympics, no successful triple axels were landed by women in international competition until Skate America in fall 2002, over a decade later. Also in the early to mid-1990s, Surya Bonaly of France made several attempts at quadruple toe loops and salchows. The Guinness Book of World Records listed her as the first female skater to perform a quadruple jump, but the ISU has not recognized even her most successful attempts (those at the 1991 and 1992 World Championships, where some part of the final revolution was completed, or "cheated," on the ice rather than in the air); the honor of first female quad officially went to Miki Ando of Japan at the 2002–2003 Junior Grand Prix final.

The post-figures era began with a handful of female skaters such as Ito, Harding, Bonaly, Kristi Yamaguchi, and Nancy Kerrigan winning medals by including at least all five of the three-revolution jumps in their repertoire. We have not seen an increase in the number of revolutions women have been performing in the air. The days of Ito's and Harding's triple axels and Bonaly's quads are now past—and few other prominent competitors have appeared to take up the challenge in competition until unsuccessful attempts at the triple axel by Yoshie Onda of Japan and the quad salchow by American Sasha Cohen during the 2001–2002 season—but the standard of jumping in ladies' skating has indeed increased dramatically. At the beginning of the 1990s, it was only a handful of the very best jumpers who attempted five different triples or any triple-triple combinations. A decade later, there are far more skaters who can perform these feats. As with the men and the triple axel, the number of female competitors at a World, Junior World, European, or U.S. championship who do attempt triple lutzes, flips, and loops now far outnumber those who do not, and it is no longer possible to reach that level of competition without at least two or three usable triple jumps.

The rules for the short program, for instance, have changed to reflect this increased depth of jumping ability. Until 1994 the senior ladies' short program required a combination of two double jumps or a double and a triple jump (the medal contenders, of course, would have been performing triples, usually lutzes) and a double jump preceded by steps. The following season the jump preceded by steps was allowed to be triple or double, and since the 1997 season the jump combination is required to include one triple and allowed to include two (a triple-triple combination). So, whereas at the Lillehammer Olympics all the ladies' short programs included one triple jump, in Nagano all included either two or three triples, in intent if not in execution. With few exceptions, the post-Nagano competitors are all skaters who reached the senior level after the demise of school figures, skaters who have spent the largest portion of their training time perfecting jumps and not the ability to draw perfect circles with their blades.

Periodically—when both Ito and Harding were doing triple axels, and up to the present, when several men plan quads—we hear that more revolutions will become necessary to win, pushing the athletic boundaries even further. But currently, it seems that the laws of physics, the limitations of human anatomy, and the increasing prevalence of injury put caps on adding more revolutions. Advances in skate technology as well as technique will probably be necessary before multiple quads or female triple axels become commonplace. Rather than adding rotations, more skaters have been increasing their jump difficulty instead through the inclusion of triple-triple and quad combinations, and also through combinations using double and especially triple loops, as opposed to toe loops, as the second jump of the combination (more difficult because it is harder to control the landing of the first jump and to generate power for the second without the toe assist). Skaters can also add difficulty by preceding or following their jumps immediately with difficult steps, thus integrating the jumps more seamlessly into the flow of the program rather than "telegraphing" them.

Whenever the jump bar is raised substantially and rewarded at expense of other skating skills and "presentation," once enough skaters can achieve the new top level of jump difficulty the pendulum then swings back to reward more complete skaters' skating skills and presentation. The two sides of the jumps/presentation dichotomy are often characterized as "athlete versus artist." The same phenomenon is often at work in both the men's and ladies' events, but because the press generally pays less attention to the men and the skating community is also somewhat more comfortable with emphasizing jumps for men and presentation for ladies, it is usually the ladies to whom the epithet "artistic" is applied as the highest compliment.

For women much more than for men, then, the "artistic impression" of their performances, including aspects of physical appearance, becomes an important criterion of skating success according to gendered codes of looking and being looked at. The following chapter examines the processes by which skating performance has become over the past century more and more *about* being looked at and consequently how it has taken on the attendant connotations of femininity.

CHAPTER FIVE

Specularity

*A*s discussed in chapter 1, the two sets of scores awarded in figure skating competitions can be seen to correspond roughly to aspects of skating that represent both sides of a masculine/feminine binary. While the competitive and athletic aspects of figure skating represent values generally accepted as masculine, the performance aspects of freestyle and dance skating—those encompassed by the second mark under its various names of "manner of performance," "artistic impression," "composition and style," or "presentation"—have allied the sport with values typically considered feminine.

The emphasis on movement quality demonstrating continuous flow as opposed to isolated bursts of movement and traveling along curved as opposed to straight or angular pathways derives simply from the physics of skating technique. These movement images and the impression of gracefulness they produce for both the participant and the spectator, however, in themselves have produced associations between skating and movement styles considered appropriate to females. Insofar as figure skating is equated with graceful movement, which is equated with femininity, skating takes on connotations of a feminine activity.

Beyond the specific visual images evoked, the very fact that judges, spectators, and therefore skaters themselves pay attention to visual imagery—the appearance of the skater's body—as a central criterion of what constitutes good skating places the skater (male or female) in the structurally feminine role of object of the gaze with respect to the other key players (judges and onlookers) in a competitive situation. In the context of a skating show or exhibition, of course, visual appeal or spectacle takes on even greater significance.

The conventions of figure skating, like those of painting and cinema that John Berger and Laura Mulvey detail, have increasingly come to epitomize this paradigm of spectatorship. The skater, while actively engaged in a display of athletic prowess, simultaneously occupies the structurally feminized looked-at position in relation to a structurally masculinized looker. Costumes that reveal the form and line of the skater's body have the effect of coding the body as erotic object and as a visual object to be valued for the beauty of the shapes it makes at the same time that they allow for greater freedom of movement and for judges to discern factors such as leg extension. Bright colors or extravagant ornamentation further code the body as a site of visual appeal. In a live competition or performance situation, the skater him- or herself is contained within the barrier surrounding the ice surface, the focus of all eyes in the arena, much as a painted or filmed image is contained within the frame or on the screen; for the television viewer, the skater's image is of course also contained within the set's frame. In either case this containment reduces the skater to an object of visual consumption for the viewer's delectation. The skater's body has become a sight, a spectacle; the male body as well as the female is thus feminized within the economy of spectatorship.

Skating as a branch of performing arts can trace its roots to Jackson Haines's performances in the 1860s and 1870s, most notably in Vienna, where Leopold Frey, Franz Belazzi, and other followers carried on the tradition Haines initiated. It was there that the practice of skating to music and of choreographing skating routines as if they were dances took hold. This led to the first attempts of couples performing waltzes, marches, and other such social dances together, the beginnings of what would eventually become ice dance. (See chapter 10.) For the most part, though, Haines's performances and those of his disciples drew on the traditions of the performing arts—the variety stage as well as ballet and circus, for instance, in an exhibition turn where "Haines appeared as a bear and Belazzi as his trainer."[1] As we have seen, the scientifically or technically minded amateur skaters of the nineteenth-century English and American schools disdained such professional show skating for its vulgar appeal to the masses, relying on the easily perceived visual appeal of costume and gesture more than on the intricacies of skating technique that only the skating-knowledgeable could appreciate. Such attitudes have persisted through the twentieth century in the proscription against spectacular but more acrobatic than skating-technique-based show-skating moves, such as backflips and pairs' Detroiters and headbanger spins, and in disdain for the costume-driven spectacles of traveling ice shows such as Ice Capades or Disney on Ice.

The next major performing skating star was Charlotte Oelschlagel, a young German woman who rose to prominence with her 1915 debut appearance at New York's Hippodrome after starring in a revue of young female skaters in Berlin before World War I. Known professionally by her first name alone, Charlotte starred in the first motion picture to feature figure skating: *The Frozen Warning*. As both showgirl and film star, Charlotte brought skating into the conventions of specularized femininity that characterized early-

twentieth-century popular entertainment. In the 1920s, she gave performances partnered with husband Curt Newmann and developed a number of
moves, including pair death spirals and the Charlotte spiral or fadeout (a
back spiral with the upper body leaning down toward the skating foot and
the free leg lifted behind to almost 180 degrees) that eventually made their
way into ladies' and pairs competitive freestyle practice.[2] Moves of this sort
furthered the development of flexibility maneuvers in the freeskating repertory that generally favor a female rather than male physique. Creating visually striking shapes while gliding on a sustained edge (spirals), in spins, or in
pairs and dance lifts thus became a characteristic function of the female skating body and so by association is considered feminine even when performed
by male skaters, particularly in shapes that rely on extreme flexibility.

Professional show skating developed its own traditions, emphasizing artistic or entertainment value over the rigorous technical concerns of competition. Even as amateur competitors disdained the style-over-substance values
of the professional milieu, they nevertheless adopted those moves invented
by professionals that fit well within the context of a competitive freestyle
program.

Lily Kronberger of Hungary had brought a live military band with her to
the World Championships in 1911 to accompany her freeskating program to
the *Pas des patineurs,* which she performed with a clear interpretation of the
music. Before World War I and for the majority of the decades prior to World
War II, though, skaters such as Kronberger and Karl Schafer who made attempts to interpret the music in their skating were rare.[3] As live accompaniment at competitions became the rule, skaters would put together their programs without music and would "request a rink-side orchestra to play a waltz
or ten-step, to which they would display their variations."[4]

The skater who did the most to transform the sport of competitive figure
skating into a spectacle, and specifically a spectacle of the skater's body, in the
process shifting its meanings firmly in the direction of femininity, was Sonja
Henie. As an adolescent in the 1920s, she introduced the use of short (mid-
thigh-length) skating skirts. Short-skirted dresses have been the norm for
female skaters' competitive attire ever since, with attached trunks and (usually flesh-colored) tights ultimately replacing the bloomers Henie sported in
her youth and with hemlines rising significantly and more or less permanently
yet again in the era of the 1960s miniskirt.

The 1920s were a period of increased social and physical freedom for
women, as manifested, among other signs, by the appearance of short skirts
and trousers as everyday apparel for adult young women. The disappearance
of ankle-length skirts on the ice both allowed women's skating for the first

time to rival the men's in athleticism and also turned female skaters into objects of potential erotic display by revealing the shape of their legs, much as the short tutu had done in ballet. Because the motions of skating cause short skirts to ripple or to fly up repeatedly, revealing the parts of the body, including hips, buttocks, and upper thighs, that they cover when at rest, even when the skater does not further reveal her crotch by performing moves that involve spreading or splitting her legs apart, such skirts no longer serve any function of modesty. The presence of a skirt, however, serves to ally the line of a skating costume with that of typically feminine apparel of various styles. Skirts suggest a social and formal context more than the sport/performance/ practice context that, for instance, a leotard without skirt, with or without tights and/or shorts would. Crucially, the skirt confirms the difference between the sexes on the social and semiotic level, because females wear skirts both on and off the ice and males do not.

When made of material light enough to ripple or otherwise move continuously as the skater moves across the ice, skirts emphasize the sense of movement and speed the skater has produced, even when she maintains a single still position while moving, as in a spiral or sustained spin position, increasing both the visual interest and the sense of athletic freedom produced by the movement. Such billowing garments make visible the effect of wind or moving air (in this case produced by the skater's movement), making the skater seem almost a part of this natural force.

With increasing athleticism in freeskating, including the early double jumps, the trend in skating clothes shifted in favor of light, close-fitting garments that allowed for greater maneuverability and also allowed judges and spectators to view directly the form of the skater's body. The advent of the short-skirted skating dress in the 1920s and 1930s marks the point at which skating attire became distinct from everyday wear—a woman's skating dress, even more than the heavy tights and belted sweaters then popular among male skaters, marked its wearer as a participant in the sport of figure skating, a fact that surely represents one reason the basic form of the garment has remained traditional for female skaters throughout the ensuing seventy years. It also marks the first time that the form of female skaters' bodies was more visible than that of their male counterparts.[5] This visibility made the attractiveness of the skater's figure newly salient. With the aesthetic (and erotic) qualities of the skater's body seemingly of equal importance to the aesthetic qualities of the skating movement, especially to members of the nonskating public for whom the fine points of that movement are lost, the semiotic weight of the skating body shifted away from the masculine realm of action and into the feminine preserve of appearance. This shift represents the beginning of public consciousness of figure skating as a specifically feminine sport as opposed to a sport (implicitly masculine) deemed suitable for female participation. The fact that the impetus for female skaters' adopting shorter skirts and form-fitting lines was to allow themselves greater scope for athleticism lends irony to this shift.

Meanwhile, variations on the basic theme of the skating dress also allowed skaters to display their individual taste and wealth. Henie, the dominant skater of the era and the daughter of a well-to-do Oslo furrier, maintained standards of richness in attire that the pretenders to her crown as queen of the ice were more than willing to emulate, as the various fur-trimmed velvet ensembles attested to at the first North American World Championships in New York in 1930.[6] The aesthetic and semiotic nuances of skating fashion have remained one source of interest in skating that has appealed to traditionally feminine sensibilities among skaters, their mothers, and skating fans ever since.[7]

Nor were short skirts the only fashion innovation Henie introduced to the skating world. Previously women as well as men had worn black skating boots; Henie was the first to wear white boots, producing a lighter, longer appearance of the leg, which was now a focal point for judges' and spectators' gaze and deemphasizing the heavy equipment on the foot. White boots quickly became the standard for female skaters, at which point Henie switched to beige in order to maintain her uniqueness. Beige boots, combined with flesh-colored tights on skaters whose flesh color is within the same range, produce a yet more unbroken line encompassing the entire leg and foot.[8]

In advising newcomers to the sport about what to wear on the ice in the late 1930s, Maribel Vinson devotes three and a half pages to the accepted outfit for women, dwelling on the correct length and style of skirt to mark the beginner as belonging on the ice and noting that "a longer skirt at once stamps you as a 'rabbit' who doesn't know any better." She also attributes the appeal of skating to feminine interests in skating fashions: "In fact it is because the stores are putting out such attractive and becoming figure-skating outfits that lots of young girls are taking up the sport!" Vinson points to several ways in which skating attire connotes (and permits) athleticism and also how it can attract the eye on the merits of its own design elements and by enhancing the visual appeal of the skater's body:

> Anything that doesn't contribute to an impression of speed and freedom of movement is undesirable. That is why the bodices of skating dresses should be molded to the figure. That is why bloomers should never be

large and bulky, (but contrariwise the too-tight, too high little panty that some good skaters are now affecting is ugly too). . . .

Color, brilliant, vivid color with plenty of depth, is most effective on the ice. For this reason white buck or calf boots are steadily replacing the old black boots among women skaters because they look best with a wide range of colored costumes, which may be white or pastel one day or a vivid splash of color the next. But black, both in dress and boots, is still good and by its comparative rarity on the rinks nowadays often seems positively distinguished.

Remember, no skirt at any time should be longer than knee length, and if you are still quite young and have a reasonably svelte figure your skirts will become shorter as your ability increases. For there is no longer any doubt that good-looking legs and good-looking skating are both shown off to better advantage on the ice if the skirt is full and several inches above the kneecap. Shorts are all right for the youngsters while they are practicing school figures but should be completely discarded for dancing and free skating, where the swish of a well-cut skirt adds so much to the grace of the movement.

Her advice for males taking up the sport is more succinct but suggests that female skaters at least did take note of the appearance of the members of the opposite sex who shared the ice with them:

> For men there are now well-cut, tight-fitting special skating trousers on sale at several metropolitan stores and specially cut tight-fitting jackets. For the average male figure skater at an average practice session short knickers (never plus fours) are probably the easiest and best. For competition black or dark-blue tights are *de rigueur*. Some rinks make the wearing of coats compulsory, but outdoors sweaters are of course best. Almost every man looks far handsomer on the ice with a belt over his sweater and a scarf around his throat than he does *sans* belt and *sans* scarf. Gentlemen readers, take this lady skater's opinion for what you think it is worth![9]

Even before first putting on skates at the age of five, Sonja Henie had loved to move to music and began studying ballet. During her competitive career, she became a devotee of Anna Pavlova after seeing the Russian ballerina perform in London and made efforts to incorporate elements of dance into her freeskating performances through the placement of her spins and jumps and choreography to reflect the mood of the music.[10] Henie's skating, although athletic and powerful for her day,[11] also incorporated elements that undercut that sense of power. Most notably, she frequently employed the toepicks of her blades for running or posing on the ice, in moves reminiscent of pointe work in ballet. Such toe steps are welcome as occasional counterpoints to the legato flow of skating movement, but Henie perhaps took their use to excess. In contrast to the strong moving out into space that characterized Henie's skating and her most forceful toe runs, other toe steps appeared mincing and ineffective.

Finally, Henie's largest contribution to public images of skating as a feminine activity came through her professional touring shows and the series of Hollywood films in which she starred. Because these vehicles were the first introduction most of the American public had to figure skating through the mass media, for these viewers the image of skating would always originally be linked to the image of the glamorous female movie star. Although the characters Henie played in the films were generally of humble origins (sometimes naive, sometimes cunning), the skating numbers within the films, as well as her performances on tour, constructed her as a "star," spectacle, and visual icon within the conventions of both 1930s film musicals and stage (or, rather, ice) extravaganzas.[12] Her costumes in the skating numbers of these films were often created on the extremely short and revealing, sequin- and feather-studded pattern that bore more resemblance to the costume of a movie or nightclub—or ice show—showgirl or circus performer than to the competition attire of the era. These costumes cemented in the public imagination the image of the female skater as sparkly and scantily dressed, a visual fantasy, well before the staid world of amateur skating embraced a comparable showiness (in more than one sense of the word) and probably contributed to later generations of skaters drawing on such fantasies for the design of their competition attire.

The British skater Cecilia Colledge, Henie's rival and successor in the mid-1930s, along with her coach Jacques Gerschwiler, was responsible for the invention of two new spins: the parallel or camel spin and the layback spin. According to Colledge, Gerschwiler, a former gymnastics instructor, "was very progressive in his ideas, and [Colledge], being his youngest and most advanced pupil, was the tool on which he would try his theories."[13] Colledge supplemented her skating training with ballet lessons and, at Gerschwiler's suggestion, "stretch" lessons from a former circus performer turned acrobatics instructor named Miss Lee. It was while watching Lee training Colledge in backbends by means of a rope tied around her waist that Gerschwiler conceived the idea of a spin performed with the back arched backward: the layback.[14] These two additions to the freeskating repertoire heightened the visual function of the skater creating interesting shapes with her body. This fact, along with the realities of human anatomy that make such positions generally easier to achieve for females than for males, probably accounts for the fact that for the first decade or so after their invention these spins remained the province of female skaters.[15]

With skating thus established in the public imagination as feminine pastime, the number of girls attracted to the sport, either for its athletic components or for the glamour of its imagery, by Henie's films and tours and by traveling shows Ice Follies, Ice Capades, and Holiday on Ice, all established in the 1930s and 1940s, increased dramatically.

Boys who encountered skating in these forums would be less likely to be attracted to the glamour—in fact, many would find that a particular reason to avoid it. At the same time, the athletic aspects of skating would hold less appeal for boys than for girls, given the wider range of other athletic options available to males. Meanwhile, while the influx of new skaters became overwhelmingly female, large numbers of young men left the sport due to the demands of World War II, as historian Wright suggests, but females who had entered the sport prior to the publicity surrounding Henie in the late 1930s did not experience a similar exodus, further increasing the disparity between the number of male and female skaters. Older skaters, male and female, lamented the scarcity of boys in their skating clubs and offered suggestions (usually involving the use of hockey games as an attraction) for attracting young male members.[16]

After the War, while Dick Button brought increased athleticism to skating, Barbara Ann Scott brought polish, glamour, and feminine delicateness. Brown describes her as a "cover girl" and "like a little doll to be looked at and not to be touched,"[17] and indeed her likeness graced the covers of Canadian magazines and dolls sold across Canada following her win at the 1948 Olympics, inspiring many Canadian girls to take up skating. Under the guidance of coach Sheldon Galbraith, Scott was also at the forefront of a new trend toward free programs specifically choreographed and skated to music rather than simply relying on music as background accompaniment.[18] In the immediate postwar era, the new "virile athleticism," lamented Nigel Brown, led skaters to "[like] music now with a 'boom' in it and [try] to land a double jump to coincide with these 'booms,'" a superficially sensationalist approach to musical interpretation that lasted "until the American male skaters at the World Championships in London in 1950 illustrated a unique combination of daring athletics, musically interpreted."[19]

Skaters now each used a specially cut phonograph record (later to be replaced by tapes and compact discs), often using three or more contrasting selections in order to display versatility. It became standard practice to design a program with each move fit to a specific musical passage or specific beat of the music, and skaters would rehearse daily to their recorded accompaniment. Music selections for freeskating continued to represent primarily the Western classical and European folk traditions. For ice dance, newly added to the roster of World Championship events in the early 1950s, standard ballroom dance rhythms, both European and "Latin," predominated. In the 1960s, specific skaters came to be identified with the music they were best known for skating to, for instance Liudmila and Oleg Protopopov with Franz Liszt's *Liebestraum.*[20]

In the 1960s, television became a significant factor in the development of competitive figure skating. In 1961, ABC, as part of their Wide World of Sports series, began televising portions of the United States Championships and, in subsequent years, the Worlds. Dick Button, after a decade as a skating professional, hung up his skates and turned his hand to skating-related business endeavors as well as to providing expert commentary for the ABC broadcasts. These broadcasts often showed entire free programs of the top competitors, as opposed to the seconds-long clips of performances that had illustrated television news reports of the skating competitions at the 1960 Olympics (where American skaters Carol Heiss and David Jenkins had won gold on home ice in Squaw Valley, California). Television coverage introduced a whole new generation of spectators to skating as something enjoyable to watch for its aesthetic appeal as well as for the sporting interest in who won. Most of these new viewers had never encountered figure skating as live spectators, much less as participants, before seeing it on television. Button's commentary in effect educated this entire generation in how to watch skating. (In Canada, Johnny Esaw at CFTO and later CTV provided a similar function.[21]) The greater visibility of skating in public media inspired new generations of potential skaters to seek out rinks where they could take up the sport, rather than being drawn to it through direct local experience. Among those who were not themselves inspired to skate, some became committed fans of the sport or of particular skaters. After being exposed to skating on television, they would make the effort to seek out live skating competitions or shows to attend in person. Meanwhile, skaters began to become more conscious of the effect of their choreographic, musical, and costuming choices on the public as well as on the judges.

More than ever before, skating became a spectator sport. With significant amounts of money coming in from outside through television contracts and ticket sales, the rules and trends within the sport itself began to respond to the interests of outside spectators as much as to the technical demands and the traditions of the sport itself. The most obvious example would be the increasing importance of freeskating and the corresponding decrease in the importance of school figures, due in part to the much greater "audience friendliness" of the former.

For the United States, the era of televised skating began with the catastrophic loss of the entire 1961 world team in a plane crash en route to that year's World Championships, which were then cancelled. Losing the generation who had been poised to continue the success American skaters had enjoyed from 1948 to 1960, along with the experience of the coaches and officials accompanying them, sent American skating into a period of rebuilding.

The first real star to emerge from this period of American skating history was Peggy Fleming, who won her first national championship unexpectedly in 1964 at age fifteen. She went on to dominate U.S. ladies' skating and to rise quickly through the world rankings to win gold medals at the 1966–1968 World Championships and the 1968 Olympics. The latter win, broadcast live via satellite from Grenoble, France, by ABC, made Fleming a household name at age nineteen. When she entered the ranks of professional skaters after following up her Olympic victory with a final World Championship win, Fleming became the best-known and highest-paid female athlete of the time.

The year 1968 was one of political turmoil throughout much of the world, including the United States, as the established power structures faced challenges from traditionally disempowered groups including youth, women, African Americans, and the working class. Although Fleming herself was a young woman from a working-class background, the image she created on the ice was that of well-groomed, well-disciplined (or docile, in Foucault's sense[22]) upper-class femininity. Her homemade skating dresses reflected the simple elegance of classic lines and her hair, teased to fullness and piled on top of her head, along with the makeup and false eyelashes then popular, attested to time and effort invested by a proper young lady and her mother/dressmaker in concerns of fashion and appearance. Fleming also drew on ballet conventions to display graceful classical positions and an upright but relaxed upper-body carriage (encouraged by the discipline of school figures and judging preferences for freeskating) and sensitive responsiveness in her movement to classical music, presenting an image of refined, unthreatening ladylikeness far removed from the headline-making disruptions of some of her contemporaries. As Fleming recounted in her recent autobiography, "I was lucky to win the Olympic gold medal when I did. I was also lucky that it was 1968. The story of the victory of a clean-cut American gave the country a break from the relentless Vietnam War and the assassinations of Martin Luther King and Bobby Kennedy. More significantly for me on a personal level, 1968 was the year that sports and the Olympics became big-time entertainment."[23]

During her final Olympic season as an amateur, Fleming gained widespread fame through her athletic accomplishments; in her subsequent professional career her public activities consisted primarily of professional show skating and television specials and commercial endorsement, in a milieu with the most tenuous of connections to sport and more obviously connected to the acceptably feminine worlds of glamour, celebrity, and show business, though always with the recognition that she had earned her entrée to the ranks of celebrity through sport. Thus, through her fame within the otherwise largely male-dominated milieu of sport, Fleming paved some steps along the way toward women's visibility in widening spheres of public life. "I don't mean to imply that in 1968 I was there to kick off the feminist movement," Fleming noted, "but the feelings of femininity that I was just learning about and trying to incorporate in skating were the same feelings that millions of woman [*sic*] were beginning to express more fully and openly in art, music, politics, marriage—in other words, in life. We wanted to be achievers, but being an achiever didn't mean that you stopped being a woman."[24]

The other major development in international skating during the 1960s was the emergence of the Soviet Union and East Germany as major competitive forces. Politically, this meant that the usual national rivalries that sometimes translated into national bias on the judges' stand, or seemed to, now fell along Cold War lines, with Eastern-bloc countries often supporting each other's skaters over Western rivals and vice versa, and with skating competitions thus serving as symbolic stagings of Cold War conflicts. With the increasing prominence of Soviet and East German skaters, the American public, including its nonskating press, came to see figure skating as a site of threats to American international strength and of Communist untrustworthiness where evidence of dishonesty in the scoring by Soviet or East German judges was always worthy of comment.

In training methods, both the Soviet Union and East Germany relied heavily on rigorous selection techniques in early childhood for determining which athletes would qualify for state-supported training and on scientific studies of the biomechanical principles involved in skating. These methods produced an approach to skating often more technical and athletic than artistically refined. Some Soviet skaters, however, drew on a culture of ballet, theatre, and folk dance performance actively supported by the Soviet system as popular expressions of national cultural heritage. For the Soviets, ballet thus represented a "Russianness" available to all social strata rather than confined to elite and, often, specifically feminine tastes as it does in the West.

Most influential in this regard was the pair team of Liudmila Belousova and Oleg Protopopov, winners of the 1964 and 1968 Olympics and the 1965–1968 World Championships. The Protopopovs, as the married couple have usually been known, raised by several degrees the level of translating classical dance to the ice. Frank Loeser commented, "They did not perform a pair routine so much as they created exquisite pas de deux."[25] Oleg Protopopov specifically identified heterosexual love as the meaning he and his wife aimed to evoke through pair skating: "First of all I see in what we try to do, a man and a woman. These pairs of brother and sister, how can they convey the emotion—the love that exists between man and woman? That is what we try to show."[26] Their performances set a benchmark for romantic heterosexuality on the ice and for classical line and expressiveness that influenced not only pair skating but also singles and dance.

Beginning with the Protopopovs' loss to compatriots Irina Rodnina and Aleksei Ulanov in 1969, the couple's classic lyricism, like the somewhat sedate athletic approach that had preceded their innovations, gave way to high-speed athleticism and ever-more dangerous tricks in pairs' performances. Rodnina, who with her partners Ulanov and later Aleksandr Zaitsev completely dominated international pair skating throughout the 1970s (equaling Sonja Henie's record of ten world championships and three Olympic gold medals), led the trend of female pair skaters as risk-taking athletes. Although she did not perform the throw jumps pioneered by her contemporaries, Rodnina did perfect athletic moves such as acrobatic lifts, side-by-side jumps, and particularly the split triple twist. As discussed in chapter 4, the athletic content of men's and especially ladies' singles freestyle also increased steadily throughout the decade of the 1970s.

The changes in skating images in the 1970s reflected changing social conditions in the world at large and the broadened popular appeal of figure skating as the first generation of skaters who had been attracted to the sport through television reached competitive maturity.

In the decade of the women's liberation movement, Fleming's successors as icons of athletic American femininity brought their own inflections to the tensions playing out between aggressive athleticism on the one hand and visual appeal on the other. For Americans, figure skating remained, thanks to its emphasis on grace and beauty, predominantly a woman's sport, and the most prominent of women's sports in public media. Television commentary often failed to distinguish between the beauty of a skater's movement and that of her own personal appearance, with phrases such as "a beautiful skater" that lacked counterparts in the discussion of men's skating (or of other sports).

While Janet Lynn was one of the early pioneers of women's triple jumps, she was better known for her musical expressiveness, graceful movement, and the almost ethereal quality of her skating. As discussed in the section on school figures in chapter 4, her competitive fate led her to be associated more directly than any other individual with the introduction of the singles' short program and the consequent increase in the value of freeskating compared to figures. Dorothy Hamill, the 1976 Olympic and world champion, who had earlier been described in terms of her athleticism in comparison to Fleming's and Lynn's artistry,[27] also drew praise for her elegant line and carriage. With her practical but elegant trademark wedge hairstyle, enhanced by the luster of an Olympic gold medal, Hamill became perhaps as well known by the general public for setting fashion among American girls and women as for her accomplishments on the ice. Perhaps because of their speed and freedom of movement, along with their simple, bright-colored costumes, no-nonsense hairstyles, and understated makeup, both Lynn and Hamill evoked associations with natural, outdoorsy wholesomeness. These were images that resonated with both conservative and feminist ideologies of femininity during the 1970s.

As the American public in general became more health- and fitness-conscious, sporty images for women gained popularity on the ice as elsewhere. Track suits or warm-up suits became acceptable on the street and on the ice, particularly for figures practice in cold rinks. Their stripes or other simple geometric ornamentation emphasized streamlined functionality. Similar stylings began to show up in competition dresses and men's stretch suits. The availability of synthetic stretch fabrics further enhanced a move toward aerodynamically sleek contours and surface luster similar to that seen in athletic apparel ranging from swimsuits to speedskating suits.

While unabashed athleticism became increasingly acceptable for female skaters, especially if performed with grace if not "artistry," a handful of male skaters were responsible for advancing the artistic possibilities of the sport. Although Janet Lynn had been hailed as a peerless artist, the impact of her free-spirited, quasi-improvisational performances seemed more an extension of herself—an unmediated manifestation of her physical grace and musicality—than a carefully crafted work of art. Her appeal as a skater and the desideratum of those who held her up as an ideal of artistic feminine skating is that of naturally spontaneous inner and outer beauty coextensive with her appeal as a young woman. For male skaters, on the other hand, there was no such tradition of valuing "natural" masculinity (which would be seen as purely athletic) and artistry or beauty within the same frame of reference.

As a child, the British skater John Curry had wished to study dance, but his parents had steered him into skating in the belief that as a sport it would be a less effeminate pursuit. When he reached age eighteen, Curry, already an accomplished skater, added daily ballet classes to his training regimen. His competitive skating during the early to mid-1970s, culminating in European, Olympic, and world titles in 1976 at age twenty-six, was characterized by strict attention to detail in search of an uncluttered, pure classical line. More than other ballet-influenced skaters such as Fleming, Curry used his dance training to display an integrity of movement more deep-rooted in both ballet and skating technique, rather than applying a balletic gloss to standard skating moves. His most memorable competitive performance was his 1976 long program to music from the ballet *Don Quixote* with its very formalist academic ballet positions and measured restraint, although two years earlier he had brought a new, more eccentric look to his skating with his interpretation of Stravinsky's *Rite of Spring*.

After turning professional, Curry produced a series of ice shows conceived more as high art dance concerts than as family entertainment, performed in legitimate theatres rather than sport arenas. For these shows, Curry worked with well-known choreographers from the worlds of ballet and modern dance, such as Peter Martins, Laura Dean, and Twyla Tharp, bringing new ideas to the possibilities for artistic movement on skates—although it was sometimes necessary for Curry to remind his choreographers of the need to move across the ice. Daily classes in edge work and fundamentals of movement instilled in his contemporaries who joined his skating company and the younger skaters who worked him a respect for making the most of even the simplest move or position.

Through their roles as performers, choreographers, and coaches, Curry, his disciples, and contemporaries who similarly sought to bring a dance aesthetic to skating furthered immeasurably the influence of art dance on skating practice. The advent of the intimate, integrated stage ice show, such as Curry's 1977 *Ice Dancing*, introduced the possibility of using skating as a medium in which to produce what aestheticians could define as "art" as opposed to simply sport or entertainment.

Philosopher Spencer Wertz, investigating the question of whether, and in what conditions, sport can be considered as art, turns to figure skating for examples. He singles out Peggy Fleming's amateur skating, particularly her 1968 Olympic-winning free program in Grenoble, as a watershed in the development of an artistic component of competitive skating. The distinction lies, Wertz argues, not so much in the intention of the skater or coach to create art, but in the degree of aesthetic control maintained over the medium of "body-on-ice":

The routines which she performed were controlled by aesthetic assessments. In observing these routines, one could see that they were more than just physical or athletic; they had an extra "something" added to them, which we would usually speak of as supplying a coherence and a fluency to her moves. The individual moves were performed and coordinated by a gracefulness consciously imparted by the performer. . . . [a]esthetic skating from Fleming on requires the individual moves to be linked— part of a continuum or unbroken unity of the entire routine. In light of this, Fleming's performances were rightfully described as "artistic."[28]

Wertz also examines a review of the professional show *Ice* performed in New York in the early 1980s, starring Fleming along with Toller Cranston and Robin Cousins, to point out how this show is distinguished as art from "arena skating" (what we might identify as vaudeville-style or "family entertainment" shows) such as Ice Follies or Ice Capades. The primary difference Wertz identifies is the use of music, choreography, and costumes (and, no doubt, lighting) to support and reveal the skating as the primary medium of expression rather than as "'gimmicks' [that] conceal the skating," along with the fact that *Ice* was staged in New York for a New York (i.e., elite, aesthete) audience rather than as a nationwide tour aimed at the masses.[29] Viewers' perception of the performance, whether competitive or commercial, as a consciously integrated whole is thus for Wertz the defining criterion by which "sport" can also be considered "art"; the two realms are not, under this rubric, mutually exclusive.

Canadian skater Toller Cranston, Curry's contemporary, was frequently judged the best freestyle skater of the mid-1970s, but his placement in the school figures limited his highest competitive achievements to bronze medals at the 1974 World Championships and 1976 Olympics. A painter by profession, Cranston brought to his skating an artist's eye, a flexible body, and a love of flamboyant costume and gesture. He popularized moves with the limbs held in unexpected angles, such as sideways toepick runs, stag jumps, the broken-leg sitspin, and his own variation on a back camel spin with the free hand holding the knee of the free leg up behind him in a high attitude and the skating arm wrapped across his chest.

With Cranston and Curry, the shapes made with the body held supreme importance, turning the male skater's body into an object for visual consumption, just as women's had always been. Both cited resistance to their innovations early in their careers from a skating culture of the 1960s and early 1970s in which simply raising one's arms above the waist or shoulders was considered unmasculine.[30]

Subsequent skaters of the late 1970s and early 1980s, including Allen Schramm and Robert Wagenhoffer of the United States, Gary Beacom of Canada, and Norbert Schramm (no relation) of West Germany, took Cranston's idea of twisted, angled, and otherwise unexpected moves and positions even further, often into the realm of the bizarre or grotesque. Without Curry's refinement or Cranston's flexibility and flamboyance, these later experimenters often produced shapes that emphasized angles rather than curves, adding an active contrast to the curving movement of skating on edges. This angularity, the occasional adoption of percussive rhythms, and the sense of exploring new territory injected enough masculine meanings into this brand of skating artistry, bringing a variety to men's skating in the 1980s that was often missing from the ladies'.

The most lasting contribution that Linda Fratianne, the 1977 and 1979 world champion from the United States, brought to the sport would include, along with cementing the importance of triple jumps in ladies skating, her popularization of the use of sequins and similar elaborate ornamentation on skating costumes. It was in this period that competitive skating costumes began to resemble the glittery apparel worn in entertainment contexts such as nightclubs, circuses . . . and ice shows. Advances in videotape technology allowed skaters literally to sparkle on the ice without creating undue glare for the cameras, and in the era of disco, glamour rock, pastel tuxedos, and leisure suits, male as well as female skaters sought to shine.

Dance, in the form of disco and jazz/show dance styles, enjoyed wide popularity in the mid-to-late 1970s and into the early 1980s, promoted by Broadway shows such as *A Chorus Line* and the works of Bob Fosse and films such as *Saturday Night Fever*, *Fame*, and *Flashdance*. These styles of movement and their associated music genres found their way onto the ice in the 1979 film *Ice Castles*, which starred skater-turned-actress Lynn Holly Johnson and was itself an example of the public fascination with expressive movement. As the 1970s gave way to the 1980s, top skaters such as 1980 Olympic men's champion Robin Cousins, 1981 world champion Denise Biellmann of Switzerland, and later Brian Orser of Canada abandoned classicism for these popular dance styles. Arrangements of familiar melodies from the classical repertoire supported by a contemporary dance beat frequently turned up in skating programs.[31]

Other skaters turned to movie soundtracks for their musical choices, usually relying on selections with sweeping, heroic-sounding melodic lines to complement the sweeping movement and upright posture that characterized skating movement. Sometimes, as with American skater David Santee's repeated use of a selection from the *Rocky* soundtrack or popular use of the theme from *Ice Castles*, knowledge of the source movie's plot or theme rendered the selection meaningful to the skaters and often to viewers, although the physical expression of these musical selections remained abstract. A few skaters also ventured to use rock instrumentals, often to the displeasure of older judges who deplored that sound. Big band, Broadway, or other earlier popular music styles, already a staple of the ice dance repertoire, offered another alternative to classical music genres that could be welcomed both by skaters in their teens and twenties and by older members of the skating community. By the 1980s, thus, any kind of instrumental music had become fair game for freestyle skating programs.

In the 1980s, as corporate sponsorship and television contracts began to turn amateur skating into more and more of a commodity for consumption by a mass audience, amateur skaters too began to take a more specialized, professional approach toward producing the winning image for competition. The emergence of more sophisticated intimate traveling ice shows, regular—and regularly televised—professional competitions, and occasional television skating specials increased the prospect of post-competitive performing opportunities and thus the incentive for skaters to develop performance skills. In this era, the soon-to-be-cliché notion of a champion skater representing a "total package" took hold. Skaters turned to specialists in skating choreography, costume design and construction, music engineering, sport science, sport medicine, and sport psychology to perform functions that had once been handled by coaches and parents, and a handful of professionals began to make careers specifically as skating choreographers, costumers, and so forth. Even professional hairstylists and makeup consultants were made available to skaters at major competitions.[32] Projecting the right look remained, as always, an important adjunct to technical skill. The preferred look was now evolving more and more along lines defined by skating practice and further from everyday fashions within the non-skating world, although the approach to image fashioning paralleled that pursued by professionals, both male and female, within the business world.

In competition attire during the 1980s, vacillations continued between images of glamour and fantasy on the one hand and functional athleticism on the other. The main trend for both male and female skaters was toward costumes that emphasized sparkle and showiness, with lustrous fabrics in bright pastel or jewel tones, ornamented by beading, sequins, and the like, often in a matching color merely to add glitter and texture, sometimes in contrasting colors to create patterns. Such costumes might suggest that skaters were dressing up, either as participants in a formal social event such as a ball (traditionally an occasion for participants, especially females, to display themselves through the clothes they wear and how they wear them) or as performers in a spectacular entertainment (where human bodies, again primarily female, may be displayed for both erotic appeal and formalist aesthetics, as well as for virtuosic feats). Alternatively, such costumes could be seen to transform the skaters' bodies themselves into glittering jewel-like objects, of primarily visual interest enhanced by their whirling movement, but seemingly devoid of personal agency. Because male skaters would wear the same color shirt and trousers, while female skaters usually wore flesh-colored tights (or bare legs), the light or bright-colored costumes covered more of the male skaters' bodies, making the effect of these colors more salient on the male than female bodies. The flamboyant styles and colors that remained popular throughout that decade in skating fashion stood out even more as unmasculine in the 1980s because everyday dress had retreated from 1970s excess to more conservative styles.

Black also became a popular base color for costumes, often with black beading or with gold or silver sequined or other glittering trim. This option allowed for images of understated elegance more in keeping with formal attire off the ice during the 1980s and also for the developing tradition of fantasy and glitter in skating attire.

The tendency to transform skaters' bodies into visual objects contrasted with the images of athletic agency occasioned by the ever-increasing importance of speed and triple jumps. Some male skaters, with Scott Hamilton at the forefront, rejected the glittery look in favor of simpler stretch suits ornamented only by geometric designs of contrasting colored fabric, with less exotic colors such as reds and blues, black, and gray the most common. Compromises between the two approaches produced stretch suits of relatively subdued colors highlighted by shinier trim or ornamentation. After Brian Boitano and Brian Orser both wore such one-piece outfits ornamented with military-style trim in 1988, the military look became a popular option for years following.

For female skaters, however, the simple or "athletic" image of the 1980s usually involved a solid-colored dress with beading of the same color; the sportier stretch fabric styles of the 1970s had largely disappeared. Instead, the trend in statement-making costuming was in the direction of more elaboration through contrasting colors and textures and toward the use of flesh-colored "illusion" fabric to give the impression of revealing more of the skater's flesh through extreme décolletage and/or bare backs while maintaining enough structural integrity to prevent dresses coming apart or shifting awkwardly during athletic moves.

In the 1988 season, perennial champion Katarina Witt of East Germany

skated her tapdance-based short program in a showgirl-style light blue sequined leotard with high-cut legs, low-cut chest, and similarly colored feathers on her headdress and sleeves and around the hips as the only perfunctory
gesture in the way of a skirt. American Debi Thomas, Witt's strongest challenger in the mid-1980s, skated an urban dance short program wearing a
black one-piece unitard with no skirt but with illusion fabric and sequin
trim typical of the era's skating dresses on the upper body. Witt's approach
invited appreciation of her body's erotic appeal, whereas Thomas's emphasized her athleticism and the shapes she created with her body, at the same
time showing off the shape of her figure and making a gesture toward the
glamour expected of competition attire.

That summer the ISU Congress passed the ruling, colloquially known as
the "Katarina rule," clarifying that clothing for skating should not be excessively theatrical—that men must wear sleeves and have a neckline that does
not expose the chest, and that ladies must wear skirts and that unitards and
bare midriffs are not acceptable (a ruling directed primarily against Witt's
feathers-only fringe but which also precluded Thomas's more sober cov-
ered-up approach). The rule also discouraged excessive decoration such as
sequins, beads, and the like for both men and ladies. This ruling occasioned
some dismay among young skaters who enjoyed the glittery style. *Skating*
magazine published a letter from one reader, complaining, "You can't get
the feeling of the music if the costumes are dull. Sequins glisten and are
pretty from a distance and close up. The ice glistens, so the skaters' costumes
should," and a reply from ISU representative Franklin S. Nelson explaining
that "what the International Skating Union and the USFSA are trying to accomplish with this rule is to keep costumes in good taste and get away from
some of the spectacular ones we have seen lately, especially in international
competitions. Some of these were felt to be more appropriate for Las Vegas
or the circus than for competitive figure skating."[34]

A few months later, USFSA president Hugh Graham discussed the problem of attracting boys to the sport because of the "mixed image our sport
has with regard to male skaters" and steps the USFSA was taking to improve
that image. These included no longer presenting male medalists with flowers on the podium and discouraging the throwing of flowers onto the ice,
promising that "the TV interview area in competitions that we control will
project a sporting image rather than a frilly flower garden." Graham noted
that "the new dress code for ladies and men should also encourage a sports
image. I am continually amazed that skaters, coaches, and parents perceive
sequins, beads, and strange outfits as an advantage to competitors. The reaction of judges is, indeed, just the opposite. Classic, well-fitting simple attire

is by far the most advantageous. We must strive to push our image as the SPORT of figure skating."[3]

Graham's reference to "classic, well-fitting simple attire" and Nelson's to "good taste," and the prohibitions on unitards for women and later on tights for men, however, suggest that while they perceive the showy excesses of 1980s costumes to be inappropriately flamboyant or theatrical, the image these officials prefer would be more along the lines of the genteel tailored clothes of earlier decades in skating fashion than of the aerodynamic, form-fitting, often bright-colored garments currently worn by athletes in other winter Olympic sports. "Theatrical" in this context seems to refer to the types of spectacular costumes worn in entertainments such as circuses, nightclub shows, and musical extravaganzas where the visual appeal of the performers' bodies is paramount, quite apart from any actions they may perform (and in the case of magicians' assistants, backup singers, showgirls, and the like, any functions these performers serve beyond the visual images they provide are generally less salient from the spectator's point of view).

Beginning in the 1980s, theme programs became popular among ice dancers, as discussed in chapters 10 and 11, often with the skaters taking on specific characters or otherwise attempting to convey aspects of some sort of narrative. Singles skaters began using characters or stories to unify their performances in programs such as Brian Boitano's Napoleon free skate in 1988 and Katarina Witt's depiction of Carmen the same year. In the 1990s, such character-driven programs became fairly common among male singles skaters as one strategy for avoiding the effeminizing effects of positioning themselves as objects of the spectatorial gaze while still earning credit for being "artistic," as discussed in chapter 8. Female skaters have not felt the need to avoid so positioning themselves, precisely because this position has traditionally been associated with femininity. Artistic ladies' skating has therefore tended to rely more on presenting the abstract beauty of the skater's body line and musical expression as a means of demonstrating artistry. When female skaters do take on theme programs, the themes often contain elements of overt seductiveness or more general sexual appeal or love interest, as with Witt's (and others') Carmen and Michelle Kwan's Salome.

The costumes for such theme programs resemble theatre costumes in the sense that they tend to approximate the kinds of clothing that might be worn on the stage or in real life by the fictional or historical characters being portrayed.[35] In other cases, costumes might remain simple and abstract in design but use colors or ornamentation symbolic of the program's theme. Rich fabrics and sparkling trim also continue to play a significant role in the design of competition wear. With the rulings that male skaters must wear trousers and not tights, one-piece outfits have become rarer, as have designs that call attention to male skaters' bodies as abstract sites of spectacle. Male skaters do sometimes wear tight-fitting clothes and perform sensual movements to showcase themselves as sexual beings, but almost always with a sense of actively controlling the relationship with the spectators, rather than simply submitting themselves to the spectatorial gaze as objects of visual consumption. Skating tradition encourages skaters to value beautiful movement for its own sake; for females the values of the skating world and the larger culture mutually reinforce the connection of such beauty to physical appearance, and so the abstractly beautiful body remains among the more common choices of imagery, while adolescent young women's desires to assert their identity as sexual beings in the face of the older generation's disapproval probably accounts for a large part of the interest in imagery that emphasizes sexuality.

A HOLLYWOOD IMAGE OF SKATING

One in a Million, Sonja Henie's first film, is the only film in her oeuvre to deal with figure skating as a competitive sport.[36] In the process, it brings together several of the issues discussed here. I want to close the chapter with a brief analysis of the film in order to pull out these issues and examine how the image of competitive skating made its way into the American consciousness through depiction in the image-driven mass medium of Hollywood film.

The plot is as follows: A group of American entertainers, headed by scheming impresario Thaddeus Spencer (played by Adolphe Menjou), are stranded in the Swiss Alps without money when they discover that the hotel where they had been booked to appear has burnt down. The troupe makes their way to a smaller inn, where the innkeeper's daughter Greta Mueller (Henie) proves to be a figure skater in training for the 1936 Olympics. Spencer spies Greta practicing on a pond behind the inn and envisions her starring in a show in which she will perform star turns as a featured skater, surrounded by supporting skaters and the troupe's own musicians and comedians. He organizes a tryout for a booking at a casino in St. Moritz and insists on payment for the tryout. Meanwhile, a pair of American newspaper men investigating the hotel fire arrive at the inn, where the younger of the two, by the name of Bob Harris (Don Ameche), is immediately smitten with Greta. He too witnesses her skating practice and learns that her father had won the 1908 Olympics but had been stripped of his title and publicly embarrassed amid accusations of professionalism by accepting payment for teaching a rich man's son to skate. According to Greta, the money had been merely a gift to allow him to purchase new skates and pay other expenses of his own training.

When Harris hears that Greta has gone to St. Moritz to give a skating exhibition in the company of the American troupe, he rushes off to stop her. Arriving after she has skated her first number, he prevents her from going on again that night, out of fear that performing with professional entertainers will compromise her amateur status and disqualify her from competing in the Olympics, a dream she and her father had looked forward to since she was six years old. Spencer cannot understand why anyone would prefer amateur trophies to the wealth of the professional performing career he envisions for Greta, but when his wife points out that Greta will attract more customers as Olympic champion than as an unknown, he agrees to wait until after the Olympics and has his manager in New York book an engagement at Madison Square Garden, promising the Olympic figure skating champion as his star.

Greta goes to the Olympics and wins. She tells Spencer she does not wish to turn professional but believes she can also win the next Olympics (scheduled for 1940). Spencer says that she is already professional because he had been paid for the St. Moritz exhibition. Mueller then sadly takes Greta's awards to a meeting of the Olympic committee to return them and asks the committee members to announce that the results had been miscalculated and another skater had actually won. The committee members, familiar with the scandal that had attended the accusations against Mueller's own amateur status, agree. Mueller tells Greta she might as well accept Spencer's offer. On learning that Greta is no longer Olympic champion, Spencer is horrified and rushes to a phone to cancel the New York booking. Harris arrives and points out to the Muellers and Spencers, and subsequently to the chair of the Olympic committee, that because Greta received none of the money paid for the exhibition and (with some fudging of the truth by Spencer) that all of the money had gone for expenses, she should not be considered professional. Greta's medal is returned and she goes to New York to star in an extravagant professional ice show.

The predominant issue at the level of the plot is that of amateurism versus professionalism. Greta's determination to compete at and win the Olympics is fueled by a desire to win the honor that her father had lost a generation earlier. As she prepares to compete, Mueller tells her he hopes that "if you do win, you'll remember the honor of that achievement is worth more than all the money anybody can offer you." In the film, the attitude of the amateur sports authorities, depicted as forbidding-looking older men, and of the Muellers themselves that one's honor is somehow tainted by engaging in commercial transactions is contrasted with Spencer's eye for the next paycheck. The fact that Mueller had needed to accept a financial gift in order to win in the first place the Olympic medal that he later lost raises the question of whether the honor of winning is necessarily dependent on already having access to material wealth.

The commercial aspects of creating a champion are ignored, however, in the depiction of Greta as a simple innkeeper's daughter who trains in isolation on readily available natural ice with only her father's coaching to guide her, with her natural talent and hard work sufficient to win her the ultimate prize. Although Greta's eventual fate as Olympic champion and future professional skating star parallel Henie's own career, the details of how she achieved this status do not. In reality, Henie's own father had spent large sums to provide her with the best coaching, costumes, and access to ice that money could buy. The mythos of the film shares with the code of amateurism the notion that the characteristics that make a skater a worthy champion are those that are inborn, not those that can be bought, although in the real world both are necessary.

Another, less explicit issue in the film is the question of specularity, the construction of the female skating star as object of the gaze by valorizing the visual appeal of skating movement and downplaying its athletic and technical demands. Championships at the time were of course determined primarily on the basis of technical superiority, particularly in school figures, but it was Henie's appealing freeskating that won over the audiences in both the brief Olympic competition scene and the extended skating show scenes within the diegesis of the film, as well as the audiences watching the film itself. Furthermore, the movie constructs this appeal precisely by means of the conventions of gendered looking that Laura Mulvey describes in her discussion of other films of the period. Both Spencer and Harris become attracted to Greta—as theatrical commodity and as love interest, respectively—in the process of looking at her skating while themselves remaining unseen by Greta, who in the first instance is unaware that her skating practice is being observed, just as the camera and thereby the movie audiences look at images of the actors while the actors and the characters they play appear to remain unaware of being observed.

Interestingly, when Harris observes Greta practicing, she is working on back loops, a move that to skaters would suggest the precise repetition demanded by school figures. This is actually one of the most visually interesting figures from an observer's point of view because of the extreme leaning and twisting of the body and swinging of the free leg necessary to produce the correct tracings on the ice. As the scene progresses, however, she breaks from this figure to perform a series of freeskating moves, suggesting her own liberation from the tedium of retracing the same marks on the ice into the freedom of unrestricted movement and "showing off" for an observer, as well as providing the observer with a more aesthetically varied set of images to enjoy.

During the scenes when she is performing for audiences within the film, Greta/Henie does acknowledge the spectators' (and the camera's) presence with her own gaze and her awareness of using her body to create a spectacle for their entertainment. The skating numbers, with their frequent poses and runs on the toepicks interspersed with spins and jumps, are choreographed with an eye more toward visual interest than toward demonstrating complexity of technical skating content. This tendency, with different particulars, could equally be applied to most skating numbers in any era that have been choreographed for shows and exhibitions versus programs designed for competition.

The discipline of school figures and the code of amateurism that played such a large role in shaping the first century of figure skating as a competitive sport had become by the century's end nearly forgotten pieces of the past. Highly demanding athleticism and increasingly sophisticated performance qualities are hallmarks of the sport as currently practiced. The ways that these aspects of current skating practice contribute to the meanings of figure skating in general and of individual programs or skaters in particular make up the subject of the remaining chapters.

PART THREE

Cultural Meanings
of Ladies'
Figure Skating

CHAPTER SIX

Critiques of Skating's Feminine Ideal

$\mathcal{F}$igure skating has long been associated with specific types of bodily images. Some aspects of these images, such as curving, flowing movement across the ice, derive from the inherent nature of skating technique. Others, such as the preference for easy movement as opposed to visible effort, or for erect upper-body carriage, are choices based on earlier skaters' and especially skating officials' ideas about the image they wanted the sport to cultivate. So, too, are aspects of external appearance, such as clothing and personal grooming. Whereas movement and carriage relate directly to what a skater does with her body while skating and thus have been incorporated into definitions of what constitutes "good" skating technique, clothing and grooming remain external and relatively superficial, especially as they relate to skaters' appearance and behavior off the ice. Unlike the technical aspects, expectations regarding external appearance are considerably different for male skaters than for females—both are expected to be well-groomed or "well put together," but according to hairstyle and clothing conventions of their respective sexes.

All these preferences, to one degree or another, influence judges' evaluations of skaters' presentation (the second mark) and all but the last their evaluations of skaters' technique (first mark). These in turn affect which skaters win competitions. This process serves to project an image that a skating federation puts forth to the rest of the skating world and to the world outside as their ideal of what a ladies' (or men's) skating champion should be. As new champions across the years exhibit characteristics that differ from the previously held ideal, understandings of the ideal change to incorporate the new characteristics, and some of the old characteristics fade in importance or disappear entirely as they no longer apply to the current favored skaters. This is a slow process, however, as skaters wishing to become champions tend to model themselves on previous champions and to present themselves within the skating world's accepted norms.

To some degree, then, skaters succeed competitively to the extent that they approximate the ideal image of the skating champion. For observers unfamiliar with skating technique or with judging criteria, judges' decisions appear to be made solely on the basis of image irrespective of the technical aspects of what the skaters have done on the ice. Often even skaters themselves, and their parents and sometimes their coaches, are unable to identify technical reasons why a skater places lower than expected in competition. They, and the public, may conclude that politics or having the correct image plays more of a role in judges' decisions than objective evaluation.

There are ideological considerations underlying evaluations of presentation and even, as I have suggested, of technique. No human being, however well trained and determined to be impartial, is ever completely knowledgeable or completely free of personal bias. Sometimes, therefore, these conclusions are indeed true. More often, however, it is the skater and her supporters rather than the judges who suffer from lack of knowledge and lack of objectivity. But as skaters repeat tales of being unfairly judged in favor of others who better represent the established skating ideal, newcomers to the sport, either as participants or as observers, become inculcated into an oral culture that believes that skating is not so much a technically evaluated sport as it is a choice among images of femininity.

These images of the ideal female figure skater have evoked associations with certain forms of off-ice femininity, as evidenced by the types of discourse surrounding the sport. In the United States, especially since the era of Peggy Fleming in the 1960s, the emphasis in the mainstream media, including ABC's televised packaging of the national championships and other competitions, has been on the ladies' singles event. The questions of what kind of young woman will represent the United States as national ladies' champion and how she will fare in international competition have been points of intense ideological investment for members of the American skating community and of the viewing public.

In Canada, figure skating is also considered a feminine sport at the recreational and domestic competitive levels, something that girls pursue while their brothers play hockey. Internationally, however, Canadian skaters have had less success in ladies' singles than in other disciplines. Petra Burka in the 1960s and Karen Magnussen in the 1970s each won world and Olympic medals, including one world gold medal each, and Elizabeth Manley won silver medals at the 1988 Olympics and Worlds. These accomplishments pale, however, next to those of Canadian men of the same period: world titles earned by Donald Jackson and Donald MacPherson and bronze medals by Donald Knight in the 1960s, Toller Cranston's bronze medals and stylistic trend-setting in the 1970s, and a string of successes in the 1980s and 1990s beginning with Brian Pockar's bronze medal at 1982 Worlds and continuing through 2000 with multiple Olympic medals and world titles won by Brian Orser, Kurt Browning, and Elvis Stojko. Indeed, in the years between 1982 and 1997, the only year in which there was not at least one Canadian man on the world podium was 1996, ironic as Worlds was held in Edmonton that year. For Canadian fans and Canadian media, therefore, the men's event takes pride of place, although the majority of fans are female, a fact that implies different dynamics of spectatorship than those addressed by American writers about the sport.

Print coverage of figure skating in mainstream publications and in the skating press has long drawn on verbal imagery suggested by the visual images of skating to promote skating in general and American ladies' champions specifically to the American public as a fantasy ideal of refined elegance and even royalty. *Time* magazine, for instance, in the 1930s reported on "five little pretenders-to-the-throne" vacated by the retirement of long-time United States champion Maribel Vinson meeting at the 1938 national championships "to vie for her crown." An account of the following year's championship referred, perhaps somewhat facetiously, to a recent tour by "Queen Sonja" and to defending champion Joan Tozzer as "blue-blood" and "statuesque."[1] Phrases such as "ice queen" or "ice princess," both with and without ironic intention, turn up regularly in discourse about ladies' skating throughout the twentieth century.

Feminist consciousness raising and populist rejections of such elite images of womanhood as ideals to identify with and aspire to changed public perceptions about such images. In the 1970s, as the American public began to show greater interest in physical fitness and sports in general and for women in particular, American skaters too began to emphasize athleticism in their freeskating with greater speed, bigger and faster jumps, and more frequent inclusion of triple as well as double jumps. But as other sports for women gained popularity, figure skating no longer held a place in public awareness as one of the more athletic activities in which women might engage.

Skaters also cultivated sportier images with short hair; lighter, more natural-looking makeup than had been popular in the previous decade; and track suits or warm-up suits (newly popular among athletic Americans in general) as attire during practices and warm-ups, and for walking around during competitions at times when it was not appropriate to wear either one's competition dress or more formal attire. Skaters were still, however, expected to avoid being seen in public at skating events wearing jeans or similar informal clothing, an example of how skating mores in the 1970s and 1980s held the athletes to an earlier generation's standard of formality rather than that practiced by teenagers and young adults in other contexts during this period. As skating gained in popularity with audiences through television coverage, the differences between contemporary popular styles of dress and self-presentation and the greater formality encouraged within the skating world led to skaters themselves and outside observers beginning to question the images of womanhood skating put forth to the outside world.

Press accounts of figure skating in mass-market (and, in the 1980s, scholarly) publications aimed at readers concerned about how womanhood and femininity are represented in public life began to include critiques of the processes by which skating chooses its exemplars and of the ideals it seems to promote. Mass-market stories no longer sought merely to convey the image of femininity skating represented, with its by-now cliché references to royalty, but to reveal the jealousies and politics of the skating world behind the image. "Feminine and nicely elegant on the outside, cold steel on the inside, the finalists in the U.S. figure skating championships proved again there is more to those fluffy little girls than meets the approving eye" noted one 1970 article.[2] Another, four years later, noted that "the title and scepter always pass to the next in line, so Dorothy Hamill figured to win the crown despite putting on a plebeian performance," and quoted "an old hand at judges' antics" on Hamill's apparently overly generous scores that "it has to be done that way. If we send her to the Worlds with a bunch of 5.5s, the Russians will automatically give her low scores because we did."[3]

The woman-oriented fitness magazine of the mid-1970s *womanSports* ran several articles that capitalized on women readers' fascination with skating as a high-profile woman's sport, yet simultaneously questioned the images of femininity it seemed to promote. The opening of one 1975 article described Hamill, "as graceful as a ballerina in her shocking pink dress that flutters ever so slightly over her well-developed thighs. Her brown hair is worn in a shortish bob, her eyes are delft blue and her cheeks are as rosy as her costume." Only the references to well-developed thighs and short hair disrupt the image of delicate femininity in this opening paragraph, but later the article quotes Hamill herself unmasking the image:

> You have to be the all-American girl, with little smiles all the time. At the championships, they watch everything you do. You can't make a face, and if you kick the ice during a practice session, forget it. A skater's reputation off the ice has a lot to do with it, too. So you can't run around with boys. And you can't run around in blue jeans, and you can't say how you really think or how you really feel. You just have to pretend that you're little Miss Goody Goody.[4]

Another article two years later focused on the importance of image in determining Hamill's successor at the U.S. championships. "With no stop-watches and no finish lines, figure skating comes close to being a Miss America Pageant on blades. Appearances and politics are part of the game" in "figuring out exactly what America is looking for in the way of a champion this year," and "it seems that winning is as much a matter of good packaging and public relations as it is talent." The article notes that what all the competitors are striving for "is an intangible called 'style,' 'personality,' 'maturity,' 'grace,' 'showmanship'" and that "constantly being watched all the way up through the ranks puts kids under a tremendous pressure to conform to the image of the ideal American girl—what both Dorothy Hamill and Janet Lynn have called the 'Goody-Two-Skates' look."[5]

A profile of Hamill as a professional noted the change in her "image in the press" from "Doris Day on skates, a slightly unreal all-American girl with a vulnerable psyche and a nervous stomach to what *People* magazine called 'a moderately spoiled,' 'sometimes rude,' 'freshly minted' superstar." The article concurred that on the Olympic podium "for a moment, she really was America's sweetheart, and you wanted to hug her" and reassured readers that during an interview for the current profile "it was easy to remember why and a relief to know that the sweetheart image—no matter how out of proportion —had some basis in reality." But the article also focused on the image construction involved in the way television broadcasts of skating present the athletes to the American public by noting that "just prior to her [Olympic] performance, an ABC feature showed Hamill in the white house with the white picket fence in Riverside, Connecticut, where she grew up, with her stuffed animals, her medals, and her china figurines." It demystified the mechanics of professional celebrity involved in Hamill's "packaging" by manager Jerry Weintraub, noting the fact that her "contracts with Clairol . . . even determine how short she must wear her hair." In the wake of articles such as the one in *People,* the author noted, Hamill herself seemed "confused by the myriad images of herself she sees in the press" that "seem to depend on what four-letter words she uses, whom she dates, how many packs of cigarettes she smokes, and how much money she makes."[6]

A 1977 profile on new U.S. champion Linda Fratianne reaffirmed the prevailing public meaning of female figure skaters. It declared that "we have trouble with most of our female athletes because they seem too invulnerable, too competent, too impervious to our affection. Not so the figure skaters. It's even easy to forget they're athletes. On the ice, they wear sequined dresses their mothers have painstakingly sewn. They glide to pretty music, twirling so fast that their panties show. They are our ruddy-cheeked girls of winter: the slightly spoiled, very graceful, all-American dreams."[7] The skaters themselves doubtless had little trouble remembering that they were athletes, especially in the late 1970s, as triple jumps started to become necessary components of championship-winning ladies' freestyle performances. For the general public, however, including journalists who through their choice of emphasis helped to shape the response of their readers, what stood out was not the difficulty of the various moves skaters performed, but the grace and ease with which the best skaters performed them.

In the 1970s, attention focused on the pressures of living up to the single feminine ideal, of proving oneself worthy of being "America's Sweetheart." The 1979 film *Ice Castles* also detailed the demands on a small-town skater suddenly thrust into the milieu of high-level competition—the image-consciousness of the other skaters at the training center who initially make fun of her small-town ways; being followed constantly and even woken up in bed by a television crew producing a news series about her ascent; making appearances at cocktail parties where she is put on display for and touched by wealthy strangers who are sponsoring her training expenses. The author of an early-1980s biography of men's champion Scott Hamilton repeatedly refers facetiously to the ladies' side of the sport as "Sweetheartville."[8]

Meanwhile, both the skating world and the mainstream press began to celebrate women's athleticism. Mainstream journalists described Janet Lynn as having a "strong, balletic style,"[9] and (citing "the words most often used by skating experts") Dorothy Hamill as "athletic, powerful, and strong."[10] Evaluations of acclaimed female skaters by male experts often balanced praise for the skaters' athleticism with reassurances of their femininity, while female commentators could be more forthright in their admiration of female strength. About Dorothy Hamill, Dick Button commented "She's a very strong, powerful, athletic girl. She has a classy look to her skating, and she's good-looking as well."[11] Ice Capades performance director Cliff MacGraham described Hamill as "a very dynamic skater. She's a very big jumper for a girl, and she has a very aggressive skating style, more so than most women. But her personality on the ice is very warm and feminine. It's the combination of the two that's so striking," while sports photographer Lyn Malone said, "She's like a gazelle and a lion out there. She knows she's the best, and if from time to time she has to prove it, by God she will."[12]

Button's commentary about ladies' triple jumps similarly blended admiration and protectionism. About the opening triples of Linda Fratianne's long programs, he commented, "That's a jump that's difficult for the strongest of men skaters, let alone girls," and "Remember she doesn't have to do this, but she has chosen to do this very difficult move."[13]

A former ladies' champion could note the increased athleticism of women's skating by comparing the current crop of competitors to the male expert himself:

> *Dick Button:* It's been twenty years since you won your gold medal.
>
> *Tenley Albright:* It's been twenty-four years since you won your gold medal.
>
> *Button:* But who's counting, who's counting.
>
> *Albright:* Not I if you don't.
>
> *Button:* All right. But it's a long time and you've had a chance to see a lot of skating in the meantime. What's the big change, or is there a change?
>
> *Albright:* Oh, Dick, look at them warm up right now. Every single one of these girls is doing fast, fast jumps with tremendous carry in the way they come out of them. It's terrific. Only you used to do that.[14]

Reports of competitions had long relied on comparisons and contrasts (for instance, of skating style, physical appearance, and family background) in describing the chief competitors. In the 1980s, however, the dualistic rhetoric of characterizing skaters as either "athlete" or "artist" began to take firmer hold. The issue, as reflected in the discourse surrounding the sport, became less one of which competitor would best live up to the single established ideal of ladies' figure skating champion, but now which of two opposing ideals would prevail. Emphasizing artistry or beauty accorded well with traditional notions of femininity, whereas an emphasis on athleticism carried connotations of masculinity and so proved contentious when applied to female skaters. Thus the two sides of this dichotomy came to carry value-laden meanings about gender ideology. On the one hand, proponents of the (stereotypically feminine) artistic side of skating, or of traditional gender roles, would sometimes describe a female skater as "athletic" to indicate that she lacked the qualities that those commentators valued most highly. On the other hand, for supporters of the (stereotypically masculine) athletic aspects of the sport, or of feminist challenges to previously masculine territory, athleticism was one of the highest—if not *the* highest—values a female skater could represent.

In the early 1980s, attention focused on the rivalry between the two American skaters Elaine Zayak and Rosalynn Sumners, emphasizing their differences along this register. *Sports Illustrated* referred to Sumners as "doll-like" and "the fair-skinned, green-eyed beauty," while Zayak's "terrier-like determination has led her to be called the Pete Rose of figure skating, but what had some of her followers concerned was that she arrived at the nationals carrying a stocky Rosean physique as well."[15] *Ms.* magazine described Zayak as "feisty and giggly," but also noted that in her 1980 senior-level debut she "dazzled the crowd and the judges by performing eight triple jumps in her final four-and-a-half-minute program," thus taking female athletic accomplishment in figure skating to a previously unheard-of level at a time when three or four triples (of two or three different kinds; Zayak herself used only three varieties of triple in her programs) represented the top level of female jump content. Zayak's jumping feats signaled a significantly greater importance to triple jumps in women's skating in the 1980s than they had held in the 1970s. The "rather shy and introverted" Sumners "performed an elegant, well-rounded program at the 1982 Nationals" to win the title Zayak had won the year before. This, such reports claim, stood as evidence that "the pendulum began to swing the other way" to reward qualities other than triple jump after triple jump.[16]

The *Ms.* article cited the 1983 ISU ruling (colloquially known as the "Zayak rule") that limited the repeated triples that had been the staple of Zayak's program (specifically, multiple toe loops and toe walleys) as evidence of this shift in emphasis. *Sports Illustrated* cited opposing viewpoints on the question of athleticism versus artistry from both a masculine and a feminine perspective. Reigning men's champion Scott Hamilton explained his decision to eschew sequined costumes in the future, complaining that "some of the outfits you see out there now remind me of bad lounge acts. . . . The professionals emphasize the artistic side of figure skating, and that's fine. But as long as we're an Olympic sport, I think the emphasis in the amateur ranks should be on the athletic side." Former ladies' champion turned television commentator Peggy Fleming, on the other hand, lamented that "the sport's going through an athletic stage right now. I've always liked the artistic side, and I think the two sides will have to come closer together. Right now the balance of power is in the hands of the triple-jump people."[17]

Interestingly, both these articles discuss excess weight as a problem that Zayak and Sumners each faced as they moved from their mid- to late teens. The articles recount Sumners's successful weight loss as part of her preparation for her win at the 1983 championships. The difference in readership addressed is clear, however, as the *Sports Illustrated* piece focuses repeatedly on the two skaters' appearance (including in the title, "The Thinner Was the Winner")—suggesting that Sumners's skating success was a direct result of her dieting success—whereas *Ms.* clearly puts her weight loss in the context of an overall "push for the top" that included curtailing social activities in favor of practice time and consultation with a sports psychologist. The *Ms.* article also expresses concern that "with our country in the throes of dietmania, the emphasis on appearance—especially on weight—has become somewhat of an obsession among several female skaters. Anorexia, common among dancers, could now become a problem in the skating world."[18]

In 1988, previews of the Calgary Olympics focused on the confrontation between reigning world champion Katarina Witt of East Germany and American Debi Thomas, who had defeated Witt for the 1986 world title and placed second to her in 1987. Descriptions of Witt's "flirtatious style" positioned her on the side of femininity and artistry, with Thomas, "a superior technical skater," aligned on the side of atheticism.[19] The Canadian magazine *McLean's*, including a home team skater in the mix, profiled Witt as "a charismatic performer" of "flamboyant, sensuous routines," Thomas as her "only serious rival" and "technically superior," and Canadian Elizabeth Manley as "technically brilliant but . . . lack[ing] the artistry" of Thomas and Witt.[20]

During ABC's short program broadcast, as Witt skated to a medley of show tunes wearing the feather-trimmed high-cut leotard (and headpiece) that served as the impetus for the ISU ruling that summer requiring ladies to wear skirts, Dick Button said "This costume all fits together. It's the quintessential showgirl number." About Thomas's techno dance number, Peggy Fleming remarked, "Well, this music is very powerful, very strong, very hard-driving," thus emphasizing the athleticism of her artistic choice of program style. Button referred to Manley as a "dynamo" and to Midori Ito, making her first appearance on U.S. television, as "a powerhouse and a very strong skater" in explanation of the fact that her presentation marks were lower than those for required elements.[21] We can interpret the latter remark to mean that because Ito's technical and athletic abilities were so extraordinary, it would be difficult for her presentation skills to reach the same standards, as indeed they did not; but by stating that her presentation scores were lower *because* her athleticism was so great, through careless wording Button almost suggests that a "powerhouse" skater by definition can never meet the highest standards of presentation, that power in itself is a negative factor when it comes to evaluating artistic impression—even though the American competitor Thomas drew praise for both her athleticism and her artistry.

Helena Michie, in an "interchapter" in her book about relationships between women in English literature and how the depiction of women as opposites alienates them from each other, examined the uses the American media had made during the 1988 Olympics of the "battle of the Carmens" between Witt and Thomas. (Both were skating their free programs to the music of Bizet's *Carmen.*) Witt chose to enact the title role by emphasizing her feminine charms and by collapsing to the ice at the end in a final death scene. Thomas, for her part, did not so much play a role as reflect Carmen's strength as a character by emphasizing her own power on the ice. Witt's image was ultrafeminine and ultrasexualized through her revealing costumes and her flirtatious playing to the judges and spectators. This was even more the case for the showgirl short program than for the Carmen long program. The African American medical student Thomas, desexualized and deracialized through her costuming and by the media discourse, according to Michie, was made to represent the chaste, healing virtue of pure athleticism that the American public was asked to identify with. For example, immediately after the free skate, ABC commentator Jack Whitaker summed up: "Katarina Witt, I guess, is the glamour girl from the unglamourous country, a consummate flirt who can work a room as good as any Las Vegas performer, and she did it here tonight. And for Debi, well, I'll tell you, if that's what young Americans are like today I'm not worried a bit and when she gets her degree I hope she'll be my family doctor. I also hope that Alberto Tomba might sweep Katarina off her feet and bring her back here to the West so we can enjoy her beauty and talent."[22] These characterizations represented a reversal of terms in the depiction of East and West from earlier Cold War depictions of East German woman athletes as "grim, unerotic, and masculine."[23]

In the event, both Witt and Thomas failed to deliver their best performances during the Olympic freeskate. (Witt placed second behind Elizabeth Manley in the free program but won gold to Manley's silver on account of their relative placements in the figures and short program; Thomas placed fourth in the free, behind up-and-comer Ito, to take home the bronze medal.) The East-versus-West, sexual-versus-chaste "binary opposition" between Witt and Thomas from the pre-Olympic buildup was disrupted by "interloper" Manley, "a reminder," as Michie puts it, "that, among other things Canada is not the United States, not perfectly and indistinguishably aligned with this country on the East/West axis. Manley's victory made clear that the majority of the fans in Calgary's Dome had, perhaps, another agenda, another fantasy than the one embodied in Debi's healing of Carmen."[24] With Witt and not Thomas capturing the gold medal despite her less-than-convincing free skate, Michie notes, American media such as *Sports Illustrated* turned their attention instead to speed skater Bonnie Blair as a better example of the triumph of pure sport over the suspect (and specifically female) sexuality as represented by Witt and by figure skating in general.

Michie focuses her analysis on the narrative that the American press attempted to make of the Witt-Thomas showdown, acknowledging the ways in which actual events did not play out according to the media script. Such narratives themselves—that is, the ways that American culture uses skating and particular skaters to play out contested values—and explications of these narratives such as Michie's can reveal a good deal about the culture that produces them. In this instance, athleticism and pure sport took on positive values associated with Americanness and straight dealing, while artistry was equated with feminine seductiveness. On the one hand, Witt's seduction of the judges and her ultimate receipt of the gold medal served Cold War rhetoric as evidence of the partisanship of Eastern European judges and thus of Eastern Europeans in general, and of the shadiness of using feminine charms to win sporting contests.[25] For feminist critics (and skating fans), the latter meaning caused the most concern, with the belief that women's skating had become more about sex appeal than athletic ability.[26] On the other hand, Witt's feminine appeal was certainly not lost on male viewers and commentators in the West and thus gained both Witt herself and the sport in general new fans, in the process provoking a subtle shift in American attitudes toward East Germans.

None of this analysis, however, really tells us much about the skating itself or about what the skating world preferred to reward. Manley won the long program with a performance that could primarily be described as athletic, with two of the more difficult triple jumps, loop and lutz, in addition to the usual salchow and toe loop, and a cheerful and outgoing style that does cast the skater in the position of being pleasing to the audience, but that had long been a standard approach adopted by so-called "athletic" skaters of both sexes to the presentational aspects of skating performance, particularly among North Americans. So the majority of judges who placed Manley first in that free program (some of whom also had Ito ahead of Witt) were certainly not favoring artistry or sex appeal at the expense of athletic accomplishment. Witt's dramatic approach, with its extended period of posing without substantial technical content (either in jumps or in spins or difficult steps) and none of the more difficult triples or difficult combinations, prevailed over Thomas and Ito, but by failing to complete her jumps cleanly or to skate with her usual power and confidence, Thomas gave away her strongest advantages.

The fact that Ito did not defeat Manley or Witt in that long program suggests that jump counts weighed less heavily in 1980s judging decisions than in the 1990s, and that if anyone suffered in Calgary for being too much the athlete and not enough the artist, it was not Thomas or Manley, but Ito. Compared to other top competitors of the era, Ito was notoriously bad at school figures, which meant that she was not in contention for a medal in Calgary even if she had won the short or long programs there, and so judges may have given her freeskating somewhat less consideration than that of the medal contenders, if for no other reason than that her lower combined placement heading into the free program meant that she skated earlier in the draw.[27] Ito's jump content in Calgary—seven triples and two double axels, including the two difficult combinations of triple toe–triple toe and double axel–half loop–triple salchow—would hold up well against the most difficult jumps performed by female skaters a decade later, and the quality of her jumps (apart from the less-preferred high wrapped position of her free leg while in the air) has never been equaled. Nor were her spins or footwork deficient in technical content. Her presentation marks, on the other hand, suffered on account of her tendency toward stiffness in her back and shoulders and a consequent lack of fluidity to her movement and subtlety to her musical expressiveness, despite the high energy and pleasing cheerfulness she brought to that Olympic performance.

Ito's mastery of all the triple jumps (to which, the following year, she added the triple axel that helped her to win the 1989 world title) may not have brought her an Olympic medal in 1988, but it did signal the arrival of a new era in women's skating, when six or seven triple jumps, usually of five different kinds, would now become the hallmark of championship-winning freestyle performances. Although 1989 and 1990 served as transitional years, with titles sometimes going to the skaters who had mastered more triples and sometimes to those who excelled at school figures and at graceful movement, as soon as figures were gone in 1991 the jumps, and especially the triple lutz, became ever more important in determining ladies' championships.

The 1992 Olympics produced contrasting profiles of the four top contenders. *Time* magazine, for instance, described "Japan's Midori Ito. . . . 4 ft. 9 in. and built like a fireplug. But can she fly!" and the three Americans who had swept the 1991 world medals, Kristi Yamaguchi, "known for her precise, delicate artistry," Nancy Kerrigan, "a Kate Hepburn–style beauty whose elegance carries over into her performing style," and Tonya Harding, "a bold, natural athlete who pays little attention to nuance, less to music," but "just gets out there and jumps."[28] This *Time* spread, incidentally, pictured both Ito and Harding, the reputed jumping specialists, performing the quintessentially feminine layback spin, next to the delicate artist Yamaguchi completing an athletic feat by stretching into the landing of a jump and Kerrigan the elegant beauty with one hand supporting her leg extended well above her head in her trademark spiral position, another beauty pose seen more often from women than men but less curved (especially as Kerrigan performed it) or explicitly feminine than the layback spin. The article thus more or less equalizes the four women's feminine image visually in balance with their verbal representation.

Women's Sports and Fitness placed the three Americans along a continuum, with Yamaguchi striking the happy medium. The photos and captions depicted Harding in a powerful but awkward-looking position in midair approaching the peak of a jump with a caption lauding her "superb athleticism," Yamaguchi in a more decorous mid-jump pose, calling attention to her "choreography [that] shows off both her jumping ability and natural grace," and Kerrigan with another view of the same spiral position and praise of her "elegance."[29]

The *Newsweek* piece on this four-way contest offered the densest analysis, pairing Kerrigan and Yamaguchi against Ito and Harding. One axis of the comparison was more developed artistic style versus triple axels, with the suggestion that as the only sport in which what women do matters more than what men do, figure skating risks losing its appeal "if athleticism overwhelms the elegance" by eliciting direct comparisons with men's accomplishments, by which standards it will suffer. In addition, the article aligned Yamaguchi and Kerrigan with middle-class stability, versus Harding's and Ito's history of financial and familial struggle. It also addressed racial questions in asking what the implications might be (for the average American "good ole boy") if, in a period of intense economic rivalry, the United States claimed Olympic victory over Japan "but on the screen there, as the band plays the 'Star-Spangled Banner,' is the All-American girl of 1992, and her name is Yamaguchi?"[30]

Scott Hamilton's commentary for CBS during the 1992 Albertville Games did even more to establish these skaters' public images. During the short program broadcast, he commented that Kerrigan's presentation scores "could be a little higher. Everything she did she did beautifully. The combination was . . . couldn't have been done better. And it's amazing when somebody can combine that kind of technical ability with this kind of beauty in their skating. . . . Everything delivered. Clean, great artistic skater." About Harding he remarked, "She is a technical skater. Her artistry is not anywhere near her ability as a technical skater. She's so strong. What an athlete." In describing Ito, however, he gave the American Harding more credit: "Her [Ito's] strength is her technical ability. If you compare spiral sequences with Kristi Yamaguchi, you can see the difference. Midori's line and presentation don't compare. . . . She's not a great artistic skater. Tonya skates with a little more fire than she does." And Yamaguchi, the eventual winner, also won his highest praise for her well-roundedness. "Probably Kristi's greatest strength is her lack of weaknesses. She does everything so well. This is a very well done combination spin. Every position is perfect."[31] Because the so-called artistic skaters performed better on that occasion, completing all their elements while Harding and Ito fell on the jump combinations, and because Hamilton points out no weaknesses in Yamaguchi's or Kerrigan's skating while disparaging Harding's and Ito's artistry, viewers are led to the conclusion that artistry is good and athleticism bad, or at best a lesser virtue, when it comes to female skaters.

According to Hamilton's characterizations and those of the *Women's Sports and Fitness* article, Harding and Ito had only athleticism to offer, Kerrigan only elegance or grace, while Yamaguchi combined the best of both. Such characterizations acknowledge Yamaguchi's technical expertise (and mental toughness) that allowed her to complete her jumps more often than Kerrigan and to perform the difficult triple lutz–triple toe combination in her efforts to match the difficulty of Harding's and Ito's triple axels. What such commentary misses, however, is the fact that Kerrigan's skating and jumping was in fact more powerful and often less graceful than Yamaguchi's. Her body type lent itself to greater elegance than Harding's or Ito's, thus occasioning the repeated descriptions of her as elegant, but a more accurate comparison of these skaters would have placed Kerrigan in the in-between position as less powerful than Harding and Ito and less refined or graceful, and also less consistent, than Yamaguchi, thus lacking the highest abilities at either extreme.

Ultimately, the Albertville results suggest that the contest was not in fact one between opposing ideals of grace versus athleticism, but rather, as with most sports contests, a test of which competitor's technique and nerves could best withstand the pressures of Olympic competition. Yamaguchi and Kerrigan (and France's Surya Bonaly, who at the time ranked among the best jumpers in the world and certainly the best in Europe, but whose basic skating technique—the way she used her blades against the ice—did not show the same technical finesse of the other top competitors) completed clean short programs and ranked ahead of Ito and Harding, who fell on their jump combinations. In the long program, Yamaguchi again made the fewest errors, faltering only on her triple loop and doubling a planned triple salchow, while Ito and Harding each suffered falls and Kerrigan popped two of her planned triple jumps to ungainly singles. Ito late in her program landed a successful triple axel, making her the only woman ever to do so in Olympic competition, to capture second place, while Kerrigan won a split decision over Harding for third in the long program but would have taken the bronze medal in any case because of her much higher placement in the short. In the end, the results came down less to which style the skating establishment preferred than to who best got the job done when it counted.

During the period of the 1980s and early 1990s, the most prominent skaters whose skating inspired the "athlete" label either came from blue-collar backgrounds, as in the case of Zayak (whose family owned a tavern), Harding, and Ito, or were black, in the case of Thomas and Bonaly. (Bonaly had been raised by white adoptive parents who professed macrobiotics, country living, and physical education.) All demonstrated in their freeskating fast, aggressive stroking and bigger and/or more difficult jumps than their competitors. But they often lacked the gracefulness and ease of movement that skating standards prize so highly. Perhaps the cultural milieux in which these skaters grew up placed less value on impressions of ease and grace in everyday movement, compared to those of the majority of skaters who come from or aspire to lives of social and economic security, or perhaps they even assigned positive value to evidence of physical effort.

The question thus arises: Are gracefulness and elegance or delicacy—that is, styles of movement and of inhabiting one's body traditionally prized as feminine—the only qualities that can define a good artistic impression on the ice? For male skaters, resisting the feminizing implications of these qualities has led to a variety of approaches to demonstrating artistry and masculinity simultaneously (see chapter 8). For the ladies, as of the early 1990s, the efforts of athletic skaters to define an artistry appropriate to their own styles of movement went largely unappreciated. Many skating experts, and mainstream sports reporters who relied on these experts for their evaluations, continued to dismiss such efforts as inartistic because they failed to live up to the expected standards of gracefulness.

By the final season of her amateur career, Debi Thomas had achieved a fair measure of graceful refinement to her movement, but her programs were still designed to emphasize other qualities. Her *Carmen* long program used aggressive skating with big, powerful jumps and fast spins in strong positions and sharply accented Spanish dance steps. It also suggested an outer-directed focus, as expressed in an uplifted torso and clean, straight lines with her arms and legs. The image presented, especially in the program's best performance at 1988 U.S. Nationals, was that of a confident and powerful woman taking command of the space around her by moving forth into it. Her short program to techno dance music, performed in a form-fitting skirtless unitard that showed off both her long lines and her musculature, contained, along with the big jumps, a high-energy step sequence involving angled limbs, shoulder isolations, and syncopated rhythms. This evoked images of contemporary urban dance derived from African American culture, congruent with Thomas's own racial heritage if not her personal experience. In 1991 and 1992, Harding similarly used heroic, outer-directed movements in the opening segments of her long programs. To the down-and-dirty pop culture rhythms of rapper Tone Loc and ZZ Top in their conclusions, with head rolls, high kicks, and sharp position changes in a combination spin that sent her ponytail and fringed skirts flying all over the place, she created, on a foundation of solid skating technique, an image of a bad girl, wild and beyond the control of the conservative social norms represented by the figure skating establishment.[32]

These images are a type of what anthropologist Mary Douglas terms "shaggy" body styles associated with lower social strata.[33] As such, they were at odds with the highly controlled and refined images derived from the elite art form of classical ballet and from the upper-class body styles in general, which skating had traditionally promoted. Conservatives within the skating world tended to perceive and to describe these intentionally unrefined styles as lacking in artistry, reserving the "artistic" label for more refined approaches to expressive movement. Similarly, the heroic style of powerful straightforward skating and straight, simple body lines that proved so successful for a male skater such as Brian Boitano was not perceived as equally artistic when performed by female skaters. Women were expected instead to demonstrate softer lines and curves in accordance with accepted notions of femininity. Skating insiders continued to describe the delicately pretty, elegant, or seductive female skaters as artistic, while dismissing those who cultivated aggressive or wild images as inartistically athletic, and the popular press mostly echoed these evaluations. Thomas's and Harding's skating offered the promise of a new direction for female artistry in skating through images of female power or of a woman breaking free of the strictures of society (as represented by rigid body control), but they never quite attained acceptance for these styles as appropriate paths for ladies' skating to pursue, either from the skating establishment or from public media. When a few years later Kurt Browning and Elvis Stojko introduced raunchy pop culture music and movement into their short programs, they achieved popular acclaim for these innovations. The mainstream culture outside the skating world considered such images more appropriate for males than skating's traditional refined, elegant, and graceful images, whereas even most mainstream publications continued to support the notion that female artistry and gracefulness must be synonymous.

One who did sense other possibilities was dance critic Anita Finkel. She noted that throughout the 1970s and 1980s the most exciting jumpers of ladies' skating competition had been girls of fifteen and sixteen who, as they matured and their jumping ability diminished, either succeeded, or not, at "offering visions of adult femininity that were comprehensive, unpitiful, strong, and directed toward beauty." Yet in 1992, while the print journalists and CBS commentators including Scott Hamilton were praising Kristi Yamaguchi's artistry, Finkel demurred: "If sheer strength, completeness, and harmonious clarity define art, then Yamaguchi, with her tentativeness and gentle evocations, rather than clear definition, of positions, shapes, and forms, offered a sketchbook in the face of a bold, decisive, and interesting canvas." That "canvas" was the work of Tonya Harding, whose "exceptional connection with the ice, her drive, her speed, her deep edges, and the clarity and stretch of her positions" gave her "the wherewithal to make her relatively short limbs and blocky torso irrelevant."[34] Whether or not Harding thought of herself as an artist in her use of skating movement, her tragedy, as Finkel perceived it even in 1992, was that the external details of her self-presentation on and off the ice—poorly designed homemade dresses, overly heavy makeup, and the like—disguised rather than enhanced the artistic point of her skating: "Tonya Harding really is a brilliant artist; the tragedy is that no one realized it, let alone valued it."[35]

By 1994, of course, examining how the apparent lack of acceptance for Harding's style had led, directly or indirectly, to criminal assault became fodder for much speculation in print and electronic media throughout America. Blame was variously placed on the sport of figure skating (and sometimes on American culture in general) for its narrow standards of gracious femininity that Harding had failed to meet, or on Harding herself for failing to meet them.[36] For feminists and other cultural critics who had become fascinated with watching figure skating before or during the crisis of 1994, the strongest reaction has been to examine the ways that skating seems to demand a disempowering femininity from its female practitioners.

Following the Tonya Harding/Nancy Kerrigan scandal in 1994, a spate of articles appeared in the popular and academic press offering a feminist critique of figure skating. The most comprehensive of these was an article by Abigail Feder, entitled "'A Radiant Smile from the Lovely Lady': Overdetermined Femininity in 'Ladies' Figure Skating," written with a focus on the 1992 Olympics in Albertville; this was published in several outlets after Kerrigan and Harding rose to further prominence in early 1994. In this article, Feder sets forth the multiple ways in which the narrative surrounding figure skating competition in general "is so overdetermined in its construction of the women skaters' femininity."[37] As in other women's sports, media representations of the athletes and the competitions defuse or apologize for female incursions into the "masculine" world of sport by emphasizing acceptable, often stereotypical, feminine attributes of the athletes both within and outside the frame of competitive activity.[38] Feder suggests that this tendency is particularly pronounced in figure skating because the technical elements of men's and ladies' singles skating are so similar that an overemphasis on gender difference in the external aspects of the sport is necessary to provide reassurance that "no matter their accomplishments, women are 'just girls' after all."[39]

As examples, Feder cites practices within the skating community—the use of the term *ladies* rather than *women* to refer to female competitors; the requirements in the short program for women to perform a spiral sequence, while men must perform an additional step sequence, and the then-current short program jump requirements in which women could perform either one triple jump or else only doubles, while men were required to include either two or three triples; the rules and practices regarding costumes; and the use of the artistic impression score (as the second mark, now known as "presentation," was then called) to reward skaters who demonstrated the acceptable image of femininity.

She also offers examples that focus on the media coverage of skating events. Introducing televised coverage of ladies' competitions with background music using lyrics referring to beautiful appearance or to wishing and dreams accompanied by soft-focus lights and images of "stars in little girls' eyes, glittery costume, and flowers from adoring crowds" or "women shown in flowing movement, in worried close-ups or applying makeup" suggests that the important thing in women's skating competitions is being considered beautiful enough to be granted approval from judges and fans. Skating telecasts accord greater athletic agency to male skaters, who are "pictured doing their most difficult jumps, raising their hands in gestures of triumph."[40] Commentary that dwells on costuming, the skaters' physical appearance, their emotions as read through facial expression (as in the quote included in the title of Feder's article), and their relationships to family all also serve to undercut the female skaters' athletic accomplishments. Dissolves in the editing of video camera shots are often used to enhance an impression of feminine flow in those skaters considered traditionally feminine, while sharp cuts often exaggerate an impression of choppiness in so-called athletic skaters (and enhance the impression of athleticism for male skaters); the choices of still photographs in print media serve similar purposes.

Feder's article caused some consternation among members of the skating community. Skaters themselves have a greater familiarity than Feder with the day-to-day concerns of skating in relation to their understandings of what skating means to them. On a daily basis, their attention would be more often on technical and athletic concerns and their own direct experiences in moving over the ice and relating to music than on questions of gender imagery. Most skaters also have little or no familiarity with academic feminist arguments about gender as a social construct; thus they would likely accept culturally determined manifestations of femininity as expressing natural, essential attributes of femaleness.

Feder invokes Frigga Haug's notion of "slavegirl competence" as "a useful framework for thinking of the way in which women both use and are victimized by the figure skating system" and states that Kristi Yamaguchi's "active participation in her own construction as a passive object of beauty was stunningly ironic." In so doing, Feder suggests that any woman who participates in skating, particularly if she includes the pursuit of beauty in any form among her goals, is necessarily being victimized.[41] The quote from Haug— "Our active appropriation of the rules makes us more self-confident in our activities; in availing ourselves of the existing order by actively 'exhibiting' our own bodies, we participate in our own construction as slavegirls"[42]— seems to place more emphasis on the "slavegirl" part of the formulation than on the "competence" involved.

This dismissal of female skaters' other forms of competence may have irked some members of the skating world. So, too, might the apparent dismissal of the fact that many female skaters themselves take pleasure in the aesthetic qualities of their sport for their own sake and not in order to become "objects of sex and pleasure" for men, to use Haug's phrase. Just as women are often said to "dress for each other" rather than for appreciation from males in everyday life, the pervasive interest among many female skaters (and mothers of skaters, and female skating fans) in skating clothing stems not from any concerns with appealing to men but from a general interest in fashion that has long been an aspect of women's culture and a means by which women communicate with each other, not merely a means of communicating their sexual desirability to men. Similarly, many women and girls share common interests in music, dance, and other arts, and those who skate transfer these interests to the artistic aspects of the skating medium. For much of the twentieth century, female skaters, coaches, and judges have maintained artistic values at the grassroots level as well as in elite competition and have passed these values on to new skaters of both sexes as they enter the sport.

It was Feder's likening of the layback spin to images of female sexual climax in pornographic representations, however, that caused the most vehement objections. Ice dancer Renee Roca, for instance, called the idea of any skater simulating sex on ice "the craziest thing I ever heard. . . . I never realized that we were porno stars on ice. Is that how some people really think of us?"[43] Coach Frank Carroll's response was "That to me indicates a sick mind. It tells us more about the writer than it does about figure skating."[44]

In a *Ms.* magazine article inspired by the Harding controversy, Kate

Rounds attributes to figure skating a "butch/femme identity" and likens its "artistic/athletic dyad" to "the classic madonna/whore construct," drawing on Mulvey's notion of the split between an active male gaze and a passive female recipient of that gaze. "By acting *and* skating butch," Rounds writes, "Harding turned the notion of passive 'receiver of the gaze' on its head. She became threatening, while Kerrigan, the femme, the acquiescent absorber of the gaze, went on to Disney World." Observing these dualities leads Rounds to the conclusion that "the not-so-subliminal message is that figure skating, in all its various forms is about sex. . . . If women's free skating is about sex, then pairs skating is about *having* sex, and men's free skating is about homoeroticism."[45]

This last observation especially draws attention to the dangers of allowing theory to dictate analysis. For men's skating to be "about homoeroticism," it is necessary to posit a male spectator. But most actual skating fans are female.[46]

An additional factor might be instances in which the skater actively chooses to address a specific subset of the skating audience as a whole. This might involve courting erotic desire from the opposite (or the same) sex, regardless of the skater's own sexual preferences. Or it might involve appealing to other-than-erotic interests more prevalent among one sex or the other, e.g., an Elvis Stojko whose traditionally masculine physicality and off-ice interests inform his skating in ways that appeal to heterosexual male viewers who are otherwise uncomfortable with what they perceive as effeminacy among other male skaters, or a female skater who chooses to emphasize and appeal to traditionally feminine interests such as fashion or ballet.

Usually, however, especially within a competitive situation, such questions of erotic appeal or any kind of specific audience appeal, or even of proving one's femininity or masculinity, would be the furthest thing from the skater's mind. Gaze-theory readings of what skating "is about" generally take as their object skating that has already been mediated by television with its framing devices and choices of camera angles, dictating what the spectator can attend to, and/or by tour and show producers with theatrical lighting and other professional production values. Such readings also presuppose a spectator who is ignorant of skating technique, and they therefore focus on how the general images such a spectator can perceive from a skating performance resonate with images from other sectors of the culture at large. The codes that the lay spectator has access to include what music a skater performs to, what kind of clothing she wears, what kind of role she appears to enact. In a professional or exhibition context, these kinds of broad cultural meanings and general audience appeal might be of prime importance to the skaters, although in a professional competition, at least, skating technique would also play a part.

In eligible competition, on the other hand, the primary audience the skaters are addressing is not the fans but the judges, and thus the technical and athletic aspects of the performance are of primary importance. Descriptions of skating performances by other skaters, parents, coaches, or judges are most likely to focus on which jumps were attempted and which completed, or on the quality of the stroking, the complexity of the connecting steps and program layout, or unique and interesting variations on spin positions and combinations of jumps or steps. For all but the most highly skilled skaters, simply performing these technical and athletic feats *well*, with enough ease and control to demonstrate mastery rather than physical awkwardness or struggle, is the challenge skaters need to meet in order to demonstrate good "presentation" as well as technical merit. Making any kind of artistic statement is at most a secondary concern. Knowledgeable fans, especially those who skate themselves, are also generally at least as interested in these aspects of a competitive performance as in the issues raised by the journalists and the academics, both those who reinforce the prevailing image of femininity in skating and those who seek to unmask it. Certainly to the extent that a skater believes that her image affects her competitive results, she (or he) would be concerned with these questions, but she would not have gotten involved with skating in the first place and would not have continued skating long enough to reach a competitive level were there not other meanings and other satisfactions that compensate for any discomfort she might feel with the dominant image.

Finally, the immediate sensations of skating, not only visual but also auditory, olfactory, and especially kinesthetic (and gustatory, for children whose enthusiasm for the ice is so great that they attempt to eat it, as the three-year-old Tonya Harding is reported to have done), are a salient source of meaning for the live spectator, knowledgeable or not, who can appreciate the rush of the skater's speed across the ice, the snap of a jump, the crunch of steel cutting into ice. Skaters themselves, whether beginners or world-class competitors, experience sensations within their own bodies and at close range, watching and watching out for other skaters on the ice, that any primarily visual theory is ill-equipped to address. Any full theory of skating meaning, therefore, including meanings about femininity, must take into account all these channels of signification.

The kinesthetic experiences of skating, for instance, provide the initial attraction that draws many skaters into the sport and inspires them to continue to pursue it even amid frustrations with competition, with the social relationships surrounding the sport, and with their own technical achievements. A television documentary about the history of women in figure skating, for instance, opens with the narrator's voice and those of well-known skaters interviewed within the documentary explaining, "More than anything else, they remember what it felt like to skate." "The swiftness. The feeling. The freedom. There's a wonderful feeling gliding on ice." "Lacing up figure skates, stepping out onto that ice, served as a woman's declaration of freedom." "Skating backwards fast and having the wind blowing your hair, I don't know, just may be like flying. You know, you just feel you're free." "Beautiful snow-capped mountains, clear blue sky. I think I was in heaven. I mean, I just loved it." "Ice has a live feeling. Warm, velvet, soft."[47]

After losing in 1997 all the major titles she had won in 1996, Michelle Kwan stated,

> I think the experience will help me a lot, preparing myself and attacking, instead of just defending something. I felt that my wings were clipped, that I couldn't fly. That's what I mean by having fun and enjoying what I love doing, and that's skating. I didn't get into the skating world just to win the Olympics or win lots of money. I really just came into skating to have fun, to look at it as a sport, to improve and work hard and see that hard work pay off. I think that's the most solid ground I've ever walked on. It's the best feeling. I just feel comfortable on the ice.
>
> It felt great to be able to fly again.[48]

The process of mastering physical skills also serves as a source of appeal. For instance, a Madison coach and former national pairs competitor describes her own attraction to the sport:

> I got learn-to-skate lessons for my birthday when I was nine, and then we just got hooked from there. So I was pretty old, relatively speaking— you know, most kids start younger, I think, if they go on to compete. . . . It was pretty challenging because I wasn't very good. I wasn't outstanding in the class. But I felt like I could do things and so I guess I felt a sense of accomplishment, even after each class, like learning how to stop, or whatever. . . . I was told this, and I tell my kids this, you know, if you go into something as fast as you can skate, and jump up in the air, that's as close to flying on your own that you're ever going to feel, and it's the coolest feeling in the world.[49]

For many competitive skaters, the process of competition itself, of striving to be the best and of doing what is necessary to outskate one's rivals, is another source of appeal. The narrative of competitiveness has often been emphasized in the men's event but obscured in the ladies' by television producers who frame the broadcasts of ladies' competitions according to narratives of stereotypical femininity, but it has already long been present within television skating coverage, coming from the skating experts providing the technical commentary.[50] Although media portrayals of figure skating, as of other sports, have de-emphasized female competitiveness, as various feminist media analyses have detailed, at the same time skating commentary has often praised champions such as Katarina Witt, Kristi Yamaguchi, and Oksana Baiul for their fierce competitiveness and determination to win. Some commentators make a habit of pointing out the determination and effort exhibited by any skater to land jumps that started out not quite right, for instance Scott Hamilton's frequent assertions that a skater (male or female) "really fought for that landing," and Peggy Fleming's occasional comments that a skater (almost always female, since she rarely comments on the men's event) "wanted very badly to land that jump."

Marsha Lopez, a writer with both academic and skating experience, argues that feminist readings of skating, particularly Feder's, miss the point because "in figure skating, the primary relationship is not between the skater and the audience, but between the skater and the ice" and that what "the skater" (generically) is trying to accomplish is "exploring and testing the limits of circular motion . . . in all its configurations. . . . The best single example is layback spin, in which the skater's body itself becomes an arc, rotating in uniform circular motion on a stationary center." Lopez likens this process to Ralph Waldo Emerson's notion of life cycles of death and rebirth flowing into transcendence of individuality. She concludes that "Figure skating . . . is about the creation of perfect circles which simulate the orbs of the universe. It is about the achievement of flow, which simulates the cycle of nature: movement (life); stillness (death)" and adds parenthetically "that female skaters are, because of their curved figure and lower center of gravity, better equipped than males to achieve this is no small irony."[51]

We can follow Lopez's example to make meaning from the skating we watch by attending to the qualities that underlie all good skating—such as flowing, curvilinear movement—to arrive at what "skating" or "skaters" in general might represent. We can also look instead at the ways each individual skater inflects these qualities somewhat differently to produce a variety of different utterances within the signifying system that is skating as a whole. One example might be to focus on stroking technique, how one skater may appear to float effortlessly on top of the ice while another carves her way powerfully into it. Such simple examples might prompt us to understand skaters according to how well they approach an ideal vision of skating technique, or according to which of two binarily opposed categories they fit into. But by attending to multiple variables of technique and self-presentation rather than just one at a time, we can produce a more specific analysis of individual skating utterances rather than analyzing only "skating" in general.

All the different channels of meaning outlined in chapter 2 come into play to produce meaning in any given skating performance. In addition to the skater's relationship to the ice, per Lopez, we can also look at her relation to the space around her as alternatives to the relationship to spectators emphasized by gaze theorists, and, in competition, the relationship to the specialized subset of spectators whose judgments will immediately affect the skater's competitive success. Each skater may choose which of these relationships to emphasize and whether to adopt a position of dominance, of equality, or of subordination within each relationship, or such relationships may come about through mere habit if the skater declines to make conscious choices about them. These choices will vary from one skater to another, often from one program to another by the same skater, and sometimes from one section of a program to the next.

In analyzing all these relationships, we must not presuppose a single, "feminized" status position on the part of all skaters (female or male), or even two oppositional alternatives of which skaters are forced to adopt one or the other. In earlier skating generations, the range of images and relationships employed was indeed more limited than today, and the number of skaters and programs to which the public had access through mass media even more limited. Nevertheless, it has always been the case that individual skaters put the stamp of their own personalities on their skating. Since the 1990s, with professional performing arts techniques finding their way even into amateur competitive performances and with the proliferation of themed programs, the range of options has expanded to the point that it is far more useful to look for differences in meaning within individual performances rather than for overarching meanings of skating in general.

Some of these meanings may explicitly address issues of gender, and we can also make the effort to tease out implicit gendered meanings in programs with other explicit emphases. In the process, however, we must not lose sight of issues unrelated to questions of gender or sexuality that may take precedence in the production of meaning from the skater's point of view.

CHAPTER SEVEN

Girls versus Ladies

*I*f the narrative of ladies' skating in the 1980s and early 1990s was of the contest between "athletes" and "artists," in the mid-1990s it took on an inflection of "girls" versus "ladies" as young teenagers began to dominate the highest levels of the sport.

Ever since Sonja Henie first won the world championship in 1927 at the age of fourteen and brought new athleticism to the ladies' side of the sport, and since British teenagers Cecilia Colledge and Megan Taylor furthered the youth movement with the introduction of double jumps a decade later, it has been known that girls in their early to mid-teens are generally more successful at the jumping aspects of freeskating than are fully grown women. In addition to the energy of youth, the relatively straight lines of an undeveloped girlish or even "boyish" figure offer less resistance to quick rotation in the air than do womanly curves. The two most renowned jumpers in the sport, Midori Ito and Tonya Harding, were more muscular and broad-shouldered than girlishly slim or womanishly curvaceous. They were also, at approximately 4'9" and 5'1", respectively, quite small.

Being able to perform triple jumps at all, let alone with any consistency, thus relies largely on body type, requiring either extreme thinness to promote quick rotation and/or considerable muscular power to allow more time in the air to complete the rotations. As female skaters grow older, like males, they tend to increase their power with increased muscle mass and also to improve their technique. Unlike for male skaters, however, for most women puberty brings a lower center of gravity and a lower strength-to–body weight ratio, which can cause jumping ability to decline significantly while the skater is still in her teens, even as other aspects of her skating continue to improve. For this reason, figure skating in the triple jump era tends to self-select for compact body types at the elite levels, limiting the range of physical images displayed among the top skaters.

Because skating is one endeavor in which girls can achieve a very high level of performance by early adolescence and may decline from that level athletically by adulthood, there have always been young teenagers among the

ranks of elite figure skaters, at times among the very best of the sport. In recent years the trend toward very young champions has become even more
pronounced and has skewed the image of figure skating from that of a woman's sport to one that favors young girls.

When school figures played an important part in a skater's advancement
through national federations' testing systems and through the ranks of senior competition, skaters were rarely able to reach the top competitive levels
before reaching physical maturity. Young competitors might be more consistent jumpers than the older seniors, but most did not have the body control
to compete with senior standards of technique and presentation. As Frank
Carroll, coach of Michelle Kwan (and before her, of Linda Fratianne, who
had also first made her mark as a young teenager), put it, "I think when girls
get to be 16 and 17 and 18 years old in figure skating, a lot of their physicality
goes and they have trouble maintaining high efficiency in the really tremen-
dously difficult things. But there's another part of their skating—the beauty,
and the edge work and those things—that they develop."[1]

As long as edge work (whether in school figures or in the connecting elements of freeskating that make up the majority of the program between the
jumps and spins) and presentation qualities that evidence the skater's understanding and fine control of how her body moves, the relationship of her
movement to music, and the visual effect of her movement for the spectators remain as important or more important than difficulty of jump content
completed, most senior competitors and most champions will be young
women in their late teens and early to mid-twenties.

Since 1991, however, school figures no longer hold back talented jumpers
at lower test levels or lesser results in senior competition until they master all
the skills involving the blades on the ice at a level comparable to their jumping ability. Each new cohort of young skaters moving up to senior level brings
an increase in the number of skaters who have been aiming from an early age
to match or exceed the jump content of the recent champions. It thus remains the responsibility of the judging establishment to reward the full range
of skating skills and of coaches to teach them, and not simply to allow skating competitions to consist of nothing but jumps.

As Carroll's statement indicates, in ladies' skating those qualities of mature presentation have traditionally been subsumed under the concept of
"beauty," whether of the skating or of the skater herself often remaining un-
specified. In addition, for female skaters, demonstrating maturity or good
presentation has often been conflated with the demonstration of one's sexuality or feminine charms along with the emphasis on physical beauty. For
instance, in an NBC interview during the 1993 World Championships, Kata-

rina Witt said to Oksana Baiul, "Well, I understand that your favorite skater is Jill Trenary, and that for you she does the ideal skating," to which Baiul replied (through an interpreter), "I love Jill as a woman. She looks like a real woman on the ice and our sport is figure skating. You must train, but basically our sport is figure skating and we must skate as women on the ice. I'm competing in ladies' figure skating and I want to show off my beauty." One example of how this emphasis relates to maturity of presentation would be Frank Carroll's urging Michelle Kwan to adopt elaborate theatrical makeup give her a more mature look to appeal to judges who were looking for "a ladies' champion, not a girls' champion."[2]

As I have noted elsewhere, and as many other feminist scholars and critics of the sport would concur, the majority of women's skating programs have either taken a purely athletic approach and so have been found wanting on artistic grounds, or else have tended to rely on a limited range of traditionally feminine approaches to artistry, which I have characterized as the lyrical/beautiful/classical approach, the perky approach, and the sexy approach, not always mutually exclusive.[3] The latter often involve the skater actively emphasizing specifically female or feminine attributes as the source of her appeal to spectators; thus the skaters who emphasize femininity also tend to be the skaters who are considered most "artistic."

In the mid-1990s, the most successful skaters included young, small teenagers such as Oksana Baiul, Lu Chen, Michelle Kwan, Irina Slutskaya, and Tara Lipinski. Kristi Yamaguchi in the early years of her senior career, 1988–1990, would also fit this description. In the 1999–2001 seasons, of a group of "baby ballerinas," as Dick Button referred to them,[4] emerged among the top ranks of the U.S. senior ladies. Some of these skaters, in their early to mid-teens, were very small, and some were even more precocious in presentation than in jumping ability.

Most of these skaters have indeed struggled with consistency on their jumps as their bodies matured or as they suffered from injuries, in some cases never regaining all the jumps or the successes they had enjoyed as younger adolescents. These facts lend credence to the argument that the technical demands of ladies' skating as it is now practiced, as had become the case in elite gymnastics, favor an undeveloped figure over that of the typical adult woman.

GIRLS' CHAMPIONS IN LADIES' CHAMPIONSHIPS OF THE 1990S

Issues of maturity versus immaturity became inextricably intertwined with those of artistry versus athleticism in ladies' skating during the years leading up to the 1998 Olympics. The results at that event, however, contradict earlier assumptions that, given a choice between mature artistry and jump-focused athleticism in ladies' skating, judges will invariably prefer the former.

The image of a barely pubescent Olympic champion, a "girls' champion," proved disturbing to members of the skating community and of the general public who look to Olympic results as determining the single ideal of femininity that the skating world endorses, at least during that Olympic cycle. Objections to this image rest on somewhat different bases than objections to beauty or sex appeal as defining the preferred image—the latter define females as holding value solely in terms of their aesthetic or erotic appeal to a male gaze, whereas the former equates female value with childishness, thus implying that adulthood, independence, and autonomy are positively valued characteristics for males but negative for females. Looked at in the context of the results of the entire four-year competitive cycle and of the succeeding years, however, the implications are more complex and ultimately more indicative of a process of judging each competition on its own merits rather than according to any single predetermined ideal.

In 1993, flirtatious, waifish fifteen-year-old Ukrainian orphan Oksana Baiul became the youngest world champion in sixty-six years, the second youngest ever. The same year, twelve-year-old Michelle Kwan was the youngest skater in two decades to compete as a senior lady at U.S. Nationals, finishing sixth. In 1994, Baiul became at sixteen the second-youngest-ever Olympic champion and retired from competition, before losing her jumps to growth spurts, injuries, and personal problems. ISU president Ottavio Cinquanta declared that "we will make more Oksanas," suggesting that charming young stars would be infinitely replaceable and longevity in the sport unnecessary.

In 1995, fourteen-year-old Kwan was favored to become the youngest-ever U.S. and possibly youngest-ever world champion, defeating Sonja Henie's record, but lost to skaters who could skate faster, jump higher, and in the case of new U.S. champion Nicole Bobek (seventeen) and world champion Lu Chen (eighteen), display more refined presentation.

As discussed in chapter 2, Kwan and her coach and choreographer sought to transform her skating and her image for the 1996 season. This transformation included both greater strength and precision in her actual skating and also external cosmetic changes such as putting up her hair, adopting elaborate theatrical makeup after having worn none the year before, and using music associated with a narrative of seduction.[5] The mainstream media made much of these external changes, suggesting that within the skating world it is attention to appearance and sexuality that mark a female skater's maturation from girl to lady. The improvements in her skating received much less comment, and what comment they did receive was primarily praise for her increasing artistry and attention to music, giving the impression that it was only prejudice on the part of the judges against a childlike appearance, and not immature qualities within her skating, that had prevented Kwan from winning the year before.[6]

At fifteen, Kwan had already missed her chance to become the youngest-ever national or world champion, but in 1996 she did become the third youngest to hold each of these titles. As an almost-unbroken winning streak stretched over more than a year from fall 1995 to fall 1996, she became the recognized favorite, the most consistent and well-rounded skater in the ladies' field, taking on an almost legendary mystique as she continued to mature as a feminine artistic skater emphasizing beauty, musicality, and dramatic storylines concerned with love and death.[7]

Also in 1996, in a battle between two "athletic" skaters, sixteen-year-old Irina Slutskaya defeated the twenty-two-year-old Surya Bonaly in the latter's bid for a sixth consecutive European title, representing yet another example of youth triumphing over experience. Bonaly had for years been the best jumper in Europe, but the new generation was catching up as her own skills began to wane. Meanwhile, tiny thirteen-year-old Tara Lipinski, in her first year in senior competition, finished third at the 1996 U.S. Championships and qualified for the World Championships, where she placed fifteenth.[8]

Despite continuing her winning streak through the first half of the 1996–1997 season, Kwan had been struggling with changes in body shape that affected her balance on her jumps and with changing to a different brand of skating boots. She won the short program as expected at 1997 Nationals, but early in her long program she fell unexpectedly and then, as she later put it, "panicked" and made several more serious errors.[9] Skating last in the ladies' free skate, Lipinski had only to place ahead of Kwan in the long program to win the national title. She rose to the occasion and won the free program as well as the competition as a whole by skating a clean program of seven triple jumps, including a history-making triple loop–triple loop combination never before completed or even attempted in competition by a female skater.[10]

Three weeks later at the Champions Series Final, Lipinski once again defeated Kwan by completing more successful jumps in both the short and long programs. Suddenly Kwan, who had defeated older and less consistent skaters not only by landing more jumps but also by radically transforming herself from little girl to mature young lady between the ages of fourteen and fifteen, was now at sixteen losing to a fourteen-year-old who had not made a similar transformation but who looked and in many ways (such as low, quickly rotated jumps and imprecise positions) still skated even younger than that. Here was evidence that the judges were not just looking for a single "mature" image for a ladies' champion; cynics and purists who valued the artistic possibilities of the sport or the fine points of skating technique complained that the judges who awarded Lipinski her gold medals were just counting the jumps and not paying attention to the quality of those jumps, much less to the quality of the rest of her skating.

At the 1997 World Championships, Lipinski won the short program while Kwan faltered on the jump combination and placed fourth; Slutskaya missed her combination entirely to place sixth. In the long program, each skated well and took first-place ordinals from three of the nine judges; taking into account second-place ordinals as well, Kwan won the free skate, with Lipinski second and Slutskaya third. Kwan did not complete quite as difficult jumps as did Lipinski or Slutskaya, but she brought more complexity to the skating between the jumps and more polished refinement to her presentation of that skating. Slutskaya was older, bigger, and more powerful than Kwan, and considerably more so than Lipinski. She also had higher jumps if not always cleaner landings than either, but although she had cut her hair and begun to wear tasteful light makeup (as did Lipinski), she still projected a more youthful image, and like Lipinski she generally received higher marks for technical merit than for presentation when she skated well, falling on the "athlete" side of the athlete-artist dichotomy.

Combined with the short program placements, these results gave Lipinski the gold medal and Kwan silver. Slutskaya had to settle for fourth place.[11] Lipinski had now managed to take away all the major titles that Kwan had won the year before, and, in doing so at age fourteen, with a birthday later in the year than Sonja Henie's, had also become the youngest-ever U.S. and world champion, feats that Kwan at fourteen had failed to accomplish. Moreover, because of new international age restrictions, it is likely that Lipinski's records will stand for years to come.

The results of the World Championships brought mixed reactions. Proponents of well-rounded, mature, artistic skating breathed a collective sigh of relief when Kwan won the long program, a sign that as long as she made no major errors Kwan's ladylike brand of skating would carry the day against the immature, athletic "jumping beans." At the same time, Lipinski, the prototypical jumping bean, still carried the world title and represented for traditionalist observers the unpleasant specter of skating as a sport in which little girls were more valued than mature young women.

Many members of the press were not kind to the new world champion. A Swiss newspaper called Lipinski "the flea who melts the ice." London *Times*

Tara Lipinski, world champion at fourteen and Olympic champion a year later, became a focus for debates about maturity in ladies' figure skating. Photo © by J. Barry Mittan.

columnist Simon Barnes referred to her as a "circus freak" and a "robotic shrimp"; he wrote that "Lipinski is very talented, and, quite obviously, a massively strong-minded person. And it is horrible to watch her: really quite disturbing. . . . Women's ice skating finds itself in the absurd position in which puberty is a disadvantage," positing, "The judges acceded to the wishes of the American corporate hunger for teeny heroines. Thus they have brought discredit upon their sport, and insulted its participants. Why have marks for artistic impression in the first place, if you don't use them to discriminate between artist and freak?"[12] French skater Laetitia Hubert, twenty-two years old, who finished sixth in Lausanne, spoke out in favor of maturity: "With such young skaters, it seems to me like we're returning to the days of baby gymnasts. Meanwhile, skaters my age are very capable of landing triple jumps but with experience and femininity added to that."[13]

Those who succumbed to "Taramania" often focused on the recordbreaking nature of her youthful accomplishments. Even those proponents of athleticism who hailed her groundbreaking triple-triple combinations could not escape the fact that her jumps were small and in some cases technically flawed.

Heading into the 1997–1998 Olympic season, with the American press playing up the Kwan-Lipinski rivalry for all it was worth, Lipinski's jump technique became a topic of hot debate. At Skate America, the opening competition of the season, Lipinski and Kwan were once again pitted against each other, unveiling the programs they would skate at the Olympics. Kwan was emphasizing sophistication and pure skating, as a change of pace from the dramatic story programs she had favored the previous two seasons, with her choices of classical music: piano music by Sergei Rachmaninoff for the short program and William Alwyn's concerto for harp and string orchestra *Lyra Angelica* for the long. Lipinski had chosen film scores for both her programs, her short program using a tune from the soon-to-be-released animated *Anastasia* and the long the soundtrack of *The Rainbow*, which Lipinski and her choreographer Sandra Bezic described as being "about a girl growing up and coming of age."[14]

When Lipinski finished second to Kwan in both programs, many observers took these results as an indication of how the two would continue to fare against each other. In the long program, Lipinski had fallen on a jump, so there was little surprise at the results. In the short, however, Lipinski's most obvious error was a slight bobble on the entrance to her combination spin, yet despite completing more difficult jumps than Kwan, Lipinski received consistently lower scores for required elements. This suggested that she had received deductions of more than just the 0.1 that the shaky spin might have occasioned. Lipinski's coach, Richard Callaghan, expressed bewilderment at why the judges had so marked down the reigning world champion, who by virtue of that position might otherwise have been expected to receive the benefit of any doubt.

Concern over Lipinski's acceptance by the judges increased three weeks later when she again finished second at an international competition, this time not to Kwan, who was widely considered to be the best all-around skater in the world, but to Laetitia Hubert of France. Hubert, a notoriously inconsistent skater who had not won a major title since the World Junior Championships back in 1992, only two weeks earlier had placed eleventh out of eleven skaters at her other fall international.

One explanation, offered by Peggy Fleming in the ABC Skate America broadcast, was that judges might have seen fit to apply a deduction for Lipinski's takeoff on the triple lutz. The lutz is unusual in that, of all those jumps that can be performed with multiple revolutions, it is the only one that takes off from an edge traveling in a direction (for most skaters, clockwise) opposite from the direction of the jump rotation itself and the landing edge (counterclockwise). The reversal of direction is supposed to occur at the instant of takeoff, occasioned by the spring off the toepick of the other foot. The counter-revolution nature of the lutz takeoff makes the triple lutz the most difficult of all the three-revolution jumps. Many skaters, usually women (for reasons that may be related to the structure of the female pelvis and hip sockets) and particularly American women,[15] have a tendency to roll off the back outside edge and onto the back inside before picking with the opposite foot. In essence, this changes the takeoff from a lutz to that of a flip jump, an error known colloquially in skating circles as a "flutz." Lipinski had a habit of doing this, as she and Callaghan later admitted in press conferences (while noting that she was hardly the only skater to do so), and in the short program at Skate America her change of edge on this jump was especially blatant, occasioning a deduction for an incorrect takeoff edge on the intended jump.[16]

Ordinarily such minutiae of technique are not considered to be of interest to the general public. In an Olympic season, however, when the technical question concerned not only the reigning United States and world champion but also one of the favorites to win Olympic gold, several sportswriters deemed Lipinski's receiving marks that might appear unjustifiably low an appropriate topic for elucidation in the pages of the major newspapers.[17] Lipinski's American supporters interpreted her loss at Trophée Lalique not so much as an endorsement of Hubert's strengths (notably, enormous speed and big jumps, and on that occasion more energy to her performance), but rather as a rejection of Lipinski for symbolizing an undesirable trend toward ladies' skating as a sport in which prepubescent girls would rule—with only the difficulty of the jumps completed but not the quality of those jumps or of the rest of the skating determining the results. The flutz explanation provided some reassurance that it was Lipinski's skating technique—and not her age or the size and shape of her body—that accounted for her mediocre scores, that figure skating really is a sport judged on technique and not simply on image.

Also in fall 1997, Michelle Kwan was diagnosed with a stress fracture in one of the toes of her left foot, causing her to withdraw not only from one of the fall internationals where she had been scheduled to compete, but also from the Champions Series Final in December. There was some doubt whether Kwan would be able to compete at U.S. Nationals at all or whether she would be able to do so at full strength, and suddenly the United States' expectations of victory at the Olympics appeared less certain than at any time since Lipinski's and Kwan's one-two finish at the 1997 World Championships.

Lipinski won the series final easily.[18] After the short program, Maria Butyrskaya, who ultimately finished third at that event, commented that "I think I am a more artistic skater and I have more elaborate choreography. . . . I'm a woman on the ice, and I think it's more interesting to watch. She [Lipinski] does more jumps, but I think artistry makes a difference. The fact that she has already lost two times proves the judges have had enough of childish skating."[19] *New York Times* sportswriter Jere Longman interpreted these remarks as an attack on Lipinski and poor sportsmanship on Butyrskaya's part, noting that "Lipinski was also faster and more graceful, and grateful, than the 25-year-old Butyrskaya, who is a heavy jumper and a stout critic."[20] In focusing on the qualities of Butyrskaya's skating that are less ideal than Lipinski's, Longman provides reasons why judges might deem Lipinski superior to Butyrskaya on presentation as well as technical merit, should they both skate without error (similar comments would apply to second-place finisher Tanja Szewczenko as well). This explanation sidesteps questions of the importance of artistic sophistication, womanly presence on the ice, and being "more interesting to watch," compared to graceful movement and successful jumps.

At U.S. Nationals, Lipinski recovered from a shaky short program to skate the long with determination, completing all her jumps including her trademark triple loop–triple loop combination and an almost-as-difficult sequence of triple toe loop–half loop–triple salchow. Because of her injury, Kwan was unable to attempt her triple toe–triple toe combination, the most difficult jump element in her repertoire, but she completed all of her seven triple jumps successfully and skated with a transcendent floating quality that was becoming her trademark. A series of 6.0s for presentation from eight of the nine judges confirmed Kwan's position as 1998 national champion and as the clear favorite for Olympic gold, while Lipinski had to settle for second place.

Heading into the 1998 Olympics, then, the conventional wisdom was that Kwan and Lipinski would finish first and second, almost certainly in that order, should both skate without serious error, while any of the other skaters who had won world or European medals during the past four years would have a good chance for the bronze medal, with hope for a higher placement only if Kwan or Lipinski should falter.

The short program in Nagano concluded with few surprises. Kwan placed solidly first and Lipinski second. Maria Butyrskaya, the twenty-five-year-old perennial Russian champion who had finally achieved major international success by winning the 1998 European title, was third; Lu Chen, the 1994 Olympic bronze medalist and 1995 world champion who had lost her world title placing second to Kwan in 1996, was fourth;[21] Irina Slutskaya, experiencing her own struggles with physical maturation as her more womanly body shape at eighteen and now nineteen years old led to more frequently missed jumps, had doubled the intended triple lutz in her jump combination and now stood fifth; and Surya Bonaly, never quite recovered from a serious Achilles tendon injury two years earlier that had essentially robbed her of her triple lutz and triple flip, disastrous for a skater whose stock in trade had been her jumping ability, was sixth.[22]

Pop culture columnist Cintra Wilson, writing for the on-line magazine *Salon* about her experience getting tickets to and watching the highly sought-after ladies' Olympic short program, opined: "The biggest faceless corporate Uncle Toms are going to get the medals. Artists with personal style need not apply. . . . OK. Tara and Michelle. Both extremely competent skaters. Both experts in exactly the kind of beauty pageant smiling and coloring-inside-the-lines rigid obeisance that the judges love. They both skate really well, particularly Michelle Kwan, who is very pretty and swanlike with her long, skinny arms. Both bore the fuck out of me, really." For Wilson, the stand-out performers of the Nagano short program were Surya Bonaly, "who kicked such preposterous amounts of ass she raised the consciousness of the whole stadium," Wilson declared in likening her to Josephine Baker, and "Lu Chen, who was like a beautiful Hong Kong movie star doing incredible stunts in a tight red dress, subtly emoting the whole time in a Ginger Rogers kind of way." Wilson found the fact that Chen and Bonaly placed fourth and sixth, respectively, in that short program, with what she calls "some truly forgettable Russian kippys" third and fifth,[23] to be evidence that "sophisticated sexual consciousness, even when adorably tempered and retro-lite, louses it all up for the judges, for some reason. They'll find any excuse to shut the girl down who looks comfortably female in the form."[24] Adult sexiness, for Wilson and her implied readers, unlike for the feminist critics of Katarina Witt's reliance on seductiveness a decade earlier, is thus to be applauded as a signifier of autonomous womanhood, whereas the fact that the chaste teenagers earned the highest scores turns figure skating competition, for a spectator who can read only the external images and not the technical details, into a contest of who can best conform to an imagined homogenized, defeminized ideal.

Wilson's commentary, oblivious to questions of jump technique or stroking quality that would do much to explain those short program results, tells us more about what types of images the readers, or at least this writer, of *Salon* consider hip than about what skating judges actually are willing or unwilling to reward. It does, however, point to the fact that there are multiple axes along which we can compare skaters' images. According to traditional skating world divisions, Kwan, Chen, and Butyrskaya would be considered the artists of the Nagano competition and Lipinski, Slutskaya, and Bonaly the athletes. As Longman had pointed out, however, if artistry is defined in terms of graceful easy movement as opposed to holding tension throughout the body rather than in terms of purposefulness and precision in evoking images, Lipinski would qualify as more "artistic" than Butyrskaya. According to definitions of skating maturity in terms of polish, the more traditionally artistic skaters would also be considered more mature, whereas definitions of maturity in terms of chronological age, body type, or exhibiting sexual consciousness would categorize the over-twenty-one Butyrskaya, Bonaly, and Chen in the mature category and teenagers Slutskaya, Kwan, and Lipinski as immature. But none of these categorizations gives as much useful insight into why the skaters placed as they did, especially in a short program, compared to an analysis of the actual technical elements.

Kwan skated first of the final group in the Olympic long program. Her performance was graceful and well measured, filled with complex edging and unusual moves such as a sequence of spins in both directions, and error-free with seven successful triple jumps. Earlier in the season, Kwan had described her long program to *Lyra Angelica* as a change of pace from the dramatic themes of her recent past, reflecting simple joy in and love for pure skating. To help her achieve the floating quality of her skating, Kwan said, "I see the ice as clouds and I'm just an angel flying around."[25] Compared to her transcendent performance at Nationals, however, the program as skated in Nagano appeared tentative and slow.[26] So Kwan had delivered a performance well worthy of Olympic gold, but not one that was unassailable.

Lipinski also completed all seven of her triple jumps, including the triple-triple combination and sequence. In terms of the difficulty of the jumps, then, she was the clear leader. Her jumps were not as big as Kwan's, but then Kwan's were not as high and did not cover as much ice on the landings as those of many of the other skaters in the competition, when they actually landed them properly. Lipinski's jump takeoffs were not always ideal—the low, whipped double axel, the triple loop combination that went up and down almost in place, and the much improved but still-present change of edge on the takeoff of the lutz—but her landings were at least as clean as Kwan's and often seemed to gain even more speed than she had had going into the jumps. Her spins were faster than Kwan's, but without as strong positions or quite as much difficulty. Nor did her program demonstrate transitional steps as complex, stroking quality as nuanced, or body carriage and line as controlled and elegant.

It would thus seem appropriate to award Lipinski the higher scores of the two for technical merit and Kwan the higher scores for presentation. The question was how much difference to allow between the scores, so that each judge would have to decide whether to give Kwan or Lipinski the higher total of the two marks, or to give them the same total and use the presentation score as the tiebreaker in the long program to give Kwan the higher placement. What most of the judges did, in fact, was to give Lipinski higher technical scores and to give both skaters the same score, most of them 5.9s, for presentation. With a majority of six judges to three, Lipinski won the free program and the gold medal.

Did the decision just come down to counting up the jump difficulty? Was technical quality, and especially artistry, being ignored? The fact that it was her high marks for presentation that gave Lipinski the win suggests not. But why did she receive such high presentation scores?

Lipinski's programs, choreographed by Sandra Bezic, certainly presented her as girlish. They used light, curved gestures with her hands and wrists often held close to or passing along her chest, emphasizing images of lightness and delicacy and directing energy and the viewer's gaze toward her body with evident awareness of herself as the object of that gaze. In this sense, her program was more stereotypically feminine than some she had skated in earlier years that instead emphasized straight lines and outer-directedness, even aggressiveness. The lightness of her movements emphasized her youth, but the conscious awareness with which she now performed them and the time she took to finish each move or position more fully than when she had seemed to rush through them in earlier years allowed Lipinski to demonstrate greater polish or "maturity" in her presentation skills at fifteen than many older skaters are able to achieve at all. In addition, Lipinski still managed to project a degree of unselfconscious and spontaneous joy in her own movement that projected a greater air of confidence and command of the space on that occasion than did Kwan's more carefully choreographed expressions of joy.

Among the bronze medal contenders, Lu Chen also delivered a musically sensitive, floaty, feminine long program interpreting the traditional Chinese story of lovers transformed into butterflies, defeating the older, equally "mature" and almost as expressive but less fluid Butyrskaya, who finished fourth, and the younger, more athletic Slutskaya in fifth. The latter's presentation still suffered from a tendency toward hunched-over posture and incompletely stretched free leg. Moreover, her Russian folk dance choreography emphasized a traditional youthful femininity that continued to make her seem less mature at nineteen than the seventeen-year-old Kwan. Ordinals among these three skaters were mixed, but again, looking at the successful jump content completed contributes as much to understanding these results as does the presentational style of each skater.

Surya Bonaly, returning to the Vivaldi *Four Seasons* program with which she had won medals in 1993 and 1994, struggled with her jumps. Toward the end of the program she threw in her trademark backflip in place of the troublesome triple lutz. This illegal move earned her deductions on technical scores already below those of the other skaters in the final group. It represented a statement that at that point she was skating more for her fans, in anticipation of a professional career, than for the judges in hopes of an Olympic medal. Some observers interpreted this move as a gesture of disrespect toward the judges and toward skating officialdom in general; in any case, it surely signified Bonaly's decision to play a game she could win—popularity with fans—rather than placing herself in the position of being determined worthy, or on this occasion more likely unworthy, according to the technical judging criteria.

At the 1998 World Championships six weeks later, with Lipinski and Chen also having announced their retirements from eligible competition, the Russian skaters swapped places, with Slutskaya earning the silver medal behind Kwan and Butyrskaya the bronze. In fourth and fifth place were Laetitia Hubert of France and Anna Rechnio of Poland, two powerful but not particularly graceful skaters. They had merited only twentieth and nineteenth places, respectively, in Nagano, but with their high speed and enormous jumps they earned high scores and judging respect when they managed to complete most of those jumps successfully.

During the seasons since 1998, while Kwan, now a mature college student, maintained her dominance of U.S. skating, a succession of younger American skaters have stolen the spotlight at Nationals. In particular, 1999 and 2000 national silver medalists Naomi Nari Nam and Sasha Cohen drew acclaim for the precocious refinement of their skating, prompting many fans and members of the media to expect the next young phenom to topple her predecessor from the highest ranks, or at least to join her there, as Kwan and Lipinski had each done to Bobek and Kwan in their turn; as interviewer Lesley Visser told Nam during the 1999 ABC Nationals broadcast, "And you, my young friend, you might be the future that the skating world has been looking for." Age rules and injuries, however, perhaps along with more focus from the judges on quality of edge work than on flexibility and pointed toes, allowed the less refined, more consistent Sarah Hughes and the older Angela Nikodinov to make a greater impact on the international scene.

Outside the United States, indeed, older skaters have been more successful. In 1999, Maria Butyrskaya defeated an ailing Kwan to win the world title, becoming the oldest-ever ladies' world champion at twenty-six only two years after Lipinski became the youngest ever. Slutskaya struggled with weight gain and technique issues in the 1999 season and lost her place on the Russian world team to two younger skaters. In the 2000 and 2001 seasons, now married and with improved presentation, she won her first Russian national championships and recaptured the European title she had held as a teenager. Slutskaya also defeated Kwan on several occasions, winning the 2000 and 2001 Grand Prix Finals and placing second behind her at the World Championships those years. With Hughes's defeat of Butyrskaya for the 2001 bronze medal, we saw mixed results favoring skaters of various ages and artistic versus athletic strengths.

The 2002 Salt Lake City Olympics once again saw the youngest of the medal contenders, sixteen-year-old Sarah Hughes, skate away with the top prize. As with Lipinski, success with very difficult jump combinations made up for a flawed lutz, and above-average edge quality, ice coverage, and "artistry" combined to establish Hughes as a strong all-around skater, able to defeat the more artistic Kwan and the more athletic Slutskaya for only the second time in her career when she skated her best and they did not. The fact that once again at skating's most watched event the younger skater rose to the occasion when the older favorites succumbed to pressure suggests that the weight of Olympic expectations may be lighter for younger skaters who enter the events more as challengers than as favorites for the top spot, that youth may provide as much of a mental advantage, in the Olympic context, as a physical one.

If, three Olympiads in a row, figure skating presents the most coveted, most publicly witnessed prize it offers women to fifteen- and sixteen-year-old girls, is there a message to be drawn from this fact? Does skating as an institution "want" to reward youth, even immaturity? Do the physical demands of triple jumps and the mental ones of performing under pressure just happen to favor younger skaters in spite of many individual judges' preferences for more mature champions?

It is easy to draw parallels among the Olympic experiences of Baiul, Lipinski, and Hughes—pointing, for instance, to the fact that none of them had won the short program and thus solidified herself, in her own mind or in those of the judges or the media, as a favorite to win the long. On the other hand, it is just as easy to point to differences: Baiul and Lipinski entered their Olympics as reigning world champions (and placed second in their Olympic short programs); Hughes was only a reigning world bronze medalist and placed only fourth in the short. Baiul was firmly on the artistic side of the athlete-artist duality in her Olympic matchup, Lipinski more on the athletic side, Hughes somewhere in between. Lipinski's closest rival was a fellow American (and a fellow teenager); Baiul was a Ukrainian facing American, French, and Chinese rivals; Hughes had to defeat both a more-favored countrywoman and a Cold War rival. Most significantly, Hughes triumphed by making fewer mistakes than her rivals, whereas Baiul defeated the "flawless" skate by Nancy Kerrigan more on the strength of charisma and musicality than technical security.

And, from the point of view of image, unlike the waifish Baiul of 1994 or the childlike Lipinski of 1998, Hughes at a similar age already possessed a body type, taller and curvier, more similar to that of the average adult young woman. As an article in Long Island *Newsday* (Hughes's local paper) noted, "The endless publicity surrounding Sarah Hughes has overlooked what ought to be one of the most important reasons for her appeal to girls dreaming of Olympic glory and parents who care about the health of their daughters. Hughes is the first figure skater since Kristi Yamaguchi in 1992 to have won her Olympic gold medal with the body not of a prepubescent waif but of a lovely teenager of normal height and weight."[27] The author goes on to explain her disturbance at the excessively small and thin, not fully grown bodies of the previous two gold medalists and of the similarly delicately built Sasha Cohen, who was also in the medal hunt in 2002, as unhealthy images for skating to offer adolescent girls as an ideal, citing examples of degenerative injuries suffered by all three of those skaters and others while still in their teens. These types of injuries are one potential health hazard that even non-elite athlete adolescents might face if lured into a cycle of poor nutrition in pursuit of unrealistic body size, with or without concurrent overtraining. Hughes, she argues, "with her obvious radiant health and normal body," could help establish a healthier ideal.

Over the years, then, what we have seen in competition results is a oscillation between medals going to newcomers and to veterans, to skaters whose most outstanding abilities could be classified as more athletic or technical or more artistic. Judges reward excellence of either kind when they see it, and only in cases of closely matched competitors with opposite strengths does an individual judge's personal bent toward favoring one or the other determine placements. Most often it will be the skater who brings something extra to her performance beyond simply ticking off elements who wins the greatest prizes, but what that something extra might be will vary from one champion to another. It is thus difficult to determine any mandated direction in what is rewarded, at best only trends in what strengths the most successful skaters bring to their performances, with Olympic results not always proving the best indicators of those trends: the sheer number of medals, including world titles, earned by skaters such as Kwan and Slutskaya who stay in the sport and continue to evolve as skaters beyond the first peak of their athleticism should diminish the fetishism attached to Olympic gold.

ISSUES WITH IMAGES

The trends toward younger skaters reaching the highest competitive levels have led to voicing of concern both within and outside the skating community that the image of ideal femininity that skating rewards and so publicly represents is one of delicacy, immaturity, and dependence rather than power, maturity, and autonomy. Concerns have also been raised about the physical and emotional demands placed on young adolescents competing on the world stage. The all-consuming lifestyle of elite competitors has for decades prompted many skaters to pursue their education through tutoring, home schooling, or correspondence courses, with many athletes not completing high school at all. Skaters (both male and female) often relocate to work at well-known training centers or with well-known coaches while still in grade school, causing families to live apart and/or to make financial sacrifices for the sake of the child's career long before it is clear whether dreams of Olympic glory will ever be fulfilled.

Similar complaints have been even more prevalent regarding elite gymnasts and ballet dancers and have prompted concerns about the health and safety of the young women involved in all these activities. In her book *Little Girls in Pretty Boxes,* Joan Ryan details how the desire to produce champions in elite women's gymnastics also produces unrealistic and harmful notions that it is possible for adolescent young women to retain prepubescent body shapes while at the same time training as hard as or harder than most adult athletes, male or female, in other sports. Such attitudes have led to incidences of life-threatening and career-ending injuries, eating disorders, and abuse by coaches.

Ryan draws parallels to similar attitudes and practices in figure skating, in particular citing instances of eating disorders and overemphasis on a slender body image among skaters and skating coaches.[28] Some of the coaches Ryan cites (often as described by former students) seem to have believed that the mere appearance of physical fitness and a body type that experience had shown to be advantageous for performing skating maneuvers was more important than actually to be as fit as possible and to perform those maneuvers as well as possible. As one anonymous Olympic skater described, "If you were skating better at a hundred and five pounds but looked better at a hundred, your coach wanted you to be a hundred."[29]

The figure skating world itself and the journalists who cover it have also expressed concern about eating disorders among skaters. One longtime judge (who prefers to remain anonymous) told me that, unlike earlier in her judging career, when skaters or their parents ask for advice about how they might be more successful competitively, she no longer tells these girls to "lose five pounds." She acknowledges, however, that "when you're judging a competition, you're not judging by a standard, but judging one against another" and therefore have to have some way to distinguish between skaters who perform the same elements equally well: "If two skate the same, most judges will give it to the one who looks nicer."[30]

In her book *Ice Time,* Debbi Wilkes discusses the case of Tracey Wainman, Canadian champion and hope for the future in 1981 at thirteen but burnt out at fourteen, unable to "tough out" her double axels and triple salchows any longer after reaching puberty. Wilkes also notes that as a television commentator she herself had "become more outspoken about a lot of things over the years, while trying to remember that these are amateurs, young people who are there out of love for the sport. I try to avoid making personal remarks about things no one has any control over, like body shape or leg length. The tiniest criticism about personal things can be devastating to a skater. But anything that affects a performance is fair game." Wilkes recounts that she had once commented that a former Canadian champion attempting a comeback would be a contender for the national title "if she can keep her anorexia under control" and that in response to this comment, "Whoo, the shit hit the fan. It was a very pertinent fact, but it was one of those things you're not supposed to talk about."[31]

As thinness has been valued as an ideal for feminine appearance within the larger culture, members of the skating community too have often tended to value thin body types. As an ideal of beauty, however, skating insiders seem not to prefer the appearance typical of adolescent girls over that of adult women. The athletic and technical criteria of judging, especially in the post-figures era, that tend to favor skaters who complete the most triple jumps (feats at which small skaters tend to have an advantage over larger skaters in terms of consistency if not always of quality) have led to an increasing preponderance of smaller, thinner skaters on the medal podiums. Judges who might prefer to see older, more womanly-looking skaters as the sport's top exemplars are unable to express that preference through placements when the younger or younger-appearing skaters complete more jumps and older and bigger skaters miss jumps or otherwise appear to flounder about on the ice.

One response the skating world has made to criticisms about skating rewarding female skaters with immature bodies has been to compare skaters' physical maturity and femininity favorably to those of the top female gymnasts. This strategy acknowledges the difficulty that adult women, especially feminists, have identifying with an infantilized image of femininity, but it also encourages the sexualized image that feminists also object to. For example, in 1987 coach Carlo Fassi predicted, "If we cancel figures, it will be like gymnastics, with young girls who can do all the jumps at age thirteen and quit at age fifteen. I don't like gymnastics any more. It's little muppets just tumbling around. Where is the beauty of that?"[32] A 1992 Olympic preview noted: "If jumps become the sine qua non of the competition, then younger and younger skaters, concentrating on a few energetic moves, could turn figure skating into another (offstage: screams, groans, shrieks, noisy wrist slittings) gymnastics. That specter, of teensy-weensy little prepubescent bubbles popping about, haunts the figure-skating beadledom. 'Look,' wails one panicky official when the dreaded comparison with gymnastics is uttered, 'ninety percent of our girls are attractive, and they all have breasts.'"[33]

Just before his death in 1997, Fassi objected to age limits as an antidote to the emphasis on jumps and the resulting increase in skating-related injuries in ladies' skating; "If that [age limits] happens, in five years, the juniors will be better than the seniors." His preferred solution was "to limit the number of triple jumps a woman could do during a long program, ensuring that spins and footwork and other forms of artistry would keep their place in the sport."[34] (Because Fassi specifically did not recommend a similar change in emphasis for men's skating, this approach, if implemented, would further reify the stereotypes of skating artistry and jumps as feminine and masculine, respectively.) Skating judge Joan Burns also advocated de-emphasizing the jumps, noting that "I keep saying that it's not necessary, that triples aren't everything. There are four elements to figure skating: jumps, spins, footwork and choreography. They all have to be good, not just the jumps."[35]

Another response to criticisms that skating rewards immaturity has been to emphasize the advanced presentation skills of the young, small champions as evidence of their maturity. One former judge, in response to a fall 1997 encounter between Kwan and Lipinski, notes:

> While watching Skate America recently, I was struck by the maturity the
> US #1 and #2 Ladies showed, and thought about the TV segment a well-

known sports journalist did. She said that judges want little girls now, and that coaches prefer immature bodies, ones that haven't developed hips or breasts yet, because these girls can jump up with less effort. Sure—a small frame is desirable, but that certainly doesn't mean the immature child is what the judges are looking for.

It is not the age or size, but the experience, that makes a mature skater. . . .

Association top judges look for maturity in not only the quality of performance, but in appearance as well—finish in style, and the confidence that comes from exposure. . . .

Every top judge worth that title knows a mature performance when they see it. Figure skating would not be as popular as it is if it weren't for the beauty of the female form.[36]

Finally, skating officials have made periodic attempts to discourage a trend toward ever-younger champions by instituting minimum age limits for international senior and even junior competition. In the early 1980s, the ISU had instituted a minimum age of fourteen for senior competition, but exceptions were sometimes granted, for instance in the case of American pair skater Natasha Kuchiki, who at thirteen qualified for the 1990 World Championships with her twenty-six-year-old partner. As commentators noted at the time, the age limit had been enacted in part to discourage the extremely mismatched pairs that had started to appear in the late 1970s, but Kuchiki at thirteen was physically mature and did not appear to be a small girl skating with a grown man. Hungarian ladies' champion Krisztina Czako also required special permission to compete at the 1992 Olympics when she was only thirteen.

Most recently, effective in 1996–1997, skaters must have reached the age of fifteen by the previous July 1 to be eligible for senior international competition and thirteen to be eligible for junior competition. Had this rule gone into effect a year earlier without any attendant exceptions, Kwan, whose birthday is July 7, would have been ineligible for the 1996 World Championships that she won, and similarly Baiul would have been age-ineligible when she won in 1993. Skaters who had not yet turned fifteen by July 1, 1996, but who had already participated in senior competitions were "grandfathered" into eligibility for that season, a ruling that allowed Lipinski to compete at and win the 1997 World Championships at fourteen.

Evgeny Plyushenko of Russia, who made his bronze-medal Worlds debut in 1998 at age fifteen, also benefited from such an exception. From time to time exceptionally talented boys as well as girls, or those from countries with small skating programs, have begun their international careers early. Any concerns about the physical or psychological hazards of young adolescents competing at the world level would thus apply to the men as well as the ladies. Added concerns that come with actually winning medals at young ages, however, would affect boys at this age much less often than girls.

Another exception that continued to apply until the 2000 season allowed skaters who had earned medals at the World Junior Championships to move on to senior competition. This rule created a paradox in 1999 when the thirteen-year-old U.S. silver medalist, Naomi Nari Nam, who had been five days too young even to qualify for that year's Junior Worlds, had to be left off the world team in favor of the two-months-older Sarah Hughes, who had met the junior medal criterion with a silver at 1999 Junior Worlds. A year later at the 2000 U.S. Nationals, once again the silver medalist, Sasha Cohen, like Nam, created a sensation with her advanced presentation abilities and was once again too young to be named to the world team. Cohen was old enough to compete at Junior Worlds, which for the first year under a new schedule was now to be held after rather than before Nationals, so she was given the opportunity to try to earn a medal and thus the right to enter the World Championships. Of the three U.S. ladies competing at that year's Junior Worlds, Cohen therefore received much more attention from the American media than is usual for junior competition. She skated less successfully than at Nationals and finished only sixth, disappointing herself and her fans in her bid to be allowed to compete at Worlds. The other Americans, Jennifer Kirk and Deanna Stellato, took home gold and silver from Junior Worlds, and once again the fourth-place finisher from Nationals had to replace the silver medalist on the U.S. world team.

As of 2000–2001, the Junior World medal exception is no longer available, and the grandfather clause that applied to Lipinski in 1997 has long since expired, so under the present rules all skaters at Worlds must indeed have turned fifteen before the previous July. Although careless journalists have sometimes claimed otherwise, the age rules were enacted before Lipinski won her world and Olympic titles and therefore could not have been conceived specifically in response to her wins, controversial as those proved to be. What is less clear is whether the motivation of the ISU congress that adopted the age limits was primarily to protect young skaters from excessive demands so early in their careers; to protect the image of skating as a sport that welcomed adults rather than children at the highest levels; to stem the tide of exceptionally young champions cashing in on fleeting competitive fame and then leaving the sport as Baiul and later Lipinski did; to lessen the advantage of the American team, with its seemingly endless supply of talented young female skaters emerging each year, over countries with smaller pools of skaters who might require longer to reach their competitive peaks; or to reserve young talent to make Junior Worlds and the expanding series of junior international events that the ISU was in the process of developing more attractive to television broadcasters.

As proved to be the case with Cohen's ill-fated and media-hounded attempt to qualify for the Junior World medal exception, imposing an age limit and then offering an opportunity to circumvent it can in fact produce more pressure on a young skater to deliver under the public spotlight than simply allowing a young skater to compete on the World stage without expectations in order to gain experience. Surely Lipinski's success in 1997 would have been that much less likely had she not had the opportunity to compete at 1996 Worlds as a thirteen-year-old and to get first-Worlds nerves and a disastrous short program out of her system while all attention was focused on Kwan and the other medal contenders.

With the depth of talent now present in the American ladies' field, and with the examples of Kwan's and Lipinski's rapid rise to the top encouraging ambitious young skaters to try to reach the top as quickly as possible, jockeying for ascendance among their peers and against the now-experienced veterans, including Kwan, skaters of the "baby ballerina" generation have been challenging themselves with ever-harder jumps and jump combinations at ever-younger ages. It is likely more than coincidence that injuries have taken such a toll on this generation. Some promising young skaters announced injury-related retirements from competitive skating after only a year in senior competition. In 2001, Stellato, Nam, and Cohen, who had each shown enough promise to be considered potential 2002 Olympians, were all forced to withdraw from Nationals (and only Cohen was able to return, and indeed earn an Olympic berth, in 2002).

In an article previewing the injury-decimated 2001 senior ladies' event, Phil Hersh of the *Chicago Tribune* suggested that career-threatening injuries were a particular problem of young female athletes and mentioned age or jump limits for the ladies as possible remedies. The skating insiders quoted, however, merely reiterated the reality of multiple triple jumps as a now-necessary part of the sport.[37] A post-event article in *International Figure Skating* quoted USFSA medical experts, expressing concern about the demands that jumps in particular and the year-round training and competition schedule that competitive skaters must follow put on skaters' bodies from young ages, but without specifically singling out girls as being more at risk than male skaters. A coach and a skater agreed with the experts' recommendations about

getting enough rest and limiting jump repetitions in practice as means to reduce the likelihood of injuries.[38]

The repetitive-motion injuries that skaters can incur through excessive
practice repetitions of the same jumps, often injuring growth plates in young
athletes and potentially leading to lifelong pain or disability, may be cause for
greater concern regarding the youth of the competitors than the acute trauma
injuries that can be expected to occur unpredictably in any athletic endeavor.
Both sorts of injuries affect male and female skaters equally and from equally
young ages. The girls may struggle more than the boys with learning the
triple jumps, but the boys who do learn them then go on to try to learn triple
axels and quadruples. Because male skaters receive less attention in general
and are less likely to reach the public spotlight before reaching adulthood,
however, and because there are simply fewer male skaters training at the
grassroots level, it is reasonable to focus on injury in skating as a "women's
sports" issue. Additionally, injuries related to bone loss as a result of insufficient nutrition are also more commonly associated with excessive weight-
control efforts.

If the demands of the sport can be seen to produce a predictable pattern of
injuries, or other problems such as eating disorders that do in fact affect
more girls than boys, concerned individuals will seek changes in those demands in order to reduce the occurrence of these problems. Whether these
changes should come through different rules, a shift in emphasis in what
judges reward most highly, or education of coaches, skaters, and parents in
healthy nutrition and training techniques remains an open question. Calls for
protective measures for girls and women that ignore similar problems affecting boys and men, however, in themselves deny personal agency to the female athletes.

To the extent that girls and their families receive unrealistic meanings
about womanhood or the role of sport in their lives through their understandings of what the sport rewards, skating associations do bear responsibility for the skating-related devastation of some skaters' lives. Readings of
skating that do not idealize girlishness at the expense of mature womanhood, especially in the form of unrealistic body images, are thus vital to the
sport's continued appeal and to the well-being of its practitioners.

ALTERNATIVE IMAGES

Contrary to Cintra Wilson's assumptions, skaters are not rated according to
inoffensiveness or "coloring within the lines," except insofar as they skate

with correct technique and do not perform forbidden non-skating elements in their programs. It may so happen that the type of personality that lends itself to perfecting the exacting techniques necessary to succeed in the sport does not also tend to go hand in hand with nonconformist self-expression. If so, fans who watch skating competitions through artistic codes are likely to be disappointed in the lack of aesthetic risk-taking among the top competitors. Skaters whose interests tend more toward unusual artistic choices than toward rote training of technical elements are rarely those who achieve the highest technical perfection and who win the most prestigious medals.

Often the places to find the most creative skaters are in the lower competitive ranks (amid a larger majority of skaters who possess neither extreme creativity nor extreme skill), in professional shows and competitions, and in the for-fun interpretive events offered at some lower-level club competitions. Except in the high-profile professional events that draw their participants from those who first achieved success as competitive athletes, these artistically but not athletically inclined skaters generally labor in obscurity because skating for art's sake does not have the same type of internationally organized infrastructure or the built-in publicity platform of the Olympics that skating as sport has. Fans looking to enjoy a wider range of approaches to skating artistry may need to look further than the top few finishers at the most prestigious competitions and should either learn to appreciate the sporting aspects of skating that determine the competitive results or to ignore those results and just enjoy the performances.

Nevertheless, some competitive skaters do find ways, or hire choreographers to do so for them, to present themselves and their skating on the ice in ways that expand or challenge the traditional images. Challenging tradition generally relies on understanding the tradition in the first place and will likely be better received if the skater has first demonstrated the ability to work within a traditional style. Creativity that uses rather than ignores skating technique to make its artistic points relies first on a mastery of that technique, including a full range of steps and turns and not just mastery of the jumps. For these reasons, the most innovative programs tend to come from skaters with more competitive experience and more life experience—that is, from older skaters, although there are exceptions. Therefore ladies' singles, the discipline that tends to feature the youngest skaters, is also that in which the programs tend to be the most generic.

The concept of theme programs as an alternative to beauty as a means of demonstrating artistry first became popular in the field of ice dance in the early 1980s and among male singles in the early 1990s (although male skaters had been exploring abstract movement approaches other than classical beauty well before that; see the chapters on men's singles and ice dance that follow). Among the ladies, the theme approach didn't really take hold until the mid-1990s, thus postdating most scholarly analyses published so far. The theme approach also seems to be more prevalent among European than among North American or Asian women, a tendency that can also be seen in the other skating disciplines.

Many female skaters who have adopted explicit narrative themes derived from the plots of the ballets, operas, musical comedies, or films that provide the music they skate to have continued to emphasize themes of romantic love or sexuality. Certainly such themes are prevalent in these other sources of cultural representation, particularly with regard to the female characters therein, and therefore female skaters drawing on these plots are likely to seize on these aspects of their representations of women in translating the source material to the ice. These are not the only options available, however, particularly for skaters who go beyond familiar plots for their choice of program themes.

During the mid- to late 1990s, while teenagers Baiul, Kwan, Lipinski, and Slutskaya were capturing the majority of the gold medals and media attention with their varying approaches to presenting athletic femininity on ice, a handful of other female skaters were exploring various unique approaches to choreography and self-representation while competing for international medals themselves, only rarely with success at just the right times to achieve exposure on the American airwaves. An observer looking for variety and risk-taking in images of women in figure skating would need to follow every network and cable skating broadcast offered within the United States even to come across such one or two such performances each year or else travel the globe to attend competitions in person, or have access to Canadian and Eurosport broadcasts that show more than just the top few contenders at each event and that often place their broadcast priorities on different events.

Lu Chen, the first skater from China to win Olympic medals or a world title in figure skating,[39] first made her mark as a young teenager in the early 1990s skating fairly generic programs to Western classical and film music, but was even then remarkable for her lyricism. In the 1996–1998 seasons, working with choreographer Sandra Bezic, she reached the peak of her expressive abilities presenting programs that showcased either lyricism or seductiveness, drawing on either Western or Chinese traditions. In 1995, however, she achieved her most impressive competitive result, winning the world championship, with a long program to the score of Bernardo Bertolucci's film *The Last Emperor*, choreographed by Toller Cranston, that combined

Western and Chinese styles of music and movement to produce striking visual imagery. As Bezic, commenting for NBC, remarked, "With this program she wants to combine her Asian heritage with a sport that has been originated in the West."[40]

The beginning and end sections of the program relied on a primarily classical skating idiom, emphasizing glide and graceful positions. Some of those positions were also classical, some more complex, relying on twisted and angled shapes beloved by Cranston, both a skater and a painter. The central section adopted more specifically Chinese music and movement, continuing the motifs of angles and twists. To percussive drums and chimes, Chen turned in place and stepped forward, arms bending in and extending, chest thrusting forward and back or hip thrusting to the side with the upper body twisted above, and walked forward on her toes. As a high string melody joined the percussive accompaniment, she moved out into the space, performing jumps and spirals interspersed with more twisted poses and a series of turns on two feet, arms curved low in front of her with elbows leading and hands fisted. In the final section of the program, the music changed again to a Western-style lyrical passage as the skating continued in the vein of a typical long program slow section with more Western-style extended positions, concluding with a series of jumps and a butterfly to back sitspin, followed by a final pose with arms wrapped around her chest, head thrown slightly back in triumph.

The forward walks on the toepicks at the beginning of the central "Chinese" section of the program suggest the mincing steps of a highborn Chinese lady. Several of the upper-body poses also suggest such a persona. The moments when she holds a position briefly motionless create a series of frozen little images emphasizing the shapes she makes with her body. In these moments, the skater serves as a visual object, like a sketch or snapshot; these images suggest delicacy, and thus femininity, within a specifically Asian idiom of body shapes. The more expansive movements of the hip and chest thrusts, the reaches and undulations, however, emphasize freedom of movement and mark her as a figure who is not restrained by bound feet, tight-fitting garments, or social constrictions on ladylike behavior. In this program, Chen moves freely between images of elegance and earthiness just as she moves between images of East and West. The recurring upper-body twists provide a visual motif that ties together the Eastern and Western movement styles, while the complexity of shapes and transitions and Chen's fluidity and expressivity with her back and arm movements give her the air of mature polish and uniqueness needed to win high presentation scores and the 1995 world title.

Chen was, then, the most successful of the skaters I discuss here as offering alternatives to the traditional images. But the fact that these skaters did not dominate the very highest echelons of elite skating attests more to the inconsistency of their technique than to an unwillingness of skating judges to reward images other than the traditional ones of beauty, sex appeal, or athletic perkiness, as evidenced by the fact that these skaters did earn medals with more individualistic programs on the occasions when they were able to deliver the athletic goods.

At 1993 Skate Canada, for instance, Olga Markova of Russia placed third with a long program skated to a piece of music called "The Cosmic Opera," wearing a streamlined solid-black dress and tights, accented by large blue oval shapes, blue gloves, and blue lining to the stiff ruffled bell shapes of the skirt, collar, and cuffs, producing a futuristic image consonant with the mysterious electronic music. The choreography, designed by Markova herself, emphasized the straight-line, angular, and twisting shapes she made with her body and her long, thin arms and legs. This was an abstract program, focused on stark geometric shapes and direct movement qualities rather than on the classical curves or flowiness associated with traditional femininity.

In 1997, Krisztina Czako of Hungary won a silver medal at the European Championships and placed sixth at Worlds skating a long program to the soundtrack of the Addams Family movie that incorporated numerous unusual and macabre touches. Most notably, during the middle slow section, she brought her foot from a spiral position behind her to hold it up in front of her, contemplating it seriously, as she slowly turned her head from side to side with her other hand holding her chin, then dismissed the foot backward with a flick from the hand that had been holding it up. This movement seemed to cause her to execute a bracket turn from forward to backward, an apparently unexpected development at which she shrugged in surprise. She then allowed the free foot to swing forward, twice, following it with her gaze as it led her through a series of double three turns. In this passage, Czako appeared bemused by body parts that seemed to be controlling her movements rather than her controlling them. Like the Addamses' disembodied hand Thing, suggested by the empty glove perched on the shoulder of her costume, images of body parts acting independently of control by a human brain are both horrifying and—because of the matter-of-fact rather than horrified attitude taken toward them both by the Addams Family cartoons, television show, and movie and by Czako's program—comical.

In the 1997–1998 season, Frenchwoman Laetitia Hubert achieved some of her best-ever as well as some of her worst results (first place at Trophée Lalique, ahead of reigning world champion Tara Lipinski, and fourth place at the 1998 World Championships; last place at Nation's Cup and twentieth

at the Olympics) skating to exotic and percussive selections by the group
Dead Can Dance. Her dress, constructed on a base of flesh-colored illusion
fabric crossed with swirling flame-like shapes of orange and copper-colored
cloth trimmed with bands of gold sequins, with a sheer yellow and beige skirt
over copper pants, and fingernails painted with matching copper polish, did
not follow the natural lines and coloring of the skater's body and thereby
promote visual appeal based on her physical characteristics. Rather, they called
attention to themselves as artificial, visual statements in their own right that
used the body as a ground or canvas, suggesting a playful or ironic use of the
body to make visual statements on subjects other than itself.

To a mysterious opening drone followed by more rhythmic musical selections, the choreography used poses, slow edgy turns, and high-speed straight-
line footwork with crossed legs, chest isolations, and arms snaking around
her head and in front of her torso to create complexity, interspersed with
some of the fastest, most powerful back crossovers around to gain speed for
her enormous jumps. Along with the complexity of the body movements and
her exhilarating speed, Hubert also displayed an economy of movement that
conveyed an image of raw power restrained by the need to keep a short leash
over her own strength in order for her to maintain enough control to land
the jumps, thus producing an image of a woman as a physically powerful, aggressive athlete. The Dead Can Dance program stepped outside conventional
images of femininity to establish its own repertoire of movements suggesting a mysterious, primal exoticism. In 1998–1999, Hubert ventured even further from the traditional images in her long program by choosing to portray
a crack-addicted prostitute through turned-in arm and leg positions and intentionally jerky rhythmic pulsing to the music. Unfortunately, injuries and
inconsistent technique prevented her from achieving similarly impressive results in competition.

Hubert's French compatriot Vanessa Gusmeroli made her biggest mark
internationally with a bronze medal at the 1997 World Championships, skating a long program set to a medley of circus music in which she used variations on skating movements to enact the roles of clown, aerialist, and so forth.
In subsequent years, Gusmeroli has skated a program based on a theme of
four elements (earth, air, water, and fire), portrayed a jewel thief and Joan of
Arc, and experimented, perhaps unwisely, with an unusual program layout
that included a prolonged series of spins, including one in the opposite direction and her trademark backspin–first combination spin, to conclude the
program. With these programs, she achieved top-six placements at the 1998
Olympics and at 1999 and 2000 Worlds.

A number of lower-ranked American skaters have also experimented with

*Vanessa Gusmeroli skates her long program in the persona
of a jewel thief. Theme programs offer alternatives to the
traditional lyrical, sexy, or perky styles of ladies' skating
programs. Photo © by J. Barry Mittan.*

unusual elements or choreographic approaches. These include Patricia Mans-
field, Alice Sue Claeys, and Alizah Allen (each of whom achieved only one
top-ten placement and televised performance at Nationals at the senior level
during the mid 1990s; Claeys had achieved some international success representing Belgium as a teenager in the early 1990s, using a more classical
style). These skaters may not have had the competitive credentials to rank as
household names even among skating fans, but their programs bring a welcome variety to the proceedings at Nationals or at sectional and regional
competitions.

  For these women, avant-garde experimentation with nontraditional elements, body positions and shapes, and themes served as examples of ways in

which women as well as men can demonstrate an artistic sensibility by emphasizing the inventiveness of their (or their choreographer's) ideas more than the beauty of their bodies.

Even among skaters whose artistic approaches are firmly anchored within more familiar styles, there are opportunities to make individual statements through the particular inflections of specific elements, as with the deep edges and control of Michelle Kwan's spirals, the extreme ice coverage before and after difficult turns in Irina Slutskaya's, or the variations on extreme flexibility moves in Sasha Cohen's, or through the particular musical genres and pieces and the associated movement vocabularies used. Butyrskaya's aggressive Swan Lake and even more so Kwan's angular, abstract explorations of dissonant twentieth-century works demonstrate inflections of a "classical" approach that does not confine the skaters to a traditional beauty-based conformity.

The powerful athleticism of skaters such as Hubert, Rechnio, Czako, or Slutskaya represents a greater technical maturity (though not consistency) than Lipinski's weaker but somewhat more difficult and more often completed jumps or Kirk's and Cohen's delicate balleticism. The presentation of these larger, more athletic, and less refined skaters may appear less "mature" in the sense of showing less refinement or polish, but through the aggressiveness of their skating these women, like Thomas and Harding before them, can present images of adult power, athleticism, and artistic choices relying on meanings other than grace, beauty, or seductiveness and feminine charm. These images can combine to represent an autonomous womanhood in which the skater is the subject of her own narrative and not of one imposed by an objectified relation to a normalizing masculine gaze.

PART FOUR

*Masculinity
on Edge*

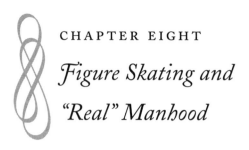

CHAPTER EIGHT

Figure Skating and "Real" Manhood

*W*hen I went to pick up some photos of figure skaters that I had taken in Norway at the 1994 Winter Olympics, I got into a conversation about skating with the man behind the camera store counter. He liked Elvis Stojko (the Canadian men's silver medalist at the recent Olympics), he told me, because Elvis "skates like a real man," but "the guy who was friends with Nancy Kerrigan" (I assume he meant Paul Wylie, who had trained with Kerrigan for many years in Massachusetts and who won the Olympic silver in 1992) gave him the creeps.

In a series of promos for NBC's sitcom *Mad About You* aired during the network's coverage of the 1993 World Figure Skating Championships, the stars of the series sit on a sofa holding hands ostensibly watching the competition in character. In one promo, Jamie marvels, "Figure skaters are so amazing." "I could do that," boasts Paul. "Then do it," she counters. "I . . . I can't," he protests. "I'm uneasy with sequins."

A 1991 *McLean's* magazine profile on Kurt Browning, after he had won his second of four world figure skating championships and was awarded the Lyle Conacher trophy for being named that year's top Canadian athlete, was titled "Real Men Do Figure Skate."[1]

What is the "realness" of the manhood that Stojko and Browning are said to embody? What is it that Wylie lacks, for one viewer at least, and why does this lack produce "the creeps"? Why should uneasiness with a fashion accessory some male skaters have been known to adopt serve as an alibi for backing up a claim of athletic prowess?

Manhood is a precarious achievement, accorded the highest status within the social hierarchy, but always subject to being judged wanting in any who profess it. Social science investigations of sex roles reveal both that traits considered stereotypically masculine tend to be more highly valued than feminine ones (or, rather, that masculine traits are viewed as more active and strong, thus more positive than passive and weak traits, which are coded as feminine), and that masculinity is a more difficult status to achieve. According to sociologist Susan Basow, "A person may be 'feminine' by exhibiting some but not necessarily all of the feminine sex-typed traits. But, to be 'masculine,' one needs to display most or all of the masculine sex-typed traits. . . . In many cases, this [greater] rigidity [of the male sex role] can lead to a constant 'proving' of one's masculinity."[2] In other words, the lower-valued feminine status serves as a kind of default position from which males must constantly strive to distinguish themselves in order to attain the higher masculine status position.

Sociologist Peter Stearns discusses modern definitions of masculinity as holdovers from early hunting societies' impulses to distinguish men from women, and men from boys still defined by their proximity to caretaking women, through ritual testing of qualities that were of particular value in the male occupation of hunting: "One was not born a man. One learned to be a man, acquiring characteristics that exaggerated some natural attributes and repressed others, such as the desire to run from danger. Not all boys could make it. In few later societies could all males fully become men; in few did all males not worry and wonder if they had the potential to do so."[3]

Later in human history, masculine value came to be associated not only with all-male associations such as the military, which replicated the virtues of the hunt, but also with working to sustain a family and with social leadership roles and spiritual quests. Because these male values are culturally rather than biologically defined, according to Stearns men measure their manhood not "by absolutes so much as by the absence, real or imagined, of the male attributes among women."[4] Men demonstrate manliness through the "signs of gender . . . assorted body deportments, clothing, customs, hairstyles"[5] that the culture they live in assigns to the male gender. In order to maintain the prestige associated with masculine status, any demonstration of qualities defined as feminine aligns the man displaying them with an inferior status position; he is seen as less than fully masculine, less than a "real" man.

Thus, once an activity such as figure skating is defined as "feminine," for a male to participate in it aligns him with the feminine connotations of the activity and a priori removes him from the status of proven masculinity achieved by dissociating oneself from feminine values. In addition to the increasing association of skating with femininity over the course of the twentieth century, skating competition by its nature lacks the structural signifiers of masculinity that characterize the first two levels in Brian Pronger's hierarchy of "masculine" sport—direct violence and symbolic struggle with an opponent or oneself—and so falls into the third category of aesthetic sports that are "the least masculine because they involve the lowest degree of aggression."[6]

The process of judging skaters on the aesthetic form of their bodies in arriving at the presentation mark is thus structurally feminizing, trivializing one according to a value system that rates activity, coded as masculine, over appearance, coded as feminine. The subjectiveness inherent in the scoring system means that judges tend to reward male and female skaters for approaching a sex-differentiated ideal appropriate to their respective sexes. Male skaters whose skating employs gestures deemed overly feminine have reported receiving comments from judges that these same sorts of gestures that would be considered to enhance a female skater's presentation in fact detract from their successful presentation of themselves as male.[7] The male skater thus is dismissed as less than masculine by the culture at large by virtue of the simple fact that he skates, and at the same time he is offered incentives within the skating world for performing (in Judith Butler's sense) a credible masculinity on the ice. [8]

Given the competitive and ultimately commercial professional rewards for thus performing their gender satisfactorily, male skaters in recent decades have employed a variety of strategies to present themselves on the ice as legitimately masculine through the creation of performance personas. In order to claim male privilege in the world beyond skating, the male skater must make additional efforts to distinguish himself as masculine not only within the context and conventions of the skating community, but also according to the norms of the broader culture. Other interested parties involved in marketing men's figure skating as a cultural commodity—the national figure skating federations, competition sponsors, tour promoters, television networks covering the events—similarly attempt to counteract the ingrained cultural discomfort with male aesthetic display by de-emphasizing this side of the sport when covering the men's competition and by emphasizing acceptably masculine, and heterosexual, aspects of the individual competitors. These efforts seem designed actively to forestall or counter the presumption of effeminacy associated with skating.[9]

CONSTRUCTING A PERFORMANCE PERSONA

Costume

In the early days of the twentieth century, men skated in suits, sweaters, and other outdoor everyday-wear suitable for cold-weather activity. These evolved into an upper-class country-club image of close-fitting jacket and bow tie and eventually to athletically streamlined variations of this image through one-piece jacket-and-shirt ensembles and to full-body jumpsuits simulating the jacketed look. The stretch suits of the 1970s and 1980s allowed for freedom of athletic movement but also clung in ways that tended to reveal the sexed contours of the body. Despite the obvious maleness of these contours, this transformation of the body surface into an erotic visual object, especially when ornamented by sequins and the like, tended to cast the male skater in a traditionally feminine role. In 1984, when these spangled one-piece outfits, a holdover from the disco era's redefinition of what to wear for a night out at a dance, still dominated, Scott Hamilton chose to mitigate the erotic effect by wearing simple stretch suits in one color ornamented only by a simple geometric shape in a contrasting color. The effect was more that of an athletic warm-up suit or speed skating suit, thus emphasizing the acceptably male sport aspect rather than the problematic "artistic" aspect of the event. More recently, several American and Canadian skaters have opted for simplicity, choosing to compete in looser trousers that either are or approximate street wear, with T-shirts, colorful button-down shirts, or black or white shirts with ties, or other adaptations of street wear displaying minimal glitter. Since the 1994–1995 season, ISU rules have explicitly required all male skaters to wear "trousers and not tights." These rules further encourage male skaters to cultivate imagery associated with off-ice social or dramatic contexts and discourage costumes that emphasize the shape of the body either in erotic or abstract formalist terms. Brian Boitano, in the years immediately following his win at the 1988 Olympics, when he was for the American public probably the single most recognizable specimen of the genus "male figure skater," was known for wearing tights in many of his professional programs and indeed numbered among his following many female and gay male fans attracted in part by the shape of his lower body thus revealed. For the most part, however, skaters who do choose to emphasize the erotic appeal of their bodies are more likely to draw attention to upper body musculature by wearing tight T-shirts than to wear tight lower garments that highlight the legs, buttocks, and genitals.

Music and Movement Quality

Competitive programs by skaters from all countries have traditionally employed music from the European high art tradition.[10] Using such "serious" music indicates that the skater takes skating and the competition seriously. Rules against the use of vocal music with lyrics in eligible competition, a restriction that seems designed to prevent skaters from interpreting the lyrics instead of the musical phrasing, reinforce this phenomenon. Even the film scores and musical theatre overtures that provide alternatives to classical pieces most often draw on classical-music conventions of rhythmic and harmonic practice and instrumentation.

Classical music also has the effect of encouraging the classical, balletic body line so many find "unmanly." Within this convention, male skaters usually avoid the curved arms, arched back, and floating quality associated with the ballerina. Instead, they tend to employ straight or angular body lines and lifted chests and to emphasize solidity and muscularity of movement, taking on commanding, heroic personas, as in Brian Boitano's 1988 free program to music from the miniseries *Napoleon and Josephine*, Aren Nielsen's 1994 and 1995 freeskate to the soundtrack of the film *The Rocketeer*, or many of the programs to historical or action-film soundtracks skated by Todd Eldredge or Elvis Stojko. These lines have the effect of sending energy, and thereby the viewer's gaze, past the ends of the fingertips or toes rather than back toward the skater's body, emphasizing the act of penetration into the surrounding space rather than the shape of the body performing this act. Russian Aleksei Yagudin's 1999–2002 long programs skated to the soundtracks of *Lawrence of Arabia*, *Broken Arrow*, *Gladiator*, and *The Man in the Iron Mask* also participate in this genre, with the simulated machine-gun fire that ended the *Broken Arrow* program proving a further literalization of the aggressive theme.

Paul Wylie during his amateur career consistently earned high artistic marks by performing this style to its utmost. A born-again Christian, when he extended his body fully into space he might have been reaching for and supported by an ineffable spirituality. His 1992 program to music from Kenneth Branagh's film *Henry V* used powerful, dramatic motions, and a footwork section with gestures suggesting a swordfight epitomized a heroic masculine energy. To the more lyrical musical passages, however, Wylie employed curved elbows and soft hands, and he even permitted himself an upper back arch in an Ina Bauer. It may be these characteristically feminine gestures that my camera-store acquaintance found unsettling, or perhaps it was simply the fact that Wylie produced such beautiful extended body lines and moved in harmony with the music throughout this and other programs.

Using percussive pop instrumentals, associated in popular culture with aggressive masculine sexuality, is one way to reject the aristocratic and feminine connotations of the balletic tradition and to assert solidarity with popular masculinities. This music also authorizes a more earthy, at times even raunchy, posture and movement style. One example is Kurt Browning's 1993 technical program to Led Zeppelin's percussion piece "Bonzo's Montreux." Browning interpreted this music by frequently running across the ice and displaying, even punching with, fisted hands. The following year he skated the technical program to "St. Louis Blues," again wearing a tight black T-shirt, belt, and stretch pants, and again raising his fists in a biceps-flexing muscle pose. The blues accompaniment suggested a more sinuous rather than

Skaters sometimes momentarily shift focus from the ice to the audience by pointing, glancing directly, or otherwise gesturing into the crowd in such a way as to dare or demand attention. Alexei Yagudin takes this one step further by aiming an invisible machine gun. Photo © by J. Barry Mittan.

choppy movement style throughout; Browning also incorporated flashes of humor by enacting the upper body movements of laughter in time with a series of descending saxophone notes and pointing at the audience during a rapid footwork sequence. Nielsen's sinuous 1995 and 1996 short program to "Stray Cat Strut," Michael Weiss's muscle-flexing, tie-dye-clad 1996 and 1997 long program to selections from Santana's *Abraxas* album, and Elvis Stojko's and Scott Davis's hip-hop short programs in 1994 and 1996, respectively, similarly used tight T-shirts and expansion, contraction, and isolations of the rib cage, hips, or shoulders to emphasize upper body muscularity and to assert a confident masculine sexuality within the conventions of contemporary popular music and dance styles.

Another option for avoiding the feminine connotations of graceful curves is to adopt angular and distorted body shapes that may emphasize sharply bent elbows or free legs and a tilted or twisted torso, particularly in spin variations or connecting glides. In the 1970s, Canadian Toller Cranston, a painter as well as a skater, used his natural flexibility to craft unusual extreme body shapes employing both curved and angular lines. Although his emphasis on the abstract visual impact of the body placed him within the "feminine" tradition, the specific shapes he used and inspired others to use did not carry the same history of femininity or refinement as the more classical lines of his contemporary John Curry, especially when performed by male skaters without Cranston's flexibility. Even while Cranston was still competing and certainly by the 1980s, skaters from both North America and the Soviet Union and other Eastern-bloc nations were employing body shapes reminiscent of his innovations, usually without the flexibility and graceful curves he achieved. By choreographing arms and other body parts to form specific shapes, these skaters could demonstrate a concern for artistry while avoiding specific shapes that carried a history of feminine associations. These might appear in more or less abstract expressionist form, or in relation to music or storylines associated with supernatural and grotesque characters that found particular resonance for Eastern European skaters—as was the case with Aleksandr Fadeev's 1989 program to Mussorgsky's *Night on Bald Mountain,* performed in a white jumpsuit punctuated by red slashes and red gloves, and Vyacheslav Zagorodniuk's 1995 depiction of a troll to the music of *The Sorceror's Apprentice*—or violent emotional states, as with Czech skater Petr Barna's 1992 portrayal of Hamlet to the music from the 1991 Mel Gibson film, in a costume complete with skull painted on his chest. More recently, Andrejs Vlascenko (a former Soviet who represented Latvia internationally in 1994 and Germany beginning in the 1996 season) skated to the music of Gounod's *Faust* enacting the struggle between good and evil, and Russian Ilya Kulik used the same music for his 1997 short program in which he wore a black costume covered with red flame shapes and claimed to be portraying Mephistopheles buying up souls.

For the former Soviet skaters, demonstrating classical ballet training and drawing on the repertoire of ballet and opera music and themes do not have the same feminine connotations as in the West, but rather serve as an expression of pride in national cultural achievements. So Vladimir Kotin in the 1980s and Viktor Petrenko in the 1980s and early 1990s, followed by Aleksei Urmanov in the mid-1990s and more recently Evgeny Plyushenko, could use ballet-inspired movements performed with forceful movement qualities as expressions of arrogance, aggression, and masculine self-assertion within the genre's conventions for representations of masculinity, inspiring ABC's Dick Button to remark on the "macho preening quality" and "Byronic" flair of Kotin's performances at the 1988 Olympics. Folk dance also served as an expression of nationalism during the Soviet period, as exemplified by Fadeev's and Plyushenko's several peasant-style programs.

Idiosyncratic Moves

Gary Beacom, who competed for Canada in the early 1980s while earning college degrees in philosophy and physics, approached freeskating as an experiment in physical principles, exploring potentials for movement that the medium of blades on ice allowed. He developed unique movements involving different types of weight shifts and reversals than those employed in standard skating techniques. In addition to the usual spin positions and double and triple jumps, sometimes from unusual entries, Beacom's programs also included a greater variety of half, single, and even one-and-a-half and double jumps from other than the usual takeoffs (but often landed intentionally on two feet), unique spin positions demonstrating difficult feats of balance and control, and complex passages of edges and footwork impossible for anyone else to duplicate. In Beacom's skating, the process of exploration was more important than the aesthetic impact of the result. Thus his creativity represented not only the masculine value of self-assertion, but a scientific more than an arts- (or even athletics-) oriented endeavor.

In the 1990s, Ukraine's Dmitri Dmitrenko similarly developed a reputation for being one of a kind, developing complex spins that changed the part of the blade he was spinning on, including rarely used parts such as the heel, and extremely complicated patterns of footwork and connecting moves with multiple unexpected changes of direction and of rhythm. Dmitrenko sometimes composes his own music, using synthesizers to incorporate unexpected and distorted sound effects, further establishing himself as the creative intelligence behind the physical performance he puts out on the ice. For both Beacom and Dmitrenko, the body is primarily an instrument for exploring ideas and physical principles, so that it is the fertility of the skater's mind more than the aesthetic appeal of his body that viewers can appreciate.

Themes and Characters

The specifications for the presentation mark in freeskating competition include "expression of the character of the music." Both male and female skaters have used this expectation to incorporate movements into their choreography that are reminiscent of the music's original provenance, for example Brian Orser including catlike bent-leg positions in his 1984 short program to music from the musical *Cats*. A number of skaters have taken this idea a step further by choosing music, designing costumes, and including numerous moves related to a single theme. This seems to be much more common among male than female skaters. I take this to be a reflection of the fact that women are expected to be "artistic" by being beautiful, whereas, in resisting this option as unmanly, men have to find other means of demonstrating artistry. Taking on a generalized persona such as cowboy or military officer (both of which have recurred in the repertory of men's programs during the past decade and a half) lets the skater demonstrate expressivity through whole-body gestures without submitting his physical appearance to aesthetic judgment; the choices of persona also tend to align the skater with an acceptably masculine set of images.

Recently, some male skaters have chosen to portray more specific characters, so that acting skill begins to come into play. Browning, for instance, skated his short program in 1991 and 1992 as a Hindu war god, "a composite of Siva and a couple of other deities,"[11] using elaborate arm movements including many positions with flexed wrists or palms pressed together to suggest Hindu imagery. In 1993 and 1994 he skated a free program using music from the film *Casablanca*, dressed in white dinner jacket and black bowtie over white shirt and black trousers, in which he took on the suave mannerisms of Humphrey Bogart's character in the film, sauntering on the backs of his blades with hands in pockets and smoking an imaginary cigarette, as well as enacting a film-noir-style chase through his skating with repeated shifts of gaze, weight, and direction. The associations with a specific actor and film genre enabled Browning to embody a masculinity that embraced both the sophisticated elegance of classic skating style and the heroic competence of the man of action confronting danger.

American Todd Eldredge skated his 1994 free program as Charlie Chaplin's Little Tramp character, to music from Chaplin's films. This role allowed Eldredge to express an extreme degree of emotional "sensitivity" (for example, hunching his shoulders, pretending to wipe a tear from his eye) in the context of a conventionalized enactment of pathos, associated with an actor-producer known for taking control of his own career as his character could not. This program also gave Eldredge the opportunity to express a whimsical mood through gestures of waking up and scratching his neck, and through stylized shapes such as outwardly flexed wrists or one leg kicked up behind his body.

The skater most associated with earning high artistic marks for his acting

Playing a role, such as Todd Eldredge's 1994 long program impersonation of Charlie Chaplin's Little Tramp, allows skaters to demonstrate artistry through expressive movement rather than physical beauty. Photo © by J. Barry Mittan.

on the ice more than for the beauty of his body line is France's Philippe Candeloro. His 1992–1993 free program cast him as Conan the Barbarian, dressed in a tunic of what appeared to be skins and furs over dark brown trousers covered with fur shin guards. The choreography highlighted his somewhat wild skating style, with innovative moves such as shooting both feet out from under him from a squat into a pike position and descending from an upright scratch spin to complete the spin on his shins; both these moves became Candeloro trademarks that he included in several of his long programs and even more of his exhibition performances.

For the 1994 Olympic season, Candeloro introduced a matched set of programs based on music and characters from the *Godfather* films, drawing on the Italian paternal side of his own family heritage as well as evoking the male-identified world of the organized crime "family." In the short program, dressed in loose brown and beige striped trousers and off-white shirt, skating to mostly tarantella rhythms, he portrayed a young tough, appearing to yell at someone in the distance, gesticulating vehemently, snatching off the chain around his neck, even directing obscene gestures at the audience. In the long program, in black trousers, black shirt closed with a gold chain across the collar, and slicked-back hair, Candeloro represented an older, more powerful figure. He glided on one foot with his limbs and hip joints bent as if seated in an armchair and then raised one hand to wave a benediction, shook the back of his hand at an unseen enemy just before entering a jump, and leaned one hip against the barrier to raise his clasped hands as church bells tolled over the sound system. He repeated his signature moves from the Conan program, given more menace by the restraint of his highly focused attention. In the 1995 season, Candeloro continued the *Godfather* theme, whitening his hair for a long program portraying an aged Don Corleone. In subsequent free programs, he enacted the Belgian comic-strip cowboy Lucky Luke and drew on French history and literature to portray Napoleon and D'Artagnan.

Candeloro explicitly stated that he plays characters in part to deflect charges of effeminacy. According to one interview, "The characterizations helped Candeloro early in his skating career when he wrestled with the notion of others that 'skating was for girls.' His solution to that problem was to act, as well as skate. He became the personality of the character he was skating. Now, his friends no longer think he is participating in a 'girls' sport.'"[12]

It can be difficult to draw a firm line between establishing a generalized thematic persona and playing an identifiable historical or fictional character: for example, Brian Boitano (who had previously been known as a jumper, in contrast to the more artistic Brian Orser) won Olympic gold in 1988 dressed in a militarily adorned blue stretch suit with red braid and epaulets, using military posture and gestures wherever the requirements of skating technique allowed, to music from the television miniseries *Napoleon and Josephine*. Was Boitano attempting to play the role of Napoleon, or simply to illustrate a general military theme? Similarly, in 1994 Stojko skated to the soundtrack of *Dragon*, the film biography of Bruce Lee, incorporating moves from his own extensive study of karate and tai chi. Stojko was not attempting to impersonate Lee, but to present himself in his own aspect as devotee of a traditionally male martial discipline.

Disrupting the Frame

As of the 1994–1995 season, the ISU outlawed moves performed without at least one skate blade in contact with the ice, a ruling that would seem to preclude a move such as Philippe Candeloro's spinning on his shins. At the Skate America competition in fall 1994, Candeloro, repeating the previous season's *Godfather* program (his third installment in the saga was not yet ready until later in the season) performed his trademark shin spin during the warm-up, to the delight of his fans. At the point at the end of the program when this spin was to occur, he made as if to enter the scratch spin, halted the movement, and stood still, facing the judges, twirling his hand to indicate the forbidden element. This intentional break in what is expected to be a seamless performance disrupted the aesthetic frame with a sarcastic comment on the framing structure of competitive rules.

In a number of pro-am competitions held under modified eligible competition rules, Scott Hamilton, competing as a professional used to the less strictly governed formats of professional competitions where entertaining the audience is the primary consideration, has included his signature backflip despite its illegality under eligible rules, gesturing to the ISU judges to indicate acknowledgment of the illegality of the move he was about to perform. At U.S. Nationals in 1991, Doug Mattis, frustrated at what he considered undermarking for his short program, similarly included the forbidden backflip element in his long program as a gesture of defiance at the judges; at 1999 Nationals, Dan Hollander announced the end of his career in eligible competition with a backflip in the long program. And the Ukrainian skater Dmitri Dmitrenko, in his comic 1994 long program, included a move where he made as if to enter a (double?) axel, aborted the movement, and gestured as if to say, "Fooled you!"

Christopher Bowman, dubbed by the media "Bowman the Showman," played similar games with the conventions of self-representation in competition. His competitive programs were usually set to powerful classical music (for instance the *1812 Overture* in his 1992 free program) with choreography that on most other skaters would emphasize the aesthetic and dramatic qualities of the movement. But Bowman would deliberately overplay or "ham up" emotional gestures and employ exaggerated facial expressions, thus drawing attention to the constructedness of the emotions he was conveying, establishing that the intensity of the performance was purely tongue-in-cheek. He would also on occasion interrupt the self-contained flow of his skating to point or mug directly at a spectator or into a television camera that happened to lie along his path. At Skate America in 1991, he further breached aesthetic distance by leaning over the barrier to grab the leg of an acquaintance in the first row. A Bowman competitive program was never a self-contained object submitted for the audience's approval, but rather a series of images simultaneously offered and disavowed. During his exhibition after winning the 1991 Skate America competition, Bowman frustrated the spectators' gaze even further by removing his jacket partway into his performance and draping it over the lens of the camera currently feeding his image to the television audience.

Through such active manipulation of the ground rules of performer/spectator relationship, these skaters position themselves as clearly in the superior status of this relationship. On a smaller scale, other skaters sometimes momentarily shift focus from the ice to the audience by pointing, glancing directly, or otherwise gesturing into the crowd in such a way as to dare or demand attention.

MARKETING MEN'S SKATING

The verbal and visual discourses surrounding men's skating competitions also construct the participants and the event in normative masculine terms.

The ways that skaters, skating officials, and the media outlets covering skating have explicitly addressed (or refused to address) the widespread perception of men's figure skating as a "gay" sport and the existence of gay skaters will be covered in the following chapter.

Signifiers of Normative Masculinity

On the opening night of the men's figure skating competition at the 1994 Olympic Winter Games, CBS ran a montage featuring the three big names of the competition—returning 1988 and 1992 gold medalists Boitano and Petrenko, and current world champion Browning—along with the current Canadian and American champions, Stojko and Davis, who had outskated Browning and Boitano at their respective national championships. To the accompaniment of a voice singing the Who's lyrics "It's a boy, Mrs. Walker, it's a boy," the feature displays photographs of the prepubescent champions (identified by captioned names) in typically boyish endeavors (e.g., Browning in full hockey gear, Davis posing in a Superman costume). "The boys have grown up and tonight begin their quest for an Olympic gold medal," a voice-over informs us, as the images change to the adult competitors skating and receiving medals, a pair of black figure skates against a Canadian flag, and Boitano posing in front of an American flag. This montage first asserts the gender of these skaters, then distances them from the delicacy of youth and positions them within a context of nationalistic contest.

Associating men's skating competitions with warfare is a common strategy. The most obvious example is the alliterative catchphrase "the battle of the Brians" used to characterize the rivalry between Boitano and Orser, the 1986 and 1987 world champions, who met in one of the closest contests ever at the 1988 Olympics. One journalist took the martial metaphor even further, noting that "The Canadian Brian also has a quad in his arsenal, but he too plans not to deploy it in the Saddledome."[13]

CBS coverage of the 1990 World Championships showed the skaters in slow motion with grimly determined facial expressions, cast as surrogate enactors of the military exploits world events were rendering remote: "The Cold War is over, but somebody forgot to tell Viktor Petrenko. Canada is one of the friendliest nations on earth, but Kurt Browning doesn't care. The U.S.A. usually wins the wars, but not this one." CBS's 1989 profiles of two favorites show Petrenko walking along the shore of the Black Sea and in his car, a real perk of skating success for a Soviet teenager, as CBS correspondent Pat O'Brien informs viewers that Petrenko is "in the driver's seat" of his career. This shot allows for a cute crosscut from Petrenko turning on his car radio to Christopher Bowman popping a tape into his dashboard cassette deck while driving the California freeways with an unidentified young woman next to him. The profile emphasizes Bowman's showbiz background (he had been a child model and attended Hollywood High School), showing a clip of him appearing on the "All New Dating Game." When it comes to signifiers of young male power—cars and access to young women—the American has the Soviet beat.

Other broadcasts have used aural and visual cues to move the image of skating from the effete old world to the pulsating new. NBC's coverage of the 1993 World Championships in Prague introduced each event with shots of castles and other venerable buildings emphasizing the city's cultural heritage, underscored with Baroque musical accompaniment. To lead into the men's event, a quick cut replaced these measured rhythms with a pounding beat and images of the top contenders raising their arms in triumph at the end of a successful performance or holding an opening pose with a look of determination while waiting for their program to begin.

Another means of verbally associating male skaters with traditionally manly attributes has been identifying skaters in terms of fathers with rugged professions. Viewers are frequently reminded that Browning, "the son of Alberta farmers," grew up on a ranch; Eldredge is "the son of a commercial fisherman" and Davis the "son of a high school football coach," and Candeloro's "father, a bricklayer, is Italian."

Covering the World Championships in 1993, NBC's Dick Enberg commented on Davis's "high-energy program," saying "Athletic Scott Davis has set the tone," and remarked that Stojko "skates with terrier tenacity." Enberg's colleague Sandra Bezic noted that "there's a reason why [Stojko's] nickname is the Terminator." During the 1994 Olympic competition, CBS's Verne Lundquist remarked that, "like Elvis Stojko, Philippe Candeloro loves to ride motorcycles."

Profiles of Stojko, not only in relation to his 1994 *Dragon* free program, often emphasized his martial arts expertise, showing him practicing karate and kung fu. Stojko himself stated during the CBS Olympic profile that "I've seen martial arts done to music and it's really cool. It's different. I like to put that on the ice and have a different side of skating instead of just the ballet side." ABC's 1996 Worlds broadcast featured a profile of Stojko riding a dirt bike and verbally identified him with his favorite animal, the wolf. Similarly, profiles of the young Russian skater Ilya Kulik aired during the 1996–1997 season (after he had moved to Marlborough, Massachusetts, to train with an expatriate Russian coach) depicted him target shooting with pistols and sparring with a punching bag.

Some skating specials have targeted a young, hip, male audience—rather than the traditional skating audience of women and young girls—by showing exhibition programs set almost exclusively to rhythmic popular music and by adopting an MTV aesthetic of canted angles, jerky camera movements, quick cuts, and zooms toward and away from video images on monitors in the background. In 1994, these included Canada's CTV Sports broadcast of *Elvis and Friends: A Helping Hand* (featuring Stojko in his role as ambassador for Ronald McDonald children's charities, in which the new world champion informed the audience that he and his colleagues were "just gonna rock and roll, have some fun") and Fox's *Fox on Ice*, billed as "skating with an attitude from some of the world's finest skaters." Subsequent made-for-TV events aiming at similar demographics included Fox's annual *Rock 'n' Roll Challenge* and the *Battle of the Sexes* in 1997, professional competitions emphasizing contemporary pop music and "celebrity judges" drawn from fields far removed from figure skating such as MTV's Downtown Julie Brown and boxer Ray "Boom-Boom" Mancini.

Skating commentary often focuses on masculine attributes. Scott Hamilton's expert input for CBS (and, in 2002, NBC) almost always emphasizes the athletic and technical aspects of the sport, particularly jumps, even in coverage of the ladies' event. Dick Button commented during Scott Davis's winning free skate, to music from *West Side Story,* at the 1993 U.S. Championships that "he likes playing this character, the role of a brash young kid who knows how to put it all together and still get the girl . . . [as Davis completes a difficult jump combination] and do that kind of a triple lutz–triple toe loop," thus conflating the persona Davis takes on in his performance and his own identity as athlete. Button introduced the 1993 Skate America competition leading up to the Lillehammer Olympics with this comparison of the reinstated professionals, Olympic champions Boitano and Petrenko: "Well, Brian is a solid, enormously powerful, straightforward skater. His jumps are high, his moves simple, his edges fast, and deep into the ice. There are no superfluous, gimcracky, or mannered movements. He fills the ice with his presence. Viktor, on the other hand, is slimmer and more supple. His spins are faster, and his steps more dancey. He courts a jazzier, much more hip look, which he overlays with suggestive arm movements and pseudosexy glances." The description of Petrenko, though accurate, sounds pejorative not only by implying that the Ukrainian clutters his programs with the superfluous movements Boitano avoids, but also by evoking feminine-coded qualities such as danciness and flirtatiousness.

Opposing Ideals

Leading into the 1994 Olympics, Western media attention focused on the veterans of the men's event—returning pros Boitano and Petrenko, and reigning world champion Browning—versus the young up-and-comers Stojko and Davis, who defeated Browning and Boitano to win the 1994 Canadian and U.S. championships, respectively. CBS, for instance, touted these five skaters, four of them North American, as the "gold medal favorites" with no mention of the younger Europeans such as Urmanov and Candeloro whose international credentials outweighed Davis's. After all three veterans took themselves out of Olympic medal contention with mistakes in the short program, with Urmanov winning both programs in contested victories over Stojko and Candeloro taking home the bronze medal, the media narrative became instead one of the proper direction that men's figure skating should take to capitalize on skating's burgeoning popularity in the North American market.

In a post–prime time interview with Stojko, Pat O'Brien (CBS's general sports anchor) remarked that "perhaps . . . figure skating is sending the wrong message, period. Because, here you are—you're a great guy, outspoken, your name is Elvis, and you're marketable and all that sort of thing. And Urmanov is a nice guy, I suppose, but he's going to go back to Russia and we won't see him until maybe the Nationals. You're here and you could promote figure skating. . . . You could be their Michael Jordan, so to speak." E. M. Swift, writing for *Sports Illustrated*, did the most to cement the opposing images of the two skaters in type, characterizing Stojko as hyper-

In the aftermath of the 1994 Olympics, Canadian silver medalist Elvis Stojko came to represent newness and the West (i.e., the New World), masculinity, wildness or roughness, naturalness, individualism, popular culture, democracy, and objective quantifiability, while the North American media tended to align Russian gold medalist Aleksei Urmanov, with his penchant for ruffles and gloves, with the figure skating establishment, conservatism and the East (the Old World), femininity, refinement, artificiality, conformity, high art, elitism, and the purely qualitative. Photos © by J. Barry Mittan.

masculine to the point of being somewhat physically grotesque but making the most of his physique:

> No one better represented this new generation than the 21-year-old Stojko, otherwise known as the quad god. . . . His movements were intentionally jerky, his poses decidedly unballetic and his jumps typically huge. Stojko, who had been landing his quadruple toe–triple toe combination all week in practice, is a veritable jumping machine, but his artistic marks have always held him back. The judges seem unable to forgive him for having the body of a Norwegian troll. His arms and legs appear too short for his muscular torso, his head and neck too large. His artistic possibilities, correspondingly, are limited. Stojko's physique was not meant to carve clas-

sical lines through the air. "The judges have to realize there's more than one style of skating," says Stojko. "Not just the classical."

. . . Stojko's long program, skated to the soundtrack from *Dragon: The Bruce Lee Story,* incorporated a few kung-fu moves amid the seven triple jumps that he landed. Stojko, a black belt in karate at 16, would punctuate a completed jump by kicking one of his stubby legs into the air or punching a fist at a phantom attacker.

Swift explicitly rejected Urmanov as inappropriately overdressed and flirtatious, therefore relying on physical charms rather than deeds to win favor —traits traditionally associated with femininity:

Urmanov, by contrast, represented everything the judges have traditionally looked for in men's skating—with the minor exception that he is virtually unable to spin. But who cares about spins these days? In winning the short program, five judges to four over Stojko, Urmanov drew gorgeous classical lines with his long limbs while gliding back and forth across the ice between triple jumps. He preened insipidly and made shameless eye contact with the judges. His costume, a billowing blue yoke of ruffled taffeta, looked like it was lifted straight off a portrait of Sir Walter Raleigh. If this is the future of men's figure skating, you may have it.

. . . The 20-year-old Urmanov also smiled fetchingly at all times, pointed his toes in a pleasing manner and waggled his knees twice at the judging panel in a peculiarly suggestive maneuver that has never been seen in Russian ballet.[14]

An implicit structuralist binary was established, with Stojko, newness and the West (i.e., the New World), masculinity, wildness or roughness, naturalness, individualism, popular culture, democracy, and objective quantifiability on one side. On the other side stand the figure skating establishment, conservatism and the East (the Old World), femininity, refinement, artificiality, conformity, high art, elitism, and the purely qualitative. Within the North American imagination, these values associated with the conservative skating establishment also tend to be gendered as feminine; certainly popular masculinities often involve resistance to their elitist ideal. Throughout the ensuing years, until Urmanov's sudden withdrawal from the 1997 World Championships with a groin injury that kept him out of competition for the entire 1998 Olympic season, American and Canadian media repeatedly returned to contrasting these two skaters as exemplars of alternative visions of men's skating that judging panels were forced to choose between, often with implicit or explicit endorsement of the values represented by Stojko and rejection of those represented by judges' apparent preference for Urmanov. In rejecting Urmanov as an appropriate champion of men's figure skating on the basis of his classical body line or frilly costumes, Stojko and his supporters in the Western press reject the concept of figure skating as a space in which men, like "ladies," are judged largely on appearance and favor instead of a view of the sport as based primarily on aggressive action in the form of big jumps and fast skating. Identification with Stojko's specific images, with the values they imply, and with his efforts to leave the world of figure skating "all shook up" (as the NBC 1994 Worlds broadcast, with its recurring allusions to Elvis Presley, put it) allows viewers to experience rooting for Stojko as a form of resistance to the perceived hegemony of the conservative, highbrow, upper-class, Eurocentric values represented by the judges.

Commentary on Urmanov most often focused on the elaborateness of his costumes and, in Dick Button's words, his "flamboyant" or "superficial and pretentious" arm movements, praising him most often, if at all, for musicality and body line—for instance, Scott Hamilton's discussion of Urmanov's extended landing positions in opposition to Stojko's bent-over landings as if they represented purely a matter of style rather than of technique. By giving less verbal acknowledgment of the athletic qualities of Urmanov's skating, such as the high speed across the ice that undoubtedly contributed significantly to his Olympic win, or of the more violent and grotesque imagery, for instance, of his 1996 *Night on Bald Mountain* short program or even the 1995 *Swan Lake* long program, Western commentary largely succeeded in obscuring the tensions playing out within Urmanov's own skating (and, often, that of younger Russian skaters such as Kulik and Plyushenko) in order to sustain a narrative of virile West versus decadent, emasculated East.

For Russians, however, the issue underlying the indulgence in elaborate costumes and arm movements and imagery that often harkens back to pre-Soviet neoromanticism or even surrealism in a post-Soviet era may be one of extravagance versus austerity much more than of masculinity or lack thereof. For North American viewers who read qualities such as lyricism and ornamentation according to gendered codes, the blurring of binary gender distinction that Urmanov's skating implies by including elements from both sides of the binary may prove, according to each viewer's valuing of this distinction, a welcome or unwelcome challenge to it; a significant portion of Urmanov's Western fans include women and gay men who profess themselves attracted to the very gender confusion that the mainstream media reject.[15]

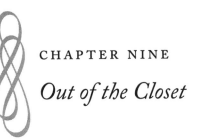

CHAPTER NINE

Out of the Closet

*T*he choice of a male rather than female sexual object is one very salient "feminine" attribute by which our culture categorizes homosexual men as failed rather than "real" men. In a binary, hierarchical understanding of gender, there are only two categories: real men and everybody else. Gay men thus occupy the same default, lower-status position as women. Verbally ascribing either homosexual or female identity to another male is a means by which many men attempt to assert their own superior status. To such thinking, the implicit corollary is that men who in other ways exhibit female gender signs or fail to make the grade as real men (e.g., by not being large enough, hairy enough, or violent enough, or by engaging in emotional and aesthetic expression) must also share in the supposed mode of sexual desire appropriate to members of this category—desire for a (real) man. There is no necessary connection between most of these signs by which men judge other men inferior on the one hand and homosexual desire on the other. But as men concerned about compromising their masculine status avoid activities that carry with them signifiers of femininity (which, attached to a man, becomes effeminacy), and so leave the field to females and to the relative minority of males for whom such concerns are less pressing (a category that includes many gay men who know that they will be excluded from the privileges of real manhood in any case and so have no status to lose), the association becomes self-perpetuating: the activity becomes further associated with the females and "unmasculine" males who pursue it, and anxious males have further reason to avoid it and to suspect the masculinity of any man who engages in it.

Thus those straight men who do engage in such activity—for example, figure skating—and who do not wish to be misperceived are thus forced to assert compulsively a sexual identity that in other contexts would be taken for granted, in response to what Eve Kosofsky Sedgwick has termed "homosexual panic," meaning "a structural residue of terrorist potential, of *blackmailability*, of Western maleness through the leverage of homophobia."[1] At the same time, people concerned with promoting the activity, women and gay men included, find it advantageous to assert the participation of straight men, given the positive value that masculinity carries with it—if real men do it, then it's worth doing.[2] Skating insiders and promoters never publicly raise the suggestion that these men might be anything other than fully masculine and heterosexual except explicitly to refute it.

A 1984 profile of then-U.S. and world champion Scott Hamilton in *Sports Illustrated,* a prime bastion of normative masculinity in sport, stated:

> Hamilton also has established his masculinity in a sport that attracts some-
> times outrageously effeminate young men. He's now self-assured enough
> to scorn the beaded and spangled costumes that most male skaters wear.
> . . . What's more, Hamilton feels he can speak out on the subject, which
> many in the sport tiptoe around. . . ."Ho-boy, wouldn't it be great, after
> the Olympics and the world's [*sic*], to jump in my Ferrari and go whip-
> ping back to Bowling Green, where a few people used to call me faggot,
> and say, 'O.K., faggot *this,* you clowns!'"[3]

The *Newsweek* 1992 Olympic preview noted that "Male figure skating has had what is euphemistically called an image problem"[4] and quotes Kurt Browning's statement in his autobiography: "Let me just say, 'I like girls.'"[5] Browning claimed he was making his sexual preference public in response to numerous inquiries from journalists following his first world champion-ship. His first Canadian television special, *Tall in the Saddle,* capitalized on his background by focusing on Wild West themes; his second, *You Must Re-member This,* included an extended sequence in the Bogart persona. Follow-ing a brief glimpse of Browning studying ballet as part of his training, he in-troduced a number skated with Kristi Yamaguchi, Josée Chouinard, and Christine Hough by informing the audience that one of the advantages of figure skating over hockey was the presence of girls.

Newspaper profiles of U.S. skaters John Baldwin, Jr., and Michael Weiss have highlighted their heterosexual status and suggested that this fact ac-counts for their consciously macho approach in skating style, putting them at odds with the traditionally feminine/effeminate values of the skating world. *Washington Post* reporter Christine Brennan, profiling local skater Weiss in her book *Inside Edge,* excerpted in the *Post* before publication, recounts his coach's fear when Weiss was still a junior skater that he might not remain in the sport because he wasn't gay.[6] Since Weiss's engagement and marriage to one of his choreographers in 1997, when Weiss was just twenty-one years old, and the birth of their daughter and son one and two years later, television coverage has made frequent references to his wife and children, perhaps re-flecting a desire on the part of the Weisses or of the networks to underscore his heterosexuality for uneasy viewers.

Baldwin was quoted as expressing the opinion that he suffered competitively for his "masculine" approach: "I think some of the other skaters get intimidated by me. I'm straight, for one. And a lot of them aren't. Their impression is, 'You're not serious.' Because I like to have fun, they think I'm not serious. I'm not a conformist off the ice. That's probably their biggest problem with me. I'm loud . . . a bit too loud and too flashy for them."

The article continues:

> And another: He openly critiques the system of judging, talking about how skaters kiss up to judges, about how your marks sometimes are no reflection of your performance, about the politics behind the fur coats. This is hardly a revelation, but the point is he's a skater and he's saying it. "It seems," he says, "that if I don't skate perfectly, I don't get the respect from the judges that I deserve. I see other skaters go out there, and nobody's perfect, and they don't skate their best, and they get respect . . . I think the judges should give me credit for my image. How can I say this? I'm not going to have my wrist limp, like this."
>
> He demonstrates. "I'm going to have a firm wrist. I'm not going to wear velvet. They think a more effeminate skater is more artistic. That's not true."[7]

On the other hand, gay skaters such as John Curry and Rudy Galindo have asserted that judges marked them down because of their sexual preference or because of their too-effeminate style. Given that Galindo and Baldwin are near-contemporaries who often competed against each other, being judged by the same judges, they cannot both be correct. Rather, such assertions are most likely the skaters' way of rationalizing results they don't understand, for instance when a stronger or technically superior skater makes more obvious errors than they do but still places higher. They might in fact both be referring to the same skaters—skaters who have not made a public issue of their sexuality and whose skating style is less aggressively masculine than Baldwin's, more so than Galindo's—each assuming that the skaters he loses to are being favored on account of a sexual orientation or gendered choice of skating style that he does not share, when in fact overall technical and athletic ability as demonstrated even within a flawed program are the primary determinants of judges' scores.

In November 1991, former Canadian ice dance champion and 1988 Olympic bronze medalist Rob McCall died of AIDS-related illnesses. The following February, *People* magazine included in its preview of the 1992 Olympics a brief feature on his partner, Tracy Wilson, who was providing expert commentary for the CBS Olympic broadcasts.[8] In October, John Curry told the London *Mail on Sunday* that he too had AIDS; wire services and newspapers throughout North America reported this news. These articles provided human interest information about well-known skaters affected by the disease. As McCall's friends were putting together a skating tribute to his memory entitled *Skate the Dream,* reporters Mary Ormsby of the *Toronto Star* and Michael Clarkson of the *Calgary Herald* noted that a number of other Canadian skaters had also recently died due to AIDS and launched an investigation polling the skating community about the disease's effect on the sport.[9] *People* picked up on the topic,[10] and ABC Sports ran a segment on the impact of AIDS on skating during their coverage of the 1993 U.S. championships. Some of the skating insiders interviewed expressed fear of the disease and of the potential for transmission within a skating context.

Some skaters, such as Curry[11] and American Barry Hagan,[12] were willing to discuss their homosexuality with the press—after they had been diagnosed with AIDS and were no longer skating professionally, much less in high-profile amateur competition. Most skaters and officials, however, responded defensively to what they perceived as media attempts to ghettoize figure skating as a gay sport or to further marginalize it through association with AIDS by minimizing the gay presence in figure skating:

> [Skate the Dream organizer Brian] Orser admitted there was some soul-searching in drawing international attention to the sport because of perceptions that AIDS is a gay disease and that some male skaters are gay. The worry was that those prejudices would prompt people to dismiss AIDS as figure skating's problem, not that of society. "To say that AIDS is a disease of gay figure skaters is really unfair speculation and it's wrong," Orser said.[13]

> Scott Hamilton . . . understands the reluctance to make an issue of the disease. "Most people need to talk about AIDS," says Hamilton, who lives with his fiancee, Karen Plage, in Denver. "But we don't want to cause unnecessary alarm. If AIDS is attached to skating, parents might not want to allow their kids to get involved in the sport."[14]

Either the *People* writers or Hamilton himself evidently felt it necessary to assert his heterosexual credentials in this context, as where he lives or with whom is not otherwise relevant to his thoughts about the media investigations.

Just how many skaters are gay became an explicit issue.

> Arthur Luiz, co-president of the newly formed International Gay Figure Skating Union, said at least half of North America's top male skaters are gay, while a Herald survey of 50 coaches estimated that number to be about 30 percent.[15]

Just like the majority in life, the majority of people in skating are straight," argues . . . Brian Boitano, who recently lashed out at the Calgary Herald investigation, calling it "a witch-hunt."[16]

Luiz comes from a perspective interested in promoting gay interests more than the skating establishment, a point enhanced by citing considerable gay contributions to the sport. The careers of skating stars, regardless of their personal sexuality, depend on figure skating maintaining a positive public profile, which high gay-identification would diminish, and so their strategy is usually to minimize or avoid the issue.

Luiz and Laura Moore founded the International Lesbian and Gay Figure Skating Union in order to lobby for inclusion of figure skating in the Gay Games contests to be held in New York in June 1994, in conjunction with commemorations of the twenty-fifth anniversary of the Stonewall riots that launched the gay liberation movement.[17] In attending this competition, I found the skaters, spectators, and organizers using the occasion as a positive assertion of gay identity and affiliation. An announcer read a short bio or personal statement from each skater before he or she took the ice, many stating that they had returned to skating specifically to train for these games or that they had always wanted to skate but were unable to do so until after "coming out" as adults. The level of the skating ranged from beginners to a handful of world-class skaters. There were relatively few women competing but a large number of men's singles competitors, particularly in the intermediate skill range, a category that included skaters who had begun as adults, childhood skaters who had returned to the sport, and professional coaches and performers who had never stopped skating. The types of programs performed included both regular competitive-style programs from skaters who also participated in regular elite or adult eligible events and also interpretive or show-type numbers and same-sex pairings.

The crowd was equally appreciative of the competitors who displayed the strongest technique and beauty in their skating and those who used their programs to make explicitly gay statements (not always mutually exclusive categories), granting standing ovations for each. Some competitors chose musical accompaniments with particular resonance in the gay community; for instance, there were two renditions of "Somewhere over the Rainbow" and a medley of Queen songs in a program dedicated to the memory of Freddie Mercury. Others used costuming to comment on social constructions of identity: one self-described "leather man" skated his program clad only in leather straps; another man wore a black leotard, black tights, and sheer wraparound skirt, the sort of attire a female skater or ballet dancer might practice in. One man, performance artist Greg Wittrock, entered the ice dressed in a full bridal gown and veil; a taped voice proclaimed "I've had enough and I want out!" and he removed this regalia to skate an angst-ridden passage in tattered black jersey and trousers to thrashing heavy metal music, then loosened his pony-tail and removed these garments to skate a flowing, lyrical section dressed in pink lingerie. A male pair team (from Canada) wore battle fatigues and tape over their mouths and skated a program incorporating moves of mutual sup-port to comment on the recent U.S. controversy about the government's pol-icy on gays in the military.

The 1994 Gay Games skating event was structured more or less as a non-elite adult club competition, with waivers obtained from the U.S. and Cana-dian federations to allow amateur or the few elite eligible skaters, and eligi-ble judges, to participate in an event that also included professionals without losing eligibility. At the 1998 Gay Games held in Amsterdam, the Nether-lands, organizers wished both to feature figure skating as an elite interna-tional competition, which would require international sanctioning from the ISU, and also to feature same-sex teams and allow for other deviations from ISU rules. For procedural reasons, the ISU did not grant the required sanction, which meant that the majority of skaters (most of them non-elite in any case) and the judges who had planned to participate would lose their eligibility by doing so. This led to cancellation of the skating competitions, resched-uled as "public practices," and accusations against the ISU of homophobia for "blacklisting" skaters who participated in the gay skating event. The blame for this mix-up, however, seems to rest with the organizers' misunderstand-ing of the purposes and procedures for ISU sanctioning.[18]

For the 2002 Gay Games, held in Sydney, Australia, organizers obtained sanctioning from the Ice Skating Institute (ISI), conformed the competition levels to the "artistic" and "spotlight" categories of ISI competition structure, and required competitors to join ISI and test to the appropriate level. ISI's emphasis on recreational rather than elite skill levels made it an appropriate format for the skating level of most Gay Games participants. In response to the fact that ISI technical competitions are more restrictive than USFSA or similar governing bodies about what elements must or must not be performed in programs at each level, the organizers chose not to include technical pro-grams in the competition, stating that "We realise that gay skaters have an inordinate need to express themselves so we are only offering the Artistic and Spotlight events for Freestyle (singles) which have no required elements."[19]

Because ISI has reciprocal arrangements with the USFSA and the Profes-sional Skaters' Association, members of these organizations would not au-tomatically forfeit their eligibility by competing. The federation governing skaters in New South Wales, Australia, however, interpreted the lack of ISU sanctioning to mean that any local skaters who participated either as competitors or as volunteers would automatically face a loss of eligibility, a decision that again caused Gay Games organizers to suspect homophobic rather than strictly procedural motivations.[20]

In a context such as Gay Games, where proving one's masculinity is less of an anxiety than in mainstream competitive venues, skaters are free to manipulate gender signifiers and so to reveal them as social constructions rather than markers of an essentialist identity. In the world of professional skating, marketability to the American and Canadian public who serve as the paying audiences, live and indirectly via television ratings that attract advertising dollars, is key. In high-level eligible competition, reputation with skating judges is always an important concern, as is protecting audience appeal for future professional opportunities and the touring and invitational competition opportunities available to eligible competitors in the current environment. Personal acquaintances of individual skaters would likely know whether or not they are gay, and other members of the skating community would have access to gossip that might or might not be accurate. Members of the public may make assumptions that particular skaters (or, in some cases, all male skaters) are gay on the basis of how they present themselves on the ice and in interviews and other public appearances. But for the most part, gay skaters, like gay celebrities in other fields, have resisted making their homosexuality public knowledge. As of the mid-1990s, the only nationally ranked and still actively competing skater to have publicly discussed the fact that he was gay was Matthew Hall of Canada, whose highest finish at Canadian Nationals had been a third place in 1989 and who—as the only active competitor to enter the 1994 Gay Games skating competition—easily won the top level of that event.

In January of 1996, *Washington Post* sports reporter Christine Brennan published her book *Inside Edge,* detailing her year spent interviewing current and former competitive skaters, coaches, judges, and other members of the skating community and following them to competitions and touring performances.[21] In the third chapter, entitled "Skating's Tragic Secret," she attempted to address the issues of gay skaters and the impact of AIDS on the skating community, without specifying whether it was AIDS or the existence of gay skaters at all that constituted the "tragic secret." She also quoted a number of well-known North American skaters' comments about how they dealt with public preconceptions of them as unmasculine. "We joke about it all the time," Kurt Browning told her. "We're always goofing around: 'Oh! That was pretty!' And it's not mean at all. It's almost making fun of everyone who's ever made fun of us." (Brennan then quotes Browning and Paul Wylie making fun of Aleksei Urmanov's "outrageous costumes.")[22]

Among the openly gay skaters Brennan interviewed were choreographer Brian Wright and current competitor Rudy Galindo, who thus became the first American skater to come out in a public forum while still actively competing. A former national pairs champion with Kristi Yamaguchi in 1989 and 1990, Galindo had been less successful in his career as a singles skater after Yamaguchi left the partnership to pursue her own singles career. His highest finish at U.S. Nationals had been fifth place in 1993; in 1995, the year covered in Brennan's book, he placed eighth.

Brennan recounted how Galindo had lost his older brother (not a skater) and two coaches to AIDS as part of her coverage of the disease's effect on the sport. Mixed in with this, she also quoted Galindo's thoughts about how judges received his unmasculine, balletic style of skating: "'When you get to Nationals, these guys skate clean, they're really butch when they skate, they're just jump-jump-jump,' he said. 'Our American judges like that. They want just conservative, just really macho men. I think the other guys are going to have to fall like twenty times and I have to go clean before they put me in that third spot.'"[23] Brennan agreed that Galindo would never win a national championship, although she reasoned differently: "But he is not being robbed. He doesn't deserve the highest marks because he is not the country's best male skater, and he is prone to falling at the worst times."[24] Although these statements were true enough at the time, Brennan had obviously not learned the lesson of the previous year's Olympics never to say "never." Nor had she evidently been paying much attention to Galindo's practices at the 1995 championship to realize that he was competing there sick with asthmatic bronchitis, which partially accounted for his poor showing in that competition, and that in addition to being one of the best spinners in the event he was also the only man other than the favorites Scott Davis and Todd Eldredge who was practicing the difficult triple axel–triple toe combination. (As of 1995, Eldredge remained the only American to have performed this combination in competition.) The Washington-area skater Brennan was following for a more extensive profile, Michael Weiss, who was in the same practice group as Galindo and who was attempting quadruple jumps, would have drawn most of her attention.

The 1996 Nationals were held in Galindo's hometown of San Jose, California, less than a month after Brennan's book hit the stores. The San Jose *Mercury,* among its daily feature stories during the week of the event, included a profile of the local competitor. Another story about a monument to Bay Area skaters dedicated while the USFSA officials were in town for

After winning the U.S. championship and a world bronze medal in 1996, Rudy Galindo embraced his position as an openly gay role model. Photo © by J. Barry Mittan.

Nationals also mentioned Galindo, included in the monument by virtue of his past pairs success with Yamaguchi. But it wasn't until later in the week that the national media took notice of him, after the favorites faltered and Galindo skated two inspired performances to win the national title.

This unexpected win, combined with the triumph-over-tragedy human interest angle of the story, drew more attention to the new champion from sources outside the skating press than previous men's champions such as Eldredge and Davis who cultivated the clean-cut all-American image had ever attracted. The fact that Galindo was "the oldest men's champion in seventy years" and "the first Mexican American champion" made catchy additions to the developing Rudy Galindo mythos, and inevitably the news reports made mention of the fact that he was the first openly gay champion, thanks to the recently published Brennan book.

In many cases, the fact that Galindo was gay served merely as one more signifier of his outsider status and therefore of the magnitude of his ultimate triumph. It was one more reason to root for him as the little guy prevailing against the entrenched conservatism of the system. Dick Button had enthused about his light, elegant style during the broadcast of the competition, as did many of the reporters commenting on Galindo's win in print. Brennan opined that not only had Galindo deserved to win the long program and thus the national title in San Jose, but he should have been placed higher than third in the short program as well, as further evidence of the arbitrary and political nature of figure skating judging.[25] There was much to like in Galindo's confident and stylish skating that year, and, as he himself put it, "I'm gay, Mexican trailer trash—who wouldn't love me?"

The link between AIDS and homosexuality remained, as articles such as *People* magazine's coupled Galindo's gayness and the fact that his brother and coaches had died of AIDS in the same paragraph, despite the fact that straight skaters (and non-skaters) are equally likely to lose people close to them to this cause.[26]

Galindo had hardly expected to win the national title and so was unprepared for the sudden attention to all aspects of his life, especially to the question about what his status as first openly gay champion meant to him. When confronted with this question at the press conference immediately following his winning performance (before drug testing and the medal ceremony), according to his later account in his autobiography, two thoughts flashed through his mind: "I don't know what I'm supposed to say, and the last thing I want to do is talk about anything that's going to get me in trouble with the USFSA."[27] So he responded, "No comment," and several publications reported this question and response in their articles about his win.

During the weeks leading up to the World Championships in Edmonton, Alberta, Galindo concentrated on continuing his training and made no attempts to take on the responsibilities of gay role model, thereby incurring disappointment or even hostility from some members of the gay community. Gary Reese published an article in the gay magazine the *Advocate* pondering the meaning of Galindo's new notoriety and whether his reluctance to discuss the gay issue constituted an attempt to "go back in the closet,"[28] and a stranger in a gay bar accosted him with the comment, "Thanks a lot, Rudy, you asshole," evidently in response to what he perceived as Galindo's betrayal of the gay cause.

After his bronze medal finish at Worlds,[29] however, Galindo was ready to address gay issues directly. In Edmonton and on tour that spring he performed his exhibition to a male choir's rendition of "Ave Maria" wearing a red scarf in the shape of a large AIDS ribbon around his neck. He accepted invitations to be the grand marshal at a gay pride parade in Ft. Lauderdale and to be the starter for a gay pride race in New York. He appeared on the cover of *Out* magazine in conjunction with a story inside about his experiences. And he published an autobiography, in which he stated that the answer he should have given to the question at the Nationals press conference was "I'm proud to have won the national championship, and I'm proud of who I am. The fact that I'm out and still won proves that in the sport of figure skating there's no longer a need to hide. I hope my example inspires others to be themselves. It's a lot easier than hiding."[30]

Galindo proved that the American public could embrace a gay skater as a national sports hero. There was no need for uneasiness about his masculinity, as he freely admitted to being both effeminate and homosexual—unlike Urmanov's, for instance, Galindo's skating and his off-ice demeanor present a coherent picture rather than dissettling ambiguity. And his is a recognizably American success story.

During the summer of 1996, due to dissatisfaction with his fall competition assignments, embarrassment from a drunk driving arrest, and recognition that another national title and world medal would be difficult to come by, Galindo decided to quit eligible skating while he was ahead and turn professional. With support from Dick Button, who organized many of the pro events, Galindo has found a successful niche in touring and pro competition.

There have not, as yet, been large numbers of skaters following Galindo's example by publicly professing that they are gay. Doug Mattis, a former national competitor and professional skater, had publicly come out (but not in print) in conjunction with skating in the Gay Games exhibitions at the request of his friend Debi Thomas, who was appearing as the featured big-name skater at that exhibition. Following Galindo's win, Mattis sought, ultimately unsuccessfully, to be reinstated as an eligible competitor, citing Galindo as an inspiration that it is possible for an openly gay skater to win competitions and for historically lower-ranked skaters to prevail when they finally skate better than the favorites. (Other skaters have been quoted as being inspired by the latter example, but, whether because they are not in fact gay or were unready to publicize that they are, did not cite that aspect of Galindo's story.) Mattis discussed his life as a gay skater in an *Advocate* article in 1996.[31]

In late 1998, Brian Orser, a much-beloved icon of Canadian skating, was "outed" in conjunction with a palimony lawsuit brought against him by a former lover. Orser had petitioned to keep the legal proceedings out of the media, but the court rejected his request.[32] He had at first feared that making his sexual preference known would hurt his popularity with skating fans and thereby his earning potential, and also that it might incorrectly associate skating with homosexuality in people's minds and discourage parents from allowing their sons to become figure skaters. According to one report, "the focus on gays in skating is what upset him most about the media coverage. 'It's totally unnecessary,' he said. 'It's putting us back in time here.'"[33] Regarding the former concern, immediate support from audiences seemed to offer reassurance that Canadian skating fans remained as loyal to Orser as ever. Regarding the latter, it would be impossible to measure exactly how much effect, if any, this revelation has had on the public's associations between skating and homosexuality or on male participation in skating, in Canada particularly.

We have seen that stereotyped perceptions of men in skating as necessarily unmasculine and by implication homosexual persist apart from the actual sexual orientation of any individual skater. Meanwhile, public perceptions of homosexuality in the wider culture outside skating are continually shifting, with some segments of the population professing strong disapproval of homosexuality itself and others objecting to closeted denial. Individual gay skaters must each weigh their own senses of whether proclaiming their gayness is a risk worth taking. Whether or not other gay skaters, male or female, will publicly admit to a gay identity remains to be seen, but, thanks to Galindo's example, the subject is no longer the unmentionable secret, "tragic" or otherwise, that it once was.

PART FIVE

Compulsory
Mating Dances

Defining Duos

*B*ecause it is a relative latecomer to organized skating competition, having originated more as a social/recreational than a competitive practice, ice dance has always found the need to define itself in terms of what it
is not, most particularly to define itself in contradistinction to the more established male-female discipline of pair skating. Thus, in order better to understand ice dance, it will be helpful first to look at pairs.

THE GENDER DYNAMICS OF PAIR SKATING

Pair skating developed as two skaters performing freestyle moves together.
They might employ shadow skating (the same moves performed side-by-side
in close proximity and in the same direction), mirror skating (the same moves
performed side-by-side in opposite directions), and moves, such as pair spins,
in which the skaters travel or rotate around a common center with the partners either separated or touching. In addition, pairs would develop moves in
which the partners play complementary rather than parallel roles, as in a pair
spiral where one of the skaters is moving backward and the other forward,
perhaps with their bodies close enough together so that they move as a unit
and produce a more complex shape than a single skater could do alone.

There is no technical reason why most such moves would need to be performed by opposite sexes, and in fact the implicit meaning in most of these
moves is the emphasis on the similarity, or symmetry, of shapes and movements made by the two bodies.[1] Many of the original concepts of nineteenth-
century "combined skating" had been pioneered by men in the days when
most advanced skaters were adult males. In the world of professional skating, teams of males performing comic and trick skating together have a long
history in ice shows related to acrobatic clown acts in circuses.[2] At the other
end of the spectrum, it remains common for young girls with some basic
skating ability to attempt to rotate around a common center formed by
joined hands, or, if they are accomplished figure skaters, to work up a routine together for a show number in a club carnival or to compete in a "simi-

lar pairs" event that occasionally may be offered at USFSA-sanctioned local competitions.

But in the first years of the twentieth century when women began participating in skating competition, pair skating proved a good opportunity for skaters who were married to each other to develop routines together and for female skaters to demonstrate their parity with males by performing the same moves alongside them. According to skating historian Nigel Brown, "Women now skated on a par with men and it was no longer necessary for the strong male to temper his virility and pace to allow his partner to complete the figure with him."[3]

So pair skating as an international competitive discipline beginning in 1908 originated as a male-female sport, and along with ice dance it remains the only Olympic sport to feature coed teams. As freestyle singles skating has increased in athleticism throughout the past century, pair skating also has come to rely more on athletic and acrobatic feats. These include not only side-by-side jumps and spins almost comparable to what the best singles skaters are capable of, but also assisted and throw jumps,[4] more complex pair spins, and acrobatic moves that combine the physics of skating with the upper body strength typical of the athletic adult male physique and the flexibility typical of females.

These factors allow "death spirals" in which the man performs a pivot anchoring the center of a circle while the lady spirals around him holding hands, using the centrifugal force and support from the man to achieve a low, almost horizontal position. Male strength allows men to lift another person with relative ease and a large, strong, skilled man to lift a small, light, athletically skilled person with the arms (or, in a real feat of strength, only one arm) fully extended overhead. Female flexibility, especially when actively cultivated, allows girls or women so lifted to produce a variety of attractive and striking positions in the air. Many lift positions and holds are adapted for the ice from similar feats long performed by ballet or adagio dancers or by skilled acrobats; skaters also develop their own variations in their quest for originality.

The more popular these moves have become, the more necessary it has become for pair skaters to perform them well in order to be competitive. Death spirals, overhead lifts, and throw jumps are required elements in the pairs' short program, and a "well-balanced" long program must contain these moves as well as all the other standard pair and side-by-side moves. Male pair skaters thus must be strong and preferably large (although for singles moves including the side-by-side moves that pair skaters must perform, especially double and triple jumps, size is often a disadvantage) and female pair skaters particularly light and flexible.

The conventions of the discipline thus require extremes of sexual difference in terms of body type, and indeed the trend toward overhead lifts as feats of strength originated with pairs in which the male partner was particularly large or happened to possess extensive weight-lifting experience.[5] Although historically there has been a preference for well-matched pairs of similar heights, such pairs are at a disadvantage when it comes to performing moves such as lifts and throws. On the other hand, the appearance of several "gorilla and flea" or "one-and-a-half" teams from the Soviet Union in the late 1970s and early 1980s, which paired a full-grown young man with a barely pubescent girl, occasioned much dismay among the rest of the skating community—in part because of the perceived unfair advantage this size difference provided and in part because of the exaggerated image of inequality such a pair produced, along with the difficulty for such a pair to achieve an impression of unison during side-by-side moves. Often, however, such teams would lose their competitive advantage as the female member of the pair finished growing. The importance of moves based on physical difference also means that "similar" pairs, either male or female, are unlikely to be physically suited to perform many of the moves that have become standard in the pair-skating repertory.[6]

In the world of theatrical dance, a choreographer might team up two (or more) dancers to perform a duet or individual partner moves together according to the demands of that particular work. The dancers would practice the moves together during the rehearsal period, but after performances have ended the dancers might never again have occasion to work with that particular partner, or to perform any of the unique moves developed for that particular piece. In competitive pair skating, by contrast, the goal is to perform the most difficult tricks as well as possible in order to achieve high scores. So pairings other than large man with small lady are rarely seen in high-level competition, and same-sex duos (or trios) have no place in the qualifying competition stream at all. In addition, skaters compete exclusively with one partner at a time. Pairings may break up for various reasons and one or both skaters might find a new partner and resume competition, but the longer a team has worked together the greater their comfort with performing even the most standard pair moves together. This factor that can become crucial when small differences in the quality of individual moves can lead to differences in competitive placement, with long-term consequences for the skaters' careers.

As a result of both the self-selection of body types within competitive pair skating and the necessity to highlight the demanding tricks, the number of thematic options available to competitive pairs remains fairly limited, circumscribed by the kinds of interpersonal relationships implied by the physical relationships between the skaters' bodies in the majority of pair moves. The emphasis on unison in identical side-by-side moves tends to suggest an equality and almost interchangeability of the sexes, particularly when both partners are of similar height and build and are costumed as identically as possible. This meaning is reinforced when the partners also engage in reciprocal pair moves, such as the pull Arabian cartwheels that were a trademark of Tai Babilonia and Randy Gardner in the 1970s.[7] Unison as reflected in pair moves contributes to the sense of "two skating as one" that can be interpreted as a metaphor for man and woman "becoming one" with each other through marriage. When pair teams choose to establish a human relationship between the two partners, most often the relationship depicted is that of a romantic couple, especially but not exclusively among pairs who are married or romantically involved with each other off the ice. As Oleg Protopopov, the influential pair champion of the 1960s, put it, "These pairs of brother and sister, how can they convey the emotion—the love that exists between man and woman? That is what we try to show."[8]

Perhaps more common, though, is an abstract, presentational approach in which the primary relationship is not that of the two skaters to each other, but rather of the skaters as a team displaying their athletic prowess to the spectators. Of all the figure skating disciplines, pair skating contains the most spectacular elements and is also the one with the greatest danger of serious injury to either partner. Often, in lifts and throws, the female partner assumes the greater degree of risk. The successful female pair skater thus must be not only small and athletic but also fearless, as witnessed for instance by the nickname of Canadian pair skater Christine "Tuffy" Hough.

Although some pairs choreography does highlight the female agency and daring involved in achieving the spectacular tricks, it is more common to aim at an impression of effortless beauty and for the extreme positions the lady attains during moves such as death spirals and some lifts at times to remove her semiotically from the realm of the human, suggesting instead an inanimate object subject to the manipulations by her partner. Commentary and training discourse that stress the male partner's responsibility for the success of pair moves—important, certainly, for reminding boys training in pairs that the safety of another human being is at stake—emphasizes the male's agency and suggests a protectionism necessary because of female vulnerability, a vulnerability that exists in this case only because of the risky feats the female partner has chosen to undertake.[9] "I think it's a more idealistic thing —she is pure, the man is stronger," says coach/choreographer and former competitive pair skater Jeff Nolt. "She goes up in the air. She hits the position in the death spiral. She is thrown in the air. In that way, she's the busier of the two. . . . Sometimes you hear it's the guy's role to show off the woman. I wouldn't teach my male partners that. I want them to be strong, if not stronger, than the woman. I think typically you look for the men to be sloppy, and just to lift the women. But they have to be better skaters than the women, because they aren't noticed as much."[10]

Typically in both pairs and ice dance there is a sexual division of labor, one shared with both ballet and exhibition ballroom dance, whereby the female partner serves as the focus of attention, presenting herself and the team as a whole directly to the audience while it is the male's function to efface himself from visual attention by presenting or drawing attention to his partner. According to this tradition, it is considered impolite or unchivalrous for the man to draw attention away from his partner and toward himself; there is no corresponding tradition of women presenting or displaying men to a spectatorial gaze. The woman as center of attention, then, remains so at the sufferance of her partner, in whom implicitly rests the power of directing the audience's gaze either to his partner or, should he choose to break convention, to himself. In one sense this tradition empowers women as performers by placing them at center stage, so to speak, and giving them the more interesting movements to perform. In another sense, however, it reinforces viewing habits whereby women are "to-be-looked-at" and thus derive meaning through appearance, in contrast to masculine meaning derived from actions.

WHAT IS ICE DANCE?

Ice dancing derives from the turn-of-the-century Viennese and English attempts to translate the waltz and other ballroom dances to the ice and to devise ballroom-style dances suitable for performance on skates. In the 1920s, informal competitions were introduced in North America and Great Britain in waltzing and in marches known as the Tenstep, or its later elaboration the Fourteenstep, and the Kilian.

The steps for these dances were soon codified into what are called "set-pattern dances," with specific edges and steps assigned to specific beats of music. In some dances, both partners perform exactly the same steps, skating in a close side-by-side dance hold known as "Kilian position." In both the European Waltz and the American Waltz, the two earliest patterns of steps set to waltz music, the partners face each other in "waltz position" (also known as "closed position"), with the lady's left hand on the man's right shoulder, the man's right hand on the lady's back, and their other hands raised and clasped to the side, as in the corresponding dance hold used in the ballroom. Because of the face-to-face position, on most steps one partner is traveling forward while the other travels backward, which means that the man and the lady perform different sequences of steps. The characteristic whirling movement of the waltz is produced by each partner successively turning a three turn, changing feet, and then stepping forward to repeat the process, either in the same direction (e.g., counterclockwise) or, with an intervening edge to change lobes, in the opposite direction. Set-pattern dances facilitate ice dancing as a social activity, because once a skater has mastered the steps of a particular dance, she or he can perform it with any partner who knows the corresponding steps and partner positions of the other part.

Standard set-pattern dances also facilitate comparisons in ice dancing competitions. With each couple performing exactly the same sequence of steps, the difficulty of the dance is held constant so judges can compare the technical skating skills and the musical expression that each couple displays while performing it. These dances came to serve a similar purpose in ice dance competition that the school figures once served in singles competition, as compulsory exercises that all competitors must perform to demonstrate their mastery of basic technical skills before proceeding to the "free" portion of the competition. This phase of competition was thus known as the "compulsory dances" or "compulsory figures," respectively.[11]

In the 1930s, while ballroom dancing enjoyed great popularity in England and live orchestras were sometimes available during evening (i.e., adult) recreational skating sessions at indoor rinks, general skating would be interrupted for "dance intervals" during which the more accomplished skaters would perform these dances, thus inspiring other skaters to learn the necessary skills to join in. Several rinks sponsored ice balls, and a number of competitions (for professionals or for professionals and amateurs alike) were held to promote the development of new dances.[12] An "original dance" event replaced the Fourteenstep at the U.S. Championships in the late 1920s, with the stipulation that "The Original Dance is any sort of a combined dance, skated to a fox-trot."[13] Throughout the 1930s and 1940s, new set-pattern dances at various levels of difficulty continued to proliferate, with a large portion of the standard repertoire deriving from the English competitions. Local clubs where ice dancing was popular would also hold intra- or interclub competitions using a variety of formats. These developments were aimed primarily at promoting ice dancing as a social activity for skating enthusiasts and as a means of interacting with skaters of the opposite sex, whether in pickup matchings for the duration of a single dance or with long-term on- and/or off-ice partners.

Meanwhile, various national governing bodies had introduced proficiency tests in the set-pattern dances and continued to refine standards for judging dance tests and competitions. In the early 1950s, the ISU developed rules, standards, and international tests for ice dance and sponsored unofficial dance competitions at the 1950 and 1951 World Championships. In 1952, ice danc-ing, consisting of compulsory dances and free dancing, became an official event at the ISU championships. Later an "original set pattern" (OSP) phase of dance competition was introduced as the middle phase of a dance compe-tition, in which each couple performed a set-pattern dance of their own com-position to the same specified dance rhythm. A few of the more successful of these OSPs were later adopted as official compulsory dances. In 1991, this phase was renamed the "original dance," and it was no longer required to re-peat the same pattern of steps on a second and third circuit of the rink.

English skaters continued to lead the sport through the 1960s, with North America and Western Europe following. Beginning in the 1970s, So-viet skaters began to claim most of the world medals. Ice dance became an Olympic event in 1976.[14]

Currently, ice dance competitions consist of one or two compulsory dances, an original dance, and a free dance. Two years before a given competitive season, the ISU selects a pool of four compulsory dances to be used during that season, and the specific dances to be used at each competition are drawn from that pool. (A separate pool is established for junior-level competition. For domestic competitions at lower levels, the individual national governing bodies such as the USFSA determine the pool of dances.) The ISU also an-nounces two years in advance the specified rhythm(s) and tempo(s) for the original dance.[15] The free dance is the opportunity for skaters to show crea-tivity through the choice of music and development of steps and other moves, with varying degrees of restrictions by the rules offered from year to year. The skaters, their coach, and often a professional choreographer choose their own music and put together their own steps for the original dance and the free dance, within the guidelines specified in the rulebook.

Because of its origins as a means of performing social dances, most spe-cifically ballroom dances, on the ice, the meanings that predominate in ice dance tend to be those inherent in the social dances from which the on-ice versions derive. In many cases, the predominant meaning of the source dance is of a particular affective state suggested by the rhythm, for instance the lightheartedness of a quickstep or the melancholy of the blues. In other cases, such as the polka or samba, ethnic affiliation takes on particular salience, with the on-ice dances designed to reproduce as authentically as possible the shapes and movement qualities associated with that dance rhythm's ethnic origins.

Ballroom dances themselves often have their origins in folk dances, which may or may not have a gendered component: some may be performed as group dances by dancers of one sex or the other, or both, others in male-female couples, often with explicit references to courting or other heterosexual behavior. As adapted for use in polite European society and by communities of European derivation in the Americas, these dances became more refined and stylized, signifying a class distinction between those performing the dances in the ballroom and their originators among the peasants of Europe and later, for the "Latin" dances, the indigenous folk of Latin America and the people of African origin who found themselves in the New World as a result of the slave trade.

Upper-class balls before and during the nineteenth century were highly formal affairs with rituals and etiquette codes governing the courtship behavior and other interactions between the sexes that took place there. Most of the dances performed involved specified steps for each participant. The waltz, with its whirling movement, close partner holds between the man and woman dancing together, and capacity for improvisation, at first proved scandalous in its suggestions of licentiousness. Eventually it gained popularity by the late nineteenth century to epitomize elegant freedom of movement and was associated with elements of romance and sexual intrigue that could occur when men and women mingled freely at dances. It was this freedom of movement and freedom of male-female association that the earliest ice dancers sought to reproduce on ice.

As the twentieth century began, dance halls and cabarets where young men and women could dance together without the supervision of older family members who would have been present at a formal dance increased the meanings that dancing now implied of liberation, especially for young women, from social restrictions. The new rhythms and movements of ragtime, jazz, and swing and the Latin dances, with their more sensual hip movements, being introduced to European and North American society signified still greater degrees of freedom, informality, and explicit sexuality than had the waltz and distanced new generations of dancers from the relative restraint of their parents' generations. By midcentury, many of these dances had gained respectability and had found their way into the most staid of ballrooms as older couples continued to perform the popular dances of their own youth and to pass them on to the next generation, again often with cruder elements stylized or refined.[16]

Thus, during the period while ice dancers were adapting more and more of these dances for the ice and codifying rules for competition, ballroom dancing was a popular form of social entertainment. The predominant unit was the individual male-female couple, so that even dances that had begun as group or solo dances were transformed in the ballroom to couple dances. The unit of ice dance competition therefore also became that of the male-female couple, and as ice dancers sought to expand their repertoire by drawing directly on folk dances as well as from the ballroom repertoire, many of these folk dances also had to be adapted for performance by couples even as they were being translated to movement on skates.

Gender theorist Judith Butler describes what she terms the *heterosexual matrix* as "a hegemonic discursive/epistemic model of gender intelligibility that assumes that for bodies to cohere and make sense there must be a stable gender (masculine expresses male, feminine expresses female) that is oppositionally and hierarchically defined through the compulsory practice of heterosexuality."[17] In other words, within the dominant social structure "masculinity" and "femininity" are assumed always to be associated with male and female bodies, respectively, and to derive meaning through their difference from each other and through heterosexuality as the relationship that defines the social structure. The dances that have become standardized within the ballroom and thereby the ice dance repertoire represent this social structuring by organizing the world within the aesthetic frame of the dance into male-female couples, most often further defined according to masculine desire for the female object. Femaleness, or femininity, with which in this matrix it is coextensive, therefore derives meaning predominantly in terms of desirability to males.

Any dance that relies on male-female pairing reproduces and thus represents a social structure organized around such couples as the social norm. Any excess or otherwise unpaired members of either sex present a problem that is generally ignored by excluding unpartnered dancers from the representational frame of the individual dance, although seeking for and switching partners *between* dances may provide as much interest in social (or dramatic) contexts as the dances themselves. In ice dance competition, unpartnered skaters (the vast majority of them female, given the demographics of the skating population) have no place in the international competitive structure and only a marginal one at lower levels of competition.[18] In the social structure represented by competitive ice dance, in contrast to "real life," everyone is a member of a male-female couple—there are no "old maids" and no re-lationships, sexual or otherwise, between members of the same sex. Even in dances in which sexuality is not foregrounded, the dance couple remains, inevitably, a *couple* expressing the mood of the dance and thus representing a world organized according to male-female dyads. In addition, many specific dances convey specific images or implied narratives, usually representative of sexual behavior, about relationships between males and females.

In compulsory dances, specific steps are assigned to the male and the female partner, with more backward steps being given to the woman. This matches the traditions of ballroom dance, in which the man usually starts the dance moving forward and the woman backward. In twentieth-century social dance practice, couples tend to improvise on the dance floor within the character of the music being played, with the man, usually the larger and stronger member of the couple, leading. Because ice dancing consists of set patterns or rehearsed programs, it is less necessary for one partner to control the movement of the couple; nevertheless, in ice dance too the male partner is expected to lead. Giving the woman the more difficult steps makes her more physically vulnerable and therefore dependent on her partner's physi-cal support, thus replicating the prevalent social/economic structures of het-erosexual couplehood in the relationships of the bodies on the dance floor or on the ice.[19]

An exception would be rock-and-roll and some disco-style dances origi-nating after midcentury, in which touching one's dance partner, or even danc-ing with a partner, is not required. Because these freeform post-1960 social dances are less easily adapted to the existing couple structure of the sport, ice dancers in the later decades of the century have mostly avoided drawing on these sources for their free dance ideas. For the rock-and-roll OSP of the 1983 competitive season and the jive in 1998, the majority of music choices and even more of the movement ideas have looked to the 1950s for inspiration. The types of dances that young skaters in the late twentieth or early twenty-first century might engage in when they dance at parties or nightclubs them-selves thus likely have less relation to the dances they perform on the ice than had been true for earlier generations of ice dancers. The leading ice dance competitors (usually young adults who have been training since childhood or early adolescence) are no longer translating their own dance culture to the ice but rather are socialized through the compulsory dance structure and the in-structions of coaches and choreographers to reproduce the dance culture of their grandparents and of the members of the ISU hierarchy who make the rules and judge the competitions.[20]

In both compulsory and original dances, the traditional character of specific ballroom dance styles circumscribes the relationship between the partners. Cultural analyst Sally Peters describes ballroom dance as role playing that "reconstructs and reiterates courting rituals that idealize the female body. . . . Here fantasies are brought to life. . . . All men are suave, handsome, and powerful, while all women are beautiful, desirable, and vulnerable."[21] The image projected by the woman may be ethereal, as in the waltz; haughty, as in the tango; or openly seductive, as in the Latin dances:[22] "As the man frames and displays the woman, he invokes his utmost artistry, making the woman a virtual icon of the feminine. In the process, his theatricalized efforts to win the woman elevate him to the realm of the idealized male."[23] The narrative of all these dances presents a more or less aloof female who eludes yet finally (or simultaneously, given that the images persist throughout the dance) submits to male desire.[24]

This vision of male/female relationship also informs role playing on the ice. A former competitor at the Canadian national level describes young skaters as being trained to perform relationships in which "the boys pursue the girls and the girls are all snots."[25] Or, as Dick Button explains, "You know, the story of ice dancing is really the same every year. It's the battle of the sexes. He tames her, but it isn't easy."[26]

In the four-minute free dance, the final phase of all upper-level dance competitions and thus the one most often televised, the skaters can choose their own styles and their own meanings. Each team's individual approach to the sport makes this phase of the competition most compelling for viewers. Because of the greater scope for personal expression afforded to the individual couples, it is in this portion of ice dance competitions that conflicting meanings about gender and male-female relations may be most clearly played out. What counts toward the overall artistic impression in the judges' and spectators' eyes is not the real-life relationship between the skaters but their performance of relationship on the ice. This performance, which we might call a relationship-persona, is constructed of images evoked by costuming, movement quality, and the physical interactions between the skaters. Off the ice, the partners might be brother and sister, they might be dating or married to others, they may even be divorced from each other (or have married for purely functional reasons such as to gain citizenship to compete at the Olympics), one or both might be gay, or they may simply not have enough in common to maintain more than businesslike relationship. On the ice, however, the received conventions of the discipline strongly code the participants as conventionally masculine or feminine and the relationships as heterosexual.

OFF THE DANCE FLOOR AND ONTO THE STAGE

Traditionally, the free dance provided an opportunity to display versatility, using three or more different pieces of music and correspondingly different styles of dancing to express the separate character of each piece. In the 1970s, the top Soviet teams pioneered an emphasis on the dramatic qualities of ice dancing, choreographing programs around a single ballroom theme and incorporating elements of ballet and theatrical training into their performances.

In 1979 Canadians Lorna Wighton and John Dowding broke with this tradition to present a single-theme program to ballet (rather than ballroom) music from *Swan Lake.* In the early to mid-1980s, teams such as Americans Judy Blumberg and Michael Seibert, Soviets Natalia Bestemianova and Andrei Bukin, and most particularly Britons Jayne Torvill and Christopher Dean (who dominated ice dance competition in the early 1980s) continued to take ice dance away from its social dance origins and toward the realm of art dance by employing less rhythmically predictable music, playing more individualized characters, and experimenting with body positions less rooted in the traditional ballroom dance holds.

Inspiration came from the classical ballet pas de deux as the high-art instance of a man and woman dancing together.[27] The ballet tradition, which reached its peak during the nineteenth century as a product of European Romanticism's fascination with (male) heroic individualism and with mystery and mysticism, presents the image of woman as ethereal, unattainable, and often the supernatural object of the male hero's desire.[28]

With few exceptions, when skaters invented original moves, they continued to reinforce images of male strength and control contrasted with female flexibility, pliability, and "to-be-looked-at-ness." Usually, the woman skates in front when the couple faces the same direction or backward when they face each other. She departs from an upright posture to create for aesthetic purposes shapes not normally seen in everyday life (and often, especially in lifts where she has no direct contact with the ice, impossible to attain without the support of her partner). She smiles at or otherwise relates directly to the audience. The man, meanwhile, maintains physical control over his own positions and movements, which remain more recognizably human, and presents his partner rather than himself to the audience as an aesthetic object. The narratives continue to be primarily about heterosexual romance.[29] Torvill and Dean's 1984 gold-medal-winning free dance to Ravel's *Bolero,* probably the most well known single program in the history of ice dance, epitomizes these trends.

The Bolero program represents a vision "of star-crossed lovers destined never to be together, who make a pact to climb to the top of a volcano and make love as they throw themselves into the fiery pit."[30] Even without this explicit narrative, the overall impression is one of eroticism or yearning, with many moments in which the skaters reach into the distance. Bob Ottum of *Sports Illustrated* commented, "This one should be shown only after the kids have gone to bed. . . . Perhaps one writer best described it when he turned to a colleague in the press gallery and whispered, 'How do you spell "lubricious"?'"[31] The music choice is a cliché of seduction scenes, but a close analysis of the performance shows just how this theme is figured in terms of sexual difference.

The program begins with symmetrical images of mutuality and equality as the skaters, facing each other, on their knees, look into each other's eyes as they sway back and curve around each other and manipulate each other's bodies. Once the skating begins in earnest, for much of the program, Jayne's focus is choreographed out and away from the couple, not acknowledging the audience, but gazing, either yearning or impassive, into the middle distance. Facing toward her, Christopher looks either at her or past her into that same distance. Although there are subsequent moments of sustained eye contact, this pattern of gaze occurs for more than half of the program's four minutes. When he looks at her, it is most often at the part of her body he is manipulating. He provides the physical impulse or initiation for almost all the changes of position between their two bodies, including lifts and dips. The initially established relationship of reciprocal support becomes one in which the woman unresistingly allows the man to position her, to control her movement.

At one point, the two skaters link their bent free legs below the knee and skate a small circle, like a slow pair spin, around a center point between them. As they gaze at each other, this moment creates a brief return of the symmetrical imagery of the opening, its circular symmetry suggesting the yin/yang symbol and, like the opening, an equal partnership between lovers through focused mutual regard and reciprocal partnering roles. To exit the move, he grasps her hand overhead and swings her around him and out of the circle.

Later, he grabs her face with one hand and brings his close to it in a brief suggestion of a kiss, perhaps to seal the pact. This moment that most nearly denotes sexual intimacy is entirely enacted by the male.

When she steps into his hand (held at waist level) and straight up, as he assists with his other hand on her upper arm, to briefly ride like a ship's figurehead into the wind, the woman takes most of the initiative in this particular lift, which might symbolize her leading the couple onward toward their intended purpose, one of the few points where her movement represents an active role in the narrative. As she steps down from the lift and glides forward on one foot, he continues to hold her other leg and uses it to spin her around and then to pull her onto a backward edge and to pull her along on it, yet another one of many instances in which he manipulates her body and the relationship between their two bodies while she seems neither to assist nor to resist. Jayne's expertise allows her to maintain skating edges as she submits to these manipulations, but this expertise is not foregrounded—rather, viewers see the man placing the woman in a variety of extreme positions.

The man's control of the woman's body becomes most evident in the climactic penultimate moment, as Christopher lifts Jayne by her armpits, swinging her feet off the ice and sharply flipping her body sideways through the air, twice. This maneuver is the most dangerous and spectacular move in the program—and the one in which Jayne's body most fully becomes a passive, manipulated object. At the conclusion, the two skaters sprawl on the ice (as if in the aftermath of sexual climax represented by those swinging flips?), reaching for something that eludes their grasp. Even at this moment, Jayne is the one who reaches across the empty ice, while Christopher reaches toward her.

The predominant pattern of gaze, in which she rarely acknowledges him, establishes a relationship in which the female becomes, on an emotional level, an inaccessible object of male regard. If she desires, the object of her desire is, evidently, not her partner, but something else "out there." And yet, because the narrative of this dance is one of eroticism, the woman's active engagement, as manifested through visual attention, with her partner or with the feats she performs with her own body does not appear to be a necessary component of that eroticism. If this ice dance represents sexual passion, her contribution seems primarily to be to lie back and win the gold for England.

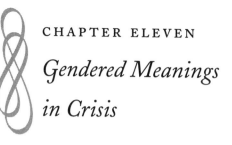

CHAPTER ELEVEN

Gendered Meanings
in Crisis

$\mathcal{F}$ollowing the 1984 season, Torvill and Dean abandoned amateur competition to create a professional ice show, where they could explore the possibilities of ice dancing without worrying about judges and rules.[1] Meanwhile, the amateurs continued to experiment with stories, music, and movements outside the ballroom tradition, and the judges approved or disapproved, often unpredictably. The Soviets Bestemianova and Bukin won their first of four world championships interpreting the story of Carmen in 1985. The following year, Canadians Karyn and Rod Garossino found themselves marked down at home and internationally with their Romeo and Juliet free dance because, the ISU later informed them, ballet was considered to be pair skating.[2] The new British champions, Karen Barber and Nicky Slater, performed an oriental-themed "Dragon Dance." Americans Suzanne Semanick and Scott Gregory took inspiration from a theme of defectors escaping from a totalitarian regime; "Scott swung his leg over Suzy and she, in one of the first sexless role reversals, swung hers over him."[3]

THE DUCHESNAYS AND DENIAL OF DIFFERENCE

Into this post-"Bolero" confusion over ice dance's identity skated the French Canadian Duchesnay siblings. Not progressing as fast they thought they should in Canada, they took advantage of their dual citizenship to represent France. From the beginning of their international career in 1986, judges did not know what to make of their aggressive style, more reminiscent of their early years as pair skaters than of the refined technique favored in ice dance, and awarded them both technical and artistic marks spanning a wider range than any of their competitors.[4] Once Dean began to choreograph their programs in 1988, they introduced a whole new range of meanings to the issue of a man and woman dancing together on the ice.

At the 1988 Olympics in Calgary, the Duchesnays skated a program called "Savage Rites." Paul and Isabelle describe it best, to an interviewer conditioned to associating ice dance with amorousness:

[Paris-Match:] Is it a parade of love, a ritual dance?

Paul: It's rather a scenario where we're two survivors in a jungle surrounded by a thousand dangers.

[Paris-Match:] With lots of sensuality, like a real couple.

Isabelle: Except in playing this couple, instead we're a Tarzan and Jane who are brother and sister. We warn and protect each other from invisible enemies.[5]

No one expected the Duchesnays to win an Olympic medal so early in their international competitive career, but the novelty and the originality of their style made an impression. "Their comedic, melodramatic tango and percussive, tribal freestyle program were favorites of the Calgary crowds, but the widely disparate scores they received indicated that many judges simply did not know what to make of their program."[6]

The following year the Duchesnays won their first world medal, a bronze. Experimentation became the name of the game as other competitors followed suit, and ice dancing's ballroom origins were stretched to the breaking point. But the gender dynamics in the Duchesnays' programs, perhaps in a conscious effort at "avoiding the incestuous connotations of an amorous relationship between skaters who are brother and sister," remained far more resistant of the traditional clichés than other ice dancing couples.[7]

The 1991 competition season, during which thematic experimentation seemed to reach its peak, provides a case in point. NBC Sports chose five programs to present in their hour of free dance television coverage from the World Championships in Munich.

Americans Elizabeth Punsalan and Jerod Swallow had a catchy free dance built around the theme of stock car racing. In black stretch suits adorned with racing colors and with Elizabeth's checkered flag skirt, they played the roles of race cars, enacting test trials, pit stops, and the race. Their matching costumes prompted ABC's coverage of this program at the U.S. Nationals to refer to them as two drivers on the same team, whereas NBC's Dick Enberg commenting on the program at Worlds wondered aloud "Who will win, twenty-year-old Elizabeth or twenty-four-year-old Jerod?" suggesting a contest between the two skaters. Rather than seeking a single coherent narrative, it might be more appropriate to consider the program as incorporating a variety of images, including the final images of defeat and victory, related to the racing theme.

This concept would seem to defy gender, but note that the mime passages more often cast the male skater as driver and the female as car than the other way around, in keeping with representational conventions whereby females are more commonly associated with the status of inanimate object (or alien "other") while males usually remain aligned with the role of human agent. At several points, Jerod's literal control of Elizabeth's body also controls the narrative imagery, as when she weaves in front of and behind him as if changing lanes to pass a slower car while both skaters glide in bent-leg spread-eagle positions, with no additional strokes to gain speed, her variations in speed relative to his achieved by his pushing or pulling her by the hand. Similarly, the program ends with Elizabeth wiping out and Jerod crossing the "finish line" with one arm pointing upward in triumph. They achieve the wipeout by Jerod pulling Elizabeth under his legs from back to front, once successfully, the second time sending her rolling across the ice. The man's choreographed control of the woman's body thus results in male victory within the final image of the performance.

The Finnish team of Susanna Rahkomo and Petri Kokko (she in tutu and red skates, he in tails) portrayed the characters of Blondie and Dagwood in presenting what NBC commentator Robin Cousins referred to as a "comedy spoof not only of the ballet, but maybe of some of their fellow competitors." Their routine deconstructed by parodying, through facial expressions, exaggeration, and off-kilter alignment, the conventions of romantic pursuit, presenting a ballerina who knows that her pursuer is a prig, knows that she is being (physically) manipulated ridiculously, and shares that knowledge with the audience; however, she chooses to play the game and let him display her as an object for mass adulation. He hauls her off the ice and around his body in a prolonged combination lift, using gravity to swing her from one position to the next like the proverbial sack of potatoes. She wraps her legs around his neck and trails upside down behind him as he glides forward standing very erect and serious. He runs after her on his toepicks, hands clasped over his heart, as she skates gleefully and ungracefully out of his reach. He grabs her foot and pulls her in a wide back inner edge curve, staying well inside the circle so that her body travels past her free leg, which is now lifted in front of her rather than behind. Her face asks the audience, "What is being done to me?" She turns her skating foot forward and smiles, but his pull on her foot turns her back to the backward edge. Still holding her foot, he skates past her, close to her so that her foot must stretch above her head and then down to pass her body. Once he lets go, she must skate fast to catch up—not to pursue him romantically, but to rejoin them so they can complete the program, with a standard ballet lift returning her to the conventions of object of display. The stereotyped roles within the narrative of pursuit are thus revealed as constructs, not inherent and inevitable in the facts of maleness and femaleness.

The top three dance teams in 1991 were the Duchesnays; the Soviets Marina Klimova and Sergei Ponomarenko, then two-time world champions who had established a reputation as traditionalists with a light, elegant touch; and another Soviet couple, Maya Usova and Aleksandr Zhulin, who leaned toward drama and passion. Like many Russian teams, both these couples were married in real life (Usova and Zhulin later divorced but until 1998 still skated together professionally) and were known for excelling both technically and artistically.

Usova and Zhulin later described their 1991 free dance as being about Paganini and his muse. In the opening moment, Maya in a short, flowing Empire-style beige dress stands posed like draped statuary as Aleksandr, dressed in brown tights and loose beige shirt, hops a circle around her crouched on his toepicks, then gestures with his hand to call her to life. One could interpret her initial arm gestures as a stylized depiction of bowing a violin and one or two of the lifts as a violinist cradling his instrument, a reading that would cast the female partner in the role of both supernatural entity (muse) and inanimate object. The program as a whole is skated largely with intense expression, incorporating repeated little runs and turns on the toepicks, knee slides, and sensuous flowing and intertwining movements enhanced by the billowing costumes, creating an overall aura of Romanticism and uncanniness. Zhulin is such a flamboyant performer that it is impossible to see him as displaying his partner any more than he displays himself, although there is never any attempt for her to display him. She remains cool and elegant, but focused into the relationship.

Klimova and Ponomarenko, having narrowly retained their title the previous year on the strength of superior compulsories and original dance but having lost the free dance to the Duchesnays, abandoned their traditional approach to meet the Duchesnays on their own territory. Their program, choreographed to music from the film *Lawrence of Arabia*, escapes gendering by representing different elements of nature, with Sergei interpreting "the sands of the desert, Marina the wind."[8] Sergei wears a brown unitard, Marina a blue one that lacked a skirt to mark her as woman. Instead, billowing panels set in the sides of the legs mark her as wind. She also evokes wind imagery by performing in several contexts an undulating curve with one or both raised arms. The assignment of elements follows spatial logic because Sergei, as sand, remains the ground supporting Marina in the air during lifts and presenting her when she skates in front of him. This logic replicates classical gender positions, with the female skater the one being offered to the audience's gaze, as well as embodying the more "ethereal" position. She does embody an active principle, clearly propelling herself into many of the lifts rather than being passively lifted. One moment in the program can be read as the wind lifting the sand into the air, not through Marina physically lifting Sergei but through her raising and rotating her arm in a gesture of conjuring as he performs two half-loop jumps, producing an image of scattering appropriate to the movement of desert sands. The relationship the two skaters perform thus is not gendered stereotypically, but it is figured as difference, as opposing elements.

In the context of these programs by their Soviet rivals, the Duchesnays had brought their controversial "Reflections" program to the European championships in Sofia in January of 1991. They dressed identically in blue-violet trousers and shirts, with Isabelle's shoulder-length hair French-braided against her head to simulate Paul's shorter curls. The choreography centered around a theme of mirror images. Isabelle describes the theme as "a single and same person, who regards her reflection in the mirror. All the aspects of her personality unwind before her. She attempts to know who she really is, why she exists."[9] It was not always possible to distinguish which skater was Paul and which was Isabelle.[10] All markers of difference seem to have been suppressed in service of the mirror image theme; the skaters' bodies are gendered as neutral.

The intention in the costuming and choreography of this program was to erase difference; the difference erased was Isabelle's identity as a female. The Duchesnays might have chosen to wear unitards, as did Klimova and Ponomarenko, which would carry connotations of dance or sport far more strongly than of either masculine or feminine gender, although they do allow direct perception of the specific form of the sexed body. Whereas unitards reveal the bulge of the penis, or lack thereof, trousers carry the symbolic weight of the phallus. In the world of figure skating, where the phallic privilege of male skaters is already precarious, this choice of costume protects Paul from the loss of status in being represented as androgynous/castrated. At the same time, in presenting Isabelle as androgynous/phallic, the choice reveals the arbitrariness of defining gender in terms of dress.

The "Reflections" costumes, unlike the more commonly seen skating dress, stretch suit, or unitard, would be appropriate worn by either a man or woman off the ice. Within the sign system of ice dance, in which women never wear trousers, they weight the neutrality semiotically toward maleness. Dressed in clothing that would not draw a second glance on the street, Isabelle is, in fact, cross-dressed on the ice. As subsequent events revealed, this instance of transvestitism profoundly disturbed the skating world, so accustomed to perceiving male/female difference as a given.[11]

The lack of emotional content in the Duchesnays' program did not go over well with the judges: "This mirror game is too intellectual. The public sulks. The judges use this to leave them on the second step of the podium."[12] According to Dean, the judges "placed it second, and we were told in no uncertain terms that there was no hope of winning the 1991 Worlds less than two months later with it. 'Too contemporary,' was the message. 'Don't be too avant garde.'"[13]

That year, the Duchesnays were determined to win the World Championship. They showed up in Munich six weeks later with a completely different free program. The previous year, they had skated a program called "Missing," in honor of the disappeared victims of Latin American dictatorships, a version of which had earlier been skated by Torvill and Dean in their professional touring show. The new program was a continuation entitled "Missing II." As in 1990, Isabelle wore a red leotard and tattered knee-length skirt; Paul wore dark trousers, a blue striped shirt with slashed sleeves, and a red tie.[14]

Although the skaters are costumed according to their respective sex, the choreography avoids narrativizing gender binarism as it constructs a narrative of mutual triumph. The program opens with delicate guitar accompaniment. The skaters' faces are serious, almost neutral, conveying a sense of disconnection and anomie. As they walk forward, Isabelle twice steps onto the heel of her blade, a position impossible to maintain; when her weight inevitably drops backward, Paul catches her each time and rotates her on her heel. She holds him by the waist as he reaches forward for something ungraspable and then as he arches backward from the upper back—a position he would be unable to sustain without support, and one seen fairly often in the context of a female skater displaying her flexibility while supported by a male partner, although in this case there is not much flexibility to highlight. Paul lifts Isabelle with one hand and swings her around his waist. Twice he braces himself against her arms and stretches himself out to a low cantilevered diagonal as she visibly steels herself to take his weight. She drops diagonally to one side and then to the other as he supports her with one hand under her armpit. Although it is clearly easier for Paul to support Isabelle's weight than for her to support his, this opening section seems to be about their common vulnerability (in actuality to gravity, metaphorically to oppression) and need for each other's support.

As the music changes tone from contemplative to upbeat, he supports her in a sequence of off-center poses reminiscent of his reach and arch at the beginning of the program; she then springs erect with a clearly choreographed smile to the viewers. Beginning with a sequence of bouncy backward side-to-side hops, from this point on they skate the program at increasingly high speed. Their exuberance and animated faces connect with the audience, who clap out the rhythm from here to the end. The skaters are no longer oppressed but in control of their destiny.

They alternate sequences of parallel skating, including a folk dance–like grapevine passage, with sequences in which Paul displays Isabelle and Isabelle displays Paul. As the two skaters continue to gain speed, they raise their fists in gestures of triumph. The program ends with Paul on his back, sliding along the ice on the back of his shirt as well as on his blades, and Isabelle riding with her hips on his knees, her back arched, and her arms flexed victoriously. This whole fast section, comprising approximately three-quarters of the program, becomes a symbolic victory over oppression and an actual victory for the Duchesnays, who succeeded in winning the 1991 world title.[15]

Many of the 1991 free dances, including the five broadcast by NBC and discussed here, drew on theatrical rather than ballroom approaches to dance and thus had to define the relationship between the male and female partner through means other than the traditional ballroom, or ballet, configurations. Rahkomo and Kokko, by foregrounding and exaggerating the conventional roles, and the Duchesnays, by avoiding them (particularly in "Reflections"), most clearly revealed gender roles as constructs. The Duchesnays best exemplify the gender crisis that seems to underlie the insistent retreat from experimental, theatrical ice dance in the years following the 1992 competitive season.

Because 1992 was an Olympic year, more was at stake for the three top couples. Each felt assured of a medal, but of course each wanted the gold. They therefore chose free dance themes that could demonstrate creativity without the risk of offending anyone. The Duchesnays were the favorites as the reigning world champions and the home team in Albertville, France; however, Klimova and Ponomarenko achieved consistently higher marks and so finished first.

Usova and Zhulin's program on the theme of statues coming to life (during which they strike poses of famous statues), skated to music from Vivaldi's *Four Seasons,* incorporated many images of symmetry and parallelism, and thus equality. It is not about sexual difference, but it does convey sexual attraction. These are passionate, eroticized statues, and the skaters' gazes are focused centripetally into the relationship, at each other's bodies and into each other's eyes.

The Duchesnays skated to music from *West Side Story,* as sister and brother Maria and Bernardo. This Maria, however, seems to be more actively involved in the street warrior culture—as one of the Sharks—than the original Maria in the musical, who lives in the female culture of "I Feel Pretty." The

lifts early in the program seem to be for the purpose of gaining a higher vantage point to keep a lookout for enemies. Later in the program, on two separate occasions, Isabelle lifts Paul off the ice, or at any rate holds him while
he flips his legs up and either over his head or around her waist. This time,
the Duchesnays erase sexual difference by making the girl one of the boys.
Again masculinity is valorized as normative, but it is not the exclusive prop-
erty of biological males. In her diagonally cut purple dress, Isabelle may be
wearing the right clothes, but not the right gender. As in the "Savage Rights"
and "Missing" programs, the man and the woman perform on the same side
in a larger struggle (in broadest terms, the struggle for individual survival),
rather than struggling between themselves for ascendancy and the power to
define their relationship (with the implicit teleology of reproduction, necessary for species survival).

Klimova and Ponomarenko's program, entitled "A Man and a Woman:
From the Mundane to the Sublime," returned to images of difference and
woman as other. Sergei wore the familiar romantic loose shirt and trousers,
given a somewhat Russian flavor by a sash at the waist; Marina wore a black
unitard with a spiderweb across her chest and floaty gray chiffon like web-
bing or wings between her arms and sides, with her curly red hair loose over
her shoulders. In these black and gray costumes, they skated a highly eroticized duet to music by J. S. Bach. Their lifts primarily display her beauty
and flexibility and his strength. At the two moments when she disappears
behind him, giving him over to the spectators' gaze (in a pivot and a spread
eagle), her hands snake under his armpits and across his chest, rooting the
display in the context of sensual indulgence. In the final tableau, she sits on
the ice while he dives into her embrace. She then bends her head to kiss
him, covering him with her hair, in a pose reminiscent of the "vampire" images of Edvard Munch, in which similarly longhaired women threaten to
engulf men within their embrace. This image and the spider imagery of her
costume suggest that in the relationship between "A Man and a Woman,"
the man is normative and the woman an exotic danger.

One could say that the Duchesnays introduced their innovations purely
through making a virtue of necessity. If they fully enacted the erotic narratives of either ballroom or classical dance, they might raise the specter of in-
cest. Also, Isabelle is close enough to Paul in age and size to claim a position
of equal rather than of little sister. The aggressiveness, intensity, and lack of
refinement in the Duchesnays' stroking and their physicality on the ice,
stemming in part from their early pairs background, highlighted supposedly
"masculine" characteristics of athleticism in the female partner to a higher
degree than the most athletic pair teams because of Isabelle's larger size; their

aggressive qualities also particularly stood out in the context of ice dancing, compared to the typical measured restraint typical of North American and British teams or to the highly refined intensity of the Soviets. Yet the necessity of a sister-brother team downplaying erotic themes and the greater physical similarity their relationship led them to perform gender representations more in keeping with late-twentieth-century ideologies of womanhood outside the world of ice dancing, showing the woman as active and strong.

BACK TO THE BALLROOM

Throughout the 1980s, as during previous decades, the ISU technical committee on dance had continued to fine-tune the rules and definitions of ice dance in response to changing ice dance practice, explicitly declaring legal or illegal innovations that prominent competitive dance teams introduced on the ice. Following the 1992 season, in response to concerns that ice dance might be removed from the Olympic Games because it had strayed too far into the realm of the theatrical, where aspects of subjective appeal to audiences and judges were overshadowing the objective technical criteria of the sport, they tightened the rules to stress once again the connection between ice dancing, including the free dance portion of the event, and ballroom dancing.[16]

Some of the new rules clarified that certain types of choreographic moves such as "i) standing, sitting or leaning on the partner's boots and/or legs, ii) pushing or pulling partner by the boot and/or leg; iii) holding of the partner's skates (boots/blades); iv) sitting or lying over the partner's leg without having at least one foot on the ice; v) lying on the ice" were not considered to demonstrate skating technique and would no longer be permitted. In addition, dance lifts are "not to display feats of strength or acrobatics. Therefore, sitting or lying on the partner's shoulder or back is considered to be a feat of prowess and is not permitted."[17] As Hans Kutschera, president of the technical committee on dance, explained,

> The ITCD (International Technical Committee of Ice Dancing) has been concerned about the free dance programs for some time. They have been trying to find a way to distinguish and separate the choreography of the free dance from that of pairs programs and exhibition skating. Particularly during the last season, numerous [*sic*] criticized the free dance for not being sufficiently competitive and athletic.
>
> The new rules attempt to establish clearer directives concerning the choice of music. The music must be suitable for dancing and it must have

a beat and a melody. The composition must be musically arranged in such a way that it is appropriate for ballroom dancing. The choreography must be technically difficult ant [*sic*] it must express the character of the music. Precise rules have been established for the composition of the free dance with respect to athletic elements. Lifts typical of pairs skating must be avoided and violations of this rule will be penalized up to 0.4. A text has been clearly written regarding the costumes which must be in keeping with the athletic nature of ice dancing. To be correct, choreography for the original dance program must reflect the character of a ballroom dance, which means there must be a preponderance of dance positions that interpret the music, and the dancers may not skate continuously in open or side by side positions. These latter positions do not correspond to the nature of dance; they are easier technically; and furthermore, they belong more appropriately to pairs skating.[18]

Most of these restrictions, along with previously existing restrictions on the number and type of lifts, jumps, and spinning movements permitted (in the free dance—with few exceptions such moves were not permitted in the original dance at all), seem designed clearly enough to place the emphasis on skating skills. Penalizing such moves with deductions, however, rather than simply specifying that they would receive no credit in the technical mark, has the effect of legislating the types of images considered acceptable in ice dance. As a feature aired by CBS during their coverage of the 1994 Olympic ice dance competition put it, "dying on the ice," as Torvill and Dean had done at the end of their influential "Bolero" program and numerous other dance teams and singles skaters had ended their programs in the intervening decade, was no longer acceptable, evidently because such acts evoked theatrical associations in addition to the fact that with only body parts other than the skate blades on the ice they could hardly be considered skating.

Another area in which the ISU clarified its policy was with regard to music. Rhythmic interpretation (and particularly "correct" expression of established social dance rhythms) had always been a more important criterion in ice dance than in other disciplines of skating, to the point of being a defining characteristic. The second mark for compulsory dances, for instance, is known as "timing and expression." In 1992, the new rules specified that music for the free dance "must be arranged and orchestrated for the dance floor" and added that "music arranged and orchestrated initially for use on the stage or in the theatre is not permitted if, in its original form it is not suitable for use on the dance floor. . . . In this case, the music must be rearranged and reorchestrated."[19] The insistence on an audible, steady beat facilitates standardized evaluation of the skaters' interpretations of the rhythms, thus enhancing the objective "sport" as opposed to subjective "theatre" associations as defined by the ISU in its discussions with the International Olympic Committee.

This insistence also specifically reinforces the association of ice dance and ballroom dance through the aural imagery employed, encouraging construction of free dances around ballroom themes and limiting the possibilities for nonballroom types of imagery. In a social dance context, whether on ice or on the dance floor, music with a steady beat serves the very practical purpose of allowing couples to join in at regularly recurring points in the music (e.g., every eight counts) and to improvise and dance to music they have not previously practiced to. For competitive original and free dances, however, which are generally rehearsed for months and skated only by the couple for whom they were originally designed, such considerations are irrelevant.[20]

Finally, the ruling that "Men must wear trousers, not tights. Ladies must wear skirts" reinforces the return to the decorum of the ballroom.[21] It also suggests that much of the discomfort with the direction ice dance had taken may derive from discomfort with a lack of clear difference between masculine and feminine images.

During the mid-1990s, in light of these new directives from the ISU, the focus returned to social dance, with a preponderance of Latin, blues, swing, and gypsy or other folk themes in free dances. As intended, complex steps once again took precedence over posing, lifts, and other highlight moves. Efforts toward originality made it somewhat more common than a decade or two earlier for the men to take positions of being displayed or supported by their partners, although almost always within the context of an assumed couple relationship.

A new development has been the frequent use of "hydroblading"—a variety of low-to-the-ice moves, some relying on a hand or elbow resting on the ice, popularized by the Canadian champions and 1996–1999 world bronze medalists Shae-Lynn Bourne and Victor Kraatz.[22] Bourne and Kraatz were not the first skaters to perform such low-to-the-ice maneuvers—some variations had been around at least since the 1930s—but they made this type of move into their signature, introducing several variations that relied on two bodies balanced against each other as staple highlights that recurred in almost all of their programs and inspiring other dance teams to experiment with similar moves of their own. In one such move, referred to as the "Shae-crusher," Shae-Lynn performs a back shoot-the-duck circling around her hand on the ice while Victor stretches out into a death-spiral-like position resting his side along hers with her body taking most of his weight. Hydro-blading offered opportunities for an edge-based expansion of ice dance's technical vocabulary, but Bourne and Kraatz drew criticism from some dance specialists for not integrating these moves better into the choreography of their programs. As Christopher Dean remarked, "I think they've got to be careful that they're not just using them as tricks, as though they're just placed in there. I think they've got to come from the choreography, they've got to develop into that move."[23] An international judge notes that hydroblading is "being discouraged. It's now outlawed to skate with a hand on the ice. It doesn't encourage good skating, it's a trick. It was a real turn-off when Bourne and Kraatz did that in the tango."[24] Because hydroblading moves became such signatures for Bourne and Kraatz and their fans would cheer loudly whenever one or both of the skaters departed significantly from the vertical, at competitions where Canadians made up a large portion of the audience these moves stood out from the flow of the dance as isolated tricks even more than in venues where the crowd was less vocal.

During the 1996 season, when they won their first World Championship bronze medal, Bourne and Kraatz emphasized the athleticism of their approach to ice dance, in contrast to the more traditional ballroom styles seen from the other top teams. The following year, in response to suggestions that they increase the complexity and danciness of their free dance, they added a hint of elegance to their primarily athletic, non-narrative approach in adopting a ballroom theme skating to the overture to *High Society,* using mostly quickstep/swing rhythms to emphasize their soft knee action and athleticism. Only their costumes and the occasional reliance on traditional dance holds suggested any gendered identity for each partner. Their particular choice of rhythms allowed Bourne and Kraatz to maintain their emphasis on athleticism and technique, without relying on the erotic narratives attached to other ballroom rhythms, while still adhering to the prevailing rules and guidelines. Both the male and female partner present themselves as athletes, both capable of assuming extreme positions and of supporting the other's weight, while the costumes, rhythms, and dance holds continue to root the performance within the ballroom tradition, as they had been advised, and within ballroom's tradition of male-female couplehood.

Meanwhile, other teams were seeking ways to branch out from the traditional themes while adhering to the music restrictions. Defending world champions Oksana Grishuk and Evgeny Platov of Russia and the French team of Marina Anissina and Gwendal Peizerat both chose Middle Eastern themes for their 1997 free dances, while the second-place Russian team of Anzhelika Krylova and Oleg Ovsiannikov combined the ballroom and the-

In their trademark low-to-the-ice move known as the
"Shae-crusher," Shae-Lynn Bourne supports Victor
Kraatz. Photo © by J. Barry Mittan.

atrical approaches with a dramatic story dance to Khatchatourian's "Masquerade Waltz."

Both of the Russian teams' free dances that year involved narratives of male control of female sexuality. In Grishuk and Platov's, "There is a story and it's basically, he fancies her, she says no, and in the end, he throws her in the dungeon"; in Krylova and Ovsiannikov's, "This is the story of a man who comes home from a waltz and finds his wife, suspects his wife of being unfaithful. . . . And of course, in the end, he kills her."[25]

As of the 1997–1998 season, the ISU technical committee on dance modified the music restrictions for free dance to require only that the music have a continuous beat and thus could derive from a stage work such as a ballet or musical comedy and could employ the original stage orchestrations. Although some dance teams interpreted this restored freedom as license to return to a more theatrical style of performance, the examples given in the ISU communication (e.g., waltzes, mazurkas, etc.) indicate that the intention was still to translate characteristic social dance forms to the ice. Another part of this communication noted that couples should not be penalized for employing a preponderance of side-by-side skating when performing dances that used such positions in their original form. Bourne and Kraatz chose to take advantage of the second of these options by performing their 1998 free dance as an Irish step dance to music from the popular show *Riverdance*, including a great deal of side-by-side straight-line footwork and up-and-down hops in place on their toes.

Several European teams, on the other hand, took a more theatrical approach to free dance. For their final eligible season as they sought to defend their Olympic title, Grishuk (who had meanwhile changed her first name to Pasha) and Platov used Michael Nymann's *Memorial Requiem* to skate an intense, relentless, abstract free dance described in various sources as being dedicated to the people of Sarajevo, to skaters who had died, or to their own life in sport. Krylova and Ovsiannikov skated a dramatic interpretation of *Carmen* involving many distorted angled and hunched-over positions and over-the-top facial expressions, particularly from Anzhelika. Although there certainly were passages of the two skaters dancing together to the musical rhythms, more of the program seemed to depict a struggle or sexual encounter in which she retained the upper hand; one reporter noted, "Krylova-Ovsiannikov skated an updated, playful version of *Carmen* that concluded with her pulling a red ribbon from his chest as if tearing out his heart."[26]

Anissina and Peizerat also took an experimental approach to well-used music from a theatrical love story, skating a sensual and mutually supportive free dance to excerpts from Prokofiev's ballet *Romeo and Juliet.* During the course of the dance, Marina twice carried Gwendal entirely off the ice supported on her hip, as if to represent Juliet's emotional strength within the relationship.

The issue in the dance community was once again that of social versus theatrical dance, this time falling more clearly along historic cultural lines. English-speaking dancers (from Britain, the United States, or in this case Canada—although Kraatz had only moved there from Germany and Switzerland as a teenager) historically have represented the traditional social dance school of ice dance, while the European taste as represented by the Russians has more often favored the theatrical.[27] Prominent Western European teams have tended to fall somewhere in between, with couples such as the Duchesnays and Rahkomo and Kokko tending toward the experimental and the-

*Marina Anissina as Juliet supports Gwendal Peizerat's
Romeo in a lift from their 1998 free dance. Photo © by
J. Barry Mittan.*

atrical, Sophie Moniotte and Pascal Lavanchy of France more traditional,
Barbara Fusar Poli and Maurizio Margaglio stressing ballroom authenticity
in the original dances and experimentation in the free dances, but none of
them with the balletic refinement of the Soviet-trained dancers. Anissina
and Peizerat draw on a more Russian tradition as Anissina is originally from
Russia but moved to France in search of a partner after both the Soviet Union
and her previous partnership dissolved. The Lithuanian team of Margarita
Drobiazko and Povilas Vanagas, although Soviet-trained, had also worked
in Britain for a while with Torvill and Dean and coach Betty Calloway and
tended to appeal more to Western tastes with their deep edges and restrained
facial expressions.

In the decade following the breakup of the Soviet Union, not only has Russia continued to field some of the most technically accomplished dance teams, but representatives from former Soviet republics, as well as from other Eastern European countries, have made up sizeable percentages of the judging panels at many events, sometimes constituting a majority. Almost always, a majority represent countries from some part of Europe. This in itself translates into a competitive disadvantage for North American skaters simply on the basis of judges' stylistic preferences. The Russian-trained teams also often bring a more extended line and greater ice speed to their skating, while the best North American dances tend to emphasize edges and footwork. Many North American experts state that only the Canadians and the Americans perform "real dance" (i.e., dance in which footwork and rhythmic steps take precedence over narrative and upper body expressiveness) and deserve to place higher than they do.

We can see something of a shift along a continuum from athleticism to social dance to theatrical dance, with Bourne and Kraatz espousing the first position in 1996 and moving to the second in 1997 and 1998, and the top European teams representing the second in 1996 and moving into the third in 1997, more firmly so in 1998 and beyond.

In the years since 1998, rule changes, along with injuries and retirements affecting some of the top teams, have led to more variety in the types of dances performed and more volatile standings in the dance event than had been the case during the mid-1990s or for most of the 1980s and earlier decades. Beginning with the 1998 season, vocal music with lyrics was permitted in the original dance to permit a wider choice of jive selections. When this option, not allowed to freestyle skaters in competition, proved popular with both skaters and audiences, vocal music continued to be allowed in the original dance and, as of the 2000 season, in the free dance as well. The only requirement for music for the free dance is now that it have a "rhythmic beat and melody, or audible rhythmic beat alone, but not melody alone" and that "the couples must skate in time to the rhythmic beat and not to the melody alone."[28]

In addition, new rules were introduced concerning the technical content for both original and free dances, specifying minimum and/or maximum numbers of required elements such as lifts or assisted jumps (now counted as the same thing, and now allowed in the original dance, with two of the free dance lifts specified as to type), "dance spins" (partnered spins using recognized dance holds), step sequences (with specific shapes, e.g., circular or straight-line, and specific partner relationships, e.g., closed or open holds or side by side), and "twizzles" by each partner. These requirements give the judges specific elements on which to compare the teams, just as freestyle judges compare skaters on jumps, spins, and step sequences. Mandatory deductions are now required for stumbles, falls, and other interruptions to the program, based on the severity of the interruption.

In recognition that many teams had been choosing to skate theme or story programs, the rules now specify that "developing a story or theme is optional."[29] In other words, the free dance is now explicitly "free" in terms of thematic content. Judges have clearer technical guidelines on which to mark the skaters, with expression of the musical rhythms still an important criterion. Faithfulness to ballroom styles is now important only to original and compulsory dances, although a number of teams continue to choose ballroom or other social dance themes for their free dances out of a preference for those styles and/or for contrast with the more dramatic approaches.

In 1999, for instance, Krylova and Ovsiannikov, skating an experiment in complex rhythms to modern African drumming, won tightly split decisions over Anissina and Peizerat's more audience-friendly romantic program to the *Man in the Iron Mask* soundtrack. Bourne and Kraatz, hampered in part by an injury to Bourne's knee, won yet another bronze medal with a foray into more contemporary social dance via hip-hop rhythms.

In a profile of the French team, focusing on yet another move in which Marina lifted Gwendal, ABC correspondent Lesley Visser stated, "In a move which has become their trademark, they perform a lift in which she appears to be holding him aloft. They see this move as a way of celebrating the opposite yet equal strengths of male and female. Yet if they are to beat the reigning European champions, they must hope that the judges are ready to embrace this feminist view."[30] The fact that Anissina and Peizerat finished first or second at every competition they entered during the 1999 through 2002 seasons while continuing to employ these reverse lifts (not actually beating Krylova and Ovsiannkov at the 1999 European or World Championships but coming as close as possible in split decisions) suggests that judges do not penalize them for this type of gender reversal. A handful of lower-ranked teams from various countries have also attempted reverse lifts with no reported effects on acceptance or competitive placements. There has been some concern, especially with Anissina and Peizerat who used these moves as a trademark in all their free dances since 1998, that, as with Bourne and Kraatz's hydroblading, women lifting men was more of a gimmick than an expression of musical interpretation or skating skill.

For the 2000 season, with vocal music now permitted in the free dance, Krylova and Ovsiannikov and Anissina and Peizerat both chose to skate dramatic programs to Carl Orff's *Carmina Burana*. Because of Krylova's debilitating back pain, the defending champions were unable to compete all season and later turned professional, allowing the French team to take over as world champions. Bourne and Kraatz, getting a late start after surgery to Bourne's knee, chose to try their hands at choreographing their own free dance to vocal selections by Harry Connick, Jr. Both the Canadians and Irina Lobacheva and Ilya Averbukh, previously ranked fourth in the world and now the top-ranked Russian team, lost ground during the season to sudden rises by the Italians Fusar Poli and Margaglio and the Lithuanians Drobiazko and Vanagas. Bourne and Kraatz ended their season early, citing a new injury, while the Russians went through a series of two new and two old free dances in various styles over the course of the season in an ultimately unsuccessful attempt to maintain a thirty-year tradition of Soviet or Russian teams on the world podium.

The Italians claimed the first world medal (silver) for that country skating to a mix of Celtic music including selections from *Lord of the Dance,* the movie *Braveheart,* and a vocal slow section by Loreena McKennit. Although some of the steps resembled those used in programs attempting to translate Irish dance to the ice, such as that of Bourne and Kraatz in 1998, Fusar-Poli and Margaglio's program belonged more to the theatrical tradition, using a narrative of conflict and resolution that showcased aggressive athleticism from both partners. Drobiazko and Vanagas, one of several teams to skate to Emma Shaplin's operatic pop hit "Spente le stelle," demonstrated a romantic expansiveness in which both partners give themselves over to a relationship more with the music and the space than with each other to win bronze.

The year 2000 also saw the sixth-ranked German champions Kati Winkler and René Lohse performing a free dance entitled "Time Goes Millennium," skated to techno-style music with ticking and tolling sounds, that featured various clock images such as arms and legs repeatedly mimicking clock hands, a rhythmically swinging lift in which Kati represented a pendulum, and both skaters looking at and listening to wristwatches while appearing to walk briskly. Except for the lifts, the moves in this program were primarily parallel, with both partners evoking similar images. Another rising team, Galit Chait and Sergei Sakhnovsky of Israel, made an unprecedented move from thirteenth place at 1999 Worlds to fifth in 2000 with a program to the *1492* soundtrack, with Sergei costumed as Columbus and Galit, through her costume and many of her body shapes, depicting the ship's sail and perhaps the ocean itself.

In the 2001 season, nearly all the top couples offered free dances drawing on dramatic emotion. This trend may have represented an effort to emulate the style of programs such as those that had brought success to 2000 world champions Anissina and Peizerat in the belief that this was the style judges preferred to see, or perhaps the preponderance of heavy free dances could be attributed to a desire for contrast with the lighter quickstep and Charleston rhythms of that year's original dance. At Worlds, the Italians' athletic aggressiveness, skating as a modern-day Romeo and Juliet to the soundtrack of the 1996 film, narrowly prevailed for gold over the French team's smoother refinement interpreting the rock opera *Beethoven's Last Night,* both teams thus ringing contemporary changes on classical high art material connecting love and death. The Russians, skating a more abstract classical-modern hybrid to a version of Bach's Toccata and Fugue with an applied dance beat, equally narrowly won the bronze medal decision over the Canadians, who, now with a new coach and a new attitude, had joined the prevailing trend toward powerful music and movement skating to Montserret Caballé's anthemic "March with Me." The relative lack of enthusiasm for the aesthetic quality of the dances from the predominantly North American crowd prompted the officials of the ISU's ice dance technical committee to request happier dances for the upcoming Olympic season.[31] The Canadians and the Italians complied, skating to a Michael Jackson medley and the disco hit "I Will Survive," respectively. The French and Russian teams chose heavier thematic approaches: Anissina and Peizerat drew some criticism regarding their use of a speech by Martin Luther King in their dance on the theme of liberty, in which "Gwendal represents humanity oppressed, Marina [drawing on French revolutionary iconography] represents freedom,"[32] while Lobacheva and Averbukh presented their response to the September 11 attacks in a program called "A Time for Peace."

As always, results depend on some combination of the skaters' technical and performance skills and the stylistic preferences and national allegiances of the judges who happen to sit on each panel. In the original dance, authentic ballroom-based interpretation of the chosen rhythms, with their traditional gender roles, remains an important consideration in ranking the various teams' dances. In the free dance, however, couples are now free to establish their own style and relationships with each new program, and the choice of subject matter and particularly the depictions of gender do not appear to show any pattern with regard to acceptance or rejection by the judges. The most significant recent controversies have centered not on the skaters' behavior on the ice, but the judges' behavior behind the scenes.[33]

The one area where the judges and officials have objected to the skaters' display of sexuality on the ice has been in objections to overly revealing costumes and what have been referred to as "gynecological" lifts and similar moves in which the woman's crotch became the focal point for the spectators' or camera's view. One elderly judge complained, "If I want a young man waving his partner's assets in my face, I can rent a porn movie. The males are acting like pimps."[34] As a result, the ISU issued a communication at the beginning of the 2001–2002 season instructing pair and dance teams to avoid such tasteless moves and judges to take deductions when they did appear. There may be a generational conflict at work here, in which the twenty-something skaters deliberately seek to test the boundaries of decency and the judges old enough to be their grandparents hold more conservative estimations of where those boundaries lie. In other instances, the skaters may simply be seeking innovative positions with which to display flexibility and creativity without considering what the moves will look like from all angles. The intentions in this ruling, as with the costume rules of several years previous, is to keep the focus modestly on athletic content rather than sexual display. Although this can be seen as another example of ISU prudery, unlike the skirt rule the effect would be to decrease rather than increase the positioning of female skaters as sexual objects.

From the point of view of gender construction, a focus on athletic skating and on rhythmic expression provides less scope for differentiation between the male and female partners. Traditional ballroom approaches rely on sexual narratives implicit in many of the standard dances, as discussed earlier in the section on ballroom dance. Theme dances, especially those with narratives attached, often foreground the sexual roles enacted by the performers. Sometimes the roles enacted return to the same basic theme of man pursuing or taming woman that is present within the ballroom dances, as well as in many of the stage sources for the music and stories behind the theatrical dances. Any dance in this context that strives to depict a romantic or sexual relationship inevitably must be a heterosexual one, since same-sex dance teams do not exist. In some cases, the female ends up dominating the relationship, as in Krylova and Ovsiannikov's "Carmen." In others, such as Torvill and Dean's "Bolero," Klimova and Ponomarenko's "Man and a Woman," or Anissina and Peizerat's "Romeo and Juliet," the emphasis is on sensuality and mutuality more than on sexual opposition. In dances on abstract themes, there may or may not be a component of gender difference built into the depiction, most commonly through the use of the woman's body to represent inanimate objects, forces of nature, or abstraction, while the man represents a human being (or "humanity"). Then, finally, there are the rare dances that explicitly disrupt conventional expectations of gender, most notably the Duchesnays' "Reflections."

PART SIX

Spectatorship

CHAPTER TWELVE

Intimate Pleasures: Skating Fandom

The pleasures and potential meanings of skating from a partici-pant point of view would cluster around the pleasure of movement—the ex-hilaration of speed or the sense of competence that comes from mastering difficult moves, the *experience* of both personal power and personal graceful-ness, often simultaneous, that can be achieved in ever greater doses as one's skating becomes more and more accomplished, and that can often prove ad-dicting. In addition, although for some skaters performing for audiences or performing for judges are at best necessary evils to allow one to make any sort of career out of what they love to do for its own sake, for others the very pro-cesses of showing off skills, striving to outdo rivals, or communicating an ar-tistic vision through the medium of skating provide pleasures even more in-tense than the mere quotidian repetition of skills on practice ice.

For fans, however, those who follow figure skating as avidly as aficionados of other cultural productions, whether in the realm of sport or art, but who do not skate themselves (or not at a level that offers the same rewards), the physical pleasures can be at best vicarious. What is it, then, about elite fig-ure skating that produces such intense devotion from the small but signifi-cant portion of those who see skating on television and feel impelled to seek out more and more opportunities to watch skating, to learn about skating, and to communicate about these experiences with others? Given the multi-ple and sometimes contradictory meanings available in this complex prac-tice, there are probably as many different answers as there are skating fans. Throughout this chapter, I will be quoting responses from fans that touch on some of the pleasures they derive from their fandom. My goal here is to examine what I think are some of the most compelling appeals, particularly to adult, middle-class, heterosexual or mostly heterosexual women, a de-scription that would include the largest portion of diehard skating fandom.[1] Most if not all of these appeals, I propose, would fall within the general cate-gories of identification, sexual attraction, and competence.

IDENTIFICATION

The first, perhaps most fundamental appeal for the spectator of any movement discipline would probably be a kinesthetic identification to the movement itself. Even as we appreciate the alienness of a virtuosity that our own
bodies lack the correct size, shape, state of fitness and training, and in some
instances sex-specific characteristics to emulate in reality, at the same time,
merely by watching another person moving in ways that we cannot, we can
experience in our own nerves and muscles a vestige of what it must feel like
to move in those ways. In the case of skating, we can experience, if only vicariously, the effortless gliding speed, the grace, the power or control or expressiveness or musicality or beauty of the skater's movement before us.

> *How do you usually feel (physically and/or emotionally) when you watch
> skating?*

Extremely excited. Very nervous when the skaters I like are skating.
Exhausted and drained when it is over.

Much like being in love, if it's good . . .

Varies but usually excited and in the wonderful but rare case uplifted.
Lu Chen and sometimes Michelle have been able to uplift me totally
into another world.

When the skating is good it can bring tears to my eyes. It varies depending on the level. olympics is better than worlds which is better
than nationals, which is better than the various week to week
competitions.

I would say I'm excited and comfortable, except when a skater I particularly care about is competing; then I'm a nervous wreck for the skater.
Physically, you don't want the details then! When I'm excited and
comfortable, all the usual symptoms of excitement: increased pulse,
etc. Skating makes you feel *alive!* It's that rollercoaster feeling—
the chills—the spills. The chance that at any time you could see one
performance that takes you off the earth.

I love the quietness, neatness, quick rotation, correct form, and absolutely gorgeous way of moving, just as I admire that in a quality
horse. I love power, too, but not showy, extravagant power. And
balance is the most satisfying thing I can think of. God, I wish I
had it.

When my sister came to watch the Skate America Exhibitions, after a
few performances, she turned to me and said, "You're jumping with

them." I said, "Huh?" and she patted my thigh and said whenever a skater went up for a jump, my thighs would twitch as if I was trying to jump too, or at least give them an extra lift. I'd never noticed that before, but I do that.

It makes me feel good. It reminds me that there is good and beauty in the world. It lifts my spirits and helps me forget some of the things in the world that are not good or beautiful.

Which skaters we most enjoy watching may be determined by which skaters most move in ways we prefer to identify with. Because skating rewards both fluid grace and explosive power from both male and female skaters, one can find examples in both the men's and ladies' events of skaters who emphasize either stereotypically male or female movement qualities, and more rarely skaters who excel at both. A distinct preference for watching one sex more than the other, then, may depend primarily on which discipline seems to provide more examples of the sorts of movement one prefers among the current crop of skaters, or it may depend on more complex interactions between the pleasures of pure movement and the social context in which it occurs.

Which discipline(s) of skating do you best like to watch?
I like watching all freestyle skating (ladies' singles, men's singles, pairs) the best, although I also sometimes like to watch the other disciplines. I like freestyle the best because I love the combination of athletic power/speed and expression.

Ladies singles, but I will watch all of it. I just am the most fascinated with the ladies, I'm not sure why . . .

Enjoy them pretty much equally with a slight favor for ladies' singles. Women have the grace.

Ladies' singles and precision. Maybe it's because I participate in these two disciplines; it's certainly the case for the latter. . . . I dislike seeing the young girls decked out in elaborate dresses, hair and makeup. I think it's worse at the lower levels and at local competitions than at the elite level.

Men's singles—seems the most daring and athletic. Because of that it is more dramatic. Ladies' singles is a little too repressed and pretty, sometimes.

Men's singles, because their skating is higher, faster, stronger, at the cutting edge of the sport.

Men's singles, because I enjoy the big jumps. They are also older and tend to have more "personality" . . . on the ice than the ladies. I also like dance, but men's singles is definitely my favourite.

Men's Singles. I love the power.

No choice here. Men's singles. I love the speed and the power most of all that a man can deliver. Perhaps that's why I'm such a fan of the most powerful skaters rather than the slower/less powerful ones.

I like watching mens and pairs. Pairs, I like the excitement of the throws and lifts and men because I like to watch the power. Ladies are ok too. Ice dance I don't understand what to look for so I don't enjoy it as much.

Men—they have more freedom than women, who always have to look pretty and sweet; they have the highest jumps and best speed. I prefer watching men's singles followed closely by pairs. I like the strength and power of some of the men especially those that are able to "take you onto the ice with them" such as Boitano and Wylie. I find pairs very exciting and I greatly admire the athletic skill required.

I've always had a soft spot for the men's singles, since that was the discipline I followed first. The men also land their jumps more often than the women, and I enjoy their programs more. My second choice would be pairs. I love the unison, the throws and jumps, and the teamwork.

Pairs—I love the complexity and intricacy of pairs elements. It's sad that more people don't understand how difficult a really nice pairs element is—everyone focuses on the singles elements.

Absolutely—ice dancing. It's the most like ballet and it's the most interesting to me, because I can relate to it the most. When it's done well, it's also the most emotional.

Enjoy all disciplines; however enjoy the intricacies of ice dance most. Especially analyzing movement down ice how lifts develop, how much of the program is performed on one foot and correct edges and unison. In general, I enjoy choreography—its implementation and use of ice and space. Mens and pairs are next on the list of favorites because usually choreography is much more sophisticated than ladies.

Other levels of identification beyond the purely kinesthetic also exist, once we situate the skater's movement within the social matrix of performance. Here the cues of the contextual frame—is the skater being judged? Is this skater an established star whose history commands our attention or a hopeful who must solicit our and/or judges' approval?—and the orientations of the skater's posture and gaze alert us to the status relationships at play.

When you watch skating, who do you find yourself identifying with?
> i dont skate but i have watched for years and sometimes you can under-
> stand exactly what they are going through for example I have
> watched Michelle Kwan grow up and to see her miss the Gold
> Medal by so little was hard for me just as it was hard for her and
> i understand that.

> Sometimes I identify with certain skaters, if something about their life
> experience is similar to mine. I do identify with them in a sense that
> they have to work hard all their lives, hoping to make the Olympic
> team, and then hoping to medal. But then they are out onto the ice
> all alone, and one slip or fall will end all those hope at once. I think
> life can be like that sometimes.

> Skaters, amazingly enough. I had to think about this a minute! I'm not
> a skater though tried when I was a kid. Weak ankles and weird fam-
> ily situation prevented me from getting lessons or being serious. But
> I am an artist and I tend to be a "powerful" and competetive female.
> You can do the psychology!

For women, the condition of being judged on one's physical appearance, both physical deportment and the externally applied clothing, hairstyle, and makeup, is a familiar one. To the extent that we understand figure skating competitions as being more saliently contests of self-presentation in this sense than of technical skills, skating's fascination for many women can be found in the process of identifying with successful skaters' negotiation of the same sorts of skills required for successful femininity under patriarchal standards.[2]

But this fascination need not imply an endorsement or even resigned ac-ceptance of these standards; the evident artificiality of skating contests and skating standards of gender presentation may call into question the apparent naturalness of such standards in everyday life. For one analyst, the fact that performance of femininity on ice is so easily disrupted by falling leads to the suspicion that "part of the appeal of the sport for women viewers is less the exhibition of femininity than the exhibition of femininity as a performance fraught with danger and possibilities of failure."[3]

I would extend this argument to suggest that, for many women, watch-ing *male* skaters in the position of being subjected to the same sorts of judgment further enhances perception that these standards are in fact socially constructed and not inherent in the biological fact of femaleness or maleness. It also allows women viewers to take a spectatorial position identified with the role of authority, the subject of the gaze rather than its object, rendering judgments on the successfulness of these men's performances of self, whether according to a personal aesthetic, the skating rulebook criteria for presentation, or socially accepted standards of masculinity. The simple act of inverting the gendering of the gaze and its object offers to women the pleasure of destabilizing the traditional power hierarchy, even if only temporarily and only in imagination.

Similarly, identifying with specific skaters, male or female, whose self-presentation actively resists positioning as receiver of the gaze offers counterexamples to the structural normalization of performer/feminine/object/powerless versus viewer/masculine/subject/powerful. Skaters who circumvent these stereotypes have access to a greater variety of performer-audience interactions and thus may appeal to fans who particularly value variety and creativity. For viewers who enjoy challenges to authority in general and to patriarchy in particular, the rewards may in fact be greater when it is a female agent who offers resistance.

> *Do you have one skater or team that you follow with more attention than others? Who is it? Why this particular one?*
> Maria Butyrskaya and Aleksei Urmanov. I find Maria very sultry, elegant, create a mood very well and her presentation is stunning. Aleksei I love his quirkiness, him being so different and yet so traditional, and just his pure AU-ness.

This resistance may come in the form of skaters such as Midori Ito, Tonya Harding, Surya Bonaly, or Irina Slutskaya, whose visibly muscular, athletic presence on the ice insists on their athletic agency even as they simultaneously concede the necessity to perform, with varying degrees of commitment and success, the expected signs of femininity. On the other hand are skaters such as Katarina Witt, Nicole Bobek, and Maria Butyrskaya who actively acknowledge and manipulate their appeal to male desire, tactically wielding their own sex appeal as a means to a larger end. When no such prominent examples happen to be available among the top women skaters or happen to appeal to the specific interests and tastes of a given viewer, however, male skaters may provide similar points of identification as skaters who are structurally positioned as feminized within the gaze-object hierarchy and who actively resist that positioning through the various strategies outlined in chapter 8.

I ask myself why Elvis a lot too. I know I fell for his "rebel" posture and unfussy skating. I find his skating exciting and real, as opposed to artificial and mannered. Also, I think I feel that Elvis skates in a sport that doesn't want stocky muscular men, the way gymnastics doesn't want tall girls. He knows that and he skates anyway.

For viewers seeking challenges to gender stereotypes, skaters of either sex who can be seen to defy the norms of their own gender can prove powerful objects of identification. The conflicting codes of both "feminine" objectification and "masculine" agency in the person of the same skater provide a potentially empowering tension in symbolic identification with a position that is neither purely powerless nor purely powerful, blurring the either/or dichotomy of a structuralist reading into an androgynous both/and.

SEXUAL ATTRACTION

One feminist observer, drawing on Laura Mulvey's notion of the split between an active male gaze and a passive female recipient of that gaze, has concluded that "the not-so-subliminal message is that figure skating, in all its various forms is about sex. . . . If women's free skating is about sex, then pairs skating is about *having* sex, and men's free skating is about homoeroticism."[4] This last observation especially draws attention to the dangers of allowing theory to dictate analysis.

For men's skating to be "about homoeroticism," it is necessary to posit a male spectator. But most actual skating fans are female, and for many of these women (U.S. media assumptions to the contrary) it is men's and not ladies' skating that elicits their fondest devotion; this would be even more true in Canada, which has produced so many more male than female stars on the international level.

Insofar as erotic attraction shapes the dynamics of skating spectatorship —and it is certainly a significant component—different meanings come to the fore depending whether the spectator is male or female, whether that spectator is primarily attracted to members of the same or the opposite sex, and whether he or she happens to be watching a male or female skater. The various permutations of each of these categories would yield at least eight possible configurations between viewer and skater, four in which the skater represents the sex that the viewer is attracted to and four in which she or he does not—or not as strongly, if we posit at least some degree of bisexuality in the patterns of desire, if not behavior, of most viewers.

For many straight men and boys who do not consider themselves skating

fans, but who occasionally watch skating on television or attend a touring
performance along with wives, girlfriends, mothers, or daughters who do
count themselves as fans, the primary pleasure to be derived may be the sight
of attractive female bodies in revealing costumes, enhanced by the peekaboo
tease of the skirts that refuse to stay down. From the point of view of the
skating-ignorant straight male gaze, this erotic attraction may be the most
salient meaning of what figure skating is about. Even for those men who do
become fans, who go on to learn more about the sport and to appreciate its
fine points and athletic meanings, the erotic charge provided by the sexual
codings attached to the athletes' bodies may remain an important stimulus
for their sustained interest. If the bodies of the athletes so coded are male
instead, then for a male viewer the erotic charge would be homoerotic, and
the appeal would presumably be greater for gay then for straight viewers,
overshadowed by distaste or even disgust for the most homophobic viewers
of either sex.

> I've always liked ladies skating best. Some people joke with me that
> those short skirts are the reason, but I think it's probably because it's
> the least jump-oriented . . . which makes the competition more
> interesting.

What's missing from this analysis, though, is the experience of the straight
female viewers who comprise the majority of skating fandom, for whom
women's skating is not purely about sex, and for whom men's skating, to the
extent that it is "about" women's attraction to specifically male forms of
physicality, must be considered hetero- rather than homoerotic.

> *Which discipline(s) of skating do you best like to watch?*
> Men's singles. Big jumps, great butts (though the butts are great for any
> of the discipline).

> Men's singles is most exciting to me because of their usually high tech-
> nical ability (the fact that many of the male figure skaters are not
> hard on the eyes doesn't hurt either).

> Men, and it's hard for me personally to say why, except that yes, the
> pulchritude factor does come in. ;-) And yes, I do find the men tend
> to exhibit a broader range of programs than the women, pairs or
> dance. Women do a lot of generic prettiness; pairs tend to be either
> "romantic" or "athletic"; and dance tends to be either overly dramatic
> to the point of bathos, or ballroom cutesy and bland.

Picture this scene: A group of women sits in the bleachers during an early-
morning practice session at an elite skating competition, watching a handful

of young men going through their paces on the ice. The aggressiveness and sometimes recklessness of the skating and jumping and the visible muscularity of many of the skaters lend the activity on the ice an aura of testosterone-steeped athleticism. Most of the skaters are intensely focused on their own practicing, oblivious to the watching fans, but some thrive on the attention and put on a good show, directing their performances to the small crowd when their turn comes to run through their programs to music, clowning for the fans' benefit when they make mistakes, or showing off with cutting-edge jump difficulty that they have little hope or even intention of performing during the competition, in an effort to outdo each other in capturing the fans' attention and affection.

Some of the women in the stands are carefully taking note of how well the skaters are practicing—who has added new moves to his repertoire since last year, who seems to have improved his style, how successful each seems to be at landing the difficult jumps, who seems to be skating strongly or tentatively—and handicapping the probable results of the upcoming competition (the "competence" approached to fandom, discussed below). Others have a favorite skater to whom they are devoted; when their favorite is on the ice, the fan avidly takes in his every move, vicariously experiencing a sense of triumph when he lands a difficult jump combination and despair when he falls or a rival pulls off a better one, and mentally storing up observations of "her" skater's demeanor and interaction with his coach and the other skaters (the identification approach, connected perhaps with a sexual attraction to the skater in terms of narrative or interpersonal relations more than as a physical body). Still others are commenting enthusiastically on which of the men's physiques are enhanced by tight practice clothes, lamenting that some of the skaters have opted for baggy sweatpants in lieu of tights or stretch suits, and speculating on what sort of undergarments the skaters are or are not wearing (the sexual attraction approach, with a focus on physical presence). The atmosphere in the stands is one of intense excitement and arousal; for many of these women, that arousal is explicitly sexual.

"This is like pornography for women!" a friend comments after the last group of men have left the practice and we head back to the main arena to watch another event. By this she means that, just as males who consume pornography make an active effort to spend time looking at female bodies or images of female bodies that they find sexually stimulating, for some of these women, attending men's skating practices serves as an opportunity to devote their attention solely to visual contemplation and consumption of attractive male bodies.[5] The same fans may watch the men's competition itself and the ladies' practices according to codes of figure skating rules and judging standards or criteria of artistry, but for the men's practices (or pair or dance practices featuring attractive male partners) they put such considerations aside in order to revel in the sexual pleasure to be derived from ogling attractive, revealingly clothed young men. This pleasure can be intense enough that some female fans would prefer to take a shuttle bus to a distant practice arena to watch another men's practice than to remain at the central location to watch actual competitions in other disciplines. For some female fans, as for some male fans, the sexual pleasure provided by attraction to particular skaters may be the first or primary source of attraction to following skating at all; for others, it is simply a subsidiary benefit.

The question arises: What is it about participation in competitive figure skating that renders these male skaters so intensely attractive to so many female fans? In the case of specific star skaters who develop large followings, as with stars in other sports or performing arts, personal charisma no doubt plays the largest role. And the focus on the visual form of the skater's body in general also provides (for instance, through tight-fitting clothing or through the medium shots that make up the bulk of televised skating performance) access to the physical signs of maleness on the athletes' bodies—well-developed muscles of the arms, chest, legs, and buttocks in addition to the genital bulge.

But to explain women's attraction to male skating in general rather than to individual skaters, I think that we need to turn again to the appeal of androgyny or conflicting codes. Different women may be most attracted to skaters at different points on a continuum between, say, the rugged warrior imagery of an Elvis Stojko or the light touch and emphasis on beautiful line and flexibility in the aesthetic approach of a John Curry or Rudy Galindo. (The same could be said of homoerotic attractions by male viewers.) But even the most effeminate male skaters exist somewhere to the masculine side of the purely feminine end of such a continuum simply by virtue of possessing a male body, a male physicality; even the most aggressively masculine exist somewhere to the feminine side of the furthest point on a continuum including all male athletes or all men in general simply by virtue of participating in an aesthetic sport in the first place. As with identification—perhaps especially in the intersection of identification with and desire for the same object simultaneously, the acknowledgment of both difference and sameness —the blurring of boundaries and the breaking down of stereotypes opens up an imagined space of multiple possibilities that transcends the limitations of a dichotomous understanding of gender.

Writers about female fandoms of cultural productions other than skating have also identified the breaking down of rigid distinctions between masculine and feminine behavior as a key element of their appeal.[6] The important point, from a methodological point of view, is the focus on the meanings received or produced by the fans themselves, which are in this instance tangential to most of those intended by the skaters and certainly to those purveyed by skating associations or television broadcasts. Nor can any preference or desire of a given subset of fans be taken as representative of all fans, even all who meet a given demographic description. What turns one person on may turn someone else off for idiosyncratic personal reasons outside the scope of the analysis at hand.

Because the point of fannish desire or sexual fantasy is the fan's desire itself and not its fulfillment in an actual sexual relationship, it matters not whether the skaters who are the object of that desire would themselves prefer a sexual partner younger (or older), more physically fit, or the opposite sex than the desiring fan, and this would be true regardless of the respective sexes of skater and fan. For some fans, regardless of sex or sexual orientation, the perception, true or mistaken, of a specific sexual identity in the object of desire is an important part of what makes him or her desirable; for others, the skater's biography is irrelevant and it is only the symbolic version of masculinity, femininity, or androgyny visible on the ice that is the source of the attraction. For (heterosexual) women specifically, the opportunity to acknowledge arousal and desire and to set aside a space in which to view men as merely objects of desire is what feels empowering in the context of a mass culture that habitually constructs women in the objectified position.

COMPETENCE: KNOWLEDGE IS POWER

Skaters go out on the ice one by one and perform a series of jumps, spins, glides, and poses that may appear more or less aesthetically pleasing and that may include one or more evident errors such as falls or may appear to have been performed faultlessly. To the uninitiated, the relative enthusiasm or coolness of the judges, the TV commentators, or longtime fans toward one performance versus another may bear little relation to the outside observer's experience of the performances or even to each other. Are there any patterns to be discerned here, or is it all just a matter of random personal preference?

To someone with little interest in skating to begin with, it doesn't matter. But for fans who like what they see in general, when they watch skating enough to seek out more opportunities to watch, developing a framework for understanding what they see often becomes an important part of their continued enjoyment. Television commentary, which often serves as the first point of entry into building such an understanding, points to several directions in which to start.

First, in many cases, is identifying the moves that recur in most skating programs. Learning to recognize jumps by their takeoffs and to identify other common moves by name confers the minimum level of technical knowledge to mark one as an initiate in discussions with other fans or with the great mass of outsiders to which one no longer belongs. One can then look outside the information regularly provided on television to acquire more advanced technical knowledge: the relative difficulty of different moves, the rules about what elements are required in competitive programs and what deductions are necessary for what kinds of mistakes, identification of the various steps and turns between elements that commentators often leave unnamed and their relative difficulty, high versus low quality in edges and other aspects of basic skating, the ranges of ability to be expected across the field at various levels. The more such knowledge one acquires, the better one can understand and predict competitive placements and explain them to the less initiated, make convincing arguments in hindsight about who "should" have placed where in a given competition (whether in agreement or disagreement with the official results), and attempt to judge competitions for oneself in real time, all sources of pleasure for fans through demonstrating competence at reading and conveying messages about skating according to the same codes as the skating insiders. Understanding and being able to explain skating's complex scoring system is a similar form of technical competence.

> *Which of these situations (watching live/while being broadcast on*
> *television/on videotape/other) do you enjoy most? Why?*
> I enjoy live the most because I get the real feeling for the strength and
> speed of the skaters. Rarely can this be caught on television. I also
> like to watch things such as stroking and listen for how loud of soft
> it is.
>
> On television . . . usually the commentary helps me with explanations
> of the judging etc. Plus the camera angles can sometimes show me
> things such as centered or traveling spins better than if I were there
> live.
>
> Live. . . . it's more varied in terms of levels and people involved. you get
> more direct sense of the skating. In local or live competitions, you get
> to see the entire field, which gives you a greater understanding to the
> scope of competition and a better understanding of just how good
> the top skaters are, and just how many stages people go through to

reach elite levels. In practices, you can see people just doing the skating, so you get to see the process of learning and perfecting.

When you watch skating, do you find yourself identifying with the skater(s)/parents/coaches/judges/other/none?

I definitely try to identify with the judges because I judge along with them. If I give out ridiculously high/low marks, I try to examine why the actual judges placed a skater where they did.

I find that during the performance of the favorite skater one identifies with the skater. During the performance of the nearest competitor one identifies with judges (Great jump but iffy landing . . .).

Familiarity with the key players—the current stars of the eligible or professional world, their recent accomplishments or claims to fame, their nationalities and other distinguishing biographical details—is another form of knowledge as competence that distinguishes the casual from the devoted fan. This kind of knowledge is readily available to fans who rely on television broadcasts with their profiles of leading skaters, supplemented by more in-depth interviews in skating periodicals. Knowledge of these skaters' histories going back more than just one year or four, of who placed where or what jumps they landed even in obscure nontelevised events, of record-book feats such as being the first (or first of a given age, sex, race, or nationality) to complete a given jump or other move, to achieve a given competitive placement, or to introduce a given artistic style may be available through longtime viewing of skating in person or on television and videotape or through reading books and magazines.

Do you have one skater or team that you follow with more attention than others? Who is it? Why this particular one?

I have a lot of faves but I tend to pay more attention to Todd Eldredge and Michelle Kwan because I've seen the highs and the lows with them.

Kurt Browning—It has been a joy to watch his talent grow from the junior ranks to the amazing profession[al] that he is today. And as a Canadian I have been most fortunate to watch this growth live on many occasions.

Midori Ito. Without doubt the strongest jumper in the Ladies singles ever, she hails from my own country. Probably, the sense of injustice done in the Calgary Olympics, still rankles. (Japanese male)

Used to be one (Curry and then Wylie), but the more I know the more skaters I like. Currently its Russians (men in particular, but the women and pairs are more interesting (as a generalization with many exceptions) than most skaters (except Nicole Bobek) from elsewhere. Quality of whole package married with connection to the music. They do seem to be, on the whole, more musical, and less afraid to show it.

Michael Chack. Because I believe his skating has a truth, grace and zest to it that is lacking from other U.S. male skaters who routinely compete more successfully.

I am also a Michelle Kwan fan, partly because I identify with her as an Asian American female and I can understand how she is handling things. I have admired her since she was 12, and by now I am loyal to her because I have enjoyed watching her growth.

Rudy Galindo and Doug Mattis, because they are out.

Brian Orser, because he is good-looking, has swift feet, and can communicate well non-verbally.

Oksana Baiul, because despite her Judy Garland-like wretchedness, she can still inspire rapture in me.

The skater I follow the most is Todd Eldredge. His skating and story slowing started fascinating me more and more in the last couple of years. Todd's story, triumphs, and downtimes present more interesting viewing than the younger skaters or those who have had everything happen right like it was "supposed" to be ala Tara Lipinski. Todd's personality is one I was attracted to, being shy myself, so it has been interesting to follow how he handles the different events in his career.

As I mentioned, there are a lot of skaters that I quite enjoy, but the one skater that I pay more attention to is Alexei Urmanov, who I noticed in Lillehammer in 1994 and really rekindled my interest in figure skating again. To me, he really embodies everything I love about the sport/art—artistry, athleticism, elegance, and grace. I'm definitely more drawn to the skaters who consider good choreography and connecting moves to be important.

Familiarity with skaters below the top tier nationally and internationally, or with the careers of well-known and not-so-well-known coaches, choreographers, or judges, also marks one as having access to knowledge beyond that readily available on television. By attending live competitions, purchasing videotapes intended for the competitors of events or parts of events excluded from television broadcasts, and trading tapes with fans in other countries to gain access to more skaters and more events than those shown on their own national television networks, fans can circumvent the networks' imposition of hegemonic media narratives and, through discussions with fellow fans, construct counternarratives that address the individual fans' rather than corporate networks' obsessions.[7] Examples might include:

- compiling a longitudinal narrative of a favorite skater's career from junior level or earlier to the present and including eyewitness reports and hard-to-obtain tapes of events that were not nationally broadcast or for which the broadcasts did not include the performance(s) of the skater in question
- focusing on the careers or styles of skaters with interesting artistic approaches but insufficient athletic ability or competitive nerve to place high enough at major events to be included in the TV broadcasts
- focusing on the technical and athletic nuances of women's competition and ignoring the ice princess imagery added by the broadcasts
- comparing American ice dance teams who do not rank among the top five or ten teams in the world to the other teams at a similar level rather than following only the medal contenders and the Americans outside their competitive context.

Which formats do you enjoy most? Why?

I enjoy watching vintage taped performances or competitions the most, because I know they're classics and I can go back and watch the stunning parts again and again!

I prefer stiff, serious judging to celebrity fluff judges, and I prefer technical minimum requirements to completely open, anything goes format. I most like to see really good skating, at a high level of accomplishment. I enjoy seeing the young up and comers, but, frankly, only in small doses.

practice sessions (local skaters) / practice sessions (elite skaters) / I love the closeness—so few viewers. i love the "behind the scenes" feel to it.

I like both the actual competitions of elite and professional skaters. Why? I like the intensity (fake though it may be), of the competitions. I like to see how people react to the pressure not only with the tech side, but how well they "sell" the programs.

I love watching the live skating best. You can really appreciate the speed, etc. and it's better to see all the skaters in a competition. There's no commentary as well.

Fans who bring technical knowledge from other sports or dance forms, aesthetic evaluation strategies from the performing arts, and historical knowledge of those arts can apply these outside competencies to their readings of skating in ways that can profitably illuminate their own understandings of what they see. By sharing this knowledge, they can offer additional perspectives previously unavailable to fans or even to skaters and other skating insiders without that outside knowledge. For example, a fan with an extensive background in ballroom dance might be able to make finer discriminations between different interpretations of tango than a fan or even a skater without such a background.

> *What do you pay most attention to while you're watching skating? What do you remember best afterward?*
>
> The program as a whole. Are they skating to music I like? How are they interpreting that music? What are they doing with the music? How do all of those elements meld together to form a whole?
>
> Probably the line skaters get during lifts and poses, the flow and expression they create as they move around each other, and the way they express the music.
>
> My own competitive sport is showing horses (hunters/jumpers), and we watch schooling interminably. . . . I'd give anything to be able to watch practices of elite skaters. Or just to sit at a good rink day after day and watch all kinds of competitive skaters. It's the best way to learn, and to be able to hear what the good coaches say would be heaven. I'd never tire of it.

In fan discussions, both in the stands at skating events and on-line in various Internet discussion forums, mastery of these types of knowledges establishes one's skating-fan credentials, just as detailed knowledge about the biography and oeuvre of a favorite skater establishes one's credentials as a fan of that skater. Status is achieved through superior knowledge or through the demonstration of inside sources of information, for instance by being the first to break the news of a change in a skater's coaching relationship or personal life. Knowledge indeed is power in establishing one's status as better informed than other fans.

Another means by which fans derive pleasure is through positioning themselves as knowing better than the purported experts. This may take the form of fans identifying with the role of coach and/or choreographer, second-guessing choices of program style or training strategy, or offering suggestions of what the skater should do next. Fans who pride themselves on knowledge about and/or taste in aesthetic matters similarly may enjoy establishing their superiority to the skaters in these matters.

What else do you do while you're watching?

When I'm watching at a friend's house we usually discuss the skating (quite loudly) and/or make wisecracks about costumes, moan about worn out music, etc.

Make smart-ass comments to whoever else is in the room about music choices, commentators, costumes.

Most commonly, though, this type of asserting superior knowledge takes the form of second-guessing the judging. The operations of national bias, for instance, are often so transparent that fans can accurately predict a judge's nationality according to which skaters the judge marked especially high or low. It is also possible to perceive patterns and to construct motivations for otherwise opaque decisions by attributing the judges' scores and rankings to stylistic preference, collusion, bribery, judging on past reputation or future potential rather than the skating at hand, or "sending messages" to skaters about the acceptability of on-ice or off-ice behavior. It is possible to perform such meta-analyses of judging behavior and to pass judgment on the judges, positioning oneself as morally and/or intellectually superior to the experts, without necessarily knowing much about skating technique or judging criteria. We can see this phenomenon both in casual fans who take great pleasure in booing scores they deem too low for well-skated performances (this had become almost an expected ritual at professional competitions, where marks, given on a ten-point scale, often cover only the narrow range between 9.5 and 10.0) and in knowledgeable fans who have memorized some or all of the relevant rules and point out at length where judges failed to apply mandatory deductions. In response to recently proposed changes in the eligible scoring system that would obscure information about how individual judges had rated each competitor, one observer noted the appeal for fans of access to that information:

The current judging system, flawed as it is, is great for the sport's popularity. Part of skating's appeal lies in the subjectivity of the scoring. Viewers delight in accusing the judges of being corrupt, idiotic or mean to cute Canadian kids. "What people love about this sport is they can all be experts," says Joe Inman, a U.S. judge. "The public will always want the score from the individual judges displayed. Many of my nonskating friends find this is one of the most exciting aspects of the sport." Nothing like an unpopular decision and a good conspiracy theory to make figure skating must-see TV.[8]

The competence appeal of skating fandom, then, includes a variety of means by which fans can establish themselves either as insiders or as superior to insiders. In these ways, skating fans resist the powerless position of being at the mercy of judges for validation of skaters' worth or of the television networks for access to viewing skating in the first place and for the kinds of meanings to be made from that viewing.

Conclusion

*W*hat fascinates me most about figure skating is the complexity reflected in the tensions, oppositions, and contradictions that give it not only shape and form but also its richness of meaning. Chief among these is probably the tension between freedom and control, which plays out on a physical level in the very muscles and movement of each skater. On a cultural or symbolic level, this tension is seen most evidently in the relation between, on one hand, the rules, structures, and traditions or expectations of skating, particularly in its incarnation as organized sport, and, on the other hand, the impulse toward self-expression and even innovation in so many of its devotees and even in the rewards for originality and musical expression within the scoring of presentation. In structure, the sport itself comprises both the compulsory (compulsory figures, compulsory dances, required elements) and "free" skating. The definitions of the competitive disciplines, particularly of ice dance, in which a couple must consist of a lady and a man, the costume rules, and in some cases the required elements impose a form of compulsory heterosexuality and insistence on sexual difference ("overdetermined" femininity and compulsively reiterated masculinity). Yet to succeed, skaters must exhibit traits and skills that fall on both sides of a masculine-feminine binary, and many of the most influential individual skaters have changed the sport vincrementally by producing challenges to traditional gender norms. Even skaters working well within the mainstream tradition must constantly construct a persona on the ice that inflects not only gender but also other aspects of social identity (often notably nationality) through the specific choices they make in performing that identity.

An analysis such as this, then, perhaps raises more questions than it answers. The most productive of these may be not simply whether a skater or a performance is sufficiently feminine or masculine or heterosexual, but more specifically what *kind* of woman or man or couple do they present or represent on the ice? How do the rules, traditions, and techniques of skating constrain meanings, and how do individual skaters negotiate those constraints to produce a variety of different possible meanings through their skating?

What kinds of choices do judges, media, and fans make among the varied images and skating values that the skaters present on the ice? How do these different sets of viewers create different narratives of success and failure? How do various skating communities, for instance in different countries or representing different functions (coaches, judges, professional skaters, amateur competitors, etc.), understand skating in general and specific events differently from each other? How do various media communities read different meanings and pass along those meanings to the public whose access to skating is primarily through the media? How do various communities of skating fans produce their own readings of the skating they consume directly or through the media that may be very different from the meanings intended by the skaters, skating associations or producers, and media?

In this book, I have touched only glancingly on these and other issues. My primary purpose here has been to investigate not so much *what* skating means in any given instance as *how,* to establish a methodology that I and others can apply to specific case studies in the future, to future events and trends as skating continues to grow and change in the twenty-first century and retrospectively to historical events, without having to define the terms and contexts of the analysis each time from scratch. For as long as skating continues to attract audiences and participants, in some cases to the point of obsession, it merits an informed critical practice.

I offer this conclusion, then, in the spirit of an introduction to what might become figure skating studies. One historical topic that has been relatively well covered, for example, is the role of champion women skaters from an American perspective. But the history of skating in the twentieth century comprises much more than just champions, the ladies' singles discipline, or Americans (plus Sonja Henie, Katarina Witt, and a handful of other prominent European-born stars). Possible further projects might include:

- archival research or oral histories drawing on the expertise of long-time skating insiders to document social issues within the skating community and the differences in skating culture between and within different countries or communities
- a history of competitive skating choreography and style(s), with reference to skating technique and competitive rules, and also trends in ice shows and in social and theatrical dance off the ice that cross-fertilized competitive skating trends
- studies of professional skating in its various guises, as performing art in both popular and elite forms and as alternative competition track

- analyses of nationalism and internationalism in skating during and after the Cold War
- documentation for English-speaking audiences of how skating was/is structured in the Soviet Union, East Germany, France, Japan, etc.
- histories of significant rule changes affecting the structure of how skating is run
- studies of the oeuvres of influential choreographers, coaches, or skaters, including interviews with the participants and close observers about their influences and intentions, as well as analysis of the works themselves
- analyses of controversial competition results through detailed analysis of the skating and, to the extent possible, after-the-fact interviews with judges and referees who worked the event or similar firsthand observers with loyalties on more than one side of the controversy
- studies of media narratives attached to prominent, particularly controversial, skating events, including different national media's responses to controversies involving skaters from each nation
- ethnographic analyses of contemporary local and/or elite skating culture and subcultures
- analyses of skating-fan culture and fan communities

Some of this work can already be found—in back issues of dance and other performing arts or cultural studies journals or similar publications, in the skating press itself, in brief chapters or passages of books on related topics, in master's and doctoral theses by former (not necessarily elite) skaters, in television documentaries. More would be welcome and would better reflect the multifaceted nature of the subject matter. Direct communication between scholars and skaters, outside the frame of mass media and the focus on celebrities, would be an important step.

The foregoing analysis is thus clearly only a beginning. Like all cultural practices, skating encodes a series of culturally specific meanings, embracing both sides of numerous binary oppositions. As skating enters the mainstream culture, those meanings become both prescriptive and descriptive, both testing limits of the surrounding culture and extending them. As such, skating not only entertains but works as a mirror to reflect back to ourselves fundamental concerns about gender and national identity, about individual expression within the strictures of rules and traditions, and about physical limitations and transcendance.

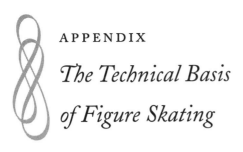

The Technical Basis of Figure Skating

FUNDAMENTALS

Figure skating blades are sharpened with a hollow along the bottom between two distinct parallel **edges**, one closer to the center of the body or the inside of the foot, and the other toward the outside of the foot. They also have a series of serrated teeth, known as the **toepick**, at the front of the blade, which provide stability and which can grip the ice for toe-assisted jumps and steps.

Skating in a straight line with the weight centered over the middle of the foot, both edges are on the ice simultaneously, creating a double tracing of parallel lines on the ice. This is referred to as skating on the "flat" of the blade. Figure skating technique is based on the fact that leaning the body slightly toward and past the center of the body, or away from the center of the body, results in skating solely on the **inside or outside edge** of the blade, respectively, and the path of travel is an arc of a circle, not a straight line. (The same is true when you lean sideways while riding a bicycle to curve to the right or left.) The mark left on the ice is a single curved line. In general, outside edges are more stable than inside edges; the most stable edge, used for landing jumps and for standard spin exits, is the back outside edge in the skater's natural direction of rotation.

Most true figure skating moves involve only one foot and only one edge of the blade on the ice at a time; excessive skating on two feet or on flats is frowned upon. The foot that is engaged on the ice is known as the **skating foot** and the one that is off the ice is the **free foot**. These terms may also be applied to other parts of the body, so that one might speak of bending the skating knee or pressing back with the free shoulder.

Power comes from pushing from one foot to the other using a deeply bent knee that straightens as the foot leaves the ice. The skating knee is almost always bent as the skater pushes onto that foot; depending on the move, it may straighten gradually or suddenly once the weight is over that leg, or it may remain bent, the degree of knee bend varying subtly throughout a held edge or within a turn on that foot. It is also possible, but requires greater skill, to gain speed and power without changing feet by varying the degree of knee bend, adjusting the configuration of the arms, shoulders, hips, and free leg, and shifting from one edge to another.

Holding the curve of a single edge indefinitely would produce a spiral pathway as the diameter of the curve decreases with diminishing speed. This is why skating terminology refers to a long extended glide on one foot as a **spiral**, even though the curves are usually so broad that skaters don't hold them long enough for the spiraling-in effect to be noticeable. Instead, the term *spiral* in skating terminology has come to mean a long edge held with the free leg lifted to or above the level of the hips—usually in back, in an arabesque position of ninety degrees or higher, although variations are possible with the free leg bent in attitude position or held to the front or the side, sometimes with the skater using one hand to hold the leg up. It has nothing to do with whether the body position is spiraled or not. Two other moves that, like spirals, emphasize gliding on edges and flexibility are the spread eagle and the Ina Bauer. The **spread eagle** is one of the oldest highlight moves in skating, performed on both feet with the feet spread apart wider and turned out 180 degrees or more, in the equivalent of ballet second position, so that one foot is traveling forward and the other backward along the same line, both on either inside or outside edges, or on flats. A variation of this move, named for the 1950s German skater who invented it, is the **Ina Bauer**, in which the feet are turned out offset from each other as in ballet fourth position rather than in the same line.

To control the curve of the edge—for instance to produce the perfect circles of a figure eight—a skater must exert muscular force to counteract the centripetal force that tends to pull the path of the blade and the free side of the body toward the center of the circle. This effort is known as **checking** (i.e., stopping) the rotation. Checking is particularly important for controlling the exit edge after a turn on the ice or the landing edge of a jump. Various forms of checking rotation and of producing rotation rely on twisting at the waist to work the upper body against the lower body, so that the hips may be facing forward along the path of the blade and the shoulders facing 90 degrees away, toward the center or the outside of the circle. Reversing the direction of this twist can produce a turn from forward to backward or backward to forward, or, with a sharp snap followed by pulling the arms in toward the center of the body, can produce the rotation in place necessary for spins and for double- and triple-rotation jumps.

EDGES AND TURNS

Two edges (inside and outside) on each blade, times two feet (left and right), times two directions (forward and backward) yields a total of eight edges: right forward outer, right forward inner, right backward outer, right backward inner, left forward outer, left forward inner, left backward outer, and left backward inner, abbreviated RFO, LBI, etc. The basic vocabulary of skating derives from the various ways of changing from one edge to the other, through changing from one foot to the other, changing direction with respect to the skater's body (forward to backward and vice versa), and/or changing the lean toward or away from the center of the body. Changing two of these factors at once (e.g., from a LFO to a RFI edge during forward crossovers, from LFO to LBI in a three turn or bracket turn, or from RFI to LBI in a mohawk turn) results in maintaining the same direction of travel with regard to the ice surface (in the examples given, counterclockwise) as the skater continues to travel along the same circular path. Changing an odd number of these factors—one, or or all three at once—(e.g., from LFO to RFO during forward stroking, from LFO to LFI in a change of edge or edge pull, from LFO to LBO in a rocker or counter turn; or from LFO to RBI in a choctaw turn) results in changing the direction of travel with respect to the ice surface (from counterclockwise to clockwise in the examples given), so that the new edge draws a circle on the ice tangent to the one previously being skated. In school figures, ice dance, and freestyle step sequences, these connecting arcs of adjacent circles are referred to as **lobes**.

The easiest of these turns, which beginners soon learn to use without thinking, are the forward-outside-to-back-inside three turns and the forward-inside-to-back-inside and back-outside-to-forward-outside mohawks. The simple figure eight used in school figures is based on drawing one circle on each foot on the edge of the same character, with a change of foot and therefore a change of direction occurring at the point where the two circles meet. The turns and changes of edge performed on one foot are the basis of most of the more advanced school figures. These include **three turns** (which rotate into the circle and leave a 3-shaped mark on the ice) and **brackets** (which rotate against the circle and make a }-shaped mark), both of which change the direction and character of the edge (e.g., forward to backward and outer to inner), but not the direction of travel. Brackets are considerably more difficult than threes. **Rockers** and **counters**, which are more difficult still, involve changing direction without changing the character of the edge (for instance, forward outer to back outer), so they also involve changing from a clockwise to a counterclockwise curve, or vice versa. All these turns are avail-

able for use during freeskating, but many skaters tend to avoid the more difficult ones.

The other basic form used in intermediate and advanced school figures is
the **loop**, or teardrop-shaped circle-within-a-circle, achieved through shifting the weight and swinging the free leg while remaining on the same edge.
The outer circles are about one-third the diameter of the circles used for all
the other figures; the body contortions involved in drawing loops on the ice
make them the most visually interesting of the school figures, but because
they remain more or less in one place rather than progressing across the ice,
they are rarely incorporated into freestyle programs and then almost always
as a contemplative moment in the "slow section" of a free program. More than
any of the turns, loops call attention to themselves as figures.

No one knows exactly why the turns from one foot to the other were named
for American Indian tribes. A **mohawk** is a turn from the forward inside
edge of one foot to the back inside of the other, or from forward outside to
back outside, remaining on the same curve. Some experts apply the term to
backward-to-forward turns on edges of the same character as well, but more
often these are simply referred to as a **step forward**; the step from back outside to forward outside in particular does not require much control or flexibility at all, and even beginners can soon do this without thinking. A **choctaw**
is a change of foot, direction, and edge character all at once, for instance left
forward inner to right back outer, which also changes from clockwise to counterclockwise. Again, some people refer to the backward-to-forward turns as
choctaws; others simply as steps forward. The usual entry into a spin, from a
right back inner (clockwise) edge to a left forward outer edge leading into a
counterclockwise spin, would be an example of a backward-to-forward choctaw. Choctaws tend to be somewhat more difficult than mohawks. Both
exist in "open" and "closed" varieties, depending on whether the new foot is
placed on the ice in front of the skating foot (heel to instep) or behind it (instep to heel). Many of the possible mohawks and choctaws turn up in the
compulsory dances that ice dancers must perform for tests and in the first
phase of dance competitions. They also appear in the new Moves in the Field
tests. Because the Moves in the Field must be performed in both directions,
unlike compulsory dances, which proceed around the rink in a counterclockwise direction and in most cases are not symmetrical, the Moves provide a
more systematic structure for learning these skills.

The turns with and without change of foot, changes of edge on the same
foot (to produce an S-shaped or slalom movement), and changes of foot
that don't involve turning but may involve crossing the free foot in front of
or behind the skating foot before setting it on the ice make up the bulk of

the technical vocabulary of ice dance. They also serve as the basis for the pure skating elements in pairs and singles freestyle skating, used as connecting moves between jumps, spins, and lifts, and as the components of specifically designated footwork sequences.

ROTATIONAL PREFERENCE

Just as most people are right-handed, most skaters prefer to rotate toward the left, counterclockwise, although a minority prefer clockwise, the equivalent of being left-handed—although left-handedness and clockwise rotational preference don't necessarily go together. (Prominent clockwise, or reverse, rotators include Toller Cranston, Denise Biellmann, Rosalynn Sumners, Todd Eldredge, Rudy Galindo, and Sarah Hughes.)

At the level of simply holding a curving edge, or with increasing skill performing one of the forward-to-backward or backward-to-forward turns described above, this rotational preference is relatively trivial. Most people prefer to do forward crossovers right over left, making a counterclockwise circle with the left side of the body toward the center, rather than left over right circling clockwise toward the right (this is one reason most public skating sessions maintain a counterclockwise skating direction) and will find it easiest to perform three turns and inside mohawks in a counterclockwise direction. Reverse rotators will have the opposite preferences. With practice, however, skaters can learn to perform these basic skating skills, as well as the more advanced turns, with near-equal facility in both directions, as required in the school figures and Moves in the Field tests.

In the high-speed tight rotations required for spins and jumps, however, this preference is magnified, so that skaters find it difficult or impossible to perform these moves in the opposite direction. Most don't find it worth the time to develop opposite or reverse spins and jumps, although a few do include the occasional reverse single or, even more rarely, double jump or slow spin for variety and choreographic interest as well as added difficulty.

SPINS

Spins are generally performed on one foot (except for the beginner's two-foot spin and the increasingly rare cross-foot spin). Spins performed on the leg leading into the rotation (left for a counterclockwise spin) are **forward spins**; those on the opposite foot (counterclockwise on the right foot) are **back spins**. (For the ballet-minded, a forward spin is the equivalent of a *pirouette en dedans*, a back spin of a *pirouette en dehors*.) A good spin should rotate in one place on the ice, drawing a series of tiny overlapping circles on top of each other. This is known as **centering** the spin. A spin that is not centered will **travel** across the ice, producing a series of loops strung out along a curve or straight line, so that the skater will end the spin several feet away from the spot on the ice where she began it.

The three basic spin positions are the upright spin, the sitspin, and the camel spin, all of which can be performed as either forward or backward spins. **Upright spins** can be performed with the free leg in any position (straight or bent next to the skating leg; held straight or bent into attitude to the front, side, or back; with the ankle of the free leg crossing the skating leg at the knee, shin, or ankle, and so on). The most common variation begins with holding the arms and free leg straight to the side in ballet second position (the leg will be more at a diagonal, slightly in front of the hips), then bending the elbows and free knee so that the hands meet in front of the chest and the free foot crosses the skating leg just below the knee, and finally lowering the free foot to cross at the ankle and pushing the hands down (or up) along the center of the body to curve in front of the abdomen (or above the head). Gradually decreasing the circumference of the circle that the extremities describe in space while rotating allows the speed of the rotations to increase rapidly. This spin is generally known as a **scratchspin** because the skater's weight is centered between the center of the spinning blade and the first tooth of the toepick, which scratches circles or loops on the ice parallel to the tracings made by the blade. When performed extremely fast, it is also known as a **blur spin**.

The **sitspin** is performed in a sitting position, with the knee of the skating leg bent and the free leg held in front. Ideally the back should be straight, not curved, the hips lower than the skating knee, and the free leg straight. When performed on an edge or flat rather than in a spin, this position is known as a **shoot-the-duck**. (In England, it is called a **teapot**). Arm position is optional. The **broken leg spin** is a variation performed with the free leg bent to the side instead of straight in front.

A **camel spin**, also known as a parallel spin, is performed with the torso and free leg stretched in opposite directions, parallel to the ice at hip level, in a position similar to a standard spiral (arabesque) position. When this spin is performed poorly by beginners, the leg and the torso may both be held too low, so that the hips stick up, resembling a camel's hump; hence the name "camel spin." When the spin is performed well, the stretch of the body should create a straight line or slight arch. Because the circumference of the rotation in a camel spin, with a diameter equal to the distance between head and free foot or approximately the height of the skater, is much greater than that in other spin positions, camel spins tend to rotate more slowly, so a fast and prolonged camel spin indicates superior technique. Variations include bending the skating knee into an attitude position or grabbing the blade of the free foot with one hand, or laying out the torso to face side or up rather than down toward the ice.

Both the sitspin and camel spin can be performed as flying spins—that is, entered with a jump. The standard **flying camel** is entered as if for a forward camel on the left foot (counterclockwise) but immediately jumped over to a back camel on the right foot. **Flying sitspins** can be either forward or back spins and can involve landing on the same foot they take off from or changing feet. A good flying spin should attain the chosen position in the air, usually but not always the same as the spinning position. The **death drop**, which appears as a particularly high and extended camel spin position in the air, folded immediately into a back sitspin upon landing, is the most spectacular and also the most difficult flying spin because of the contrast between the high air position and the low spinning position.

The **layback spin** is a common variation of the upright spin in which the free leg is usually held in a back attitude position and the head and upper body arched backward so that the skater is facing up toward the sky or ceiling or even further back, behind herself. This spin is required for female skaters in the short program (although a **sideways leaning spin**, tilted sideways from the waist and hips instead of arched backward, may be substituted) and some lower-level tests, so most learn to master it well enough to include in free programs as well. A true layback position in a back spin is very difficult to maintain and therefore very seldom seen. A handful of male skaters perform versions of the layback or sideways leaning spin, but the majority do not have the natural upper back flexibility to perform the layback effectively and do not make the effort to increase this flexibility. The higher center of gravity in the male body also interferes with men's ability to perform this spin. Particularly supple female skaters may display their flexibility by grabbing the blade of the free foot while spinning and pulling it up toward the back of the head. The **Biellmann spin**, a related spin that requires even more flexibility, popularized by 1981 world champion Denise Biellmann, involves grabbing the free blade and pulling the foot straight up above the head so that the legs are approximately in a full split with the back and head arched upward.

A **combination spin** includes more than one position and may or may not include a change of foot. The current short program rules for junior and senior men and ladies require a combination spin with "only one change of foot and at least two changes of position." The easiest combination that would meet these requirements would be a forward camel to forward sitspin followed by a change of foot to back sitspin and a back scratchspin or other upright variation (a few concluding revolutions in a neutral upright position, however, would not be counted in the number of positions or revolutions). The change from forward camel to sit position, decreasing the circumference and swinging the free leg around from back to front in the direction of the spin, allows the spin to gain speed from the position change, and it is much easier to change feet in the sit position where most body parts remain close to the spinning center of the body. For added difficulty, skaters may include more positions, including variations that involve twisting, leaning, or holding up the free leg with one hand; switching to a camel position at the change of foot; making the change from back spin to forward spin; and/or making the change by means of a jump over rather than a step. Combinations in the free program, of course, may include more than one change of foot as well and jumps on the same foot while spinning in sitspin position.

JUMPS

Skating jumps are defined primarily according to the edge they take off from and whether or not they involve a toe assist. There are a variety of small jumps of one revolution or less that are useful for transitions, for variety within jump sequences and step sequences, and as connecting moves. Jumps that achieve great height and emphasize the position attained in the air, such as the split, Russian split, stag jumps, and the mazurka jump, in which the legs cross in the air like scissors, stand out as choreographic elements in their own right.

There are six jump takeoffs that allow for multiple rotation and that may be performed with one, two, three, or even four revolutions in the air before landing on a back outside edge. Roughly in order of difficulty, they are the salchow, toe loop, loop, flip, lutz, and axel. The double and triple versions of these jumps have become increasingly important over the years as a measure of technical and athletic ability, with attention paid to clean takeoffs and landings. During a jump, the skater's body travels in three directions simultaneously: horizontally—continuing along the direction of travel prior to leaving the ice; vertically—up off the ice and then back down; and around. A good double or triple jump achieves as much distance across the ice surface and as much height as possible, as well as tight rotation around the central axis of the body. In jumps of more than one revolution (and some of the single jumps as well) the free leg is generally crossed in front of the landing leg in the air, then unwraps upon or just before landing and swings back as the skater lands with a bent skating knee and opens the arms to check the rotation.

Because of the muscular force needed to achieve jump height and rotation, and the speed needed to maintain good ice coverage, these jumps leave little room for error. If the skater does not land with her weight precisely positioned over the landing edge or does not check the rotation hard enough or soon enough, she will be forced to continue rotating on the landing foot (usually turning a backward outside three turn followed by a forward inside one, known as a "double three," before controlling the desired back outside edge), or will continue rotating and be forced to step onto the other foot (a "step out" or "fall out," depending on how serious the lack of control is), or will have to place her free foot on the ice (a "touchdown" or "two-foot," depending on how long the blade remains on the ice and whether it provided any stability to the landing or simply didn't get out of the way in time), or must lean forward or sideways far enough that her hand touches the ice before she is able to control the landing edge. Or she may not be able to keep the landing foot under her at all and will find herself sitting or lying on the ice. If the rotation is incomplete, the skater may land facing forward or sideways relative to the direction of travel rather than backward; if she doesn't fall or put her free foot down, she may force the blade to rotate onto the back outside edge, which would be considered "cheating" the landing. Any of these errors would occasion a specified deduction from the required elements score if committed during a short program; in a free program they would result in the skater's receiving no credit or only partial credit for the jump attempted. It is also possible that the skater might land with most of the weight over the toepick so that the blade scratches or scrapes the ice before achieving a gliding edge, or that the skater lands bent forward or sideways at the waist but does not touch the ice with her hand, or that the free leg and/or arms flail wildly before achieving a controlled position, or that the landing edge produces a tight circle rather than a bold curve. These errors would not require any deductions, but compared to another skater who landed the same jump with good form and control would produce a jump of lower quality and therefore, everything else being equal, probably a lower score.

Most of these jumps are named after the men who invented them in the late nineteenth and early twentieth centuries. All jumps will be described from the counterclockwise perspective, to be landed on the right back outer edge. The clockwise version of each jump would involve the same edge on the opposite foot and would land on the left back outer edge.

An **edge jump** is one that takes off from any of the forward or backward edges from one foot only, without the other foot touching the ice. Although it is possible to scrape or spin the takeoff of some of these jumps (and in double and especially triple axels some degree of scraping may be inevitable), proper technique demands that the jump results from "a clean spring starting from a true edge"[1]—that is, the edge of the blade should bite into the ice and push against it to produce the elevation of the jump. For a counterclockwise jump, which would land on the right back outside edge, the takeoff edges in the same direction would be left back inside, right back outside, left forward outside, and right forward inside for the salchow, loop, axel, and inside axel jumps respectively. It is also possible to take off from an edge traveling clockwise and reverse the direction of rotation at the time of takeoff, thus jumping from the right back inside to right back outside in the **walley** jump, and from left back outside to right back outside in the almost-never-seen **toeless lutz** jump. This reversal of rotation is extremely difficult; double walley jumps are virtually unheard of, and skaters usually don't learn the single until after they have already mastered some of the easier double jumps. A few do, however, learn to perform the single walley on the opposite foot in the opposite direction as well.

The **salchow**, named for the Swedish world champion of the early twentieth century Ulrich Salchow, takes off the back inside edge of the left foot. The most common entrance to this jump is a LFO-to-LBI three turn. On the single jump, bringing the free side of the body forward and around toward the left after the turn is enough to produce the necessary rotation without pulling in the arms or free leg close to the body. Because the takeoff edge curves into the circle in the same direction as the rotation in the air, the skater's actual rotation in the air with respect to a fixed point is slightly less than 360 degrees. The takeoff and landing must both be on clean backward edges, however; if the skate blade begins to turn forward before taking off, or has not yet turned completely backward by the time of landing, the jump would be considered cheated. Pulling in tight from a controlled back inside edge easily produces additional rotation, which is why the salchow is usually the first jump that skaters learn to double, and the first or second to triple. There have been only a handful of attempts at quadruple salchows in competition, including some (unsuccessful) by Surya Bonaly and Sasha Cohen. The first attempt ratified as successful was by American Timothy Goebel (who thus became not only the first skater to land a quadruple salchow, but also the first American to land any successful quad in a major competition) at a junior international competition in March 1998; Miki Ando of Japan became the first female skater to land an officially ratified quad, the salchow, in December 2002.

The next edge jump is the **loop jump,** which takes off from the right back outside edge and lands on the same edge. Theoretically, if the skater did not jump, but performed the rotation without leaving the ice, the blade would draw a loop on the ice, which is where the jump gets its name. (In practice, however, if a skater does perform the motions of a loop jump without leaving the ice, the actual tracing produced is a double three and not a loop.) This jump is usually approached directly from back crossovers with the skater establishing the upper body position while gliding backward on the right outside edge of an uncrossing stroke before springing into the air (often with the left inside trailing on the ice without weight on it until the last moment before jumping; if the left, i.e., free foot does not leave the ice before the actual jump takeoff the two-footed takeoff would be considered incorrect). The loop is more difficult than the salchow or toe loop because the free leg is already in crossed position at takeoff, so the rotation is initiated from the upper body and the edge of the skating foot only. Most skaters find it easier than the flip and lutz because the coordination of timing and weight shift need not be so exact. Because the loop takes off from the same edge as the standard jump landing, it is possible to enter a loop jump from the landing of a previous jump, i.e., to perform it as the second jump of a combination. The fact that the free leg remains in front makes both controlling the landing of the first jump and generating the lift and rotation for the second more difficult than when a toe loop is used as the second jump.

There is also a transitional jump known as a **half loop** that takes off from the right back outside edge, just as the loop does, but lands on the left back inside. Because it rotates backward to backward, it is actually a whole-revolution jump, just slightly less than 360 degrees rotation. It is not performed as a double jump, because the back inside landing is much harder to control than the back outside. The half loop is used primarily in step sequences or as an isolated choreographic element, and in the middle of jump sequences (where it is one version of what commentators often refer to simply as a "hop,") and multiple-jump combinations followed by a double or triple salchow or occasionally a double flip. The axel–half loop–double salchow is seen fairly often from intermediate-level skaters, and a few senior-level skaters perform a double axel-half loop-triple salchow version.

The most difficult (but oldest) of the standard edge jumps is the **axel** or Axel Paulsen jump, first performed in the 1880s by Axel Paulsen of Norway. The axel is the only major jump with a forward takeoff, from the left forward outer to right back outer, and the change of foot means that the skater must transfer her center of gravity from the left side to the right while rotating in the air to be correctly positioned for landing. The single axel thus consists of one and a half revolutions, placing it at an intermediate level of difficulty between single and double jumps. The double axel involves two and a half revolutions, the triple axel three and a half. First performed in competition in 1978, the triple axel is the most difficult jump now expected of all senior-level male competitors at international events; some top junior men include it as well. The only women to complete this jump successfully in international competition have been Midori Ito of Japan (beginning in 1989) and Tonya Harding (in 1991), until fall of 2002, when a handful of young skaters, mostly from Japan, managed to land the jump. The approach to the axel is usually a series of backward crossovers in either the same or the opposite direction to the rotation of the jump, followed by a step forward onto the forward outside takeoff edge. Advanced skaters who perform single axels with ease can learn to perform a **delayed axel** with the legs straight and apart for the ascending part of the jump, involving only one quarter rotation, with the remaining one and a quarter rotations occurring on the way down. The delay in rotation gives a sense of suspension in the air rather than the usual smooth up and down arc. An even more spectacular variation is the **tuck axel**, in which the free (soon to be landing) leg is held extended in the air at hip level while the takeoff leg bends up next to the body.

The **waltz jump** takes off and lands on the same edges as the axel, but with only one half revolution from forward to backward. The free leg swings past the jumping leg and the half rotation and weight shift from left to right happen gradually (not sharply as in a ballet *tour jeté),* so that at the halfway point of the jump the legs are stretched in a wide second position in the air and the weight centered between them, with the front of the body facing into the circle. This is usually the first jump with a true back outside edge landing that beginning skaters learn. More advanced skaters often use waltz jumps as the first jump in their warm-up sequence to get the feel of the edges on the ice before attempting multiple-revolution jumps. Waltz jumps sometimes turn up in footwork and connecting sequences in programs, often with variations in the leg, arm, or back positions. Back when the double axel was the most advanced jump most female skaters performed, occasionally a skater would include a sequence of waltz jump, single axel, double axel in a program to demonstrate the progression from easy to intermediate to difficult jumps all based on the same takeoff.

The **one-foot axel** bears the same relation to the axel as the half-loop does to the loop jump: it uses the same takeoff and, except for the fraction of arc between landing with the weight over the left as opposed to right foot, the same amount of rotation as the standard jump (in the axel, left forward outside takeoff and one and a half revolutions), but it lands on the left back inside edge instead of the right back outside. Again, the inside edge landing is less stable and more difficult to control, so the jump is not performed as a double or triple. The one-foot axel may be used as a choreographic element in its own right, usually followed by a change of foot and additional steps. It can also occur as the introductory element in a jump combination or sequence that begins forward and continues with backward jumps. A one-foot axel followed immediately by a salchow (double, triple, or quadruple—the latter has been attempted in competition, although not successfully) is a true jump combination unusual in the fact that it does not conclude with a toe loop or loop jump.

Another forward-to-backward jump performed on one foot is the **inside axel**, taking off the right forward inside edge and landing on the right back outside as usual. It has the word *axel* in its name just because it is rare enough that no one ever felt the need to assign it its own name. It shares with the axel the distinction of a forward takeoff, but because the takeoff edge is different, technically it is a completely different jump. Because there is no weight shift involved, skaters sometimes learn this jump as a preparation to learning the true axel, in order to get used to rotating one and a half times in the air. Because the inside edge takeoff is less stable than the outside edge of the axel, and because the free leg does not swing through to assist with the height and rotation, it's hard to gain much power with an inside axel and so it is almost never performed as a double. Inside axels generally occur in programs as part of jump or step sequences.

Both the axel and the inside axel are sometimes performed in "half" (one-instead of one-and-a-half-revolution) varieties, landing forward on the edge of one foot and the toepick of the other. As such they are sometimes referred to simply as "hops" and usually occur in the middle of jump or step sequences.

Toe jumps are jumps that take off from the edge of one blade and the toepick of the other. The picking leg remains straight and acts in a similar manner to a pole-vaulting pole while the skating leg bends and releases to produce the jump. Technically, both blades should leave the ice at the same time, but in practice the picking leg usually comes off just a split second later, so that the weight is over the picking leg after takeoff and the jump feels more like an edge jump that takes off that foot than like an edge jump that takes off the same leg as the corresponding toe jump. For instance, both the salchow and the flip (which is occasionally referred to as a "toe salchow") take off from the left back inside edge, but because the flip also takes off from the right toepick, the feel and the technique of the jump have more in common with the loop than with the salchow. If the skater waits too long to leave the ice after getting her weight over the picking leg, however, so that the rotation of the jump begins with the pick still in the ice, the power of the jump will be dissipated and the jump will be cheated. For instance, a double toe loop that involves taking off forward from the left toepick, instead of backward from right edge and left pick, is known colloquially as a "toe axel." This is not a new variety of jump (there are no toe jumps with forward takeoffs), but a common error on the double toe loop, especially when performed at the end of a jump combination. In a single toe loop, this error would become a "toe waltz jump."

The **toe loop** is the easiest toe jump, comparable in difficulty to the salchow. It takes off from the right back outside edge and the left toepick. The skater approaches the RBO edge from a RFI-to-RBO three turn, a LFO-LBI three turn followed by a change of foot, or the landing of a previous jump. She reaches her left leg behind her, places the left toepick in the ice, and jumps, pulling the right leg back and around the left and reaching forward and around with the right arm and shoulder to achieve the rotation. Turning the body toward the assisting foot at takeoff slightly reduces the rotation required in the air, and the toe-assisted takeoff adds power, making the toe loop the easiest jump to add a third or even fourth revolution to. Skaters have been attempting quadruple toe loops in competition since the mid-1980s. Kurt Browning was officially credited with the first successful attempt at the 1988 World Championships, and numerous other skaters have achieved both better and worse results since then. Surya Bonaly is the only woman to have performed this quad in competition; none of her attempts was officially recognized as complete. Because the takeoff position for the toe loop (right back outer edge, with the free foot swinging back) is the same as the standard landing position, the toe loop is the most common jump used at the end of a jump combination.

The **toe walley** is a counter-rotational jump taking off from the clockwise right back inside edge and reversing rotation at takeoff, like the walley jump described briefly above, assisted by the left toepick. It is usually approached from a LFO-to-LBI three turn and a step to the RBI edge. The takeoff edge is thus in the opposite direction from the rotation and landing edge, although the toe assist facilitates the change of direction. The toe walley is slightly more difficult than the toe loop, but so similar that they are considered the same jump for the purposes of limiting repetitions of triples (and, as of 1998–1999, quads) in the long program. Skaters are therefore much less likely to perform toe walleys than toe loops, although some commentators assume that any jump approached from a LFO three followed by a change of foot and vault from the toe is a toe walley, because the edge on the right foot is often too brief to discern in real time.

The **flip jump** (which has nothing to do with the backflip used in professional and show skating) takes off from the left back inside edge and right toepick. For this jump it is particularly important that the edge not be too deep, but rather forms almost a straight line. The unstable inside edge and the precision necessary for aligning and timing the vault from the toepick make the flip somewhat trickier than the loop for most skaters, considerably more so than the salchow or toe loop.

Performed with only half a revolution from backward to forward, landing on either toepick and the forward edge of the other foot, the **half flip** can be a simple transitional move in the middle of a step sequence. It is also the standard takeoff for the **split jump** and other large half-revolution jumps that emphasize position in the air rather than rotation. A Russian split jump performed with one quarter rotation on the way up and an additional three quarters (instead of the usual one quarter) on the way down, so that the jump lands on the standard back outside landing edge, is in effect a full single flip jump with a split position at the peak, known as a **split flip**.

The **lutz**, like the walley and toe walley, is also a counter-rotational jump, from the left back outside edge and right toepick. The picking technique is similar to the flip jump, but the upper body action necessary to reverse the rotation is different and even trickier to master. Almost all skaters find single and double lutzes more difficult than the corresponding flips, but when it comes to triples some find that the power and stability of the outside edge takeoff allow for more control than the inside edge of the flip. A handful of skaters have attempted a quadruple lutz in practice, and Michael Weiss of the United States has attempted it in competition occasionally, but it has yet to be performed successfully in competition. Skaters usually approach the lutz with a series of clockwise back crossovers and then a long LBO edge heading toward the corner of the ice surface. Because the upper body turns toward the outside of the circle before jumping, the skater can't see where she's heading with her head straight over her shoulders. While holding the entry edge, the skater will often look back over her right shoulder to judge the distance to the barrier, or on practice sessions to make sure there aren't any other skaters in the way; this is one way to recognize the most common lutz approach.

A **jump combination** is two (or more) jumps performed in immediate succession so that the landing edge of the first jump becomes the takeoff edge for the next. If the second jump is a toe jump, usually a toe loop, the other foot will of course touch the ice in the form of the toepick assist, but any step to an edge on the other foot or turn (e.g., a three turn) on the ice precludes a true combination. A series of jumps linked together with any such intervening steps or turns is called a **jump sequence** or **jump series**. From the normal back outside landing edge, the possible second jumps in a true combination are the toe loop and loop. Other possible true combinations are a one-foot axel or half loop, landing on the back inside edge, followed by a salchow or flip, and any reverse (opposite direction) jump, for example, a reverse walley, followed by a lutz. Because jumps with inside-edge landings and reverse jumps are almost always performed as singles, however, these unusual combinations generally turn up in free programs, if they are performed at all, and never appear in the required jump combination in the short program. A repeated triple or quad in the long program must be performed as part of either a jump combination or jump sequence, but because sequences are allowed, the distinction between sequences and true combinations is less vital there.

Notes

NOTES TO THE INTRODUCTION

1. Among the American sportswriters who have made figure skating their beat, the most prominent include Philip Hersh of the *Chicago Tribune,* Jere Longman of the *New York Times,* Joann Barnas of the *Detroit Free Press,* E. M. Swift of *Sports Illustrated,* and, most notably, Christine Brennan, formerly of the *Washington Post,* later of *USA Today,* and author of two nonfiction books about elite skaters and skating. For citations of scholarly writing addressing figure skating as subject matter, see the notes to chaps. 6 and 8.

2. See Laura Mulvey, "Visual Pleasure and Narrative Cinema," (1975), rpt. in *Feminisms: An Anthology of Literary Theory and Criticism,* ed. Robyn R. Warhol and Diane Price Herndl (New Brunswick: Rutgers University Press, 1991). For instance, in addition to the *Ms.* article by Kate Rounds discussed in chap. 6, Sandy Flitterman-Lewis's "Tales of the Ice Princess and the Trash Queen: Cultural Fictions and the Production of 'Women,'" in Cynthia Baughman, ed., *Women on Ice: Feminist Essays on the Tonya Harding/Nancy Kerrigan Spectacle* (New York: Routledge, 1995), draws directly on Mulvey's notions of "the sadistic voyeurism of narrative and the fetishistic scopophilia of display"; Flitterman-Lewis finds Harding's experiences in Lillehammer and the way CBS conveyed them to the American public to fit neatly into the paradigm of sadistic voyeurism, while Kerrigan became the quintessential object of display: "As everything else dissolves around the viewer and the object of desire, looking at the performing woman becomes an activity of intense libidinal investment. And it is this body, this image, and this product that the name Nancy Kerrigan has come to signify in the constructed social imagery surrounding the two skaters" (173). Robyn Wiegman and Lynda Zwinger attempt to develop a theory of what they call "heterovisuality," the ways that television in particular depicts women's sports according to narratives of heterosexuality defined in terms of the visual. They attribute the disjunction between "the athletic female body, cultural norms of femininity, . . . and accepted forms of female social bonds" to, in part, "the active/passive split that traditionally governs the visual scenarios in which the female body appears—what feminist film theory has defined as the implicitly masculine structure of the gaze" ("Tonya's Bad Boot, or Go Figure," in Baughman, *Women on Ice,* 105). In terms of figure skating, "the athletic female body strains under the regime of aestheticized female beauty, negotiating a narrow space of acceptance between muscular strength on the one hand and the 'grace' and 'loveliness' of a thin, fashion-ready and heterosexualized body on the other" (109).

3. See, e.g., Melanie Thernstrom, "The Glass Slipper" (148–161), Lynn Spigel, "Cool Medium on Ice: Tonya, Nancy, and Television" (193–203); and Jane Feuer, "Nancy and Tonya and Sonja: The Figure of the Figure Skater in American Entertainment" (3–21), all in Baughman, *Women on Ice.* Some of the articles in the Baughman anthology allude to ways that Harding might serve pro-feminist functions: her physicality, muscularity, and athleticism, her frankly commercial interests in winning (as exemplified by her comment about seeing dollar signs when she skated), and her traditionally masculine and/or blue-collar taste in music and interests such as shooting pool and fixing truck engines reveal that the image of upper-class femininity that figure skating and the American media in general promote is not inherent in all women's, or even all female figure skaters', bodies. Harding's very existence therefore disrupts prevailing assumptions about a coherent, essentialist, pure femininity. Wiegman and Zwinger, for instance, state of women's sports in general that:

> It is hardly a surprise to recognize that the female body, muscled and in motion, perhaps (gasp) sweating or (double gasp) not at all conscious of, perhaps not even self-conscious about the buoyancy of her breasts—such a female body violates the classic visual paradigm in which the female body is defined by and articulated as the locus of heterosexual masculine desire. Or perhaps it is most accurate to say that such a female body threatens to violate this paradigm, threatens to dismantle the heterosexualized femininity in which women's bodies . . . are cast. (105)

Referring to Kerrigan and Harding specifically, they note:

> But these nice ice girls who love their mothers and have high school chumlike relationships with their closest rivals are serious athletes who could deck the prince as easily as waltz off with him, who don't need fairy godmothers to dress them for the ball because they have their own gold (American Express cards), who are in the game for bottom lines never acknowledged in the how-to-be-a-nice-girl handbooks (magazines, television, movies, Connie Chung interviews). It's a precarious kind of disavowal we are engaged in when we see only the image and not the business. And of course it is the unmasking of this disavowal by a noncomplying player that has pretty soundly rattled nearly everyone on and near the ice. (114)

They then go on to cite various descriptions of Harding in masculine terms.

See also the article by Kate Rounds discussed in chap. 6, and Elizabeth Kissling, "Skating on Thin Ice: Why Tonya Harding Could Never Be America's Ice Princess," paper presented at the annual meeting of American Folkore Society, Oct. 1994, Milwaukee.

4. Originally, the man's arms were not supposed to travel above chest height; this was later modified to no higher than his shoulder, and as of 1997–1998 no

higher than his head (ironic because overhead lifts do exist in the context of exhibition and some divisions of competitive ballroom dance). These dance lifts are usually developed anew for each new dance to enhance the musical interpretation or thematic content and to suit the abilities of the particular team performing them. They aren't standardized and expected of all dance teams the way pairs lifts are, and they would contribute to the presentation score just as much as to technical merit.

NOTES TO CHAPTER ONE

1. Ferdinand de Saussure, *Course in General Linguistics*, trans. Wade Baskin (New York: McGraw-Hill, 1966).

2. Stanley Fish, *Is There a Text in This Class* (Cambridge: Harvard University Press, 1980).

3. For discussion over whether sport is or can also be art, with examples frequently drawn from figure skating, see the section "Sport and Aesthetics" in *Philosophic Inquiry in Sport*, ed. William J. Morgan and Klaus V. Meier (Champaign, IL: Human Kinetics, 1988).

4. For a discussion of these processes, see Stuart Hall, "Encoding, Decoding," in *The Cultural Studies Reader*, ed. Simon During (London: Routledge, 1993), 90–103. For a history of this shift in emphasis, see During's introduction to that anthology.

5. For the structural anthropologist Claude Lévi-Strauss, human societies make sense of the world by dividing it into a series of related binary oppositions. See Claude Lévi-Strauss, *The Raw and the Cooked*, trans. John and Doreen Weightman (New York: Harper & Row, 1969). Not all aspects of reality, however, fit easily into one side or the other of the relevant binary, and it is most often the exceptions that exist at the intersections between opposites that prove the most potent symbols in the myths Lévi-Strauss analyzes. According to cultural analyst John Fiske, these exceptions occupy "anomalous categories" that "draw their characteristics from both of the binarily opposed ones, and consequently they have too much meaning, they are conceptually too powerful" (John Fiske, *Introduction to Communication Studies*, 2d ed. [London: Routledge, 1990], 118).

6. Skaters at various levels of accomplishment express similar sentiments. Olympic medalist Paul Wylie says, "I think the whole activity of skating on ice is always a little bit mystifying, in its own way. I don't think anybody or anything can take away that power. It's a really neat human, cultural activity. I mean, it's kind of weird. You take a tool. You strap a blade to your skate. You go out on the ice and you perform all sorts of maneuvers that you couldn't do without the frictionless surface" (qtd. in Michael Knisley, "In This Sport, Everything Figures; The Lillehammer Games Exposed Figure Skating's Dirty Little Secrets," *Sporting News*, Mar. 7, 1994, Olympic section, 12).

A pair skater who has competed internationally representing both the United States and Greece says,

> I am a music fanatic. I always have some type of music playing in my car stereo, on my home stereo, or in my walkman as I am walking around. I am especially linked with classical music because I think it has such depth and integrity. The music is powerful and can be incredibly expressive and emotional. . . . It's hard to express the emotion felt when hitting a line. . . . your freeleg [*sic*] fully extended, arms outstretched, and your back and abdominal muscles supporting your position. . . . listening to Puccini's, "O Mio Babbino Caro" or stroking as fast as you can into a reckless and exhilarating footwork sequence to Orff's, "O Fortuna, O Fortune." (Mark Naylor, personal communication, Apr. 21, 1993)

A former pairs competitor, now coaching, says, "I was told this, and I tell my kids this, you know, if you go into something as fast as you can skate, and jump up in the air, that's as close to flying on your own that you're ever going to feel, and it's the coolest feeling in the world" (Cesca Supple, personal interview, Oct. 1997).

Adult recreational skaters offer the following reasons for their addictions to the sport:

> For me, the watchword is "passion." I came to this sport looking for nothing more than an alternative to the Nordic Trak that wasn't so boring, and found the fountain of youth! It is artistic, it is passionate, it is challenging, it is creative, and in all probability, it has changed my life. (Don Cardoza, posted to the rec.sport.skating.ice.figure newsgroup, May 18, 1998; qtd. by permission)

> I love to go fast; I love the feeling of the cold wind in my face; I love the adrenalin rush that I get from attempting an axel when I'm going real fast; I love being the first person out on the ice and having that whole wide open space all to myself early on Sunday morning when everybody else I know is still home in bed; sometimes I even like to fall! . . .
>
> I love the fact that in skating I am only competing against myself. I look at competitions as a challenge to myself, a learning experience. Of course, placing well feels great, but skating well and living up to the challenge that I've placed on myself feels even better.
>
> I also love the fact that skating has so many goals; big ones like passing a test, little ones like learning a new move or just getting that axel a little further around. Setting goals and reaching them really helps my self-confidence. When I have to do something that I am nervous about, such as giving a presentation at work, I remind myself that this is another challenge just like skating; and I'm probably the only person in that room

who can do a lutz! (Debbie Mulrooney, posted to skaters-l mailing list, Oct. 31, 1996; qtd. by permission)

Peace—the intense feeling of inner stillness that comes from fully concentrating all of the body and mind on something

Excitement—the rush of excitement before, during, and after performance. Also the excitement of FINALLY having something go right after you've been working at it a long time

Solitude—the privacy of concentration, especially during patch or while working on dance footwork, but also on any other aspect of skating.

Companionship & comaraderie . . .

Exercise, conditioning . . .

Body awareness—becoming aware of where the bits and pieces are and what happens when you move them (and how to keep from moving them if you don't want to)

Sanity—I can't really think about anything but skating while I'm skating, so it provides a wonderful breather in the middle of the day. . . . calming me after a bad morning, getting me ready for a possibly strange afternoon

Perspective—skating puts my work into perspective. Work puts skating into perspective.

Flying—the wonderful frictionless sensation of flying (not even during jumps. . . . . maybe MAINLY not in jumps)

Goals—a never-ending supply of goals to work toward [and] . . . a growing list of goals reached. They don't even have to be enormous goals to bring satisfaction. . . .

Facing up to fear—working at something that scares you until finally one day you realize that you are doing the move without even thinking about it. Also doing something that scares you even though it's still scarey, and realizing that you CAN do it and you WILL.

An appreciation of what goes into skating . . .

An opportunity to serve and be useful. (Janet Swan Hill, posted to skaters-l mailing list, Nov. 6, 1996, qtd. by permission)

7. Nigel Brown, *Ice-Skating: A History* (New York: A. S. Barnes and Company, 1959), 105.

8. The sense of leaving one's mark on the world is more prominent on natural ice than on artificial ice, since the tracings left by the blade stand out more against a dark surface than on ice produced over white-painted floors, as is the case in most arenas, and since the marks will remain until the next change in the weather or until enough people skate over them to obliterate them. This sense is particularly prominent in the once-celebrated practice of carving one's name into the ice on one foot.

For discussions of the gender associations of these aspects of sport, see, for instance, Pierre Bourdieu, "How Can One Be a Sports Fan?" in *The Cultural Studies Reader*, ed. Simon During (London: Routledge, 1993); and Brian Pronger, *The Arena of Masculinity* (New York: St. Martin's, 1990).

9. Mulvey, "Visual Pleasure and Narrative Cinema."

10. John Berger, *Ways of Seeing* (London: British Broadcasting Corporation, 1972), 46, 47; Mulvey, "Visual Pleasure and Narrative Cinema," 436. Berger's book offers a discussion of this tendency in the realms of film and visual arts in general.

11. For instance, the 1960 USFSA rulebook specifies:

2. Manner of Performance.

a. The general carriage, except in planned positions, should be erect but without stiffness.

b. The head should follow out the line of the back.

c. The free leg should be carried as gracefully as possible, moderately extended and controlled without stiffness, knee and hip turned out, the toe pointed down and out. It should swing freely to assist the movement but at all times with control.

d. The skating knee should be used with great flexibility, continuously straightening and bending to give that beautiful easy glide and effortless "run" that is the essence of skating.

e. The arms should be held easily; like the free foot, they can be used to assist the movement. In general, they should be held out on a line with the waist of the skater. The elbows should be softly curved, never bent outward in "akimbo" position, nor should the shoulders be raised.

f. The hands should follow out the line of the arms, palms generally towards the ice, not being allowed to dangle, droop, or curve sharply in a stereotyped or affected manner. Never, except in a few planned positions, should there be deviation from the above.

g. The fingers should be held easily; they should not be spread or clenched or held rigidly straight.

h. Speed should be gained as inconspicuously as possible, and maintained without "pumping" the arms, bending from the waist, or scrambling with the feet.

i. In general, everything violent, angular or stiff should be avoided. There should be no visible strong effort and the impression should be given that the entire program is executed with ease.

(United States Figure Skating Association, *USFSA Rulebook, 1960 Edition* [Boston: USFSA, 1959], 6–7)

12. Judith Butler, "Performative Acts and Gender Constitution," in *Perform-*

ing Feminisms: Feminist Theory and Theatre, ed. Sue-Ellen Case (Baltimore: Johns Hopkins University Press, 1990), 270.

13. See Marcel Mauss, "Techniques of the Body," *Economy and Society* 2.1 (1973): 70–88.

14. See, e.g., Mary Douglas, *Natural Symbol: Explorations in Cosmology* (New York: Pantheon, 1970), particularly the chapter entitled "The Two Bodies"; Jonathan Benthall and Ted Polhemus, eds., *The Body as a Medium of Expression* (New York: Dutton, 1975).

15. Michel Foucault, *Discipline and Punish: The Birth of the Prison,* trans. Alan Sheridan (New York: Vintage, 1979), 136.

16. Details are available in the rulebook and schedule information from the USFSA and ISU (see "For Further Reading and Viewing" for contact information). For handy overviews, see www.sk8stuff.com/m_basic.htm and related links, and www.frogsonice.com/skateweb/faq/rules.shtml.

17. Foucault, *Discipline and Punish,* 184.

18. A coach says:

> I think [competition is] important because it gives them first a way to judge how they're doing against other skaters, to be able to rank themselves, to give them goals, to give them something to work on. It motivates them and it's very rewarding, because then they get to go home with their little trophies, their little rewards, and say, "Yeah, I did a good job." You have something to look forward to, you have something to work toward. I think it's very important. I don't push it on everybody, and I make sure that they're going to the right competitions. I don't like to send kids to competitions who aren't ready or who aren't—who are just going to get wiped out, because that's not fair to them. So I try and pick and choose the competitions. . . . It's not for everybody, but I think it is important. So you just find a competition where they can do well and put them at a level where they can do well and feel proud of what they've done. You don't want it too easy or too hard because that's not fair to their poor little psyches. (Susi Wehrli-Thompson, personal interview, July 1996)

19. At the ISU championships—that is, the World and Junior World Championships, the European Championships, and potentially the Four Continents Championships (an event initiated in 1999 for skaters representing non-European countries)—qualification rounds were instituted in 1993 for events with more than thirty entrants to reduce the field to thirty for the short program, with a further cut being made to twenty-four for the long. Skaters perform their long programs in two groups for two separate panels of judges, and the top fifteen skaters in each group advance to the short program. It has never yet been necessary to hold such initial rounds for pairs or at Four Continents, and in the dance

event the cut to thirty is made after the compulsory dances. Beginning with the 1999 season, the qualification round results contribute toward the final results, counting for 20 percent of the final score, with the short program reduced to 30 percent and the long to 50 percent rather than the one-third and two-thirds factors that they carried in the past and continue to carry in competitions with fewer entrants. This change allows smaller countries whose skaters do not qualify for the final phases of the event to participate in the offical championships rather than just in a preliminary event. For the top skaters, this change means that they can no longer afford to take it easy during qualification rounds and save their strength for the subsequent phases later in the week, and the revised weightings result in more instances than are seen in the two-program format of gold medals going to skaters who do well in the two earlier phases and then fail to win the final freeskate.

20. The ISU criteria for marking the required elements are:

- A. Jumps: the height, length, technique, and the clean starting and landing of the required jumps;
- B. Jump combinations: the perfect execution of the two jumps in relation to their difficulty;
- C. Spins: strong and well-controlled rotation, number of revolutions in the required position, speed of rotation (in fast spins), centering of the spin. In flying spins, the height of the jump and the position in the air and landing;
- D. Step and spiral sequences: the difficulty of the steps used, the swing, carriage and smooth flow of the movement in conformity with the character and rhythm of the music;
- E. Difficulty of the connecting steps/movements;
- F. Speed.

The ISU provides the judges with a table setting forth the point deductions required for each of the possible errors a skater might make on any of the required elements.

For presentation, the criteria are:

- A. Harmonious composition of the program as a whole and its conformity with the music chosen;
- B. Variation of speed;
- C. Utilization of the ice surface and space;
- D. Easy movement and sureness in time to the music;
- E. Carriage and style;
- F. Originality;
- G. Expression of the character of the music. (*The 2001 Official USFSA*

Rulebook [Colorado Springs: United States Figure Skating Association, 2000], 120–121)

For pairs, unison is also a criterion under the second mark.

21. The criteria for technical merit are:

A. Difficulty of the performance (with no credit being given for portions thereof which are missed);
B. Variety;
C. Cleanness and sureness;
D. Speed.

For presentation, they are:

A. Harmonious composition of the program as a whole and its conformity with the music chosen;
B. Variation of speed;
C. Utilization of the ice surface;
D. Easy movement and sureness in time to the music;
E. Carriage and style;
F. Originality;
G. Expression of the character of the music. (United States Figure Skating Association, *The 1999 Official USFSA Rulebook* [Colorado Springs, CO: USFSA], 116)

22. Jeroen Prins, interview with Katja Rupp; J. Prins, personal communcation.

23. Jean Senft, CBC broadcast of 1993 World Championships men's short program.

24. See Amy Rosewater, "New Scoring System Is in Developing Stages," *New York Times*, Oct. 4, 2002; Hilary Kraus, "Scores Shrouded in Anonymity: Judges Row Shouldn't Cause a Row When Skating Scores Announced," Associated Press wire story, Oct. 22, 2002; and Philip Hersh, "A season of confusion awaits: 2 sets of scoring systems on tap; 3rd on the way" *Chicago Tribune*, Oct. 24, 2002.

25. See Melanie Campbell, "Proposed Judging System Has Many Benefits: Undergoes Testing at Skate Canada," www.skatecanada.ca/english/mcscie02/news.

26. "Passion on Ice," *Newsweek*, Mar. 15, 1993, 73.

27. Tom Weir, "Figure Skating Never Lacks for a Story," *USA Today*, Jan. 14, 1994.

28. Bernie Lincicome, "Here's a Sure Cure for Winter Blahs," *Chicago Tribune*, Feb. 20, 1992. A decade later, Lincicome was still expressing similar sentiments; see "Skating as Sport in Olympics? Go Figure," *Rocky Mountain News*, Jan. 14, 2002. For another perspective, see Karlo Berkovich, "Can We Really Call

Figure Skating a Sport? By Strict Dictionary Definition It Is, but Then Again So Are Bowling and Fishing" *Kitchener-Waterloo Record*, Dec. 14, 2001.

29. See, e.g., Franklin Foer, "Howard Kurtz and the Decline of Media Criticism," the Wayward Critic, *New Republic Online,* May 4, 2000, www.thenewrepublic.com/051500/foero515, which compares media critic Kurtz to "an East German figure-skating judge, docking reporters for technicalities."

30. Noel Streatfeild, *Skating Shoes* (New York: Random House, 1951).

31. *Ice Castles,* dir. Donald Wrye, with Lynn-Holly Johnson and Robbie Benson. Columbia Pictures, 1979.

32. But from an axel takeoff, at a time when only one man had ever performed a triple axel in competition and only the strongest jumpers among the women performed triple jumps at all. The two times Lexie is shown performing this "triple" it is not shown completed—the first time the scene cuts from a shot of Lexie taking off for the jump at a practice session to a scene in a car with her coach berating her for "show-off acrobatics"; the second time the shot of the takeoff is followed by slow-motion shots of her falling into the patio furniture. Actress Lynn-Holly Johnson, a former competitive skater herself, performed much of her own skating for the film. According to a *Skating* magazine article at the time, skater Staci Loop was flown in to double for Johnson in some skating scenes. "She donned a blonde wig and performed double Axels and triple loops which were crucial to Lexie's climatic [*sic*] winning performance, however, the triple loops were later edited out" (Debbie Stoery, "Silver Screen Skating," *Skating,* Nov. 1978, 26). During a scene of Lexie competing elsewhere during the film, she is shown matter-of-factly performing double axels along with the other double jumps, so the film is not asking us to believe that a double axel is actually a triple jump. Are we supposed to believe that Lexie can perform triple axels but not any of the easier triple jumps that female skaters were actually performing at the time? Or does the film count on viewers not knowing one jump from another and find the forward takeoff of the axel and its additional half rotation more dramatic than using Loop's triple loop or any of the backward takeoffs edited to make a double jump look like a credible triple?

NOTES TO CHAPTER TWO

1. Roland Barthes, "Myth Today," in *Mythologies,* trans. Annette Lavers (New York: Noonday, 1972), 113–159.

2. Roland Barthes, "The Third Meaning," in *Image, Music, Text,* essays selected and translated by Stephen Heath (New York: Hill & Wang, 1977).

3. CBC broadcast of men's free skate, 1995 World Championships.

4. Susan Leigh Foster, *Reading Dancing: Bodies and Subjects in Contemporary American Dance* (Berkeley: University of California Press, 1986); see esp. chap. 2, "Reading Choreography: Composing Dances."

5. Choreographers for the Next Ice Age, a professional skating troupe organ-

ized along the lines of a ballet or modern dance company, note the difference in emphasis between competitive and art skating. Company codirector Nathan Birch said that Next Ice Age skaters have to be willing to check the soloist mentality at the door; his colleague Tim Murphy then elaborated that, as hard as it is to train for Olympic competition, it's much harder to train for Next Ice Age. Competitors are pampered, but in Next Ice Age, "the choreographers are pampered" (at least until opening night, when they give the works over to the performers) (Question and answer session at Next Ice Age open rehearsal, Kennedy Center Eisenhower Theatre, Washington, DC, Sept. 22, 2001). Who gets to be pampered —made the focus of others' attention, with his or her needs or vision taking precedence—is also whose meanings the collaborative work is structured to support. In competitive skating, it is the skater; in an artistic dance company on ice, it is the choreographer.

6. For further discussion of this example, see chap. 6.

7. It is not unknown for skaters to attempt jumps that they land successfully in practice only rarely, or even never. Including such moves may be a form of prevarication, in hopes that the judges will interpret the failure of such an attempt as the exception rather than the rule. In the short program, judges assign base marks to each program as attempted and then take required deductions from the base mark as necessary. If a skater is not entirely confident of an easier jump she could include, she might attempt a more difficult jump instead, believing that if a deduction is likely in any case it would be preferable to have the deduction taken from a higher base mark. An experienced judge, however, can usually tell from the nature of the failure whether the skater was capable of succeeding or not and will take this into account in setting a short program base mark or in deciding whether to give partial credit for an unsuccessful attempt in the free program. One judge says that she marks falls and two-footed jump landings in her notes as "could be" or "no way" (Debby Fortin, personal communication). From watching practices at the competition venue and the warm-up before each group of skaters competes, judges often have a general sense of which jumps each skater has mastered and which she is still in the process of learning.

Occasionally a skater may include a jump she has little expectation of landing successfully to send a message other than the false one that she expects to land it. If it is a jump none of her competitors are expected to include, for instance Surya Bonaly's and more recently Sasha Cohen's attempts at quadruple jumps, the attempt itself may signal that she is bored with the standard repertoire of jumps at her competitive level and is setting herself new challenges, and it marks her as an adventurous and potentially history-making athlete. Michelle Kwan's attempt at a triple lutz–triple loop combination at 2001 Skate Canada could be seen as an answer to criticisms that she had been playing it safe and neglecting to "up the ante" in her jump content while her rivals were attempting (but less often completing) more difficult triple-triple combinations than the triple toe–triple toe Kwan had been including since 1995–1996. Sébastien Britten (a skater who excelled at most skating techniques except for jumping and who won the 1995 Canadian title when world champion Elvis Stojko withdrew from the national championship because of injury) included triple axel attempts in his 1995–1996 programs as a way of letting the judges and especially the Canadian Figure Skating Association know that he was working seriously toward mastering this jump, which the CFSA had determined was a prerequisite for male skaters to be sent to senior international competitions.

8. *The 2001 Official USFSA Rulebook,* 122–123. Skaters may repeat only two different jumps of three or more revolutions (only one at the novice level) one additional time, and at least one time the repeated jump is performed it must be part of a jump combination or sequence, which adds the information that not only can the skater perform the jump, she can also combine it with other jumps.

9. Ibid., 123.

10. Senft, "Judge's Seat," CBC broadcast of 1995 Europeans, men's long program.

11. Ibid.

12. Ricky Harris, *Choreography and Style for Ice Skaters* (New York: St. Martin's, 1980), 50, 57.

13. Qtd. in Randy Harvey, "This Time, Eldredge Takes Charge," *Los Angeles Times,* Nov. 1, 1996.

14. This was even more true through the 1994 season, when missing the combination could carry deductions as high as 0.5, since lowered to 0.4, or 0.6 and 0.5 respectively for omitting it entirely, and when ladies were not permitted to perform a second triple jump as the isolated jump out of footwork.

15. *USFSA Rulebook,* 144.

16. See, e.g., chap. 7, "Sports, Inc.: The Influence of the Mass Media," in Mary A. Boutilier and Lucinda SanGiovanni, *The Sporting Woman,* Champaign, IL: Human Kinetics Publishers, 1983; Garry Whannel, "Fields in Vision: Sport and Representation," *Screen* 25, 1984.

17. Ricky Harris advises young skaters to develop movements by starting with everyday gestures and stylizing them (33).

18. See Susanne Langer, *Feeling and Form* (New York: Charles Scribner's Sons, 1953).

19. See Marsha Lopez, "Does Figure Skating Exploit Females?" *American Skating World,* Aug. 1995, 25.

20. Peter Paul Moormann, "Figure Skating Performance: A Psychological Study," Ph.D. diss., Leiden University, 1994, 7.6.1.

21. Ibid., 7.6.3.

22. Ibid., 7.6.5.

23. Rudolf Laban, *The Mastery of Movement,* 4th ed. revised by Lisa Ullmann (Plymouth, UK: Northcote House, 1950, 1988), 84–85.

24. An extreme example would be perceiving meaning simply in the title of a musical work, as in Tonya Harding's choice to skate the soundtrack from "Much Ado About Nothing" at the Lillehammer Olympics, during the height of the controversy surrounding her. During the CBS broadcast of the event, commentator Verne Lundquist referred to this music choice as "ironic," which author Marsha Kinder interpreted as "sarcastic," although in fact the choice of music for that year's programs had been made months earlier, well before the plot against Kerrigan supposedly formed. See Marsha Kinder, "Tonya, Nancy, and the Dream Scheme: Nationalizing the 1994 Olympics," in Baughman, *Women on Ice*, 246. Less extreme would be American audiences' recognition of the opening phrase of Russian skater Ilya Kulik's 1996 short program to music from the soundtrack of the Addams Family movie, despite Kulik's unfamiliarity with the characters and attitude associated with the music.

25. Kurt Browning, *Kurt: Forcing the Edge* (Toronto: HarperCollins, 1991), 151–152.

26. Moorman, "Figure Skating Performance," 6.6.6.

27. A male pair skater comments, "Make-up is the final touch. The make-up itself cannot be too theatrical in nature; it is meant to simply augment fair skin complexions under bright lights and present women as attractive [*sic*] as possible. In my opinion, make-up is of least importance. However, this may be just a male's perspective" (Mark Naylor, personal communication, Apr. 21, 1993).

28. *The 2001 USFSA Rulebook*, 146. Note that the ruling discourages "excessive" decoration such as beads, sequins, and feathers but does not forbid their use entirely. The rule goes on to state that "any ornamentation attached to the clothing must be firmly fastened so as not to fall off while skating under normal competitive conditions."

For synchronized skating, in which up to twenty-four skaters may be on the ice at once in close contact, the rules are more restrictive for reasons of safety: "No feathers, sequins, rhinestones, jeweled trim or other materials or items that could be dislodged upon contact shall be permitted on the skaters' clothing. . . . The use of hair pins and bobby pins is prohibited while skating in any synchronized team skating competition" (158).

29. Ibid., 136.

30. Keith Johnstone, *Impro: Improvisation and the Theatre* (New York: Theatre Arts Books, 1979), offers a chapter on "Status" that discusses very usefully performers' (actors') use of varying status positions with regard to each other and to the performance space. For a feminist discussion of status relationships between performer and audience, see, e.g., Elin Diamond, "Brechtian Theory/ Feminist Theory: Towards a Gestic Feminist Criticism," *Drama Review* 32.1 (1988).

31. Foster, *Reading Dancing*, 65.

32. Jay Miller, "The Maturation of Michelle," *Skating*, June 1996, 23.

33. ABC coverage of 1995 Skate America.

34. Qtd. in Susan Reed, "At Rainbow's End," *People*, Mar. 18, 1996, 116. The ABC broadcast of the 1996 World Championships reported a briefer version of the remark: "Her coach Frank Carroll said, 'The judges wanted a ladies' champion, not a girls' champion.'"

35. Aired during the ABC coverage of 1996 U.S. Nationals.

36. Analysis based on ABC coverage of 1995 Skate America.

37. See Edward Said, *Orientalism* (New York: Vintage, 1978).

NOTES TO CHAPTER THREE

1. Historical information in the beginning of this chapter, where not otherwise indicated, comes from Nigel Brown, *Ice-Skating: A History* (New York: A. S. Barnes, 1959), and Julia Whedon, *The Fine Art of Ice Skating: An Illustrated History and Portfolio of Stars* (New York: Harry N. Abrams, 1988).

The prehistory and early history of figure skating as an organized sport has, to date, primarily been written as collections of interesting anecdotes, aimed at skaters and/or skating fans, uncluttered by reference lists, footnotes, or other scholarly apparatuses. Many of the documents and artifacts still in existence that can illuminate this history are housed in the figure skating museum and archives at the USFSA's headquarters in Colorado Springs and have served as the source material for the popular histories, such as the books and *Skating* magazine or television retrospectives, cited throughout this section. A thorough critical history of the sport's origins could be written, should a market for such a work exist, by a scholar with enough weeks available to pore through the archives in detail within the museum's five-hours-per-day opening schedule. Because of limitations of time and space, that is not my project here. Nor do I wish simply to duplicate the efforts of Brown and Whedon, or of Benjamin Wright, Lynn Copley-Graves, and others (see "For Further Reading and Viewing"), by combing the archives for the same and perhaps some fresh anecdotes. Rather, I wish to sketch the outlines of where figure skating came from and how later practitioners have understood that history in order to illuminate more recent practices.

2. *Frostiana*, qtd. in Whedon, *Fine Art of Ice Skating*, 52.

3. Brown, *Ice-Skating*, 70.

4. Ibid., 112–116.

5. H. E. Vandervell and T. Maxwell Witham, *A System of Figure-Skating: Being the theory and practice of the art as developed in England, with a glance at its origin and history* (London: Macmillan, 1869), 232–234.

6. Ibid., 63.

7. Ibid., 231.

8. Miss L. Cheetham, in Douglas Adams, *Skating* (London: George Bell, 1894), 86.

9. Reprinted in *Skating*, Dec. 1976, 14.

10. Montagu S. Monier-Williams, *Figure-Skating* (London: A. D. Innes, 1898), 8; qtd. in Brown, *Ice-Skating,* 120.

11. Brown, *Ice-Skating,* 140.

12. Helga K. Van Horn, "The Leadville Ice Palace: The Grandest Ice Palace of Them All," *Skating,* July 1981, 40–42.

13. Vandervell and Witham, *A System of Figure-Skating,* 36–57.

14. Brown, *Ice-Skating,* 105.

15. Ibid., 125.

16. Ibid., 127.

17. Qtd. in Susan A. Johnson, "And Then There Were None: A Fond Remembrance of Compulsory Figures at the World Championships, Part I," *Skating,* Mar. 1991, 10.

18. The European Championships, on the other hand, remained a men-only competition until ladies' and pairs events were added in 1930, the first time that the World Championships themselves were held outside of Europe (in New York). See Benjamin T. Wright, *Skating in America* (Colorado Springs: USFSA, 1996), 40.

19. Ladies' world bronze medalist in 1992 and 1993, Olympic bronze medalist in 1994 and 1998, world champion in 1995, and world silver medalist in 1996.

20. 1999 and 2000 silver and 2001 bronze medalists at the World Championships; Olympic bronze medalists and world champions in 2002.

21. U.S. and world champion; 1987 world silver medalist; 1988 U.S. champion, Olympic and world bronze medalist.

22. European champion 1991–1995, world silver medalist 1993–1995.

23. For the accomplishments of African Americans in skating, see the Black Ice Web site, www.pdm-blackice.com/History.html. For the contributions of an early pioneer, see "Mabel Fairbanks: Breaking Down Barriers," Women's Sports Foundation, www.womenssportsfoundation.org/cgi-bin/iowa/athletes/article.html?record=71.

NOTES TO CHAPTER FOUR

1. As one Englishman wrote, "Now there are certain attributes that are supposed to belong to those of high birth. The fact that a man is born into [the] society of gentlemen imposes upon him certain duties and, to some extent the ideas of his class. He is expected to have a broad education, catholic tastes, and a multiplicity of pursuits. He must not do anything for pecuniary gain; and it can easily be seen that he must not specialize. It is essentially the mark of a bourgeois mind to specialize." H. J. Whigham, "American Sport from an English Point of View, *Outlook,* Nov. 1909; qtd. in Eugene A. Glader, *Amateurism and Athletics* (West Point, NY: Leisure Press, 1978), 16.

2. Nigel Brown, *Ice-Skating: A History* (New York: A. S. Barnes, 1959), 23; no source given for quoted portion.

3. Pierre de Coubertin, *Memoires Olympique*, qtd. in Glader, *Amateurism and Athletics*, 134. Taking part in a competition "open to all comers," that is, in a competition that did not insist on strict amateurism, would mean that one might have competed against professionals and so violated criterion number 2 without necessarily having been aware of doing so.

4. Benjamin T. Wright, *Skating in America* (Colorado Springs: USFSA, 1996), 20.

5. See ibid., 57, 59, 61–62, 65, 94.

6. Ibid., 143.

7. Ibid., 187; Debbi Wilkes and Greg Cable, *Ice Time: A Portrait of Figure Skating* (Scarborough, ON: Prentice Hall Canada, 1994), 27.

8. Qtd. in Wright, *Skating in America*, 183.

9. Charles DeMore, "Amateur Status Rules Changes," *Skating*, Sept. 1970, 16–17.

10. See Wright, *Skating in America*, 336.

11. Qtd. in Susan A. Johnson, "And Then There Were None: A Fond Remembrance of Compulsory Figures at the World Championships, Part I," *Skating*, Mar. 1991, 13.

12. Qtd. in Arthur R. Goodfellow, "The Origin of School Figures: Where They Came From, Who Discovered Them," *Skating*, Oct. 1988, 33.

13. Howard Bass, *This Skating Age* (Boston: Branford, 1959), 69–70.

14. See, e.g., Ernest Jones, *The Elements of Figure Skating* (London: Methuen, 1931); Maribel Y. Vinson, *Primer of Figure Skating* (New York: Whittlesey House, 1938); Frederic Lewis, *Modern Skating* (Chicago: Reilly & Lee, 1938); T. D. Richardson, *The Art of Figure Skating* (New York: Barnes, 1962).

15. T. D. Richardson, *The Art of Figure Skating* (New York: Barnes, 1962); see chap. 12, "New Figures," 88–92.

16. Per Cock-Clausen, "In My Opinion: 60/40," *Skating*, Dec. 1965, 8.

17. ABC Sports, coverage of 1988 Olympic Winter Games, ladies' figures competition, Feb. 1988.

18. Wright, *Skating in America*, 397.

19. ABC Sports, coverage of 1988 Olympic Winter Games, ladies' figures competition, Feb. 1988.

20. Ibid.

21. CBS coverage of 1989 World Junior Championships.

22. "Reflections on Ice: A Diary of Ladies' Figure Skating," narr. Susan Saint James, prod. Kathie Farrel, exec. prod. Ross Greenberg, HBO, Jan. 25, 1998.

23. The United States Figure Skating Association began holding National Championships (senior level) in 1914. Over the years, as the number of skaters and the standards at the highest levels of competition rose, progressively lower levels were added. The current levels are senior, junior, and novice (considered "elite" levels—thus novice competitors are newcomers not to skating but to elite

competition); intermediate and juvenile (sub-elite developmental levels for younger skaters, now with their own national competition; older skaters who do not meet the age limits may still test to these levels and compete at nonqualifying competitions); and prejuvenile, preliminary, pre-preliminary, and beginner/no test (nonqualifying levels).

24. One solution briefly employed at the Figure Skating Club of Madison, Wisconsin, was to mark off two strips of patches at the far end of the rink for those skaters who chose to buy patch time and to make the reduced ice area that was left available for a low-level or no-jumps-allowed freestyle session.

25. Eugene Turner, "Turner's Turn," *Skating*, Jan. 1983, 5.

26. Marsha Lopez, "Does Figure Skating Exploit Females?" *American Skating World*, Aug. 1996, 24–25.

27. Beverley Smith, *Figure Skating: A Celebration* (Toronto: McClelland & Stewart, 1994); John Misha Petkevich, *Figure Skating: Championship Techniques* (New York: Sports Illustrated/Winners Circle Books, 1989); Josef Dedic, *Single Figure Skating for Beginners and Champions* (Prague: Olympia, 1982).

28. Dedic, *Single Figure Skating,* 90.

29. Wright, *Skating in America,* 81.

30. ABC broadcast of the 1980 Olympic Winter Games, introduction to men's competition, Feb. 1980; Dick Button, *Dick Button on Skates* (Englewood Cliffs, NJ: Prentice-Hall, 1955).

Similarly, an article in *Skating* magazine in 1944 praised athleticism and visible strong effort in skating, dismissing "the type of skating which belongs with eighteenth or nineteenth century art—art which embodied only the beautiful, the graceful, the sweet and frilly, the effeminate" in favor of "art of the twentieth century [which] is manly, dynamic, and intense. . . . Have I any objection to beauty and grace?" the author asked. "No; my objection is to the concept that they are the only criteria for 'good art.' My objection is against rules which attempt to confine skating to these two rather effeminate qualities. May I repeat art of today is a dynamic, manly thing, and in free skating, anything whatever (provided it is skating) that is aesthetically effective should be considered good skating!" William H. Grimditch, Jr., "Dynamism," *Skating*, Jan. 1944, 3–4, 33–34.

31. When I was studying skating in the 1970s, coaches taught the crossed position but did not insist on it. Today, double jumps with uncrossed legs are not considered acceptable, so no one gets as far as learning triples without mastering the crossed position.

NOTES TO CHAPTER FIVE

1. Brown, *Ice-Skating: A History,* 89.

2. Beverley Smith, *Figure Skating,* 23.

3. Brown, *Ice-Skating,* 183.

4. Frank Loeser, "Loeser on Music," *Skating*, Oct. 1979, 7.

5. Up until the 1920s and 1930s, recreational and competitive skaters (i.e., amateurs, as opposed to professional show skaters who sported various types of theatrical costumes) had practiced their sport dressed in normal outdoor winter clothing, with groups of self-professed expert skaters such as the Gilets Rouges in France and London's Skating Club in England distinguishing themselves from the masses by wearing distinctive styles of jackets.

As in other contexts, the clothing an individual chose to wear revealed much about his or her social status. Over the course of the nineteenth century, male fashion in general followed a trend toward simplicity and uniformity, while female attire retained the function of displaying wealth and status and providing visual interest to any social gathering through variety of line and color, rendering the wearer as much an ornament to her husband or other male companion as she was herself ornamented.

J. C. Flugel in his *Psychology of Clothes* discusses what he terms the "great masculine renunciation" of personal ornamentation among Western males as an effect of the rejection of aristocratic privilege following on the French Revolution (J. C. Flugel, *The Psychology of Clothes* [London: The Hogarth Press Ltd., 1930].) Such solidarity between middle-class and working-class masculinity can also be seen within North American culture, founded as it was largely on the rejection of European class distinctions, as I discuss further in chapter 8.

For comments related to skating fashion in particular, see "Elements of Skating [*sic*]. News from the USFSA Hall of Fame and Museum: Skating Fashions in the Twentieth Century," *Skating*, May 1980, 13–14.

6. Arthur R. Goodfellow, "When the Worlds First Came to America," *Skating*, Mar. 1981, 22–27. The narration and interviews with Henie's competitors Fritzi Burger and Cecilia Colledge in the HBO special "Reflections on Ice" also indicate that Henie led the rivalry not only in who was the best skater of the era but also in who would be best-dressed on the ice.

7. Indications of the interest in skating fashion can be seen in the frequent mentions in competition reports of what competitors were wearing and in articles devoted specifically to the topic of what to wear in publications addressed to skaters. For instance, the British magazine *Skating Times* in the late 1930s carried a regular column entitled "Fashion Feature," under the byline "by the Fashion Editress," addressing such questions as "Colour on the Ice" (*Skating Times*, Nov. 1938, 94, 96).

The USFSA's *Skating* magazine also periodically ran features on skating costume. See, e.g., T.W.B. [Theresa Weld Blanchard], "A New School Figure Costume," *Skating*, Mar. 1937, 19; Jane Vaughan Sullivan, "Competition Clothes," *Skating*, Dec. 1943, 8; Marion F. Paterson, "Dresses—Olympic Style," *Skating*, Apr. 1956, 8–9; "Competitors Reveal the *Appropriateness *Basic Design *Color Choice of Ice Dress," *Skating*, Feb. 1964, 22–24, 38; Ronay Titus, "The Look of Champions," *Skating*, May 1964, 22–23; Mary Richardson, "Mod Colors Swing Cut Stretch Cloth," *Skating*, Apr. 1967, 26.

8. In the 1990s, it became fashionable for female skaters, especially ice dancers, to use flesh-colored tights that cover the skating boot as well as the leg in order to create such an unbroken line. The use of colored tights and matching bootcovers, seen occasionally in the 1980s and 1990s, similarly avoids an abrupt change of color at the ankles; often such tights are the same color as or a continuation of the pants of the skating dress, a variation that avoids the usual change of color and thus the visual focus at the groin and buttocks.

9. Maribel Y. Vinson, *Primer of Figure Skating* (New York: Whittlesey House/ McGraw-Hill, 1938), 17–21.

10. Sonja Henie, *Wings on My Feet* (New York: Prentice-Hall, 1940); Raymond Strait and Leif Henie, *Queen of Ice, Queen of Shadows: The Unsuspected Life of Sonja Henie* (New York: Stein and Day, 1985).

11. According to Frank Carroll, "Maribel [Vinson Owen], told me that Sonja could probably have been Olympic champion at any sport she chose, that she was a tremendous athlete, had a perfect body for sport and was very, very naturally strong. Sonja's style of skating was very old-fashioned, and, you know, we would imitate her and make fun of her. And Maribel would be livid and just say, you know, 'You have no idea how fast she was, how good her figures were, and what a fabulous skater she was, and so just all of you stop it'" ("Reflections on Ice").

12. For further discussion of these conventions, see Jane Feuer, "Nancy and Tonya and Sonja: The Figure of the Figure Skater in American Entertainment," in Baughman, *Women on Ice*, 3–21; and see the analysis of *One in a Million* at the end of this chapter.

13. Cecilia Colledge, "The Birth of a Camel," *Skating*, July 1987, 11.

14. Cecilia Colledge, "Breaking the Back of the Layback," *Skating*, Nov. 1987, 7. Colledge also refers to this procedure with the rope in HBO's "Reflections on Ice" documentary.

15. Dick Button is credited with being the first male skater to perform the camel spin, as well as with introducing the flying camel. Camel spins are now required elements for both sexes at some levels of testing and competition, while the layback is similarly required for females but not for males. Male layback spins remain rare, especially with a true backward rather than sideways arch.

16. Harry A. Sims, "Where Are the Boys?" *Skating*, Dec. 1954, 14–16; "Bring in the Boys," *Skating*, Dec. 1955, 7–8, 38, 40.

17. Brown, *Ice-Skating*, 177.

18. Smith, *Figure Skating*, 38. Brown credits Scott's 1948 Canadian teammate, Marylyn Take, with taking "a very bold step at musical interpretation, presenting a programme largely dominated by ballet movements" (*Ice-Skating*, 184) and praises the "brilliance and natural talent as an artist" (182) of French skater Jacque-

line Du Bief, the 1952 world champion. Other prominent skaters of the period praised for their musicality include the Americans Tenley Albright and Hayes Alan Jenkins (Loeser, "Loeser on Music," 7).

19. Brown, *Ice-Skating*, 184. See William H. Grimditch, Jr., "Dynamism," *Skating*, Jan. 1944, 3–4, 33–34, for an argument in favor of such a "virile" style of performance.

20. Loeser, "Loeser on Music," 7.

21. Debbi Wilkes and Greg Cable, *Ice Time: A Portrait of Figure Skating* (Scarborough, ON: Prentice Hall Canada, 1994), 106–119.

22. Foucault, *Discipline and Punish*.

23. Peggy Fleming with Peter Kaminsky, *The Long Program: Skating toward Life's Victories* (New York: Pocket Books, 1999), 7.

24. Ibid., 10.

25. Loeser, "Loeser on Music," 9.

26. Qtd. in "Colorado Dispatch: Indepth Tidbits on the Championship Scene," *Skating*, May 1969, 10.

27. Hamill herself had stated, "The way Peggy Fleming and Janet Lynn skated was an art. But that's just not my style. I became a sport skater because of my first coach, Gustave Lussi. . . . He was a technician. He always worked on spins and jumps, and never on graceful moves. So I always concentrated on higher and more powerful jumps, and faster spins." Qtd. in Judy Klemesrud, "Dorothy Hamill Prepares for Stardom," *womanSports*, Feb. 1975, 42. Her later coach Peter Burrows said that "Fleming was really a ballerina on ice, whereas Hamill is more of an athlete." Qtd. in Jane Leavy, "Dorothy Hamill, Winner," *womanSports*, June 1977, 36.

28. Spencer K. Wertz, "Artistic Creativity in Sport," in *Sport Inside Out: Readings in Literature and Philosophy*, ed. David L. Vanderwerken and Spencer K. Wertz (Fort Worth: Texas Christian University Press, 1985), 514.

29. Ibid., 515.

30. Keith Money, *John Curry* (New York: Alfred A. Knopf, 1978); Toller Cranston, interviewed on ABC coverage of 1976 Olympics.

31. The heroine of *Ice Castles* performs to Walter Murphy's "A Fifth of Beethoven," and one cannot watch videotapes of competitions from this period without encountering the ubiquitous disco *Firebird* arrangement.

32. See Mary Ann Purpura, "Total Image," *Skating*, May 1981, 40–42.

33. "In Reply," *Skating*, Oct. 1988, 11.

34. "From the President's Desk," *Skating*, Feb. 1989, 6.

35. This would be a different meaning of "theatrical" from the one used in the ISU and USFSA costume rulings, which seems to refer to the flamboyant and showy presentational qualities of the clothes themselves, not whether the clothing depicts a particular character. For an earlier expression of a similar idea, see "Among other Things: Gossip by A.C.B.," *Skating Times*, Jan. 1939, 191–214. The

author addressed the question of "fancy dress" in championship skating, stating, "For myself I, too, think that it is better that competitive sport should be conducted on severe lines, leaving sartorial effect for those of the stage whose business it is to please the eye and entertain. . . . There is plenty of room for both competitive and stage skating, but perhaps it would be well to keep them apart."

36. *One in a Million,* dir. Sidney Lanford, with Sonja Henie, Don Ameche, and Adolphe Menjou, Twentieth Century Fox, 1937.

NOTES TO CHAPTER SIX

1. "Five Little Pretenders," *Time,* Mar. 7, 1938, 23; "Fine Figures," *Time,* Jan. 30, 1939, 38.

2. Pat Ryan, "A Little Murder Set to Music," *Sports Illustrated,* Feb. 16, 1970, 18–19.

3. Jeanette Bruce, "The Divine Right of Queens," *Sports Illustrated,* Feb. 18, 1974, 66–70.

4. Klemesrud, "Dorothy Hamill Prepares for Stardom," 40–43.

5. Deborah Larned, "Sold on Ice: What's Beneath the Sparkling Surface?" *womanSports,* Feb. 1977, 25–33.

6. Jane Leavy, "Dorothy Hamill, Winner," 26–28, 36, 47–48.

7. Janice Kaplan, "The New Ice Queen Cometh," *womanSports,* Feb. 1978, 32–35, 47–48.

8. Michael Steere, *Scott Hamilton: A Behind-the-Scenes Look at the Life and Competitive Times of America's Favorite Figure Skater, an Unauthorized Biography* (New York: St. Martin's, 1985).

9. William Johnson, "This Is It, For Heaven's Sake," *Sports Illustrated,* Mar. 5, 1975, 38.

10. Leavy, "Dorothy Hamill, Winner," 36.

11. Qtd. in Klemesrud, "Dorothy Hamill Prepares for Stardom," 43.

12. Both qtd. in Leavy, "Dorothy Hamill, Winner," 36.

13. ABC coverage of 1976 and 1978 U.S. Nationals, respectively.

14. ABC broadcast of 1976 Olympic Winter Games.

15. E. M. Swift, "The Thinner Was the Winner," *Sports Illustrated,* Feb. 1983, 75–76.

16. Emily Greenspan, "Battle of the Blades: The Competition That May Change Women's Figure Skating," *Ms.,* Jan. 1984, 90–93.

17. Swift, "The Thinner Was the Winner," 75.

18. Greenspan, "Battle of the Blades," 92, 90.

19. "Calgary Gold," *Newsweek,* Feb. 15, 1988, 76–81.

20. Anthony Wilson-Smith with Ann Walmsley and Shaffin Shariff, "Fire on the Ice," *MacLean's,* Feb. 1988, 25; Ian Austen, "Chasing a Crown," *MacLean's,* Feb. 1988, 30; Ann Walmsley, "Power Play," *MacLean's,* Feb. 1988, 32.

21. ABC broadcast of 1988 Olympic Winter Games.

22. Ibid. Tomba was a popular Italian skier, known for his good looks and womanizing playboy lifestyle, who won two gold medals in Calgary.

23. Helena Michie, *Sororophobia* (New York: Oxford University Press, 1992), 169.

24. Ibid., 171–172.

25. For discussion of nationalism in judging at this event, see Ellie McGrath, "The Skunks of Calgary," *Time,* Mar. 7, 1988, 66.

26. See, for instance, Penny McCann, "Seductive Spectacle," *Broadside* 9.7 (May 1988): 9: "If skaters, their coaches, and the skating industry as a whole think that alluring costumes and seductive spectacle will improve the aesthetics and popularity of their sport, they are sadly mistaken. Not only were the events in February demeaning to women, they were insulting to the intelligence of figure skating fans who proved themselves during the Olympics to be considerably knowledgeable of the intricacies of the sport." Even in the 1990s, what many female skating fans continued to associate most with Witt was her use of sexuality as a competitive strategy in 1988 (as well as in many of her professional performances since then) and in some cases found it hard to forgive her for skewing the emphasis in women's skating away from athletic accomplishment.

27. At the 1982 and 1984 World Junior Championships and the 1990 World Championships, for instance, Ito won both the short and long programs but, after placing nineteenth, thirteenth, and tenth respectively in the school figures, ended up finishing sixth, third, and second overall. In 1989, a sixth-place finish in figures and a favorable order of finish among the other top competitors, combined with wins in the short and long program, allowed her to win the world title that year. With the elimination of school figures in the 1990–1991 season, Ito was favored to dominate the ladies' event, but injuries and the pressure of expectations caused her to skate less well at the 1991 World Championships and 1992 Olympics than she had in 1988–1990.

28. Martha Duffy, "Spinning Gold," *Time,* Feb. 10, 1992, 55.

29. Susanna Levin, "Heavy Medal," *Women's Sports and Fitness,* Jan./Feb. 1992, 32–36.

30. Frank Deford, "Jewel of the Olympic Games," *Newsweek,* Feb. 10, 1992, 46–53.

31. CBS broadcast of 1992 Olympics.

32. After winning Skate America in 1991, Harding performed an exhibition to George Thoroughgood's "Bad to the Bone" utilizing a similar wild style, as did her short programs in 1991 and 1992. For a more detailed description of Harding's 1992 long program as performed at that year's Olympics, see my article "What Tonya Harding Means to Me, or Images of Independent Female Power on Ice," in Baughman, *Women on Ice,* 53–77.

33. Mary Douglas, "The Two Bodies," in *Natural Symbol: Explorations in Cosmology* (New York: Pantheon, 1970).

34. Anita Finkel, "Firebirds and Firecrackers," *New Dance Review*, Apr.–June 1992, 6.

35. Ibid., 7.

36. For a representative sampling of such articles in the mainstream press during the 1994 controversy, see "Living on the Edges," *Newsweek*, Jan. 24, 1994, 71–72; Martha Duffy, "With Blades Drawn," *Time*, Feb. 21, 1994, 52–58; Clarence Page, "Tonya's Doing It Her Way," *Chicago Tribune*, Jan. 23, 1994; Caryl Rivers, "Skating on Stereotyped Ice," *Boston Globe*, Jan. 20, 1994; Mary Schmich, "Kerrigan Attack: Now It Figures," *Chicago Tribune*, Jan. 14, 1994; Jill Smolowe, "Tarnished Victory," *Time*, Jan. 24, 1994, 41–54; and, retrospectively, Abigail Feder, "The Femininity Trap: Tonya and Nancy," *Village Voice* Jan. 3, 1995.

37. Abigail Feder, "'A Radiant Smile from the Lovely Lady': Overdetermined Femininity in 'Ladies' Figure Skating," *Drama Review* 38.1 (spring 1994): 62–78. Excerpts from this article also appeared in the *Village Voice*, and it was reprinted in Baughman, *Women on Ice*.

38. For further discussion of this tendency in the coverage of women's sports, see Mariah Burton Nelson, "I Won. I'm Sorry," *Self*, Mar. 1998, 145–47; Mary A. Boutilier and Lucinda SanGiovanni, *The Sporting Woman* (Champaign, IL: Human Kinetics Publishers, 1983), esp. chap. 7.

39. Feder, "'A Radiant Smile,'" 63, drawing on Susan Brownmiller, *Femininity* (New York: Linden Press/Simon & Schuster, 1984).

40. Feder, "'A Radiant Smile,'" 64.

41. Ibid., 71–72.

42. Qtd. in ibid., 72.

43. Qtd. in Marsha Lopez, "Does Figure Skating Exploit Females?" *American Skating World*, Aug. 1996, 25.

44. Qtd. in ibid.

45. Kate Rounds, "Ice Follies: Reflections on a Sport Out of Whack," *Ms.*, May/June 1994, 26–33.

46. See chapter 12 for a discussion of erotic attraction as a component of figure skating fandom among female fans.

47. "Reflections on Ice."

48. Qtd. in Steve Milton, *Skate Talk: Figure Skating in the Words of the Stars* (Buffalo, NY: Firefly Books, 1997), 142.

49. Cesca Supple, personal interview, Oct. 1997.

50. Because of the nature of the sport, skaters generally direct this kind of competitive toughness toward their own performances and not against their competitors. In effect, the challenge each skater faces in competition comes not from the other skaters but from the elements she has chosen to perform. How well she succeeds provides the basis for a narrative of triumph or failure with each performance, irrespective of her ultimate placement relative to the other skaters. Of course, the narrative of skater versus skater is also available.

Strategy in choosing which elements to perform and with how much difficulty to combine them (and at the lower levels, choosing which level to compete in) does of course come into play, especially in the short program, as skaters must weigh the likelihood of completing an element against the technical weight accorded to its difficulty. Successfully completing a particularly difficult program puts additional pressure on one's competitors to do the same.

One-upmanship during practice sessions at competitions provides another means by which skaters directly interact with their opponents and may affect their performances for better or for worse depending if they are inclined to respond in kind during the competition or to become easily rattled. For example, during the 1992 Olympics in Albertville, Katarina Witt and Paula Zahn, commenting for CBS, discussed the unnerving effect on Midori Ito of Surya Bonaly performing a backflip and eliciting cheers from the French fans while Ito's music was being played for her to run through her program. Witt's disapproval was ironic, considering that in her own competitive days she had been known to draw attention during other skaters' practice run-throughs by improvising to their music.

Refusing to give way when on a collision course with another skater, and thus forcing the other to do so—in effect, playing "chicken"—during practice sessions is another form of such gamesmanship. Ice dance teams in particular have been known to skate dangerously close to their rivals at full speed as a means of intimidation. (And less advanced, slower skaters are often intimidated by being on the ice with faster skaters even if the latter are not intentionally trying to be intimidating.) Sasha Cohen drew media attention during the 2002 U.S. Nationals for a number of unintentional bumps and near misses, especially with defending champion Michelle Kwan, during the competition warm-ups.

More benignly, during the warm-up period of practice sessions at high-level domestic competitions in the United States, it is common for skaters who have already been sent to international competitions to wear the USA team jackets they received on those occasions, while less experienced competitors must wear jackets or sweaters without such prestigious logos.

Skaters' efforts to outdo each other with more attractive or more expensive clothing on and off the ice has been an aspect of the feminine culture within the sport since at least the days of Sonja Henie. This probably accounts in part for the continuing use of elaborate beading and sequins on many skating dresses even in the face of efforts by skating officials to encourage simplicity in athletic attire. Ice dancers in particular, with two compulsory dances per competition (four per season) plus original dance and free dance, and two skaters to dress for each dance, are particularly known for going to great lengths and great expense to reflect the mood or style of each dance within their costumes, often with alternate versions for minor competitions and for practice sessions. For freestyle, on the other hand, a generically stylish dress, no matter how elaborate, could serve a skater for a variety of different programs, and practice clothes are even less often program-specific. Those who indulge in such fashion competitions (by no means all ladies' competitors, even at the highest levels) of course are likely to spend the money for multiple expensive practice dresses.

Most often such direct rivalry relates to behavior outside the frame of competition itself. Media accounts of this type of narrative as related to female skaters often therefore portray them as illegitimate (the most egregious example of course being the 1994 attack on Nancy Kerrigan) or petty (as with rumors of skates or other equipment being sabotaged by other skaters). For examples, see Christine Brennan, *Inside Edge: A Revealing Journey into the Secret World of Figure Skating* (New York: Scribner, 1996), 106, and Joan Ryan, *Little Girls in Pretty Boxes: The Making and Breaking of Elite Gymnasts and Figure Skaters* (New York: Doubleday, 1995), 133–134.

51. Lopez, "Does Figure Skating Exploit Females?" 24–25.

NOTES TO CHAPTER SEVEN

1. Qtd. in Steve Milton, *Skate Talk: Figure Skating in the Words of the Stars* (Buffalo, NY: Firefly Books), 138.

2. Qtd. in ABC broadcast of the 1996 World Championships.

3. Ellyn Kestnbaum, "'Artistry' and the Female Skater," *American Skating World*, Aug. 1996, 14–15, 19, 22.

4. ABC broadcast of 2000 U.S. National Championship. The allusion is to a similar group of precocious dancers who had taken the ballet world by storm in the 1930s.

5. See Brennan, *Edge of Glory*, 79–86, for an account of this transformation.

6. For example, during coverage of the short programs at the 1996 U.S. National Championships on ESPN, Peggy Fleming commented that Kwan was "really feeling the music so much more than she did just even a year ago. She's really grown up." At that year's World Championships, ABC sportscaster Brent Musberger remarked that "this time [at that year's Nationals, as opposed to the previous year's Worlds], the judges saw her with a more objective eye. It was all right to make her a champion now. Her time had come." During the same broadcast, Dick Button said of Irina Slutskaya, "She's really more of a teenager than Michelle Kwan, who's two years younger than she is. It's very interesting, the relationship between the two of them."

7. Kwan's 1995–1996 long program had been set to music from various tellings of the biblical story of Salome. In 1996–1997 her short program was to Jules Massenet's *Dream of Desdemona* and her long program to Azerbaijani music but costumed and choreographed to reflect the Indian theme of "the love story behind the Taj Mahal." As skating fan and journalist Lorrie Kim has pointed out, these program themes also each contain elements of racial difference or exoticism, representing at least a cursory attempt to acknowledge Kwan's "exotic" status as Chinese American within white-dominated American culture, but with-

out directly drawing on the specifics of her own Chinese heritage. Kim contrasts this approach to earlier attempts to portray the Japanese American Kristi Yamaguchi as an all-American California girl (several posts to the rec.sport.skating.ice.figure Internet newsgroup and personal communications). In some more recent programs, such as her portrayal of "The Fate of Carmen" and the "Lament d'Ariane" in her 1999 short and long programs, Kwan continued to draw on musical works with similar themes, although in general her work has moved in the direction of more abstract depiction of the musical content.

8. Lipinski had been fifth in the short program at Nationals, behind Kwan, veteran Tonia Kwiatkowski, Bobek, and 1995 U.S. junior champion Sydne Vogel, despite Bobek's having made an error on her jump combination and Lipinski completing the most difficult jumps of the event. Her jumps were still small and sometimes whipped or spun barely off the ice, however, and her presentation still appeared vague and childlike. Bobek's withdrawal from the long program with an ankle injury and Vogel's mistakes there allowed Lipinski to earn her spot on the podium. The USFSA International Committee decided not to name Bobek, the previous year's national champion and a reigning world medalist, to the world team, a decision that caused a fair degree of controversy considering that they had done so in similar circumstances in the past. Instead, they sent the thirteen-year-old Lipinski to the World Championships along with Kwan and Kwiatkowski. Lipinski fell twice during her short program at Worlds, finishing twenty-third in that phase and almost not making the top-twenty-four cutoff for the long program, but she rallied with a strong long program to pull up to fifteenth place overall.

9. At the post-competition press conference, Kwan said, "I guess I wasn't concentrating enough. I panicked in the middle of the performance after the (first) fall. Just mind games. . . . I have to learn something from this. I have to get my head together and learn how to take defeat" (qtd. in Jay Miller, "Fresh Faces," *Skating*, Apr. 1997, 14).

10. This combination had been completed, probably for the first time in any competition, the previous season by France's Eric Millot at the 1996 Champions Series Final and World Championships. The young American Timothy Goebel had also performed it when he won the silver medal at the 1997 World Junior Championships, two months before Lipinski did so at the National Championships. But Lipinski did it under more celebrated circumstances, and in their enthusiasm for the feat many journalists have forgotten to include the qualification that Lipinski was the first *female* skater to land this combination; even the USFSA media guide, the source of information for many of these journalists, lists her simply as the first skater to do so.

Kwan actually placed third in the long program at that 1997 Nationals, to take the silver medal. Nicole Bobek, sixth in the short program after errors on two of the jumps, placed second in the long and pulled herself up to third overall with a clean and well-skated program that was, however, too light in technical content, including only four triple jumps, to challenge for first place in the long program.

11. Vanessa Gusmeroli of France, another newcomer who had skated a strong short program, challenged Lipinski for the lead in that phase. She managed only a distant fourth in the long but took the bronze medal ahead of Slutskaya because of her higher short program placement.

12. Qtd. in Brennan, *Edge of Glory*, 161.

13. Debbie Becker, "Lipinski's Title 'A Big Shock, but I Love It,'" *USA Today*, Mar. 24, 1997.

14. Brennan, *Edge of Glory*, 216.

15. Janet Swan Hill, an adult skater and low-level USFSA judge, has suggested in posts to the skatefans e-mail discussion list that the large number of female skaters and the consequent competitiveness among them in the United States may encourage these skaters to attempt to add the double and triple lutz to their repertoires as soon as possible, concentrating on adding a rotation and actually landing the jump rather than on first perfecting the takeoff technique on the single and double lutz.

In countries with smaller skating populations, skaters would not necessarily need a double lutz to advance in the equivalent of U.S. juvenile and intermediate competitions, or a triple lutz to contend for their national titles, so there would be less pressure to rush the jump into their programs before having mastered the technique. Skaters who place high enough in their national championships to compete internationally, however, generally do aim to learn the triple lutz as soon as possible, often before the triple loop or flip, in order to be able to include the more difficult combination in their short programs, and so in international competitions we are seeing more and more flawed triple lutz attempts from skaters representing smaller skating countries.

Coaching techniques or emphases may also play a part in this tendency, given that the ladies' fields in Russia and at times in recent years other countries such as Japan, France, Ukraine, and Hungary have been, if not as deep as that in the United States, often comparably competitive at the top levels, yet it is less common for female skaters from these countries, particularly the former-Soviet countries, to change edge on their lutz entries. Many of these skaters, however, do experience more difficulty in landing the jump consistently than either Kwan or Lipinski.

Previous skating generations, those who had reached the senior level before 1991, spent much of their training time working on school figures, which gave them a greater understanding of the different edges and also slowed their progress through the competitive ranks, so that correct double lutzes, and triples from those few skaters who performed them, were more common than is currently seen with ladies' triples. Before 1991, triple lutzes from women were rare and were not necessary to compete successfully (Jill Trenary, for instance, won the 1990

U.S. and World Championships without one), so it tended to be only those skaters who were exceptionally strong jumpers with particularly good lutz technique who performed them. During the early 1990s, enough women were performing triple lutzes that even if some of them made errors on this jump or elsewhere in their programs, there were generally enough other top skaters who did perform the triple lutz to fill the medal stand at major championships. It was not until about 1995, however, that a majority of senior ladies and many juniors, including those who had little hope of winning important medals, began including triple lutzes in their programs.

16. For an even more obvious example of this error, see almost any lutz performed by Nicole Bobek or Sarah Hughes.

17. See, e.g., Philip Hersh, "Suddenly, Olympic Medals for American Skaters Are Not a Sure Thing," *Chicago Tribune,* Nov. 20, 1997; Mike Penner, "If Lipinski Still Has an Edge, It Might Be the Wrong One," *Los Angeles Times,* Dec. 14, 1997; Jere Longman, "Lipinski's Imperfect Lutz Is Good Enough for First," *New York Times,* Dec. 20, 1997.

18. The German Tanja Szewczenko did offer an impressive challenge. Szewczenko's jumps were much higher than either Lipinski's or Kwan's, and at age twenty she presented a more mature presence on the ice than Lipinski, but she did not have the fluidity and gracefulness of the Americans or the jump difficulty to match Lipinski's triple-triple combinations, nor the stamina to sustain as much speed throughout her program because of lingering effects of a combination of viruses that had kept her out of competition for almost two years previously.

19. Qtd. in Longman, "Lipinski's Imperfect Lutz Is Good Enough for First."

20. Ibid.

21. Chen had missed almost the entire 1997 season due to injury, showing up undertrained at 1997 Worlds, where she had placed twenty-fifth in the short program and so failed to qualify for the free skate.

22. Tanja Szewczenko had had to withdraw from the competition after another bout with illness in the Nagano flu epidemic. Nicole Bobek succumbed to a combination of health problems and her own unreliable jumping technique, placing seventeenth in the short program and so dashing any hopes of an American medal sweep.

23. Butyrskaya and Slutskaya—forgettable, perhaps, because Wilson, like most of the general public, may follow skating only at the Olympics, and thus would have seen Bonaly and Chen at the 1992 and 1994 Olympics but would have missed the emergence of the Russian ladies near the top of the international rankings in the interim. Or because the Russians lacked the signifiers of hip exoticism that Wilson could impute to the Black French Bonaly and the Chinese Chen, especially considering that Butyrskaya's short program to "Fever" showed as much sexual consciousness as Chen's interpretation of Astor Piazzola or Bonaly's of Duke Ellington.

24. Cintra Wilson, "Ice Follies," Feb. 20, 1998, www.salon.com/wlust/feature/1998/02/20feature.html.

25. ABC coverage of 1998 U.S. National Championships.

26. The lack of attack or full commitment to the movement stood out to me when watching it on television. For the lack of speed, I rely on commentator Chris Howarth's remark after Lipinski's long program during the British Eurosport broadcast of the 1998 Olympics: "Tell you what, it was faster across the ice [than Kwan's program] as well," and Howarth's comment during the Eurosport broadcast of Kwan's long program from the World Championships in Minneapolis, Minnesota, six weeks later:"Already she's achieving more speed across the ice than in Nagano." I attended those World Championships in person and noted that Kwan was by far the slowest skater in the final group of six, average on the speed criterion among the twenty-four skaters who skated in the long program. In Nagano, where Kwan reportedly skated more slowly and in the presence of more top skaters such as Lipinski, Chen, and Bonaly (who did not attend the World Championships and so left room for weaker skaters to fill out the bottom of the field there), it would probably be fair to say that Kwan was not in the top half of the field in terms of speed, despite the higher quality of most of her skating. Skating against other American skaters at Nationals, Kwan no longer appeared as slow in 1997 and 1998 as she had compared to Bobek and Kwiatkowski in 1995, and only Bobek at her best could match her for security and depth of edge and for extension of her body into space, characteristics that, along with actual speed, contribute to the sense of "filling the ice." Compared to European and Asian skaters who are used to filling larger, Olympic-sized ice surfaces, American standards of speed do not measure up to those of the fastest skaters in the world.

27. Susan Jacoby, "Finally, a Figure Skater with a Figure," *Newsday*, Mar. 4, 2002.

28. Joan Ryan, *Little Girls in Pretty Boxes.* See esp. chap. 3, entitled "Be Thin and Win: Image."

29. Ibid., 98.

30. Anonymous skating judge, personal interview. It is less usual for judges to be unable to distinguish between skaters at the highest levels, although different strengths and weaknesses among skaters may lead to the overall value of their performances balancing out to a similar level, so that judges must determine which quality to give the most weight. As this judge put it, you might have a judge who really loves jumping, a judge who really loves a balletic style, and another judge who really loves an athletic style; "a judge can't really part from what he feels himself; he has to set his own standard for what he thinks is good and what is poor."

At lower levels, however, the numbers of skaters involved are such that two or more skaters may indeed demonstrate almost identical abilities. At a regional competition in the United States, for instance, there might be over a hundred inter-mediate ladies entered who will be seeded into initial, or elimination, rounds from which the top few skaters in each group will advance to a final round. The best skaters at this level can all skate fast and aggressively, perform jumps up to dou-ble lutz consistently on their own and in double-double combinations, and per-form combination spins with all the basic positions and often difficult variations as well. In the final round, some skaters will make mistakes and be ranked at the bottom of the group, and some will attempt a double axel or triple salchow and probably be ranked at the top if they succeed. But in the middle of this group will be several skaters who attempt pretty much the same technical content and perform it pretty much equally well (and a decision among two or more such skaters may well span the difference between fourth and fifth place, the cutoff point after which skaters will advance to the next competition), so judges will seize on any detail that will allow them to distinguish one skater from another; physical appearance is one area where one skater may make a significantly better impression than another.

31. Wilkes and Cable, *Ice Time*, 96, 124–125.

32. Qtd. in Brennan, *Edge of Glory*, 132.

33. Deford, "Jewel of the Winter Games," 50.

34. Brennan, *Edge of Glory*, 134.

35. Qtd. in Ryan, *Little Girls in Pretty Boxes*, 103.

36. Patty Staunton, "Unmasking Judging: Maturity," *American Skating World,* Dec. 1997, 10.

37. Phil Hersh, "Women Jumping to Contusions: Injuries in Practice Harm Many U.S. Senior Hopefuls," *Chicago Tribune,* Jan. 19, 2001.

38. Lois Elfman, "Go Boston: 2001 U.S. Nationals Breaks Record," *International Figure Skating,* June 2001, 58–60.

39. See the chapter "China: A Rising Power" in Beverley Smith, *A Year in Figure Skating* (Toronto: McClelland & Stewart, 1996), 125–144. Chen's notable accomplishments include bronze medals at the 1992 and 1993 World Champion-ships and 1994 and 1998 Olympics, silver at 1996 Worlds, and gold in 1995.

40. NBC coverage of 1995 World Championships.

NOTES TO CHAPTER EIGHT

1. Trent Frayne, "Real Men *Do* Figure Skate," *McLean's,* Jan. 14, 1991, 47.

2. Susan A. Basow, *Gender Stereotypes: Traditions and Alternatives,* 2d ed. (Monterey, CA: Brooks/Cole, 1986), 7.

3. Peter Stearns, *Be a Man: Males in Modern Society,* 2d ed. (New York: Holmes & Meier, 1990), 17.

4. Ibid.

5. Brian Pronger, *The Arena of Masculinity* (New York: St. Martin's, 1990), 54.

6. Ibid., 20. But from a participant's, as opposed to a spectator's, point of

view, skating certainly does involve struggle with oneself and with natural forces. It is only the value placed on producing an appearance of ease that renders this struggle invisible to the outside observer. Watch beginners, or skaters of any level attempting to learn a new move, and the struggle will be evident.

7. John Curry [as told to Fiona Barton], "All My Friends Have Died of AIDS. Now It Is My Turn," *Mail on Sunday*, Oct. 4, 1992, 48–49, and Rudy Galindo in Christine Brennan, *Inside Edge*, 68. Criticisms or ridicule of Russian skater Aleksei Urmanov's presentational style by North American skaters, commentators, and journalists, discussed later in this chapter, similarly suggest that to these observers Urmanov fails to present himself as sufficiently masculine on the ice. Whether any judges are disturbed by these qualities is unclear. Although compared to the most aggressively masculine of his competitors Urmanov may embody some feminine characteristics, compared to Curry or Galindo he is a much more powerful and less refined skater.

8. Butler, "Performative Acts and Gender Constitution," 270. See chap. 1 for discussion of the concept of performing gender.

9. For a discussion of several of these trends in men's figure skating and the media that cover it in Canada, see Mary Louise Adams, "So What's the Problem with *Wussy* Sports?" *Borderlines* 46 (Apr. 1998): 12–15, and Adams, "To Be an Ordinary Hero: Male Figure Skaters and the Ideology of Gender," *Avante* 3 (1997): 93–110.

10. In exhibitions, by contrast, which exist specifically for the purposes of entertainment, American popular music genres serve as the most frequent accompaniment, with even skaters who don't speak English performing to songs with English-language lyrics.

11. Kurt Browning, *Kurt: Forcing the Edge* (Toronto: HarperCollins Publishers, 1991), 152.

12. Mike Spence, "Candeloro," *Skating*, Oct. 1994, 27.

13. Jill Smolow, "The Soaring, Spinning Battle of the Brians," *Time*, Feb. 15, 1988, 58–59.

14. E. M. Swift, "Stepping Up: A New Generation Took Over As the Old Guard Took Spills," *Sports Illustrated*, Feb. 28, 1994, 46–47.

15. For a more detailed analysis of the Stojko-Urmanov dualism in the North American media, see chap. 10 in Ellyn Kestnbaum, "Figure Skating and Cultural Meaning," Ph.D. diss., University of Wisconsin–Madison, 1999.

NOTES TO CHAPTER NINE

1. Eve Kosofsky Sedgwick, *Epistemology of the Closet* (Berkeley: University of California Press, 1990), 20.

2. See, e.g., Gib Twyman, "Boitano Pokes Fun at Misconceptions," *Deseret News*, Feb. 14, 1999.

3. Bob Ottum, "Wow! Power," *Sports Illustrated*, Feb. 6, 1984, 91.

4. Frank Deford, "The Jewel of the Winter Games," *Newsweek,* Feb. 10, 1992, 47.

5. Browning, *Kurt: Forcing the Edge,* 104–5. Elsewhere in the book, Browning finds opportunities to note that other male skaters of his acquaintance "like girls," notably Viktor Petrenko and Canadian/French ice dancer Paul Duchesnay.

6. Brennan, Christine, *Inside Edge,* 185.

7. Mark Ziegler, "Skate Expectations: Father's Obsession Molded Son," *San Diego Union-Tribune,* Feb. 8, 1995.

8. "After a Partner's Death, Tracy Wilson Looks Back—and Ahead," *People,* Feb. 24, 1992, 82.

9. Mary Ormsby, "Skaters Facing Up to AIDS," *Calgary Herald,* Nov. 11, 1992; Michael Clarkson, "Deaths Create Massive Vacuum" and "Skating's Spectre," *Calgary Herald,* Dec. 13, 1992.

10. Susan Reed, Fanny Weinstein, and Lorenzo Benet, "Fear on the Ice," *People,* Jan. 25, 1993, 39–45.

11. Curry, "All My Friends Have Died of AIDS," 48–49. Curry notes in passing that (presumably when he was competing in the 1960s and 1970s) "I already had to fight against prejudice in the ice-skating world. Some judges said quite openly they wouldn't put me first because I was 'queer.'"

12. See Reed et al., "Fear on the Ice," 42.

13. Clarkson, "Deaths Create."

14. Reed et al., "Fear on the Ice," 41.

15. Clarkson, "Skating's Spectre."

16. Reed et al., "Fear on the Ice," 41.

17. Arthur Luiz, personal interview, Apr. 18, 1993.

18. See Sandra Loosemore, "Gay Games fiasco not ISU's fault," CBS Sports-Line, Aug. 14, 1998, cbs.sportsline.com/u/women/skating/aug98/loosemore81498.htm; Lorrie Kim, "Gay Games Organizers Dodge Responsibility for Fiasco," www.plover.com/rainbowice/fingerpoint.html; and "Figure Skating: ISU draws boos from Gay Games," www.sportserver.com/newsroom/sports/oth/1998/oth/mor/feat/archive/080598/mor58297.html.

19. See www.gaygames.com/en/games/gg6 and www.sydney2002.org.au.

20. See Stacy Farrar, "NSW ice skaters face ban for Gay Games participation," www.ssonet.com.au/showarticle.asp?ArticleID=1919.

21. For a more detailed review of problems with *Inside Edge,* in light of the USFSA's temporary decision during the spring of 1996 to revoke Brennan's press credentials at their events, see the unpublished letter to the *Washington Post* by Ellyn Kestnbaum and Sandra Loosemore on Loosemore's Web site at www.frogsonice.com/skateweb/articles/brennanletter.shtml.

22. Brennan, *Inside Edge,* 67.

23. Ibid., 68.

24. Ibid.

25. Conveniently, Brennan forgot her recently published assertion that Galindo would never win because he was not the best skater in the country and, if she ever knew in the first place, that speed and power, height and distance traveled on jumps, correct takeoff edge on the lutz jump, and complexity of footwork are equally important criteria as jump difficulty, flexibility, and elegance. But the latter, Galindo's strong points, are more evident to the untrained eye than the former, areas in which his short program as performed in San Jose did not match the two that placed ahead of him. A good case could be made for placing Davis behind Galindo in that short program due to a deduction on the double axel, but despite Eldredge's completing a less difficult combination (triple axel–double toe vs. Galindo's triple axel–triple toe) and his relatively flat performance quality, it was probably his power more than his reputation that kept him in first place in the short.

26. William Plummer, "Redemption Song," *People*, Feb. 5, 1996, 126.

27. Rudy Galindo with Eric Marcus, *Icebreaker: The Autobiography of Rudy Galindo* (New York: Pocket Books, 1997), 213.

28. Gary Reese, "Thin Ice," *Advocate*, Mar. 5, 1996, 33–35.

29. Thanks to Stojko's fall in the short program and Urmanov's in the long, Galindo's fourth in both programs was good enough for third place overall. Eldredge, taking his second-place finish in San Jose as a wake-up call, had renewed his training and focus to finally capture the world title.

30. Galindo and Marcus, *Icebreaker*, 230.

31. Lorrie Kim, "A Long Program," *Advocate*, June 11, 1996, 31–33.

32. See, e.g., Martin Cleary, "Ex-lover's Suit Upsets Skater Orser." *Ottawa Citizen* Nov. 19, 1998; D'Arcy Doran, "Orser Wanted Palimony Suit Details Hushed," *Toronto Star*, Nov. 19, 1998; Beverley Smith, "Support Pours in for Orser," *Toronto Globe and Mail*, Nov. 20, 1998.

33. Beverley Smith, "Orser: 'I've Never Had to Lie about it,'" *Toronto Globe and Mail*, Dec. 9, 1998.

NOTES TO CHAPTER TEN

1. A related team discipline known as "fours," usually consisting of two men and two women, was also popular before and after World War II and was briefly revived in the United States and Canada in the early 1990s. Here symmetrical patterning of movement around a common center was the most salient feature, with highlights such as a combined four-person death spiral providing choreographic contrast.

2. Examples include the Ice Follies' well-known "Frick and Frack" of the 1930s and teams such as the Armenian-born "Ari and Akop" who performed in various televised skating performances and with the Ice Theatre of New York in the 1990s.

3. Brown, *Ice-Skating*, 157.

4. In a throw jump, the female member of the pair sets up and performs a standard jump while the male member performs a parallel setup while holding onto her torso; instead of jumping himself, he adds additional energy to the direction of her jump, so that she is able to jump higher and/or further than she could on her own. Thus some pair skaters are able to achieve enough additional air time in throw jumps to complete triple revolutions on jumps that they can perform only as doubles on their own. Because of the extra momentum and height, the landing of a throw jump requires greater strength on the part of the lady to control it.

Occasionally in exhibition or pro performances, pairs have reversed roles to have the lady "throw" the man in a single axel. Same-sex pairs can also perform throw jumps. But in these cases the throw does not increase the size of the jump as much beyond what the jumping partner is capable of achieving on his or her own. The greater the size differential between the partners and the greater the strength of the throwing partner, given comparable technique, the greater the extra momentum.

5. Brown, *Ice-Skating,* 158.

6. A handful of same-sex pairs were entered in the figure skating competition at the 1994 Gay Games. Most of these, including both of the all-female pairs, were skaters of beginning or intermediate levels of accomplishment. Jean-Paul Martin and Marc Hird of Montreal brought a fairly high level of skating and pair skills to their program, including lifts by each partner of the other, with the larger of the two lifting the smaller one overhead. Their program was designed more as an artistic or show number than to conform to competitive rules (since there were no other pairs at their level to compete against or other competitive forums for male pairs to compete in); they later performed this and other routines at various benefit skating shows in New York and Montreal. See Abigail Feder, "Gay Games IV," *Village Voice,* June 21, 1994; Roger Rubin, "Same-Sex Pairs' Flair," *New York Newsday,* June 24, 1994.

7. In an "arabian" or arabian cartwheel, a move borrowed from acrobatic dancing, a skater kicks her feet up behind her, first one then the other, while leaning forward with the upper body; ideally the feet should follow a circular arc as high as possible above the lowered head. It is similar to and more spectacular than the move skaters and gymnasts refer to as the "butterfly." Solo skaters often use this move as an entrance into a flying spin. By joining hands and pulling against each other, two skaters can take turns performing the move and providing additional support to allow the partner to achieve greater power and height while doing so.

8. Qtd. in "Colorado Dispatch," 10.

9. Judge Janet Swan Hill, for instance, described attending a pair seminar where coaches continually referred to the female partner during lifts as the male's "precious cargo" (personal communication).

10. Qtd. in Lorrie Kim, "Beyond Spirals with Jeff Nolt," *6.0* (spring 2001).

11. Pair skating competition had never included a compulsory phase of this nature. In the early 1960s, the ISU therefore instituted a short program of required moves as the first phase of pairs competitions, but unlike compulsory figures or compulsory dances, the arrangement of the specified moves was left to the discretion of each individual pair. The short program introduced into men's and ladies' singles competition in 1973 was modeled on the pairs short program, and since the elimination of figures from singles competition in 1991 the structure of singles and pairs competition has been identical (except at large championships where qualifying rounds are required for singles).

12. Brown, *Ice-Skating*, 169–172.

13. That is, to music with a foxtrot rhythm, and employing movements and dance holds reminiscent of the foxtrot as performed on dance floors. IEV Rules (*Skating*, Nov. 1928, 5), cited in Lynn Copley-Graves, *Figure Skating History: The Evolution of Dance on Ice* (Columbus, OH: Platoro Press, 1992), 29.

14. See Copley-Graves, *Figure Skating History*, for further details about the development of ice dance competition.

15. For the 1998 season, for instance, the rhythm was the jive and for 1999 the waltz. Beginning with the 2000 season, original dances have been combinations of related rhythms, specified in pools of four or five from which each team must choose two or three. For the 2000 Latin Combination, the choices were rumba, cha-cha, mambo, merengue, and samba; the 2001 Rhythm Combination the choices were march, charleston, quickstep, and foxtrot, with the latter two rhythms being by far the most frequent choice; the 2002 selection was a Spanish Medley of paso doble, tango, flamenco, and waltz orchestrated in a Spanish manner, and for 2003 the theme was "Memories of a Grand Ball," with waltz, polka, march, and galop as the choice of rhythms.

16. For further discussion about the development of social dance forms, see, e.g., Belinda Quirey, *May I Have the Pleasure? The Story of Popular Dancing* (London: Dance Books, 1987); John Martin, *The Dance* (New York: Books for Libraries, 1980), 24–32; Julie Malnig, *Dancing Till Dawn: A Century of Exhibition Ballroom Dance* (New York: Greenwood Press, 1992).

17. Judith Butler, *Gender Trouble: Feminism and the Subversion of Identity* (New York: Routledge, 1990), 151 n. 6.

18. Solo skaters may often be found practicing on their own the steps that they would perform with a partner. There are many accomplished ice dancers who are unable to participate in competition because of the lack of a suitable partner. These often include skaters who excel at factors such as edge quality and musical interpretation but cannot succeed in singles competition because of inability, perhaps due to body type or to prior injuries, to master or maintain the more difficult jumps. The imbalance in partner matching almost always in the direction of excess females leads to a "seller's market" in favor of potential male partners. Particularly in the United States, families of talented daughters who

possess sufficient wealth may offer to pay for a male skater's training and even living expenses in order to secure a partner for their daughter, a practice that of course favors female skaters whose families can afford thus to buy a partner. (A similar arrangement in the context of a pairs partnership is detailed in the film *The Cutting Edge*.) In recent years, there has also been a trend toward American female dancers teaming up with partners from other countries. Of the three top-ranked couples at the 1999 U.S. Championships, for instance, two of the men were originally from Russia and one from Great Britain.

In the United States, nonqualifying competitions sometimes offer "solo dance" as a competitive event to accommodate unpartnered skaters. In Great Britain, solo dance competitions including phases equivalent to the original or free dance are a recent innovation.

For testing purposes, rules about who may partner a test candidate, in terms of professional/amateur status and how many higher tests the partner has passed, have been relaxed over the years to allow test skaters to hire a partner for the duration of a test. As of 1996–1997, a solo dance test track has been introduced to allow skaters, generally girls, for whom even that option is not feasible to be tested only on their own steps of the dance. Testing with a partner of the same sex, even one's coach, however, is not allowed.

19. The compulsory dances used in competition are the same set-pattern dances that make up the syllabus of ice dance tests and that serve as a repertoire that ice dance enthusiasts can perform for fun in social contexts such as the "dance intervals" still scheduled during public skating sessions at many British rinks and at "dance weekends" held annually by various rinks throughout North America. Because the steps are standardized, one can simply ask a new acquaintance in such a setting, "Do you care to tango?" and both partners know exactly what is expected of them in terms of steps. Knowing exactly how to position oneself in relation to one's partner in order to facilitate and not to impede the partner's progression from one step to the next develops through experience performing these dances with different partners and also through experience skating with that particular partner. So two relatively inexperienced skaters who may be able to perform their own steps well when skating by themselves or with an experienced partner would likely find themselves pulling each other in inappropriate directions the first time they skate together and would certainly not have the unison that would be expected of longtime frequent partners. Each would always have to make constant minute adjustments to accommodate the body type and skating style of the new partner. Nevertheless, "leading" is in theory supposed to be the responsibility of the male, although in practice if the female partner is the stronger or more experienced skater she is likely to take more of an active role in controlling the couple's trajectory.

20. In the 1980s and 1990s, ballroom dance enjoyed a resurgence of interest among young adults. Observers attribute this interest to the fact that the physical

proximity and structured holds and steps promote greater intimacy between dance partners than do freeform dance styles and to a return to monogamy and nostalgia for traditional gender roles in reaction to the AIDS crisis and other anxieties deriving from the 1960s breakdown of sexual stereotypes (Rebecca Smith, "Ballroom Dancing," *Dance Magazine,* Apr. 1995, 54–57; Peter Shaw, "Clean Dancing," *Commentary,* Oct. 1988, 53–54). As Shaw notes, however, "Couples dancing, it is true, has not been restored to its role as a social ritual, or a means of meeting members of the opposite sex, and actual participation in dancing has so far been limited to a few dance-instruction studios, a few reopened nightclubs, and—typically enough of the present age—a few health clubs where dance instruction has been introduced for its exercise benefits" (54). Thus, although adults in their twenties or thirties might take up ballroom dance for similar reasons that they might take up ice dance—as a means through which to meet new friends or to share an activity with a life partner, and as a form of exercise—the dances they learn belong to the traditions and rituals of earlier generations of the twentieth century, not to the day-to-day culture of the current era. For competitive skaters, who generally begin training well before adolescence (when they might be expected to become interested in the social attractions of dancing or skating with a partner of the opposite sex), ballroom traditions would have even less contemporary relevance. Ice dancers study ballroom dance in order to enhance their competence in their sport; they don't, for the most part, take up ice dance because ballroom dance is already a meaningful part of their lives that they wish to extend onto the ice, as was the case with the (adult) skaters of 1890s Vienna or 1930s London who originated the sport.

21. Sally Peters, "From Eroticism to Transcendence: Ballroom Dance and the Female Body," *Michigan Quarterly Review* 30.1 (1991): 26–27.

22. Ibid., 28–29.

23. Ibid., 36.

24. Peter Shaw argues that "couples dancing enacts a complex mutuality between the sexes" in which "though the man appears to be holding and controlling the woman, the two of them are actually together constructing a ' frame' or circle with their arms. Each exerts a degree of force on his side of the frame, slightly pushing against the other. . . . In other words, not compliance but resistance makes the male lead possible." The same is true of ice dancing in ballroom dance holds. By focusing on the experience of the dancers rather than any hypothetical observers, Shaw concludes that "each partner accepts the constraints and enjoys the prerogatives of a frankly sex-stereotyped role. . . . His is a role of responsibility, as it was once universally believed to be his sexual role in life. Her role is to make it possible for him to lead and thereby help him provide her with pleasure, as it was once universally believed to be her sexual role in life." Since the pleasure referred to is that of being put on display while executing "those attractive maneuvers that social dance reserves for her alone," this participant-oriented

point of view also reserves the role of to-be-looked-at for the female ("Clean Dancing," 54). In Shaw's perspective, the female occupies the more privileged position, but one dependent on the power of the male to provide her that privilege.

25. Tina Chen, personal interview, Mar. 26, 1993.

26. ABC coverage of 1988 Olympic Winter Games. This comment was inspired by the gold-medal-winning free dance of Soviets Natalia Bestemianova and Andrei Bukin, but it seems intended to apply to the meanings inherent in the discipline itself.

27. Blumberg and Seibert incorporated moves from George Balanchine's *Prodigal Son* into their 1984 free dance to Rimsky-Korsakov's *Scheherezade.* (Anita Finkel, "The Sport of It," *Dance Magazine,* Feb. 1984, 14–17.) For Russian skaters, ballet remains a vital element of the national culture, and ballet classes from a very early age were a required component of the Soviet system of figure skating training.

28. For discussion of these meanings in the ballet tradition, see Ann Daly, "The Balanchine Woman: Of Hummingbirds and Channel Swimmers," *Drama Review* 31 (spring 1987): 8–21; Susan Foster, *Choreography and Narrative* (Bloomington: University of Indiana Press, 1996), esp. chap. 5; Christy Adair, *Women and Dance: Sylphs and Sirens* (New York: New York University Press, 1992), 82–118; Belinda Quirey, *May I Have the Pleasure? The Story of Popular Dancing* (London: Dance Books, 1987), 74–76. For a challenge to this position, see Sally Banes, *Dancing Women: Female Bodies on Stage* (London: Routledge, 1998).

29. An exception is Torvill and Dean's 1983 free program to music from the Broadway show *Barnum,* which was about circus tricks, not romance. According to Copley-Graves, the program's unveiling at the British championships drew mixed responses "because its athleticism did not portray the traditional relationship between man and woman" (*Figure Skating History,* 312). However, with tricks such as "Jayne's leg swing under Chris's other leg like an elephant, Jayne rolling into the ring like drums, Jayne falling off the tightrope and rescued by Chris," in addition to moves in which both equally played trombones or painted on clown faces, the program was hardly designed to challenge male normativity and control. Their 1984 paso doble OSP, which portrayed more literally and more memorably than most that dance's bullfight origins in which the man represents the matador entering the ring and the woman represents his cape, similarly relegated the role of non-human to the woman.

30. Sandra Stevenson, "Perfect Torvill and Dean," *Guardian,* Feb. 26, 1984, 24.

31. Bob Ottum, "Notable Triumphs, Wrong Notes," *Sports Illustrated,* Feb. 27, 1984, 63.

NOTES TO CHAPTER ELEVEN

1. "By the Olympics, we'd already begun to feel stifled by the rules and regulations of amateur competition," Torvill said, citing rules outlining what ice dancers were not allowed to do in competition "so that the judges can evaluate every-

one on an equal basis." Qtd. in Donald Chase, "Torvill & Dean: So Nice on Ice," *Saturday Evening Post,* Jan./Feb. 1987, 48. Dean expressed the team's artistic aspirations: "We felt that as people, as dancers, as skaters, we wanted to move on. We wanted to do things, skating-wise and choreographically, that hadn't been done before, to have *thought* behind what we're doing, so that it wasn't just coordinated movements to a piece of music. As well, it had to have rhyme and reason, a concept, a story" (87). As professionals, Torvill and Dean could explore themes and relationships well beyond the stereotyped roles of the standard ballroom dances that competitive ice dancing relied on.

They experimented with programs in which the male as well as the female partner displayed his body and flexibility and moments in which each offered the other emotional support through gestures of physically supporting part of the other's weight. They also performed comic numbers based on a principle of one-upmanship: a slapstick tango involving extremes of stylized violence including Jayne "kicking" Christopher in the crotch, and "The Red Hat," in which the two take turns tricking each other out of possession of a red hat by exchanging it for a less desirable black one. In both these battles, Jayne emerges as the winner.

Blumberg and Seibert, after turning professional following the 1985 season, performed a number based on the concept of tango as a male challenge dance, with both skaters costumed identically in black trousers and white shirts, in which each partner dipped the other and performed other reciprocal actions.

2. Copley-Graves, *Figure Skating History,* 335. The objection seems to have been that the music used—probably the theme from Franco Zeffirelli more so than that from the Prokofiev ballet—was lyrical rather than rhythmic and that the skating therefore also lacked a steady rhythm.

3. Ibid., 325.

4. Ibid., 340. There had, however, been role reversals in earlier dances, as in Blumberg and Seibert's 1983 homage to Ginger Rogers and Fred Astaire, which included a set of pull-throughs, with Michael pulling Judy past him in a low-to-the-ice horizontal position and Judy doing the same to Michael.

5. "—Est-ce une parade d'amour, une danse rituelle?

Paul. Il s'agit plutôt d'un scenario ou nous serions deux survivants dans une jungle et environnés de mille dangers.

—Avec beaucoup de sensualité, comme dans un vrai couple.

Isabelle. Sauf qu'en fait de couple, nous sommes plutôt des Tarzan et Jane qui seraient frère et sœur. Et chacun, tour à tour, avertit et protege l'autre d'ennemis invisibles."

Jean-Francois Chaigneau, "Dans le coeur du public, nous sommes les premiers," *Paris-Match,* Apr. 22, 1988, 22.

6. E. M. S[wift], "So Much for Originality," *Sports Illustrated,* Mar. 7, 1988, 45.

7. "Cela [the Duchesnays' 1992 West Side Story free program] permettait de

mettre en valeur leur caractère en évitant les connotations incestueuses d'une re-
lation amoureuse entre des patineurs qui sont frère et sœur." Dean qtd. in Alain
Giraudo, "L'heure de verité pour les Duchesnays," *Le Monde,* Feb. 14, 1992. Since
Dean is English, I may just be undoing Giraudo's translation into French.

8. Robin Cousins, NBC coverage of 1991 World Figure Skating Championships.

9. "Le thème justifie ce costume, car nous ne sommes qu'une seule et même
personne, qui regarde son reflet dans la glace. Tous les aspects de sa personnalité
défile devant elle. Elle tente de savoir qui elle est réellement, pourquoi elle existe"
Isabelle Duchesnay, qtd. in Martine Carret, *Isabelle et Paul Duchesnay: Notre Passion* (Paris: Robert Laffont, 1992), 97–100. The feminine pronoun agrees with the
noun *personne;* it does not necessarily imply the sex of the person referred to. Later
in the same paragraph, Carret refers to "l'être qui s'interroge sur lui-même" (the
being who examines himself), using a masculine pronoun to agree with the noun
l'être.

10. Giraudo, "L'heure de verité," 10.

11. Marjorie Garber, in her analysis of transvestism, claims that the cross-
dressed individual is "both a signifier and that which signifies the undecidability
of signification," a " 'third' . . . which questions binary thinking and introduces
crisis." Marjorie Garber, *Vested Interests: Cross-Dressing and Cultural Anxiety* (New
York: Routledge, 1992), 37, 11. Isabelle's declaration, perhaps defensively in response to disapproval from ISU officials, that "L'Union international de Patinage
exige que les costumes soient décents. Je suis couverte de la tete aux pieds, il est
difficile de faire plus!" ([The International Skating Union demands that the costumes be decent. I'm covered from head to foot, it's hard to do more!]; qtd. in
Carret, 97) suggests that female modesty itself, if it lacks distinction from male
dress and thus "questions binary thinking," was more disturbing than the less
modest but explicitly feminine costume trends the ruling was meant to discourage.

12. "Ce jeu de miroir est trop intellectuel. Le public boude. Les juges en pro-
fitent pour les laisser sur la deuxième marche du podium." Giraudo, "L'heure de
verité," 10.

13. Jayne Torvill and Christopher Dean with John Man, *Torvill & Dean: The
Autobiography of Ice Dancing's Greatest Stars* (Secaucus, NJ: Carol Publishing Group,
1996), 251. In fact, it would have been difficult for the Duchesnays to win using
the "Reflections" program as skated in Sofia. Technically they could not match
the edge quality or facility of turns of the top Russian couples and habitually
placed behind them in the compulsory dances. In addition to power and speed
that drew on their youthful training as pair skaters, the Duchesnays' most valuable assets were Dean's choreography and the intensity they brought to their
performances. "Reflections," which relied choreographically a good deal on one
skater pushing and pulling the other by the free leg (an interaction the ISU subsequently decided to forbid) and other tricks such as lifts, connected with simple

crossovers and other two-footed skating, was virtually devoid of the intricate footwork that contributes the most technical content to an ice dance program.

14. "Missing II" caused its own controversy in that the Duchesnays distributed a press release connected to the free dance that expressed their hopes for peace; many saw this move as playing politics in an attempt to sway the judges.

15. The audience connection that was missing in "Reflections" seems to have been key to the superior artistic marks awarded to "Missing II." The upbeat music probably helped; geography may also have played a role, as the Duchesnays trained in Oberstdorf, Germany, not far from Munich, and thus may have benefited from a sizable contingent of local fans in the stands.

16. See, e.g., the feature "Danse/Dance," *Patinage,* Oct.–Nov. 1992, 20–23, and Nancy Rappaport, "Shall We Dance? The Twists and Turns in the World of Ice Dancing," *International Figure Skating,* Dec. [1996]/Jan. 1997, 12–14.

17. From ISU Rule 510, reprinted in "Danse/Danse," 20.

18. In "Danse/Dance," 21.

19. The United States Figure Skating Association, *The 1992–93 Official USFSA Rulebook* (Colorado Springs: USFSA, 1992), 98–99.

20. Similarly, requirements that original or original set pattern dances must progress around the ice in a constant direction without retrogression and without crossing the center line of the ice surface except at the ends of the rink would be very practical for dances intended for use on social dance sessions where four or more couples might be performing the same dance at the same time, following each other around the pattern and/or starting at opposite ends of the rink, in that such a pattern would minimize the likelihood of collisions that would be far more serious at twenty-some miles per hour on the ice than at the brisk walking pace achieved by dancers on the floor. Such considerations would also prove useful in practice sessions when several couples would each be practicing their own dances at the same time; however, the fact that free dances are not subject to such restrictions and therefore traffic is a problem in any case at practices where more than one couple are practicing free dances obviates safety as the reason for the requirement in the original dance. When asked about the reasoning behind this requirement, an international judge explained that "the only reason is to keep it from being a free dance, to give it some structure" (Robert Horen, personal interview, July 16, 1998).

21. *The 1992–93 USFSA Rulebook,* 98–99. Language requiring skirts for female competitors in all disciplines had already been in place since the 1989 season, but as we have seen not all the top dance couples had adhered to this rule; adding the statement to the rules for the original and free dances stressed that it applied to dance as well as freestyle. The ban on tights (or unitards) for male dancers was new as of the 1993 season and further encouraged a reliance on social rather than stage dance conventions in ice dance. When tights were banned for male freestyle

skaters two years later, the clothing requirements for dance then matched those for freestyle and the language was removed from the dance portion of the rules, retained in the general section on clothing.

22. The term *hydroblading*, coined by Bourne and Kraatz's "stylist," Uschi Keszler, derives from the skaters' practice of supporting their weight by holding onto water bottles placed on the ice with their hands while learning the techniques of skating with such deeply bent knees and extreme body lean. In competition, of course, no such props are permitted.

23. Commentary during Fox broadcast of 1996 Champions Series Final.

24. Robert Horen, personal interview, July 16, 1998.

25. Nicky Slater, Eurosport coverage of 1997 European Championships; Dick Button, ABC coverage of 1997 World Championships.

26. "Without Olympic Champs, Ice Dancers Move Up at Worlds," *Buffalo News*, Apr. 4, 1998.

27. Canadian judge Jean Senft has explained, "I do think North Americans and Europeans look at ice dancing differently. . . . The former prefer athletic performances with intricate footwork, and the latter prefer theatrical, dramatic performances with more emphasis on upper body movement and facial emotion." Qtd. in "Ice-Dance Judge 'Felt' Fix Was In: Canadian Suspected Placings Pre-determined," *Toronto Sun*, Feb. 18, 1998. American judge Robert Horen says, "We do have our traditionalists, but so do some of the Europeans, for instance the British. The French tend to be more creative. But you would see the same thing in the opening ceremonies at the Olympics in France, versus the opening ceremonies in Atlanta. Americans in general tend to be more conservative. Or, I don't know, maybe the French see that as traditional. . . . There was mixed reaction in the U.S. to Punsalan and Swallow's race car program, but they loved it in Europe" (personal interview, July 16, 1998). Along these lines, we can interpret Torvill and Dean's *Bolero* as representing an approach more within the Russian than the English tradition.

28. *The 2001 Official USFSA Rulebook*, 140.

29. Ibid.

30. ABC coverage of 1999 Grand Prix Final.

31. "The main point stressed by all committee members was that for the Olympic year there is not supposed to be sad or dramatic music." Ice Dance Technical Committee Meeting, notes by Tanja Brand, www.ice-dance.com/technical/2001committeenotes.htm. "Aleksandr Gorshkov summed it up best, at the dance meeting, 'Ice Dance can not afford any more sad free dances. It will be the death of dance at the olympics.'" Ginny Conway, personal communication, Apr. 2001.

32. Tracy Wilson, NBC coverage of 2002 Olympic Winter Games, Feb. 18, 2002.

33. See, e.g., Beverley Smith, "Ice Dance Judging Triggers Uproar: Brave Judges at Kitchener Grand Prix Find Themselves on International Hotseat As

Russian Referee Shows Displeasure," *Toronto Globe and Mail,* Dec. 20, 2001; Amy Shipley, "Skating Dances Around Judges' Choices," *Washington Post* May 12, 2002.

34. Sandra Stevenson, "Dirty Dancing: The Innovation of Ice Dancers Is Turning the Skating World Upside Down with Indecent Exposure Officials Could Do Without," *National Post,* Jan. 16, 2002.

NOTES TO CHAPTER TWELVE

1. The quotes in this chapter are drawn from a survey I distributed in fall 1998 via several Internet forums where skating fans gather to discuss their favorite sport. The sample is thus skewed in favor of those who are computer-literate and devoted enough in their love of skating to seek out electronically others who share their interest. There is also a heavy bias toward English-speaking fans. The purpose is not to attempt any statistical conclusions about skating fans in general or even about this particular subset of fans; the substantive responses are excerpted for anecdotal value only. Demographic information is provided for informational purposes: The fans in this sample were overwhelmingly female (74 female, 4 male), American (63 American, 10 Canadian, 3 Japanese, 1 each British and Polish), heterosexual (only two respondents, both female, identified themselves as "gay" or "bisexual," and one refused to answer), and in early or middle adulthood (5 teens, 18 twenties, 26 thirties, 17 forties, 10 fifties, 2 sixties). Surveys of other segments of the skate-fan population would likely produce different trends in the types of responses. The historical moment at which the survey was conducted also affects the responses; for example, many of the respondents cited the depth of talent in the international men's field as opposed to the ladies' and the consequent competitiveness or feeling that "anyone could win" as a reason for choosing men's singles as a favorite discipline; in other years, fans for whom the level of competition was a primary determinant of favorite discipline might choose a different event.

2. For the importance to women's sense of identity of competence in meeting the demands of patriarchal standards of femininity and valuing the skills required to do so, see Sandra Lee Bartky, "Foucault, Feminity, and the Modernization of Patriarchal Power," in *Feminism and Foucault: Reflections on Resistance,* ed. Irene Diamond and Lee Quinby (Boston: Northeastern University Press, 1988), esp. 77–78.

3. Judith Mayne, "Fear of Falling," in Baughman, *Women on Ice,* 85.

4. Kate Rounds, "Ice Follies: Reflections on a Sport Out of Whack," *Ms.,* May/June 1994, 26–33.

5. Lorrie Kim, personal communication.

6. See Janice Radway's identification of the utopian nurturing hero as a key source of appeal of romance novels to their readers in *Reading the Romance: Women, Patriarchy, and Popular Literature* (Chapel Hill: University of North Carolina Press, 1984) and see Susan J. Douglas, *Where the Girls Are: Growing Up Fe-*

male with the Mass Media (New York: Times Books, 1994) on the attraction of the Beatles for teenage girls in the 1960s: "Their music bridged safety and danger as well. Drawing from the 'hard' rock 'n' roll of Chuck Berry and Little Richard, as well as from the 'soft' call-and-response layered harmony styles of the girl groups, the Beatles pushed the conventional musical codes of masculinity and femininity up against each other in a way that evoked making love with your clothes on . . . suggesting that male sexuality wasn't so threatening, female sexuality was perfectly normal, and the two could exist together harmoniously" (117). Analyzing "slash" fan fiction by and for women that depicts sexual relationships between male heroes of television and other mass media narratives, Henry Jenkins acknowledges the utopianism of the genre in its celebration of male-male experience "at the expense of developing alternative feminine identities" and proposes that "Slash may, finally, be more important because of its questioning of sexuality and popular culture than for its specific answers." Henry Jenkins, *Textual Poachers: Television Fans and Participatory Culture* (New York: Routledge, 1992), 190.

7. See Jenkins, *Textual Poachers*, for analysis of similar practices among media fans in light of Michel de Certeau's theory of reading as "poaching" alternative meanings from authoritative texts.

8. E. M. Swift, "Figuring It Out: How Will Skating Get Its House in Order After the Salt Lake Scandal?" *Sports Illustrated,* May 13, 2002, 19.

NOTE TO THE APPENDIX

1. *The 1999 Official USFSA Rulebook,* 109.

For Further Reading and Viewing

Listed here are resources that readers may find useful for learning more about figure skating. References are cited in the notes to each chapter.

This list is not exhaustive. Except in the historical section, I have tried to list only books that are still in print or books and magazine/journal articles recent enough that there is a good chance of finding them in local public or college libraries, particularly those with large collections and/or located in ice-friendly climates.

HISTORIOGRAPHICAL WORKS

Even the more serious historiographical works listed here lack scholarly apparatus such as notes citing specific facts to specific sources, and in some cases even lack reference lists or detailed indexes.

Brown, Nigel. *Ice-Skating: A History.* New York: A. S. Barnes and Company, 1959.
> A readable narrative, with opinions and analysis by the author, covering the history of skating from its prehistoric origins to the mid–twentieth century.

Copley-Graves, Lynn. *Figure Skating History: The Evolution of Dance on Ice.* Columbus, OH: Platoro Press, 1992.
> A narrative of ice dancing from its origins through 1990, pieced together from copious archival sources. Lists of all major competition results and diagrams for set pattern dances in the margins provide additional reference material.

Wright, Benjamin T. *Skating in America.* Colorado Springs: USFSA, 1996.
> A detailed history of the United States Figure Skating Association and the place of American skaters in world competition, gleaned from material in association archives and back issues of *Skating* magazine.

HOW-TO MANUALS FROM EARLIER ERAS

Almost all these books are out of print. Most are available in the open library at the World Figure Skating Museum at USFSA Headquarters in Colorado Springs, and many may be found unexpectedly in local public or university libraries. These older technique manuals provide a look at how skating was taught and practiced and what was valued in earlier eras. These and other similar publications provide their authors' insights, as skating experts, into what the skating world valued when each was published. The numbers of chapters devoted to school figures compared to freeskating, pair skating, and ice dancing proves most illuminating.

Bass, Howard. *This Skating Age*. Boston: Branford, 1959.
A British skating journalist's perspective.

Jones, Ernest. *The Elements of Figure Skating*. London: Methuen, 1931.

Lewis, Frederic. *Modern Skating*. Chicago: Reilly & Lee, 1938.

Lussi, Gustave and Maurice Richards. *Championship Figure Skating*. New York: Barnes, 1951.

Monier-Williams, Montagu S. *Figure-Skating*. London: A. D. Innes, 1898.
From the era when skating was first making the transition from pastime to organized sport; includes a chapter on skating for women by an accomplished woman skater of the day.

Ogilvie, Robert S. *Basic Ice Skating Skills*. Philadelphia: Lippincott, 1968.
Billed as "An Official Handbook Prepared for the United States Figure Skating Association" by a professional instructor. Includes sections on fundamentals and the basics of freestyle, figures, and dance, illustrated with photographs and diagrams.

Richardson, T. D. *The Art of Figure Skating*. New York: Barnes, 1962.

Vandervell, H. E., and T. Maxwell Witham. *A System of Figure-Skating. Being the theory and practice of the art as developed in England, with a glance at its origin and history*. London: Macmillan, 1869.
The earliest published scientifically theorized approach to skating technique.

Vinson, Maribel Y. *Primer of Figure Skating*. New York: Whittlesey House, 1938.

———. *Advanced Figure Skating*. New York: Whittlesey House, 1940.

BIOGRAPHIES AND AUTOBIOGRAPHIES

Many biographies, authorized and unauthorized, are available about recent skating stars, and many have written autobiographies. Fans or researchers interested in specific skaters of course would seek out the works devoted to their object of interest. The following is just a sampling of works useful for illuminating particular periods in skating history.

Browning, Kurt. *Kurt: Forcing the Edge*. Toronto: HarperCollins, 1991, 1992.
The man credited with the first successful quadruple jump in competition and the only skater to win world titles both with and without school figures. Browning's eligible career also straddled changes in rules regarding amateurism; he was just beginning to realize his potential as an artistic as well as athletic skater when this book was produced.

Button, Dick. *Dick Button on Skates.* Englewood Cliffs, NJ: Prentice-Hall, 1955.
   Autobiography of the first American to win Olympic gold in figure skating
   and the first skater to perform a triple jump.

Cranston, Toller, with Martha Lowder Kimball. *Zero Tollerance: An Intimate
Memoir by the Man who Revolutionized Figure Skating.* Toronto: McClelland &
Stewart, 1997.
   Personal thoughts and reminiscences from the flamboyant painter-skater.

Fleming, Peggy, with Peter Kaminsky, *The Long Program: Skating Toward Life's
Victories.* New York: Pocket Books, 1999.
   Fleming discusses the decisions that led to her advancement of balletic
   qualities in women's skating in the 1960s, her experiences as a female sport
   celebrity after her Olympic win, and her recent bout with breast cancer.

Galindo, Rudy, with Eric Marcus. *Icebreaker: The Autobiography of Rudy
Galindo.* New York: Pocket Books, 1997.
   Discusses his personal struggles and his historical position as the first openly
   gay U.S. champion.

Gordeeva, Ekaterina, with E. M. Swift. *My Sergei: A Love Story.* New York:
Warner, 1996.
   Love story of pair skating greats Gordeeva and Grinkov, until Grinkov's un-
   timely death in 1995. Also valuable for the insights into skating practice, and
   daily life, in the last years of the Soviet Union.

Hamilton, Scott, with Lorenzo Benet. *Landing It: My Life On and Off the Ice.*
New York: Pinnacle, 1999.
   Personal history focusing on Hamilton's much-discussed childhood illness
   and recent testicular cancer, along with accounts of his competitive career
   and the development of Stars on Ice as an intimate touring ensemble.

Hennessy, John. *Torvill and Dean.* New York: St. Martin's, 1983.
   Celebration of the team that dominated and transformed ice dancing in
   the early/mid-1980s as they headed into their Olympic-gold-medal-winning
   season.

Henie, Sonja. *Wings on My Feet.* Englewood Cliffs, NJ: Prentice-Hall, 1940.
   The three-time Olympic champion who made figure skating famous via
   Hollywood recounts how she got there.

Money, Keith. *John Curry.* New York: Alfred A. Knopf, 1978.
   Heavy on photographs, this book celebrates the artistic vision of the 1976
   Olympic champion, who brought the values of classical ballet and modern
   dance not only in his competitive skating but even more in his professional
   work producing dance concerts on ice.

Steere, Michael. *Scott Hamilton: A Behind-the-Scenes Look at the Life and Com-*

petitive Times of America's Favorite Figure Skater, an Unauthorized Biography.
New York: St. Martin's, 1985.

A sportswriter's account of the U.S. and world figure skating scene in the early 1980s, focusing on the man who dominated the men's competition in that era.

Strait, Raymond, and Leif Henie. *Queen of Ice, Queen of Shadows: The Unsuspected Life of Sonja Henie.* New York: Stein and Day, 1985.

Emphasis on the less savory aspects of Henie's life, contributed by her brother.

Torvill, Jayne, and Christopher Dean with John Man. *Torvill and Dean: The Autobiography of Ice Dancing's Greatest Stars.* Secaucus, NJ: Carol Publishing Group, 1996.

The skaters' own accounts of their early lives and the early years of their partnership, as well as their experiences as professional skaters and choreographers continuing to expand the artistic possibilities of ice skating and their 1994 return to Olympic competition.

SCHOLARLY AND FEMINIST CRITIQUES OF SKATING

Baughman, Cynthia, ed. *Women on Ice: Feminist Essays on the Tonya Harding/Nancy Kerrigan Spectacle.* New York: Routledge, 1995.

Feminist reactions, ranging from personal accounts to jargon-laden scholarly critique, to the crime that riveted America's attention during the 1994 Olympic season.

Lopez, Marsha. "Does Figure Skating Exploit Females?" *American Skating World,* August 1995, 25.

Part of a special feature on women in skating. A former skater's reactions to the skating world's reactions to feminist critiques.

Michie, Helena. *Sororophobia.* New York: Oxford University Press, 1992.

An account of relationships between women in English literature; includes an "interchapter" about the Debi Thomas–Katarina Witt rivalry in 1988.

Rounds, Kate. "Ice Follies: Reflections on a Sport out of Whack." *Ms.,* May/June 1994, 26–33.

Reflections on how the culture of figure skating (as seen through the American mass media) led to the violence against Nancy Kerrigan at 1994 Nationals and contributes to the sexual objectification of all skaters.

Ryan, Joan. *Little Girls in Pretty Boxes: The Making and Breaking of Elite Gymnasts and Figure Skaters.* New York: Doubleday, 1995.

An investigation into the harmful physical and psychological effects of elite women's gymnastics on many of its practitioners, with many parallel stories from competitive figure skating included, especially in the chapter on eating disorders.

SKATING APPRECIATION

Bezic, Sandra, with David Hayes. *The Passion to Skate: An Intimate View of Figure Skating.* Atlanta: Turner Publishing, 1996.
Colorful coffee-table book from the perspective of one of the most successful skating choreographers in North America.

Brennan, Christine. *Inside Edge: A Revealing Journey into the Secret World of Figure Skating.* New York: Scribner, 1996.
Gossipy behind-the-scenes reports by a journalist following the 1994–1995 eligible and professional skating seasons in the United States.

Brennan, Christine. *Edge of Glory: The Inside Story of the Quest for Figure Skating's Olympic Gold Medals.* New York: Scribner, 1998.
Journalistic accounts of the major events in the year leading up to the 1998 Olympics.

Milton, Steve. *Skate Talk: Figure Skating in the Words of the Stars.* Buffalo, NY: Firefly Books, 1997.
Extended statements on various topics by prominent skaters and other key players in the world of figure skating.

Smith, Beverley. *Figure Skating: A Celebration.* Toronto: McClelland & Stewart, 1994.
A coffee-table book offering an overview of skating's past and present at the height of its popularity.

———. *A Year in Figure Skating,* ed. Dan Diamond. Toronto: McClelland & Stewart, 1996.
A large-format, photo-intensive account of the 1995–1996 international skating season.

———. *Talking Figure Skating: Behind the Scenes in the World's Most Glamorous Sport.* Toronto: McClelland & Stewart, 1997.
Based on extensive interviews; includes chapters on skating parents, coaches, judges, choreographers, and other topics.

Whedon, Julia. *The Fine Art of Ice Skating: An Illustrated History and Portfolio of Stars.* New York: Harry N. Abrams, Inc., 1988.
Reproductions of archival illustrations make this book a mini-trip to the World Figure Skating Museum without the travel.

Wilkes, Debbi, and Greg Cable. *Ice Time: A Portrait of Figure Skating.* Scarborough, ON: Prentice Hall Canada, 1994.
A Canadian former Olympic medalist turned broadcaster offers insights on her own career and on the skaters and skating she presents on television.

Yamaguchi, Kristi, with Christy Ness and Jody Meacham. *Figure Skating for Dummies.* Foster City, CA: IDG Books, 1997.

Guidance from the 1992 Olympic champion and her coach (Ness) on beginning skating technique, recognizing elements, and appreciating the finer
points of program construction and choreography, competitive rules, judging, and scoring. An excellent starting point for fans seeking illumination
as to what they are seeing on the ice.

SKATING TECHNIQUE

Berman, Alice. *Skaters Edge Sourcebook.* Kensington, MD: Skaters Edge, 1995.
(Order from Skaters Edge, Box 500, Kensington, MD 20895; 301-946-1971)
    Comprehensive reference guide for participant skaters, covering rinks, equip-
    ment, books, videos, and other publications, as well as listing elite champions
    and contact information for fan clubs.

Harris, Ricky. *Choreography and Style for Ice Skaters.* New York: St. Martin's,
1980.
    Aesthetic theory of choreography as applied to skating programs rather than
    stage dance, with practical exercises for developing creativity and expression.

Ogilvie, Robert. *Competitive Figure Skating—A Parent's Guide.* New York:
Harper & Row, 1985.
    What to expect from the world of competitive skating, covering topics such
    as equipment, coaching, skating clubs and practice sessions, testing, and
    competing. Includes a chapter for parents, also useful for fans and other non-
    skater observers, on how to recognize freestyle elements. The chapters on
    school figures are, of course, now out of date.

Petkevich, John Misha. *Figure Skating: Championship Techniques.* New York:
Sports Illustrated/Winners Circle Books, 1989.
    One of the most thorough how-to books around. Although no book can re-
    place the personal instruction of a qualified coach for learning skating skills
    and the book does cover advanced skills that cannot be self-taught, this book
    is the next best thing to supplement a beginning or advanced beginning
    skater's progress when lessons are hard to come by.

United States Figure Skating Association. *The 2002–2003 Official USFSA Rulebook.* Colorado Springs: USFSA, 2002.
    Updated each year, the official rulebook is a must-have for coaches and
    skaters who test and compete within the USFSA system; skaters who fail tests
    or lose competitions because of rule violations that could have been easily
    avoided have no one to blame but themselves. The outline of testing require-
    ments and competition rules can also provide outsiders with insight into how
    figure skating is structured within the United States below the elite level and
    details relevant to elite competition often glossed over by television commen-
    tators and print journalists.

PERIODICALS

Blades on Ice
7040 N. Mona Lisa Road, Tuscson, AZ 85741
602–575–1747 / www.bladesonice.com/mag
> Available at large bookstores, newsstands, and by subscription. Photo features, profiles, and topical articles.

International Figure Skating
Subscription Department, 55 Ideal Road, Worcester, MA 01604
IFSMAG@aol.com / www.ifsmagazine.com
> Available at large bookstores, newsstands, and by subscription. Profiles of prominent international skaters and others influential in the skating world and articles on topical issues, with a focus on the business side of figure skating.

Patinage Magazine
39 Bld de la Marne, F-76000 Rouen, France
> French skating magazine with an art- and fashion-oriented fan focus. Articles often appear in both French and English.

6.0 Skate Magazine
P.O. Box 559, Newton, NH 03858
603-382-1702 / six0skatemag@aol.com
> Bills itself as "the alternative skating magazine for the twenty-first century."

Skating
20 First Street, Colorado Springs, CO 80906-3697
719-635-5200
> Official publication of the U.S. Figure Skating Association. USFSA members receive *Skating* as a benefit of membership; subscriptions are also available to non-members. Includes test and competition results; reports of major competitions; profiles of prominent and up-and-coming U.S. skaters and other important U.S. skating figures; articles on synchronized, adult, basic skills, and Special Olympics skating, sports medicine, sports psychology, etc.

Spotlight on Skating
208 Mohawk Rd., Ancaster, ON, L9G 2W9, Canada
spotlightonskating.com
> A skating magazine with a Canadian focus.

VIDEO RESOURCES

Commercially available skating videos fall into several major categories:

- feature films in which skating plays a central role (e.g., the various Sonja Henie vehicles and movie versions of ice shows of the period such as *Ice Fol-*

lies of 1939; Ice Castles, The Cutting Edge, and other Hollywood or independent products with skaters as central characters)

- edited tapes of skating broadcasts, for example, of Olympic and occasionally World Championship competitions (high production values and some backstage material not aired in the original broadcasts, but even more mediated by what the producers found significant or memorable about the event than the original broadcasts)

- compilations of classic programs from professional competitions and shows or amateur exhibition tours (This and the previous category provide fans who could not record the original broadcasts and researchers new to the subject matter access to high points in the history of skating as sport and art form since the 1980s.)

- historical overviews of skating history relying on archival footage and recent interviews (e.g., the first *Magic Memories on Ice* video; the HBO documentary *Reflections on Ice: A Diary of Ladies' Figure Skating,* both heavily Americentric)—the only readily available access to extended clips and in some cases whole programs by amateur skaters from the 1970s and earlier

- videographic documents (without the commentary, interviews, and other accoutrements of television broadcasts) of competitions ranging from local club events to World Championships, and various club shows, produced for purchase by the participants but often available to any interested purchasers without restrictions (in recent years the USFSA contract with ABC television has precluded commercial sale of these tapes from U.S. Nationals) —often the only way to see skaters at lower levels, including some future stars, other than attending the events in person

- instructional materials for skaters and coaches about technique and choreography

- instructional materials for judges about how to recognize proper technique and errors and how to apply the presentation criteria

These last three categories offer an inside view unavailable through the mass media.

Rather than listing specific titles in each category, instead I will provide contact information for sources through which skating videos of various kinds can be ordered; their catalogs provide detail on most of the tapes available.

International Skating Union
Chemin de Primerose 2, CH-1007 Lausanne, Switzerland
Telephone: 41 21 612 66 66 / Fax: 41 21 612 66 77
info@isu.ch / www.isu.org/publications/publications.html
   The source for ISU-produced technical information.

Ledin Photo & Video
22645 15 Mile Road, Clinton Township, MI 48035
586-790-9097 / www.ledinvideo.com
> An event video company that provides tapes of competitions and ice shows, particularly at Michigan and Ohio skating clubs for the participants and other interested observers to purchase.

R & J Video
Ron Singson, P.O. Box 70287, Stockton, CA 95267v
209-476–0124 or 209-275-5506
> Another source of videotapes of some non-televised skaters and events.

Rainbo Sports Shop
4107 Oakton Street, Skokie, IL 60076
Telephone: 847-982-9000 / Fax: 847-982-9008 / Order toll-free: 800-752-8370
www.rainbowsportsshop.com/video.htm
> One of the largest shops specializing in all forms of ice and roller skating equipment and paraphernalia, including commercial skating videos.

USFSA
20 First Street, Colorado Springs, CO 80906
719-635-5200 / www.usfsa.org
> Sells some compilation videos of elite competitions and training materials.

Video Sports Productions
P.O. Box 2700, Dept. 902, Westfield, NJ 07091
800-USA-1996 or 201-276-7790 / www.skatetape.com
> Offers a wide variety of skating-related videotapes, including tapes of U.S. Nationals as far back as 1981.

Another good source of skating on tape is fans who have recorded skating broadcasts on their home VCRs. A few even have tapes going back twenty to twenty-five years. Even for more recent events, Canadian and Japanese networks often offer more thorough coverage (more skaters, short as well as long programs) than their U.S. equivalents of many eligible events. For major championships such as Olympics, Worlds, and Europeans, the cable channel Eurosport will often show all or almost all of the competitors in each phase of the event. Cable subscribers throughout most of Europe receive the same video feed and music, with commentary provided in the local language by former skaters teamed with full-time sports announcers. Although the British Eurosport commentators, for instance, do reveal personal preferences and admit to putting on their "patriotic hats" when a British skater takes the ice, in general the broadcasts are much less packaged than those on American or Canadian networks—the commentary offers more detail about technique, rules, and judging standards, less about personalities, with less effort to construct a viewing position rooting for or against certain skaters on the basis of nationality or style. If the commentary is in an unfamiliar language, of course it is possible to ignore it completely to watch the skating almost unmediated. On the other hand, skating fans in Europe and Japan often do not have access to professional competitions and other events produced for American broadcast (or to the midranked U.S. skaters included on broadcasts of U.S. Nationals). Tape trading, often with the necessity of converting tapes between the different broadcast standards used in different parts of the world, or in the case of older tapes from Betamax format, is thus an invaluable resource for witnessing a wider range of international approaches to skating.

ON-LINE RESOURCES

Skateweb by Sandra Loosemore

www.frogsonice.com/skateweb

Skateweb is the most complete guide to figure skating resources on-line, with links to virtually every other major skating site, including news sources; chat rooms, discussion boards, and mailing lists; skating clubs and competitions; and official and fan-produced Web sites for prominent and not-so-prominent skaters. The ideal starting point for anyone looking to research figure skating on-line.

Figure Skater's Website by Don Korte

www.sk8stuff.com

Reference material on skating from an adult participant point of view. Includes handy video illustrations for non-skaters to learn to recognize elements and overviews of the U.S. test and competition structures.

Ice Skating Institute

www.skateisi.com

Official site of the largest recreational skating association that offers an alternative test and competition structure to the national federations whose primary focus is elite competition.

International Skating Union

www.isu.org

Official site. Provides competition schedule information, updates on rule changes, and a discussion board, along with offering for purchase historical publications and rulebook and instructional materials used for training international judges and promoting the sport of figure skating worldwide.

Rainbow Ice by Lorrie Kim

www.plover.com/rainbowice

Site for topics related to lesbian, gay, bisexual, and transgendered issues in the sport of figure skating.

news://rec.sport.skating.ice.figure
    News and discussion on figure skating topics.

news://rec.sport.skating.ice.recreational
    Participant skating discussion, with an emphasis on adult figure skating.

Silent Edge by Ellen Edgerton
www.silent-edge.org
    Provides information and links of interest for those concerned about sexual
    abuse and exploitation in figure skating (and in all sports), and other advo-
    cacy issues for skaters.

Skatabase by Ellen Edgerton
www.silent-edge.org/skatabase
    Searchable database of past competition results and jumps landed at various
    events.

Skate Canada
www.skatecanada.ca/english/info/index.html
    The Canadian national figure skating federation offers useful technical
    information on their official Web site.

Technical Figure Skating by Kevin Anderson
nsn.nslsilus.org/eakhome/skating/kevinnew
    Includes video clips of all major skating elements and a more extensive
    bibilography of skating books and videos than provided here.

United States Figure Skating Association
www.usfsa.org
    Official site. Provides news about U.S. skaters; information, including re-
    sults, about domestic and international competitions, television broadcast
    schedules, and USFSA programs; and discussion boards and an on-line store.

Index